CONSCIENCE

CONSCIENCE

theological and psychological
perspectives

edited by
C. Ellis Nelson

NEWMAN PRESS
New York / Paramus / Toronto

Library of Congress
Catalog Card Number: 73-75245

ISBN 0-8091-1767-3   '

Published by Newman Press
Editorial Office: 1865 Broadway, N.Y. N.Y. 10023
Business Office: 400 Sette Drive, Paramus, N.J. 07652

Printed and bound in the
United States of America

ACKNOWLEDGEMENTS

Guilt, Ethics and Religion: From *Talk of God* by Paul Ricoeur. Royal Institute of Philosophy Lectures, Vol. 2, 1967-68. London and Basingstoke: St. Martin's Press and Macmillan, 1969, pp. 100-117. Reprinted by permission.

The Decline and Fall of Conscience: From *Ethics in a Christian Context* by Paul Lehmann, pp. 327-343. Copyright © 1963 by Paul L. Lehmann. Reprinted by permission of Harper and Row Publishers, Inc.

A Conscience above Moralism: From an essay originally entitled "Conscience in Western Thought and the Idea of a Transmoral Conscience" by Paul Tillich, *Crozer Quarterly,* Vol. XXII, No. 4, Oct. 1945, pp. 289-300. Used by permission.

The Nature of a Liberating Conscience by Paul Tillich: From *Ministry and Medicine in Human Relations,* edited by Iago Galdstone. New York: International Universities Press, Inc., 1955, pp. 127-140. Reprinted with permission.

How the Bible Speaks to Conscience: From *Christ and Conscience* by N. H. G. Robinson. London: James Nisbet and Company, Ltd., 1956, pp. 171-178. Used by permission.

Protestant Problems with Conscience by Hans Schär: From *Conscience,* edited by the Curatorium of the Jung Institute, Zurich. Evanston, Illinois: Northwestern University Press, 1970. This article, found on pp. 113-130, was translated by R. F. C. Hull and Ruth Horine. Reprinted by permission.

A Catholic View of Conscience by Josef Rudin: From *Conscience,* edited by the Curatorium of the Jung Institute, Zurich. Evanston, Illinois: Northwestern University Press, 1970. This article, found on pp. 137-158, was translated by R. F. C. Hull and Ruth Horine. Reprinted by permission.

Conscience and Church Authority by Avery R. Dulles, S.J.: From *Conscience, Its Freedom and Limitations,* edited by William C. Bier, S.J. New York: Fordham University Press, 1971, pp. 251-257. Reprinted by permission.

An Anglo-Catholic View of Conscience: From *The Elements of Moral Theology* by R. C. Mortimer. London: A. & C. Black Ltd.; New York: Harper and Row, Publishers, Inc., pp. 75-83. Reprinted with permission.

The Christian Conscience Today: From *Christian Morality Today* by Charles E. Curran. Notre Dame, Indiana: Fides Publishers, Inc., 1966, pp. 13-25. Reprinted with permission.

The Mature Christian Conscience by Ewert H. Cousins: From *Conscience, Its Freedom and Limitations,* edited by William C. Bier, S.J. New York: Fordham University Press, 1971, pp. 369-378. Reprinted with permission.

The Struggle of Conscience for Authentic Selfhood: Excerpts from *Three Issues in Ethics* by John Macquarrie, pp. 111-123. Copyright © 1970 by John Macquarrie. Reprinted by permission of Harper and Row, Publishers, Inc. and SCM Press Ltd.

Conscience and Superego: A Key Distinction by John W. Glaser: From *Theological Studies,* Vol. 32, 1971, pp. 30-47. Reprinted by permission.

Elements of Personality: From *Self and Society* by Nevitt Sanford. New York: Atherton Press, 1967, pp. 73-86. Reprinted by permission.

Superego and Conscience by Gregory Zilboorg, M.D.: From *Ministry and Medicine in Human Relations,* edited by Iago Galdstone, M.D. New York: International Universities Press, Inc., 1955, pp. 100-118. Reprinted with permission.

Guilt and Guilt Feelings: From *The Knowledge of Man: Selected Essays by Martin Buber,* edited by Maurice Friedman, pp. 123-136. Copyright © 1965 by Martin Buber and Maurice Friedman. Reprinted by permission of Harper and Row, Publishers, Inc.

The Development of Moral Values in Children by E. Mansell Pattison, M.D.: From *Pastoral Psychology,* Februray, 1969, pp. 14-30. Reprinted with permission.

The Development of the Normal Conscience by Dorothea McCarthy: From *Conscience: Its Freedom and Limitations,* edited by William C. Bier, S.J. New York: Fordham University Press, 1971, pp. 39-61. Reprinted with permission.

Contents

ix

II

PSYCHOLOGICAL PERSPECTIVES

Preface

Sigmund Freud, in his introduction to the book *Wayward Youth* written by his friend August Aichhorn, said that he accepted it as a byword "that the three impossible professions are teaching, healing and governing." Because he was busy with healing, Freud said he did not give much attention to education; but he respected those who did. Freud also stated that educational work was "not to be confused with, nor exchanged for, psychoanalytic means of influence. Psychoanalysis of the child may be drawn upon as a contributory help, but it is not an appropriate substitute for education."

To Freud's list of "impossible professions" we could add those of ministers, social workers, parents and other persons who by circumstance or choice find themselves working or living with individuals who are struggling with their consciences. Such people have one thing in common: each is caring for, or trying to help someone else who is less mature, less well-informed, or less able to handle his conflicting emotions and is unable to function smoothly in a decision-making process which involves moral values. It is an impossible job because it demands a theory of how the human mind is formed and functions; it requires an intensive knowledge of the private history of the person one is trying to help; it presupposes that the helping person understands the options that are open for action; and above all, it assumes that the relationship between the two is conducive to the creation of new insight and behavior. But that is not all. The helping person cannot treat matters of conscience as a problem others are having while he remains calm and reasonable. To the contrary, the helping person's mind is flooded with his own struggles with conscience—some of which are probably not clearly worked out—and this experience clouds the issues and makes the helping relationship complex and the result uncertain.

With such formidable obstacles, our temptation is to fall back on common sense or conventional folk wisdom and say, "We'll

1

muddle through this problem." Or, if we are religiously inclined, we may say, "God will, in his own time and way, provide the necessary guidance." This latter may be the better of the two answers because it forces the responsibility for decision on the person who needs help, but neither answer is adequate.

Although the lure of reason and understanding in the human mind is faint compared to the emotions, it is persistent. If we are going to help ourselves and others face the problems and opportunities of making life more rewarding, then we must follow our natural curiosity about how human beings develop their capacity and skill in living together. This requires a better understanding of conscience because conscience comes from our common life, and in turn it is the element in our individual lives which forms the values of society. We can apply to conscience the comment attributed to Winston Churchill, "We build our buildings and then are shaped by them." The content of our conscience—what we consider right and wrong—is formed by our parents and others who raise us from infancy; most of us then absolutize that code and pass it on to our children. Thus we form the values of our social life and in turn are formed by them. So the job re-creating— or at least re-evaluating—our own moral values while at the same time attempting to help others form a proper conscience comes close to being impossible.

The focus of our inquiry is that of the individual, but the reason for our concern is social. Today technology in medicine, communication, agriculture and the labor-saving methods of manufacturing have changed the conditions of human life. We find ourselves engaged in an intensive struggle to adjust our values to fit our new human situation. Here, progress is exceedingly slow.

This collection of writings is for the people who attempt to do the impossible job. It is intended primarily for students who have a basic understanding of modern social science, especially psychology, and a concern for a theological interpretation of personality. Many ministers and parents would likewise have such a background.

This audience helps to give a focus to the articles, focus being a serious problem in dealing with conscience. Conscience means too many things! For example, in popular usage conscience is often thought of as a feeling of guilt when we do something we consider wrong. In the newspapers we read that a person takes a stand on a public issue because of his conscience. In theological literature, conscience may be reported as the voice of God speaking to concrete ethical matters about which a Christian should make a decision. Some of this linguistic confusion is rooted in our lack of clarity about the way the mind functions; some of it is caused by our predilection to call something "moral" if we think we ought to do it rather than because the act is a genuinely responsible thing for us to do. Moreover, many religious people assume that their conscience is in practice their religion. Yet when they see non-religious people with high ethical standards they are uncertain as to the role of religion in the forming of conscience.

One finds, therefore, many different definitions in the selected articles. The state of psychology is not such that there is a common dictionary. Is theology much better? To ask the question is to answer it; we should not expect these essays to present a comprehensive, systematic point of view about conscience. Rather, they were selected to sharpen the perception of those of us who have the impossible job. The focus is on the powerful inner-urgings that warn, haunt, threaten, cajole or lure us whenever we are facing alternate ways of acting. The following questions help sharpen the focus: How is conscience formed? What are the developmental stages of conscience? What is the relation of conscience to other functions of a person's mind, particularly his reason? What is the source of morality? What forces or factors change a person's moral standards? Can moral decisions be made more rationally than they usually are? Is conscience the same as the superego, or is it a zone within a person's life in which he can increasingly work out his ethics in a conscious way? Is guilt a reaction to the breaking of commonly understood moral standards, or is guilt a "feeling" that is more related to a person's personality structure? Few of these questions are new. In fact, they have engaged the minds of some of our best theologians and philosophers for thousands of years. What is new is psychological data about conscience which have been accumulated during the last half century. Although social scientists make no secret about their work, their writings are not widely read by scholars in the humanistic tradition; and, contrariwise, there are not many theologians or philosophers who have made a serious study of psychiatry. On each side there are some thinkers who have attempted to understand the other side, and today there are some writers who have been trained both in theology and in psychiatry. The underlying problem they all have had to treat has been how our modern empirical data about man is used in forming our doctrines of man and in shaping our child-rearing practices.

This collection of writings is not an encyclopedia. You will not find here some of the excellent articles on conscience by great theologians and philosophers, some of which are remarkably true to our modern knowledge of the mind. Nevitt Sanford, for example, said that McDougall (in 1908) wrote "an account of conscience that has still to be surpassed." (See Sanford's *Self and Society*, page 111.) However, McDougall's chapter on the self-regarding sentiment is not included both because the ideas are not expressed in the language of our present generation and because it lacks the precision of analysis that we expect today. One could likewise select from St. Augustine's *Confessions* classic statements about the way the self deludes the self or about how the self can convert one form of desire to another. Yet for the same reasons such passages are not included.

The assumption that was used to select these writings is illustrated by that old story about the three blind men who were trying to discover the nature of an elephant. One touched his trunk and described the elephant as a rope that could move about with great force. Another touched the legs and described the elephant as a tree. A third felt the sides and reported that the elephant was more like a wall. None of the three was incorrect, given the area he explored; but each explanation was incomplete.

I assume that there is one true description of the nature and function of conscience but that we do not know exactly what it is at the present time. What we have is much better than three blind men. We are, I think, in the stage where theology and psychology are often talking about the same thing—each with its specialized language. If this is the case, then these essays can be used as an exercise in translating from one field of thought to another. When it is not the case of different language games being played but rather of a substantial difference in ideas, the reader will be able to form an image of what one writer has in mind and contrast it with images from other writers. In such cases, we will just have to say we do not yet know exactly what the conscience is, all the while working and living on the basis of what we think is the most accurate account.

The use of different languages to describe the same thing brings us to another matter—the repetition of certain key ideas. This is to be expected because many of these articles were written to treat conscience as a whole. Thus, some writers give a brief survey of the way conscience is formed or how the parents are "introjected" into the child's personality. However, we did not want to delete these repetitious paragraphs, for that would destroy the author's development of ideas or the proportion he assigned to the parts of his essay. If paragraphs treat topics already read, you may feel free to skip or skim over those passages. However, we would suggest that you *not* do so because by reading several versions of the same thing, you will be better able to understand the shades of meaning and add depth and range to your knowledge.

Since the articles were not selected to cover the whole range of matters related to conscience, is there a "party line" that determines which articles were used? The main consideration was whether the essay was about the questions indicated earlier and was written within the context of—and respect for—a modern knowledge of the mind. There is a preference for the Freudian type of psychology because it is so widespread and seems to offer the best basis for analysis. Some of the psychological writers chosen are psychiatrists who deal with people in an everyday setting and with problems that are often related to conscience.

The theologians selected have no common ideology or metaphysics. What is common is their intuitive way of probing the self and their ability to sense or describe what many psychiatrists see in their clinical work. Without exception the theological writers find an element in conscience different from the Freudian superego, but what they do with this difference varies one from another. The theologians are all from the Christian tradition. The limitation of space required that we not try to cover too many points of view, and the pressing issue just now is a better understanding between Protestants and Catholics on moral development.

There is no particular rationale for the sequence of articles in the theological section. However, the Protestant and Catholic background of the writer may be discerned by the topics he treats and

often by the way he uses the Christian heritage. It is also significant to note the extent to which both of these Christian traditions
incorporate the thought of Greek moralists as well as their common theological predecessors. In the light of their own heritage
and present church situation, Protestants and Catholics treat the
matter of authority, the need and difficulty of following the spirit
of God in moral matters, and the necessary but risky process of
individual decision-making. Such comparisons make it easier to
understand how the complex matter of morality may be viewed in
the years ahead as the ecumenical movement draws Christians
together.

The articles in the psychological section are from some writers
who deal with conscience as a part of the psychic structure and
others who are concerned with practical matters such as the formation and education of conscience. Since it may be nearer to the
truth to say a person *is* a conscience rather than he *has* a conscience,
the education of conscience is a consideration of the whole person
and becomes more like therapy than like something which can be
assigned to the classroom. But therapy is not limited to the work
of psychiatrists. In the sense of defining personal problems and
helping individuals work through them mentally and emotionally,
therapy goes on all the time in thousands of ways. One can guess
that about 90% of the population has no other shapers of conscience
and helpers in moral matters than their parents, friends, ministers
and teachers. This section is directed toward helping people who
are not professional therapists but who in everyday life are trying
to do the "impossible job" of helping someone achieve clarity
about, and support from, his conscience.

Next to the service of selecting these articles about a common
theme from hundreds of essays on conscience, this collection provides the convenience of having them together for ready reference.
The latter point, although not important to a person who lives
near a university library, may be of practical significance for others.
There are very few books devoted entirely to conscience. Those
available are usually surveys—telling the reader second-hand what
other people think about the subject. Moreover, conscience
seems to be a matter about which scholars write a chapter or give
a lecture or two. Some of these chapters and lectures, now out of

print or located in journals difficult to obtain, are made available here.

No bibliography is appended to this selection of essays. Conscience is so broad a subject and it has connections with so many fields of thought that a thorough bibliography would take several hundred pages. There are, however, numerous references and footnotes cited in the essays to help a person pick up the trail of writers in whom he develops an interest. These references lead to others so that the matter of finding additional articles becomes self-generating.

This reader, part of a longer project on conscience, was made possible by the Auburn Studies in Education. To the Board of Directors of Auburn Theological Seminary, the Committee supervising the research grants, and especially to the Dean of Auburn Theological Seminary, Robert W. Lynn, I want to express my appreciation and thanks.

I also want to record my appreciation to Padraic O'Hare for help in selecting articles. To Robert Springer, S.J., Professor of Moral Theology at Woodstock College, I owe a special note of thanks for his guidance about the whole project.

The careful reader will discover that the spelling of some words in certain articles reflects their English origin. In some translated articles the language may not always conform to standard American usage. Also, the notes found at the end of each essay are not uniform. These discrepancies in style were allowed to remain because the articles are reproduced in the form in which they were copyrighted.

C. Ellis Nelson
August, 1972

I
THEOLOGICAL PERSPECTIVES

1 Guilt, Ethics and Religion

PAUL RICOEUR

Of all the methods of analyzing human situations, phenomenology is one of the most difficult for Americans to appreciate. We are inclined to respond favorably to pragmatic, empiric, or idealistic ways of interpreting life because we are acquainted with these approaches and they yield data which appear to be based on fact or reason. The phenomenological approach, as used by Ricoeur, requires the reader to open himself to evidence that comes from an examination of words, ceremonies, myths, subjective feelings, and deductions based on these data. Moreover, the results of this type of study do not correspond to any field of academic study. Rather, they commend themselves to the reader only to the extent that they correspond to his self-understanding. Conscience as a topic is not a major feature of this article,* for Ricoeur prefers to deal with the more primordial awareness of guilt and how this experience causes ethics and religion to emerge.

At the outset, I would like to thank the Royal Institute of Philosophy for inviting me to add my contribution to the general theme of the present session. Mr. Vesey suggested that I speak on the notion of guilt from the twofold perspective of Ethics and of the Philosophy of Religion. I was very happy to accept his proposal, for it gave me the oppor-

* From *Talk of God*, Royal Institute of Philosophy Lectures, Vol. 2, 1967-68 (London and Basingstoke: St. Martin's Press and Macmillan, 1969), pp. 100-117. Reprinted by permission.

11

tunity to gather together my own reflections on this difficult topic, which up to now have been somewhat scattered. My principal task will be to determine the distinction between ethical discourse and religious discourse on the question of guilt. These will be the two main divisions of my analysis.

But, before treating these two respective discourses with a view to distinguishing them and understanding their relationship, I suggest that first we come to an agreement about the meaning of the terms in question. Allow me, then, by way of preface, to develop a semantic analysis of the very term 'guilt'.

1. *Guilt: Semantic Analysis*

I propose, first, to consider this term, not in its psychological, psychiatric or psychoanalytic usage, but in the *texts* where its meaning has been constituted and fixed. These texts are those of penitential literature wherein the believing communities have expressed their avowal of evil; the language of these texts is a specific language which can be designated, in a very general way, as 'confession of sins', although no particular confessional connotation is attached to this expression, not even a specifically Jewish or Christian meaning. Some decades ago, Professor Pettazzoni of Rome wrote a collection of works covering the entire field of comparative religions. He called this precisely *Confession of Sins*. But it is not from the comparative point of view that I take up the problem. My point of departure is in a *phenomenology of confession* or avowal. Here I understand by phenomenology the description of meanings implied in experience in general, whether that experience be one of things, of values, of persons, etc. A phenomenology of confession is therefore a description of meanings and of signified intentions, present in a certain activity of language: the language of confession. Our task, in the framework of such a phenomenology, is to re-enact in ourselves the confession of evil, in order to uncover its aims. By sympathy and through imagination, the philosopher adopts the motivations and intentions of the confessing consciousness; he does not 'feel', he 'experiences' in a neutral manner, in the manner of an 'as if', that which has been lived in the confessing consciousness.

But with which expressions shall we start? Not with expressions of confessions that are the most developed, the most rationalised, for example, the concept or quasi-concept of 'original sin' which has often guided philosophical thought. On the contrary, philosophical reasoning should consult expressions of the confession of evil which are the least elaborated, the least articulated.

We should not be embarrassed by the fact that behind these rationalised expressions, behind these speculations, we encounter myths, that is, traditional narratives which tell of events which happened at the origin of time and which furnish the support of language to ritual actions. Today, for us, myths are no longer explanations of reality but, precisely because they have lost their explanatory pretension, they reveal an exploratory signification; they manifest a symbolic function, that is, a way of expressing indirectly the bond between man and what he considers sacred. Paradoxical as it may seem, myth thus demythologised in its contact with physics, cosmology and scientific history becomes a dimension of modern thought. In its turn, myth refers us to a level of expressions, more fundamental than any narration and any speculation. Thus, the narrative of the fall in the Bible draws its signification from an experience of sin rooted in the life of the community: it is the cultural activity and the prophetic call to justice and to 'mercy' which provide myth with its sub-structure of significations.

Therefore it is to this experience and to its language that we must have recourse; or rather, to this experience *in* its language. For it is the language of confession which elevates to the light of discourse an experience charged with emotion, fear, and anguish. Penitential literature manifests a linguistic inventiveness which marks the way for existential outbursts of the consciousness of fault.

Let us, therefore, interrogate this language.

The most remarkable characteristic of this language is that it does not involve expressions which are more primitive than the symbolic expressions to which myth refers. The language of confession is symbolic. Here I understand by symbol a language which designates a thing in an indirect way, by designating another thing which it directly indicates. It is in this way that I speak symbolically of elevated thoughts, low sentiments, clear ideas, the light of understanding, the kingdom of heaven, etc. Therefore, the work of repetition as applied to the expressions of evil is, in essence, the explicitation, the development of different levels of direct and indirect significations which are intermingled in the same symbol. The most archaic symbolism from which we can start is that of evil conceived as defilement or stain, that is, as a spot which contaminates from the outside. In more elaborated literatures, such as that of the Babylonians and especially of the Hebrews, sin is expressed in different symbolisms, such as to miss the target, to follow a tortuous path, to rebel, to have a stiff neck, to be unfaithful as in adultery, to be deaf, to be lost, to wander, to be empty and hollow, to be inconstant as dust.

This linguistic situation is astonishing; the consciousness of self, so intense in the sentiment of evil, does not, at first, have at its disposal an abstract language, but a very concrete language, on which a spontaneous work of interpretation is performed.

The second remarkable characteristic of this language is that it knows itself as symbolic and that, before any philosophy and theology, it is *enroute* towards explicitation; as I have said elsewhere, the symbol 'invites' thought; the myth is on the way towards *logos*. This is true even of the archaic idea of defilement or stain: the idea of a quasi-material something which contaminates from the outside, which harms by means of invisible properties—this idea possesses a symbolic richness, a potential of symbolisation, which is attested to by the very survival of this symbol under more and more allegorical forms. We speak even today, in a non-medical sense, of contamination by the spirit of monetary profit, by racism, etc.; we have not completely abandoned the symbolism of the pure and the impure. And this, precisely because the quasi-material representation of stain is already symbolic of something else. From the beginning it has symbolic power. Stain has never literally signified a spot, impurity has never literally signified filth; it is located in the 'clear-obscure' of a quasi-physical infection and of a quasi-moral indignity. We see this clearly in rites of purification which are never just a simple washing; ablution and lustration are already partial and fictive actions which signify, on the level of body, a total action which addresses itself to the person considered as an undivided whole.

The symbolism of sin such as is found in Babylonian and

Hebraic literature, in Greek tragedies or in Orphic writings, is certainly richer than that of stain, from which it is sharply distinguished. To the image of impure contact, it opposes that of a wounded relationship, between God and man, between man and man, between man and himself; but this relation, which will be thought of as a relation only by a philosopher, is symbolically signified by all the means of dramatisation offered in daily experience. So too the idea of sin is not reduced to the barren idea of the rupture of a relation; it adds to this the idea of a power which dominates man. Thus it maintains a certain affinity and continuity with the symbolism of stain. But this power is also the sign of the emptiness, of the vanity of man, represented by breath and by dust. So the symbol of sin is at one and the same time the symbol of something negative (rupture, estrangement, absence, vanity) and the symbol of something positive (power, possession, captivity, alienation). It is on this symbolic foundation, in this network of images and nascent interpretations that the word guilt should be resituated.

If we want to respect the proper intention of words, the expression guilt does not cover the whole semantic field of 'confession'. The idea of guilt represents the extreme form of interiorisation which we have seen sketched in the passage from stain to sin. Stain was still external contagion, sin already the rupture of a relation; but this rupture exists even if I do not know it; sin is a real condition, an objective situation; I would venture to say, an ontological dimension of existence.

Guilt, on the contrary, has a distinctly subjective accent: its symbolism is much more interior. It describes the consciousness of being overwhelmed by a burden which crushes. It indicates, further, the bite of a remorse which gnaws from within, in the completely interior brooding on fault. These two metaphors of burden and of biting express well the arrival at the level of existence. The most significant symbolism of guilt is that which is attached to the theme of tribunal; the tribunal is a public institution, but metaphorically transposed into the internal forum it becomes what we call the 'moral consciousness'. Thus guilt becomes a way of putting oneself before a sort of invisible tribunal which measures the offence, pronounces the condemnation, and inflicts the punishment; at the extreme point of interiorisation, moral consciousness is a look which watches, judges, and condemns; the sentiment of guilt is therefore the consciousness of being inculpated and incriminated by this interior tribunal. It is mingled with the anticipation of the punishment; in short the *coulpe,* in Latin *culpa,* is self-observation, self-accusation, and self-condemnation by a consciousness doubled back on itself.

This interiorisation of guilt gives rise to two series of results: on the one hand, the consciousness of guilt marks a definite progress in relation to what we have described as 'sin'; while sin is still a collective reality in which a whole community is implicated, guilt tends to individualise itself. (In Israel, the prophets of the exile are the artisans of this progress (Ezek. 31:34); this preaching is a liberating action; at a time when a collective return from exile, comparable to the ancient Exodus from Egypt, appeared impossible, a personal path of conversion opened itself to each one. In ancient Greece, it was the tragic poets who assured the passage from hereditary crime to the guilt of the individual hero, placed alone before his own destiny.) Moreover, in becoming individualised, guilt acquires degrees; to the egalitarian experience of sin is opposed the graduated experience of guilt: man is entirely and radically sinner, but more or less guilty. It is the progress of penal law itself, principally in Greece and Rome, which has an effect here on moral consciousness: the whole of penal law is actually an effort to limit and to gauge the penalty in function of the measure of the fault. The idea of a parallel scale of crimes and sins is interiorised, in its own turn, in favour of the metaphor of the tribunal; moral consciousness becomes itself a graduated consciousness of guilt.

This individualisation and this gradation of guilt surely indicate a progress in respect to the collective and unqualified character of sin. We cannot say as much for the other series of results: with guilt there arises indeed a sort of demand which can be called scrupulosity and whose ambiguous character is extremely interesting. A scrupulous consciousness is a delicate consciousness, a precise consciousness enamoured of increasing perfection; it is a consciousness anxious to observe all the commandments, to satisfy the law in all things, without making an exception of any sector of existence, without taking into account exterior obstacles, for example, the persecution of a prince, and which gives equal importance to little things as to great. But at the same time scrupulosity marks the entrance of moral consciousness into its own pathology; a scrupulous person encloses himself in the inextricable labyrinth of commandments; obligation takes on an enumerative and cumulative character, which contrasts with the simplicity and sobriety of the commandment to love God and man. The scrupulous consciousness never stops adding new commandments. This atomisation of the law into a multitude of commandments entails an endless 'juridisation' of action and a quasi-obsessional ritualisation of daily life. The scrupulous person never arrives at satisfying all the commandments, or even any one. At the same time even the notion of obedience is perverted; obedience to a commandment, because it is commanded, becomes more important than love of neighbour, and even love of God; this exactitude in observance is what we call legalism. With it we enter into the hell of guilt, such as St Paul described it: the law itself becomes a source of sin. In giving a knowledge of evil, it excites the desire of transgression, and incites the endless movement of condemnation and punishment. The commandment, says St Paul, 'has given life to sin', and thus 'hands me over to death' (Rom. 7). Law and sin give birth to one another mutually in a terrible vicious circle, which becomes a mortal circle.

Thus, guilt reveals the malediction of a life under the law. At the limit, when the confidence and tenderness, which are still expressed in the conjugal metaphors of Hosea, disappear, guilt leads to an accusation without accuser, a tribunal without judge, a verdict without author. Guilt has then become that irreversible misfortune described by Kafka: condemnation has become damnation.

A conclusion of this semantic analysis is that guilt does not cover the whole field of the human experience of evil; the study of these symbolic expressions has permitted us to distinguish in them a particular moment of this experience, the most ambiguous moment. On the one hand, guilt expresses the interiorisation of the experience of evil, and consequently the promotion of a morally responsible subject—but, on the other hand, it marks the beginning of a specific pathology, wherein scrupulosity marks the point of inversion.

Now the problem is posed: what do Ethics and the Philosophy of Religion make of this ambiguous experience of guilt and of the symbolic language in which it is expressed?

2. *Ethical Dimension*

In what sense is the problem of evil an ethical problem? In a twofold sense, it seems to me. Or rather, by reason of a double relationship, on the one hand with the question of freedom, and, on the other hand, with the question of obligation. Evil, freedom, obligation constitute a very complex network, which we shall try to unravel and to order in several stages of reflection. I shall begin and end with freedom, for it is the essential point.

In a first stage of reflection, I say: to affirm freedom is to take upon oneself the origin of evil. By this proposition, I affirm a link between evil and liberty, which is so close that the two terms imply one another mutually. Evil has the meaning of evil because it is the work of freedom. Freedom has the meaning of freedom because it is capable of evil: I both recognise and declare myself to be the author of evil. By that fact, I reject as an alibi the claim that evil exists after the manner of a substance or of a nature, that it has the same status as things which can be observed by an outside spectator. This claim is to be found not only in the metaphysical fantasies, such as those against which Augustine fought—Manicheism and all sorts of ontologies which conceive of evil as a being. This claim can take on a positive appearance, or even a scientific appearance, under the form of psychological or sociological determinism. To take upon oneself the origin of evil is to lay aside as a weakness the claim that evil is something, that it is an effect in a world of observable things, whether these things be physical, psychic or social realities. I say: it is I who have acted: *ego sum qui feci*. There is no evil-being; there is only the evil-done-by-me. To take evil upon oneself is an act of language comparable to the performative, in this sense, that it is a language which does something, that is to say, that it imputes the act to me.

I said that the relationship was reciprocal; indeed, if freedom qualified evil as a doing, evil is that which reveals freedom. By this I mean to say, evil is a privileged occasion for becoming aware of freedom. What does it actually mean to impute my own acts to myself? It is, first of all, to assume the consequences of these acts for the future; that is, he who has acted is also he who will admit the fault, who will repair the damages, who will bear the blame. In other words, I offer myself as the bearer of the sanction. I agree to enter into the dialectic of praise and blame. But in placing myself before the consequences of my act, I refer myself back to the moment prior to my act, and I designate myself as he who not only performed the act, but who could have done otherwise. This conviction of having done something freely is not a matter of observation. It is once again a performative: I declare myself, after the fact, as being he who could have done otherwise; this 'after the fact' is the backlash of taking upon oneself the consequences. He who takes the consequences upon himself, declares himself free, and discerns this freedom as already at work in the incriminated act. At that point I can say that I have committed the act. This movement from in front of to behind the responsibility is essential. It constitutes the identity of the moral subject through past, present, and future. He who *will* bear the blame is the same who *now* takes the act upon himself and he who *has* acted, I posit the identity of him who accepts the future responsibilities of his act, and he who has acted. And the two dimensions, future and past, are linked in the present. The future of sanction and the past of action committed are tied together in the present of confession.

Such is the first stage of reflection in the experience of evil: the reciprocal constitution of the signification of *free* and the signification of *evil* is a specific performative: *confession*. The second moment of reflection concerns the link between evil and obligation. I do not at all want to discuss the meaning of expressions such as 'You ought' nor their relation with the predicates 'good' and 'evil'. This problem is well known to English philosophy. My contribution to a reflection on evil will be limited to this problem: let us take as our point of departure the expression and the experience 'I could have done otherwise'. This is, as we have seen, an implication of the act by which I impute to myself the responsibility for a past act. But the awareness that one could have done otherwise is closely linked to the awareness that one *should* have done otherwise. It is because I recognise my 'ought' that I recognise my 'could'. A being who is obligated is a being who presumes that he can do what he could do. We are well aware of the usage to which Kant put this affirmation: you must, therefore you can. It is certainly not an argument, in the sense that I could deduce the possibility from the obligation. I would rather say that the 'ought' serves here as a detector: if I feel, or believe, or know that I am obligated, it is because I am a being that can act, not only under the impulsion or constraint of desire and fear, but under the condition of a law which I represent to myself. In this sense Kant is right: to act according to the representation of a law is something other than to act according to laws. This power of acting according to the representation of a law is the will. But this discovery has long-range consequences: for in discovering the power to follow the law (or that which I consider as the law for myself) I discover also the *terrible* power of acting *against*. (Indeed, the experience of remorse which is the experience of the relation between freedom and obligation is a twofold experience; on the one hand, I recognise an obligation, and therefore a power corresponding to this obligation, but I admit to having acted against the law which continues to appear to me as obligatory. This is commonly called a transgression.) Freedom is the power to act according to the representation of a law *and* not to meet the obligation. ('Here is what I should have done, therefore what I could have done, and look at what I did.' The imputation of the past act is thus morally qualified by its relation to the 'ought' and 'can'.) By the same fact, a new determination of evil and a new determination of freedom appear together, in addition to the forms of reciprocity which are described above. The new determination of evil can be expressed in Kantian terms: it is the reversal of the relation between motive and law, interior to the maxim of my action. This definition is to be understood as follows: if I call a maxim the practical enunciation of what I propose to do, evil is nothing in itself; it has neither physical nor psychical reality; it is only an inverted relationship; it is a relation, not a thing, a relation inverted with regard to the order of preference and subordination indicated by obligation. In this way, we have achieved a 'de-realisation' of evil: not only does evil exist only in the act of taking it upon oneself, of assuming it, of claiming it, but what characterises it from a moral point of view is the order in which an agent disposes of his maxims; it is a preference which ought not to have been (an inverted relation within the maxim of action).

But a new determination of freedom appears at the same time. I spoke a moment ago of the *terrible* power of acting against. It is, indeed, in the confession of evil that I discover the power of subversion of the will. Let us call it the *arbitrary,* to translate the German *Willkür,* which is at the same time free choice, i.e. the power of contraries, that which we recognised in the consciousness that one could have done otherwise, and in the power not to follow an obligation which I simultaneously recognise as just.

Have we exhausted the meaning of evil for Ethics? I do not think so. In the 'Essay on Radical Evil' which begins *Religion within the Limits of Reason Alone,* Kant poses the problem of a common origin of all evil maxims; indeed, we have not gone far in a reflection on evil, as long as we consider separately one bad intention, and then another, and again another. 'We must conclude', says Kant, 'from many, or even from a single conscious evil action, *a priori* to an evil maxim as its foundation, and from this maxim to a general foundation inherent in the subject, of all morally bad maxims, a foundation which in its own turn would be a maxim, so that finally we could qualify a man as evil.' [1]

This movement towards greater depth which goes from evil maxims to their evil foundation is the philosophical transposition of the movement of sins to sin (in the singular) of which we spoke in section 1, on the level of symbolic expressions, and in particular of myth. Among other things, the myth of Adam signifies that all sins are referred to an unique root, which is, in some way or other, anterior to each of the particular expressions of evil, yet the myth could be told because the confessing community raised itself to the level of a confession of evil as involving all men. It is because the community confesses a fundamental guilt that the myth can describe the unique coming-to-be of evil as an event which happens only once. The Kantian doctrine of radical evil is an attempt to recapture philosophically the experience of this myth.

What qualifies this re-examination as philosophical? Essentially the treatment of radical evil as the foundation of multiple evil maxims. It is therefore upon this notion of foundation that we should bring to bear our critical effort.

Now, what do we mean by a foundation of evil maxims? We might well call it an *a priori* condition in order to emphasise that it is not a fact to be observed or a temporal origin to be retraced. It is not an empirical fact, but a first disposition of freedom that must be supposed so that the universal spectacle of human evil can be offered to experience. Neither is it a temporal origin, for this theory would lead back to a natural causality. Evil would cease to be evil, if it ceased to be 'a manner of being of freedom, which itself comes from freedom'. Therefore, evil does not have an origin in the sense of an antecedent cause. 'Every evil action, when pushed back to its rational origin, should be considered as if man had arrived at it directly from the state of innocence.'[2] (Everything is in this 'as if'. It is the philosophical equivalent of the myth of the fall; it is the rational myth of the coming-to-be of evil, of the instantaneous passage from innocence to sin; *as* Adam—rather than *in* Adam—we originate evil.)

But what is this unique coming-to-be which contains within itself all evil maxims? It must be admitted that we have no further concept for thinking of an evil will.

For this coming-to-be is not at all an act of my arbitrary will, which I could do or not do. For the enigma of this foundation is that reflection discovers, as a fact, that freedom has already chosen in an evil way. This evil is already there. It is in this sense that it is radical, that is anterior, as a non-temporal aspect of every evil intention, of every evil action.

But this failure of reflection is not in vain; it succeeds in giving a character, proper to a *philosophy of limit,* and in distinguishing itself from a philosophy of system, such as that of Hegel.

The limit is twofold: limit of my knowledge, limit of my power. On the one hand, *I do not know* the origin of my evil liberty; this non-knowledge of the origin is essential to the very act of confession of my radically evil freedom. The non-knowledge is a part of the performative of confession, or, in other words, of my self-recognition and self-appropriation. On the other hand, I discover the *non-power* of my freedom. (Curious non-power, for I declare that I am responsible for this non-power. This non-power is completely different from the claim of an outside constraint.) I claim that my freedom has already made itself not-free. This admission is the greatest paradox of ethics. It seems to contradict our point of departure. We began by saying: evil is what I could have not done; this remains true. But at the same time I claim: evil is this prior captivity, which makes it so that I must do evil. This contradiction is interior to my freedom, it marks the non-power of power, the non-freedom of freedom.

Is this a lesson in despair? Not at all: this admission is, on the contrary, the access to a point where everything can begin again. The return to the origin is a return to that place where freedom discovers itself, as something to be delivered—in brief to that place where it can *hope* to be delivered.

3. *Religious Dimension*

I have just attempted with the aid of the Philosophy of Kant to characterise the problem of evil as an ethical problem. It is the twofold relation of evil to obligation and to freedom, which has seemed to me to characterise the problem of evil as an ethical problem.

Now, if I ask what is the specifically religious way of speaking about evil, I would not hesitate for a moment to answer: the language is that of Hope. This thesis requires an explanation. Leaving aside for a moment the question of evil to which I shall return later, I would like to justify the central role of hope in Christian theology. Hope has rarely been the central concept in theology. And yet we now know, since the work of Johannes Weiss and Albert Schweitzer, that the preaching of Jesus was concerned essentially with the Kingdom of God; the Kingdom is at hand; the Kingdom has drawn near to us; the Kingdom is in your midst. If the preaching of Jesus and of the primitive church thus proceeds from an eschatological perspective, we should rethink all of theology from this eschatological viewpoint. But this revision of theological concepts, taking its point of departure from the exegesis of the New Testament, centered on the preaching of the Kingdom-to-come, finds support in a parallel revision of the theology of the Old Testament. Thus Martin Buber contrasts the God of the promise—God of the desert and of the wandering—with the popular gods who manifest themselves in natural epiphanies, in the figure of the king or in the idols of the temple. The God who comes is a *name,* the god who shows himself is an *idol.* The God of the promise opens up a history, the god of epiphanies animates a nature. But the New Testament did not put an end to the theology of the Promise, for the Resurrection itself, which is at the centre of its message, is not only the fulfillment of the promise in an unique event, but the confirmation of the promise which becomes for all the hope of final victory over death.

What follows from this for freedom and for evil, which ethical consciousness has grasped in their unity? I shall begin by a discussion of freedom, for a reason which will become clear in a moment. It seems to me that religion is distinguished from ethics, in the fact that it requires that we think of freedom under the sign of hope.

In the language of the gospel, I would say: to consider freedom in the light of hope, is to re-situate my existence in the movement, which might be called, with Jürgen Moltmann, the 'future of the resurrection of Christ'. This 'kerygmatic' formula can be translated in several ways in contemporary language. First of all, with Kierkegaard, we could call freedom in the light of hope the 'passion for the *possible*'; this formula, in contrast to all wisdom of the present, to all submission to necessity, underscores the imprint of the promise on freedom. Freedom, entrusted to the 'God who comes', is open to the radically new; it is the creative imagination of the possible.

But, in a deeper dimension, freedom *in the light of hope* is a freedom which affirms itself, *in spite of* death, and in spite of all the signs of death; for, in a phrase of the Reformers, the Kingdom is hidden *sub contrario,* under its contrary, the cross. Freedom in the light of hope is freedom for the denial of death, freedom to decipher the signs of the Resurrection under the contrary appearance of death.

Likewise, the category of 'in spite of . . .' is the opposite or reverse side of a vital thrust, of a perspective of belief which finds its expression in the famous 'how much more' of St Paul. This category, more fundamental than the 'in spite of', expresses what might be called the logic of superabundance, which is the logic of hope. Here the words of St Paul to the Romans come to mind:

But the free gift is not like the fault, for, if many died through one man's fault, *how much more* have the grace of God and the gift conferred by the grace of that one man, Jesus Christ, abounded for many. . . . If because of one man's fault, death reigned through that one man, *how much more* will those who receive the abundance of grace, the free gift of righteousness, reign in life through the one man, Jesus

Christ. . . . Law came in to increase the fault; but where sin increased, grace abounded all the more. . . .' (Rom. 5:15, 17, 20)

This logic of surplus and excess is to be uncovered in daily life, in work and in leisure, in politics and in universal history. The 'in spite of . . .' which keeps us in readiness for the denial is only the inverse, the shadow side, of this joyous 'how much more' by which freedom feels itself, knows itself, and wills itself to belong to this economy of superabundance.

This notion of an economy of superabundance permits us to return to the problem of evil. It is from this point of departure, and in it, that a religious or theological discourse on evil can be held. Ethics has said all it can about evil in calling it: (*i*) a work of freedom (*ii*) a subversion of the relation of the maxim to the law (*iii*) an unfathomable disposition of freedom which makes it unavailable to itself.

Religion uses another language about evil. And this language keeps itself entirely within the limits of the perimeter of the promise and under the sign of hope. First of all, this language places evil *before* God. 'Against you, against you alone have I sinned, I have done evil in your sight.' This invocation which transforms the moral confession into a confession of sin, appears, at first glance, to be an intensification in the consciousness of evil. But that is an illusion, the moralising illusion of Christianity. Situated before God, evil is installed again in the movement of the promise: the invocation is already the beginning of the restoration of a bond, the initiation of a new creation. The 'passion for the possible' has already taken possession of the confession of evil; repentance, essentially directed towards the future, has already cut itself off from remorse which is a brooding reflection on the past.

Next, religious language profoundly changes the very content of the consciousness of evil. Evil in moral consciousness is essentially transgression, that is, subversion of the law; it is in this way that the majority of pious men continue to consider sin. And yet, situated before God, evil is qualitatively changed; it consists less in a transgression of a law than in a pretension of man to be master of his life. The will to live according to the law is, therefore, also an expression of evil—and even the most deadly, because the most dissimulated: worse than injustice is one's own justice. Ethical consciousness does not know this, but religious consciousness does.

But this second discovery can also be expressed in terms of promise and hope.

Indeed, the will is not constituted, as we have seemed to believe in the context of the ethical analysis, merely by the relation between the arbitrary and the law (in Kantian terms, between the *Willkür* or arbitrary will and the *Wille* or determination by the law of reason). The will is more fundamentally constituted by a desire of fulfilment or achievement. Kant himself in the dialectical part of the *Critique of Practical Reason* recognised this intended goal of totalisation. It is this precisely which animates the *Dialectic of Practical Reason,* as the relation to the law animates the *Analytic.* Now this tendency toward totalisation, according to Kant, requires the reconciliation of two moments which Rigorism has separated: 'virtue', that is, obedience to pure duty, and 'happiness', that is, satisfaction of desire. This reconciliation is the Kantian equivalent of hope. This rebound of the philosophy of will entails a rebound of the philosophy of evil. If the tendency toward totalisation is thus the soul of the will, we have not yet reached the foundation of the problem of evil so long as we have kept it within the limits of a reflection of the relations of the arbitrary and the law. The true evil, the evil of evil, shows itself in false syntheses, i.e. in contemporary falsifications of the great undertakings of totalisation of cultural experience, that is, in political and ecclesiastical institutions. In this way, evil shows its true face—the evil of evil is the lie of premature syntheses, of violent totalisations.

Evil 'abounds' wherever man transcends himself in grandiose undertakings, wherein he sees the culmination of his existence in the higher works of culture, in politics and in religion. And so these great simulacra, the cult of race, the cult of the State, and all forms of false worship, are the very birth of idols, substituted for the 'Name', who should remain faceless.

But this greater deepening of our understanding of evil is, once again, a conquest of hope: it is because man is a goal of totality, a will of total fulfilment, that he plunges himself into totalitarianisms, which really constitute the pathology of hope. As the old proverb says, demons haunt only the courts of the gods. But, at the same time, we sense that evil itself is a part of the economy of superabundance. Paraphrasing St Paul, I dare to say: Wherever evil 'abounds', hope 'super-abounds'. We must therefore have the courage to incorporate evil into the epic of hope. In a way that we know not, evil itself co-operates, works toward the advancement of the Kingdom of God. This is the viewpoint of faith on evil. This view is not that of the moralist; the moralist contrasts the *predicate* evil with the predicate good; he condemns evil; he imputes it to freedom; and finally, he stops at the limit of the inscrutable; for we do not know how it is possible that freedom could be enslaved. Faith does not look in this direction; the origin of evil is not its problem; the end of evil is its problem. With the prophets, faith incorporates this end into the economy of the promise, with Jesus, into the preaching of the God who comes, with St Paul, into the law of superabundance. This is why the view of faith on events and on men is essentially benevolent. Faith justifies the man of the *Aufklärung* for whom, in the great romance of culture, evil is a factor in the education of the human race, rather than the puritan, who never succeeds in taking the step from condemnation to mercy, and who thus remains within the ethical dimension, and never enters into the perspective of the Kingdom which comes.

Such are the three 'discourses' which may be held about guilt: the semantic discourse is mainly a phenomenology of confession by means of an interpretation of symbolic expressions; the ethical discourse is an explanation of the relation between freedom, obligation and evil (it relies on the performatives through which I take on myself the origin of evil and constitute myself as a responsible will); the religious discourse is a reinterpretation of freedom and evil in the light of hope—in Christian terms, of hope in the universal resurrection from the dead.

If I consider these three discourses as a whole, they offer a kind of progression, which could be compared to the progression from the aesthetic stage to the ethical and the religious stage in Kierkegaard's philosophy. I should accept this comparison, if I did not find it disparaging and discouraging.

NOTES

1. *Religion within the Limits of Reason*, §§ 83-9.
2. *Ibid.*, § 62.

2 The Decline and Fall of Conscience

PAUL LEHMANN

Probably nowhere in the vast literature about conscience can we find our modern dilemma more
clearly stated than in this passage. Starting with the
Greek tragedians and ending with Sigmund Freud,
Lehmann explores shifting views of conscience.* His
critical analysis shows how our modern knowledge
of self "naturalizes" conscience and makes it just
another object for therapy. Without denying the need
for psychological clarity in self-understanding, Lehmann presses the ethical questions: How can there
be ethics if conscience is—or can be—domesticated
by parents or society? How can we make moral judgments that are not merely a reflection of our personal history? Although not reprinted here, the
author in the chapter that follows this selection develops the idea that "the community of believers,"
if taken seriously as the context of ethical decision-
making, would change our false reliance on the individual's conscience and would open up the deeper
meaning of the biblical notion of "heart" as the
source of ethical reflection.

The semantic, philosophical and theological
pilgrimage of conscience begins with the
Greek tragedians of the fifth century before Christ and ends with
Sigmund Freud. It is a moving, tortuous record of decline and fall
which forces upon us in our time the frankest possible facing of a

* From *Ethics in a Christian Context* (New York: Harper and Row,
1963), pp. 327-343. Reprinted with permission.

sharp alternative: either 'do the conscience over' or 'do the conscience in'! Ethical theory must either dispose of the conscience
altogether or completely transform the interpretation of its ethical
nature, function, and significance.

When we describe the present ethical condition of conscience
as one of decline and fall, we have two considerations chiefly in
mind.[1] By the *decline* of conscience we mean the fact that the
power of conscience to shape behavior both through judgment and
through action has steadily lost persuasiveness and force. By the
fall of conscience we mean the rejection of conscience as formative
of, or important for, ethical behavior. What is of utmost significance for ethical theory, however, is that the conscience which has
been rejected is the conscience which has declined; it is *not* the
conscience which is intrinsic to ethical action which has been rejected. And this discrepancy provides the clue to a constructive
interpretation of the ethical nature and function of conscience.

1. *The Enemy of Humanization*

The original semantic environment of the *conscience* was
Greek. The Latin, *con-scientia*, was a translation of ἡ συνείδησις,
which appears initially to have had two main uses, a technical-
philosophical usage and an ethical usage.[2] The technical usage
referred to a state of consciousness such as would be expressed
as 'I am conscious of this or that within myself', or 'I am conscious within myself that this or that is the case'. Whatever it is
that 'I know together with, or in common with myself' appears to
include the implication of being 'desirable' or 'undesirable', but in
the cognitive rather than in the ethical sense. Thus, Alcibiades declares that he is conscious that if he did not shut his ears against
Socrates, 'and fly as from the voice of the siren', his 'fate would be
like the others,—he would transfix me and I should grow old
sitting at his feet'.[3]

The moral use of ἡ συνείδησις denotes the moral quality of
the self's own acts or behavior, as in such variant phrases as 'to be
a witness for or against oneself', 'to hug a secret to oneself', usually
a guilty secret. Indeed, unless stated otherwise the connotation of

ἡ συνείδησις is bad. Euripides makes Orestes say that he suffers conscience (ἡ σύνεσις, i.e., self-knowledge! knowledge privy with himself concerning himself) in that he knows with himself that he has done terrible things.

> ORESTES: I call it conscience.
> The certain knowledge of wrong, the conviction of crime.
> MENELAUS: You speak somewhat obscurely. What do you mean?
> ORESTES: I mean remorse. I am sick with remorse.[4]

And Menander declares that he who knows anything at all with himself, no matter how brave he is, will be reduced to terror by that knowledge.[5]

Now something like a structure or configuration of meaning emerges from the foregoing uses of 'conscience', which are merely samples of innumerable others.[6] The structure suggests that ἡ συνείδησις is connected with the fixed order of things as they are. Gradually this connection tends to be traced to the gods or to God as the orderer of the universe. Conscience is also an order intrinsic to the nature of man. It refers, moreover, always to specific acts and to acts that are past. And finally, its function is that of pain. Thus Plutarch can say that conscience is 'like an ulcer in the flesh'; [7] Polybius 'asserts that there is no witness so fearful, nor accuser so terrible as that which dwells in the soul of every man'; [8] and Philo describes the conscience with great vividness and force: 'It is born with every soul . . . is at once both accuser and judge. . . . Never does it depart by day or by night, but it stabs as with a goad, and inflicts wounds that know no healing, until it snap the thread of that soul's pitiful and accursed life.' [9] The meaning of conscience, then, is that human nature is so constituted that if man oversteps the moral limits of his nature he is certain to feel the pain of τῆς συνειδήσεώς. Just as the delight of a journey lies in the absence of mishap, so the absence of conscience is a great joy. As a nurse or governess will watchfully guard her charges, so the proper office of conscience is to protect man from physical and moral harm.[10] What is to be noted above all is that according to the original semantic environment of conscience, the ethical significance of conscience is not that it is a teacher of morals. Its ethical significance is that it resides in human nature as the bearer of ethical negation and futility in the relationship between man and the order of things in which he lives.

2. *The Domestication of Conscience*

If now we shift the perspective and turn from the original semantic environment of conscience toward the apex of its cultural journey, we come upon the clearest and most influential account of its ethical nature and significance through the mind of Thomas Aquinas. The account centers upon the distinction already alluded to between *synderesis* and *conscientia.* 'There is in the soul', Thomas wrote, 'a natural habit of first principles of action, which are the universal principles of the natural law. This habit pertains to synderesis. This habit exists in no other power than reason. . . . The name *conscience* means the application of knowledge to something. . . . Conscience . . . is the application of any habit or of any knowledge to some particular act.' [11] The first principles of moral action are known to all men without deliberation. But the behavioral implementation of this knowledge requires a kind of liaison between the principle and any given action. This bond between the principle and the act is the conscience. What a man knows together with himself is that this or that particular, freely chosen action is in accordance with natural law. *Conscience is, thus, the bond between law and responsibility.*

Thomas is not unaware of the variety of meanings which have been attributed to *conscience.*[12] But following the advice of Aristotle that one should follow the more common signification of terms, Aquinas adheres to the tradition which derives *conscience* from *conscire,* 'to know together'.[13] As the analysis proceeds, however, a significant transformation of the ethical meaning and role of conscience takes place. The fierce and awesome internal arbiter and enemy of man is brought under the discriminating differentiation and control of the reason in the act of judging both what man knows and what man does. 'Judgment', Thomas notes, 'is two-fold: of universal [principles], which belongs to synderesis; and of particular activities, which is the judgment of choice and belongs to free choice' (i.e., the conscience).[14] Thomas explains the operation of this twofold judgment in terms of the contrast between scientific and moral knowledge, between what one 'is conscious of' and what one 'has a conscience about'.[15] In both cases there is a 'knowing together with ourselves', a 'bond betwixt two'. But in the first case, 'through scientific knowledge we look for what should be done' and 'proceed from principles to conclusions'. In the second case, 'we examine those things which already have been done and consider whether they are right' and 'reduce conclusions to principles'.[16]

This brings us to the passage in which the transformation of the ethical meaning and role of conscience is vividly formulated. 'We use the name of conscience', Thomas wrote, 'for both these modes of application [i.e., the two cases just mentioned]. For, in so far as knowledge is applied to an act, as directive of that act, conscience is said to prod or urge or bind. But, in so far as knowledge is applied to an act, by way of examining things which already have taken place, conscience is said *to accuse or cause remorse* when that which has been done is found to be out of harmony with the knowledge according to which it is examined; or to *defend or excuse* when that which has been done is found to have proceeded according to the form of the knowledge.'[17]

Something like a *domestication* of conscience has occurred. The ominous, sometimes even wildly terrifying fury of the guilty conscience has been tamed by a divine infusion of the rational soul which lightens the dark torment of negation and futility by an intrinsic power to distinguish between good and evil, and so either to defend or to accuse, to excuse or to cause remorse. The easy conscience has become the companion of the uneasy one. It must be borne in mind that the environment of conscience has also been markedly transformed from an indifferent or hostile order of inscrutable arbitrariness into an order of intellectual stability and understanding. This is the meaning of Thomas's suggestion that *synderesis* is common both to men and to angels.[18] But the change in the environment of conscience does not diminish the significance of the transformation of the conscience itself. Indeed, it is this very change which makes the domestication of conscience possible. Originally conscience had but a single function and that was negative and unbearable. Now conscience has acquired a double function, a negative and a positive one, and has become bearable. Originally conscience was that in a man which above all things else he could not endure. Now conscience can be lived with; the knowledge which a man has together with himself could be counted upon as still against him, but sometimes also—and this is the important change—as on his side.

3. *Duty's Inner Citadel*

The Thomistic view of conscience is the classic statement, if not the origin, of the popular notion of the conscience as a built-in human device for spot-checking right from wrong. The pervasive hold of his position over popular morality has reached beyond the confines of the Christian ethical tradition. Within the Christian tradition its formidable influence upon ethical thinking, instructed and uninstructed alike, is due to the pivotal role of conscience in moral theology. But there is another view of conscience, strikingly similar yet strangely different, whose influence upon ethical theory and practice is perhaps second only to that of Aquinas. This influence has been initiated without the benefit of clergy. Indeed, the roles have been reversed; for the clergy have not so much bestowed as received the benefits of conscience which have been secured by Immanuel Kant.

For Kant, as for St Thomas, conscience is a faculty of judgment. It is concerned with the evaluation of action in accordance with universal moral principles and is both internal and intrinsic to human nature. With Kant, as with Thomas, the conscience both accuses and excuses. 'For conscience is practical reason which, in every case of law, holds before man his duty for acquittal or condemnation.' [19] The law, of course, is the moral law. And what makes the conscience that 'marvellous faculty in us' [20] is its function in bringing the moral law and the moral will together. *Conscience is the bond between duty and obligation.*

The argument in brief is this. The moral worth of actions is defined by the fact that the will is determined by the moral law. This means that all incentive is excluded from moral action except the constraint of the moral law itself. Thus 'morality of moral worth can be conceded only where the action occurs from duty, i.e. merely for the sake of the law'.[21] But an action done *from* duty is not in and of itself an action done *according to* duty. One may, for example, act *from* duty simply because the law of duty constrains, while one really desires to act in another way. The moral will is at variance with the moral law. Conversely, one may act *according to* a sense of duty without a clear command of the moral law. As Kant puts it, 'it is a very beautiful thing to do good to men because of love and a sympathetic good will or to do justice because of a love of order. But this is not the genuine moral maxim of our conduct'.[22] When this happens, a disparity has occurred between what the law of duty requires objectively (an action *from* duty) and what it requires subjectively (an action *according to* duty, i.e., as an obligation). In short, the command and the maxim of the action do not correspond. 'It is', however, 'of the utmost importance in all moral judging to pay strictest attention to the subjective principle of every maxim. . . .'[23] In the case of a good act, in the pure and proper sense of the phrase, the subjective principle of *respect for the law* (obligation) combines with the constraint of the law itself (duty). Thus, 'duty and obligation are the only names which we must ever give to our relation to the moral law'.[24] An act done both *from* duty and *in accordance with* duty is an act done both from respect for the moral law and in accordance with the moral law as the sole determining ground of the will.

Although duty and obligation define the relation of men to the moral law and thus also the moral worth of their actions, the question still remains as to how one knows that this or that action has actually met the conditions of morality. The answer is given by the moral consciousness, i.e., the consciousness of the ethical subject in the performance of a moral act. Such a man is conscious of his transcendental freedom, i.e., of his own existence as 'determinable only by laws which he gives to himself through reason'.[25] And he is also conscious of a capacity for judgment, i.e., the consciousness that at the moment of acting 'he was in possession of his freedom'.[26]

Thus, as Thomas had analyzed the moral consciousness in terms of a compound of synderesis and conscience, Kant analyzes the moral consciousness in terms of the moral reason and conscience. As Thomas had derived the content of synderesis from the *natural* law, Kant finds the moral reason informed by the *moral* law and respect for the moral law. What a man knows in conscience is that, in the case of any given action, duty and obligation either correspond or do not correspond. If duty and obligation are adjudged by the conscience to correspond, the conscience acquits; if duty and obligation do not correspond, the conscience condemns.

This brings us to the strangely different countenance of conscience under the careful scrutiny of Kant as compared to Aquinas. Kant's stress upon law and upon the *pure* (in contrast to the prime) principles of morality has brought a corresponding accent to the conscience in operation. The judgmental function of conscience has acquired an astringent quality. Whereas Aquinas had analyzed the conscience as a faculty of judgment, Kant makes an important addition. Conscience for Kant is *juridical as well as judgmental.* It functions not simply as the intellect or reason in the act of distinguishing good from evil but as a *tribunal.* As Kant puts it in a particularly forceful passage, 'the consciousness of an internal tribunal in man . . . is conscience. . . . This power is not something which he himself makes but it is incorporated in his being. . . . It follows him like his shadow, when he thinks to escape. . . . In his utmost depravity he may indeed pay no heed to it, but he cannot avoid hearing it. . . . Now this original intellectual and moral capacity, called *conscience,* has this peculiarity in it, that although its business is a business of man with himself yet he finds himself compelled by his reason to transact it as if at the command of another person . . . God.' [27] Thus an inner faculty of reason becomes an inner voice of judgment and the way is open for a virtual identification of the voice of conscience as the voice of God. Kant himself had cautiously written: 'the subjective principle of a responsibility of one's deeds before God'. But plainly the identification is not far removed.

The identification of the voice of conscience with the voice of God is not completely absent from the conscience as domesticated by Aquinas. In a precise sense, the juridical and the judgmental functions of conscience always belonged together as two sides of a coin. Yet just as the marked stress upon the awesomeness of duty inevitably overshadowed the pure rationality of the moral law, so the marked stress upon the inwardness of conscience heightened its juridical significance over its judgmental significance. The result was an operational detachment of conscience from synderesis, of the tribunal of moral judgment from the transcendent character of moral freedom. And this meant that actions could be appraised as good or bad with a heightened sense of moral certainty in proportion to the inner depth of conscience. In a more intimate and volitional sense than ever, a resurgence of the uneasy conscience had occurred. Kant had outdone the classical dramatists and moralists in juxtaposing the guilty conscience with a rational order of responsibility. And he had undone St Thomas in reaffirming the radical character of negation in relation to achievement in the evaluation of moral behavior. In the classical view, the guilty conscience, like the mark on the forehead of Cain, was the bearer of the tragedy of man's life in the world. Thomas (and moral theology with him) had displaced the tragic conscience by the easy conscience as the bearer of the dignity, and the promise of man's life as a rational being under grace. Kant had once again restored the tragic conscience to its due place in a rational analysis of the moral life. Kant has made it impossible for reason either to ignore or to suppress the conscience in the analysis of ethical sensitivity and responsibility.

However, despite the magnificence of Kant's demonstration of the impotence of conscience to shape behavior on the classical and the Thomistic model, his own achievement must also be reckoned as an extension of the conscience in decline. Perhaps it may be said that Kant was the principal architect of the decline of conscience since he most directly prepared the ground for its fall. For Kant had displaced the human significance of conscience as the link between the internal nature of man and the order in which his life is sustained. He had substituted the legal significance of conscience as an internal voice of an external authority. It is this authoritarian conscience which has so conspicuously lost its ethical persuasiveness and force today. Consequently, we must face the question whether a recovery of the ethical significance and role of conscience is either possible or desirable. If Thomas and especially Kant may be regarded as the architects of the decline of conscience, Sigmund Freud must be regarded as the principal architect of the fall of conscience.

4. The Dethronement of Conscience

There is a passage in the *New Introductory Lectures* which

vividly expresses both Freud's rejection of Kant and a hint of his own considered view of the conscience.

The philosopher Kant once declared [Freud remarks] that nothing proved to him the greatness of God more convincingly than the starry heavens and the moral conscience within us. The stars are unquestionably superb, but where conscience is concerned God has been guilty of an uneven and careless piece of work, for a great many men have only a limited share of it or scarcely enough to be worth mentioning. . . . It is a very remarkable experience to observe morality, which was once ostensibly conferred on us by God and planted deep in our hearts, functioning as a periodical phenomenon. For after a certain number of months the whole moral fuss is at an end, the critical voice of the super-ego is silent, the ego is re-instated, and enjoys once more all the rights of man until another attack.[28]

Clearly, what Freud had discovered clinically was that the conscience did not, as Kant had claimed, express and facilitate the moralization of man. On the contrary, the net effect of the Kantian account of conscience was the dehumanization of man. Indeed, the Freudian exploration of the intimate connection between mental and moral disorder has compounded the evidence confirming the fatal role of conscience in the Western ethical tradition. With Freud the line beginning, as it were, with Euripides comes full circle round. Dramatist and scientist have met in a common documentation in depth of the ethical futility of conscience. 'The stars are unquestionably superb, but where conscience is concerned God has been guilty of an uneven and careless piece of work. . . .'

Nevertheless, Freud seems to have regarded the conscience as an inevitable rather than as an expendable datum of human nature. There is a bond between the environment of decision and the intrinsic human response to that environment which makes or breaks the emerging humanity of man. In this, Freud was in agreement with Euripides, Thomas, and Kant. But unlike the theologian and the philosopher, Freud shares the pessimism about the conscience which informed its original semantic clarification. A passage in *Totem and Taboo* is virtually a prosaic duplication of the metered melancholy with which Orestes voices the suffering of conscience.

Taboo conscience is probably the oldest form in which we meet the phenomenon of conscience. For what is conscience? According to linguistic testimony it belongs to what we know most surely; in some languages its meaning is hardly to be distinguished from consciousness.

Conscience is the inner perception of objections to definite wish impulses that exist in us; but the emphasis is put upon the fact that this rejection does not have to depend on anything else, that it is sure of itself. This becomes even plainer in the case of a guilty conscience, where we become aware of the inner condemnation of such acts which realized some of our definite wish impulses. . . . Whoever has a conscience must feel in himself the justification of the condemnation, and the reproach for the accomplished action. But this same character is evinced by the attitude of savages towards taboo. Taboo is a command of conscience, the violation of which causes a terrible sense of guilt which is as self-evident as its origin is unknown.[29]

The more Freud observed the results of conscience in operation, the more he endeavored to find an explanation of its origin and formation. His earliest conjectures are characterized by an ambivalence which the latest position tried not so much to discard as to reconstruct. Two conceptions of conscience seem to persist side by side as Freud tries to deal with the fact that human nature appears unable either to avoid or to endure conscience. 'It has long been our contention', he wrote, 'that "dread of society" (*soziale Angst*) is the essence of what is called conscience.' [30] Yet this contention had not been of such long standing as to displace an earlier suggestion that 'as a substitute-formation there arises an alteration in the ego, an increased sensitiveness of conscience, which can hardly be called a symptom'.[31] The point here is that conscience is a neurotic manifestation arising from a hiatus between the instinctual drives of the organism and reality, as presented to the organism in its environment. The ego is the focal point of this hiatus and responds by repressing the conflict between what Freud elsewhere calls the 'pleasure-principle' and the 'reality-principle'.[32] In a later and perhaps more crucial discussion, a different formulation occurs which appears to contradict 'the long-standing contention' that conscience is a social manifestation. It may be, however, that Freud is attempting a rather more precise formulation of the relation between two hitherto disparate conceptions of conscience. '. . . That part of the fear of the superego which may be called social anxiety', Freud notes, 'still represents an internal substitute for an external danger, while the other part, fear of conscience, is entirely endopsychic.' [33] Here the term 'conscience' appears to be applied to internal psychic responses rather than to external social pressures upon the individual.

By whatever developmental route Freud arrived at his most fully elaborated view of conscience, the several elements of it are already before us. The instinctual drives, the ego responses both to these drives and to the super-ego, provide the clinical and conceptual materials which were destined to play such a formative role in the fall of conscience. As is well known, the basic elements of the psychic apparatus are the *id*, the *ego*, and the *super-ego*. The human organism arrives in the world equipped with an unorganized chaos of instinctual drives: hunger, self-preservation, sexuality, love. These drives press for and require gratification. In their elemental form they constitute the id. The id possesses the capacity to differentiate between the inexorable reality of the outer world and an inner dynamism of response, and for this part of the id Freud uses the term 'ego'. 'One can hardly go wrong,' he declares, 'in regarding the ego as the part of the id which has been modified by its proximity to the external world and the influence that the latter has had on it. . . .' [34] And just as the ego is a modified part of the id, so the super-ego is a modification of the ego. If the ego is that part of the id which protectively selects and orders its chaos anent the external world, the super-ego is that part of the ego which responds to and transmits the restrictions imposed by the external world via external authorities. 'We have posited a special function within the ego,' says Freud, 'to represent the demand for restriction and rejection, i.e., the super-ego. We can say that repression is the work of the super-ego—either that it does its work on its own account or else that the ego does it in obedience to its orders,' [35] The super-ego, at first shaped by the demands of authorities external to the ego, chiefly parental, gradually displaces these authorities and functions by its own power as a kind of internalized echo of external authorities. 'The super-ego takes the place of the parental function, and thenceforward observes, guides and threatens the ego in just the same way as the parents acted to the child before.' [36]

Thus, for Freud, the neurotic and the societal aspects of the phenomenon of conscience meet in the super-ego and its operation. In a word, conscience *is* the super-ego. Whether conscience has a positive function is not entirely clear. Freud speaks of a 'distance between an ego ideal and the real ego' [37] due apparently to the dissatisfaction of the ego with itself. But whether this ego ideal is the cause or the consequence of the dissatisfaction is ambiguous. It is, perhaps, also ambiguous whether the super-ego (as the repository of parental and cultural ideals) [38] contributes positively to the socialization of the individual. Indubitably, however, the decisive operation of conscience is negative, i.e., judging and condemning, 'exercising the function of a censor'.[39] The exercise of this function is at once so intense and so aggressive as to leave the ego almost prostrate before it. As Freud describes the sequence of conscience formation its range and oppressiveness seem virtually complete. There is 'first, instinct renunciation due to dread of loss of love. . . . Then follows erection of an internal authority, and instinctual renunciation due to dread of it—that is dread of conscience. In the second case, there is the equivalence of wicked acts and wicked intentions; hence comes the sense of guilt, the need for punishment. The aggressiveness of conscience carries on the aggressiveness of authority.[40] This aggressiveness appears to be reinforced by the super-ego of the neighbor, a phenomenon which Freud explores in terms of the relations between 'psyche' and 'alter'. 'Now it is, of course, very probable', he writes, 'that my neighbor, when he is commanded to love me as himself, will answer exactly as I have done and reject me for the same reasons. I hope he will not have the same objective grounds for doing so, but he will hope so as well. Even so, there are variations in men's behavior which ethics, disregarding the fact that they are determined, classifies as "good" and "evil". As long as these undeniable variations have not been abolished, conformity to the highest ethical standards constitutes a betrayal of the interests of culture, for it puts a direct premium on wickedness.'[41] The social pessimism which Thomas Hobbes had described in political terms three centuries earlier is here established clinically.[42] What Freud seems to be saying is that 'good' and 'evil' are deterministic variants of the social and endopsychic conflict between 'psyche' and 'alter', between which the conscience operates to maintain an uneasy truce. The truce is particularly uneasy because the very obedience of 'psyche' to the demands of the super-ego provides the occasion for 'alter' to express its own aggressions unhindered by any anxiety over their being returned. This means that conscience has exchanged its ethical role and function for a psychoanalytic one. Although Freud recognized that conscience is the result both of innate constitutional and concrete environmental factors, he was unable to arrive at a depth-psychological account of the origin and significance of conscience that was otherwise than heavy with guilt and inexorability. At the end, neither individual fulfillment nor cultural development can break the stranglehold of conscience upon man's 'task of living with his fellows'. For conscience is simply 'the price of progress in civilization'.[43]

The ethical consequences of this grim doctrine are enormous. Freud seems to have done with meticulous precision what God had allegedly done with uneven carelessness, 'The moral fuss is, indeed, at an end.' But there is no 'waiting for the next attack' except for those constitutionally unable to pay the price of conscience. For the normal human course there is a way of coming to terms with the ever-present threat of dehumanization aimed at the ego by the super-ego. This is the way of the therapeutic transformation of the ethical role and function of conscience into a psychoanalytic one. Therapy seeks to illuminate the struggle between the ego and the super-ego and thereby to achieve an accommodation of the human psyche to its natural and social environment. Mature self-knowledge leads to serenity through a manageable reduction of the tensions arising from involvement in the stresses and strains of living. Consequently, an appeal to conscience in the name of morality or contrariwise to morality in the name of conscience is ethically sterile because humanly false, i.e., irrelevant to human nature as it actually behaves and develops. The clinical data have exposed a moral bondage upon mankind from which there is no egress. Under this bondage, the sensitivity to what it takes to make and to keep human life human is severely restricted to an attainable adjustment between self-conscious self-awareness and the relevant limits imposed by external environment. The tragic nobility of Orestes has given way before the precarious tranquillity of the measurably uninvolved life. If the uneasy conscience cannot be made easy it can at least be made evident; if it cannot be domesticated, it can at least be subdued.

> Thus conscience does make cowards of us all;
> And thus the native hue of resolution

Is sicklied o'er with the pale cast of thought,
And enterprises of great pith and moment,
With this regard their currents turn awry
And lose the name of action.[44]

Hamlet was a Freudian before Freud, a pitiful replica of Orestes, and the prototype of twentieth-century man.

Freud's greatness, like Kant's, is marked by his dedication to follow his findings regardless of consequences. On the boundary of the ethical disintegration and psychoanalytic confirmation of conscience, he has exposed the long-overdue need for a reconsideration of 'the knowledge of good and evil' as the environment of human wholeness. That he was unable himself to move toward such a reconsideration is not so much to be held against him as against the failure of the Western ethical tradition to provide an adequate context for conscience. The fall of conscience, as Freud documents it, is the rejection of the hostile conscience through the demonstration of its ethical impotence and uselessness. Such a fall could be the prelude to a rise of conscience if the loosing of conscience from its barren ethical moorings should prove to be a way of loosing it for a context within which its potential ethical role and significance could acquire ethical reality.

NOTES

1. A full-length study of what has happened to conscience in the Western cultural tradition is overdue. A carefully documented and sufficiently comprehensive account of what might be called 'the shape of conscience', i.e., of an interpretive framework other than that offered by moral theology in which the ethical nature and behavioral effectiveness of the conscience might once again be clearly and persuasively understood, is not at hand. Obviously, such a discussion of conscience goes beyond the limits of the present book. All that can be attempted here, and indeed is necessary to the concerns of this essay, is some indication of the principal episodes of the decline and fall of conscience and a concluding hint of a constructive ethical interpretation.

2. The paragraphs in this chapter dealing with the Hellenistic and biblical environment and usage of the word 'conscience' are heavily dependent upon the succinct but carefully documented discussion of conscience by C. A. Pierce, *Conscience in the New Testament,* Alec R. Allenson, Inc., Naperville, 1955 (SCM Press, London, 1955).

3. Plato, *Symposium,* 216, Jowett translation. The Greek text says: 'χαὶ ἔτι γε νῦν σύνοιδ' ἐμαυτῷ. . . .'

4. Orestes, ll. 395ff. *The Complete Greek Tragedies,* edited by David

Grene and Richard Lattimore, Vol. IV, University of Chicago Press, Chicago, 1958, p. 214.

5. Fragment 632 (Koch collection, 1880): '. . . ἡ σύνεσιζ αὐτὸν δειλότατον εἶναι ποιεῖ'. Pierce, *op. cit.*, p. 25.

6. How innumerable may be gleaned from the analytical index of Greek sources which Pierce has provided, *op. cit.*, pp. 131-47.

7. *De Tranquilitate Animi*, 476F-77A; quoted by Pierce, *op. cit.*, p. 47.

8. See Pierce, *op. cit.*, pp. 40-41.

9. *De Decalogo* 87; quoted by Pierce, *op. cit.*, p. 46.

10. See Pierce, *op. cit.*, pp. 50-51.

11. *De Veritate*, Q. 16, art. 1; Q. 17, art. 1. We quote from the English translation entitled *Truth*, by James V. McGlynn, S.J. Chicago, Henry Reguery Company, 1953.

12. He alludes to Bonaventura and Alexander Hales, who use the word 'conscience' variously for the object of which one is conscious, for a power, a habit, or an act. See *De Veritate*, English translation, Q. 17, art 1; and also p. 449.

13. See Aristotle, *Topica*, II, 1, 109a, 27. *De Veritate*, Q. 17, art. 1, Reply.

14. *De Veritate*, Q. 16, art. 1, Answer 15. The bracketed word appears in the English translation, p. 307.

15. The phrases are mine, not Thomas's.

16. *De Veritate*, Q. 17, art. 1, Reply. The first case is clearly *synderesis;* the second is *conscience.*

17. *De Veritate*, Q. 17, art. 1, Reply. Italics mine.

18. I.e., to the next higher order of beings. Ibid., Q. 16, art. I, Reply. See on this point especially, Étienne Gilson, *The Christian Philosophy of St. Thomas Aquinas,* Random House, New York, 1956 (Gollancz, London, 1957). Or perhaps a more existentialist interpretation of St Thomas is possible, and the environment of conscience is to be understood as an order of providence and charity. I am indebted to Professor Richard Kalter of Berkeley Divinity School, New Haven, for clarifying discussions of St Thomas' views on conscience and for this suggestion in particular growing out of his own studies looking toward the completion of a Th.D. dissertation on 'Conscience and Providence in the Thought of St Thomas Aquinas'. The re-examination of moral theology by Roman Catholic theologians considered in the foregoing chapter seems also to point to this possibility.

19. Immanuel Kant, *The Metaphysical Elements of Ethics, Werke,* Vol. V, Hartenstein edition, Modes und Baumann, Leipzig, 1938, Introduction, Part XII, par. b, p. 227. Translation mine.

20. Immanuel Kant, *Critique of Practical Reason,* Beck edition, University of Chicago Press, Chicago, 1949, p. 204.

21. *Ibid.*, p. 188. See also pp. 180ff.

22. *Ibid.*, p. 189.

23. *Ibid.*, p. 188.

24. *Ibid.*, p. 189.

25. *Ibid.*, p. 203.

26. *Ibid.*, p. 204.

27. Kant, *The Metaphysical Elements of Ethics,* Part II, par. 13, pp. 271-72. Translation mine.

28. Sigmund Freud, *New Introductory Lectures on Psychoanalysis,* translated by W. J. H. Sprott, W. W. Norton and Company, New York, 1938 (Hogarth, London), p. 88. Kant had actually written 'the moral law within'. But as we have seen this was functionally identical with conscience.

29. Sigmund Freud, *Totem and Taboo,* in *The Basic Writings of Sigmund Freud,* translated and edited by Dr A. A. Brill, The Modern Library, New York, 1938 (Kegan Paul, London), pp. 859-60. In a footnote Freud expressly alludes to the Oedipus myth, according to which the guilt of Oedipus is not canceled by the fact that it was incurred without his knowledge and will and even against them. The essay itself marks the beginning of Freud's effort to bring his clinical findings to bear upon the question of the origin of conscience, illuminating thereby also the nature of conscience. Other essays which have to do particularly with Freud's reflections upon the conscience and with the emergence of his final position on the problem are: *The Origins of Psychoanalysis,* 1910, in *General Selections,* edited by John Rickman, Hogarth Press, London, 1937; *Group Psychology and the Analysis of the Ego,* translated by James Strachey, International Psycho-analytic Press, London, 1922 (*GPE*); *The Problem of Anxiety,* translated by Henry A. Bunker, W. W. Norton and Company, New York, 1936 (*A*); *The Problem of Lay Analysis,* Introduction by Dr L. Terenczi, Brentanos, New York, 1927; *Civilization and Its Discontents,* translated by Joan Rivers, Hogarth Press, London, 1930 (*CD*); *New Introductory Lectures in Psychoanalysis* (*NIL*). The abbreviations in parentheses will be used below in identifying sources. I wish to acknowledge with special appreciation the kindness of Mr Donald Miller, a candidate for the Ph.D. degree in the history and philosophy of religion at Harvard University in making available to me his preliminary researches in connection with a dissertation upon Freud's doctrine of the conscience. Mr Miller is, of course, not accountable for the use which I have made of his findings. His assistance has helped, however, both to confirm my previous understanding of Freud's position and to facilitate the consideration of Freud for the limited purpose of the present chapter.

30. *GPE,* p. 10.

31. Sigmund Freud, *Repression,* in *General Selections,* Rickman edition, 1915, p. 109.

32. Sigmund Freud, *Mental Functioning, General Selections,* Rickman edition, 1910, p. 57.

33. *A,* p. 114.

34. *NIL,* p. 106.

35. *Ibid.,* p. 98.

36. *Ibid.,* p. 89.

37. *GPE,* p. 70.

38. *CD,* chap. 1.

39. *Ibid.,* p. 93.

40. *Ibid.,* pp. 82-83.

41. *Ibid.,* p. 60.

42. *Bellum omnium contra omnes,* 'the war of all against all', had been the maxim in the light of which Hobbes had proposed a theory of

the political community by social contract. *Leviathan,* chap. 13. This precedent is worth recalling here not only in connection with Freud's researches but in support of Freud against those among his disciples and critics who imagine that ethical humanism offers a persuasive alternative to social pessimism. It may be that the physiological basis of Freud's social pessimism is too slender a foundation for it and certain revisions are required as regards Freud's account of the emergence of the super-ego. But this does not mean, for example, that a 'humanistic conscience' as 'the expression of man's self-interest and integrity', as 'the reaction of our total personality to its proper functioning and disfunctioning' (Erich Fromm, *Man for Himself,* p. 158) reduces or eliminates the 'direct premium on wickedness'. It means rather that the integrity of a humanistic conscience is directly proportional to its sensitivity to the dehumanizing pressures upon it.

43. *CD*, p. 90.
44. *Hamlet,* Act III, Scene 1.

3 A Conscience above Moralism

PAUL TILLICH

There is an inevitable connection between selfhood and conscience, according to Tillich.* Somewhere back in mankind's distant past primitive conformism broke down, and individuals became conscious of themselves as beings who could be held responsible for their actions. This coming into self-consciousness was mankind's giant leap forward; but it also produced law and a guilty conscience. Much of Western thought, especially Christian theology, has been a struggle to extradite mankind from the burden of guilt or the demands of a moralistic conscience. According to this analysis, Luther's discovery of "justification by grace" opened up a new way to overcome the despair caused by guilt and new vistas of what life could become. Thus, a new joyous conscience could emerge which shaped human situations for greater creativity in contrast to the negativism of the moral conscience.

The famous theologian, Richard Rothe, in his *Christian Ethics* has made the suggestion that the word *conscience* should be excluded from all scientific treatment of ethics since its connotations are so manifold and contradictory that the term cannot be saved for a useful definition. If we look not only at the popular use of the word with its complete lack

* The essay was titled "Conscience in Western Thought and the Idea of a Transmoral Conscience" and is from *Crozer Quarterly*, Vol. XXII, No. 4, Oct. 1945, pp. 289-300, used by permission.

of clarity, but also at its confused history, this desperate advice is understandable. But, though understandable, it should not be followed. For the word *conscience* points to a definite reality which in spite of its complexity can and must be described adequately, and the history of the idea of conscience, in spite of the bewildering variety of interpretations it has produced, shows some clear types and definite trends. The complexity of the phenomenon called "conscience" becomes manifest as soon as we look at the manifold problems it has given to human thought: Man shows always and everywhere something like a conscience, but its contents are subject to a continuous change. What is the relation between the form and the content of conscience? Conscience points to an objective structure of demands making themselves perceivable through it, and represents, at the same time, the most subjective self-interpretation of personal life. What is the relation between the objective and the subjective sides of conscience? Conscience is an ethical concept, but it has a basic significance for religion. What is the relation between the ethical and the religious meaning of conscience? Conscience has many different functions: it is good or bad, commanding or warning, elevating or condemning, fighting or indifferent. Which of these functions are basic, which derived? These questions refer only to the description of the phenomenon, not to its explanation or valuation. They show its complex character and the reason for its confused history.

I
The Rise of Conscience

The concept of conscience is a creation of the Greek and Roman spirit. Wherever this spirit has become influential, notably in Christianity, conscience is a significant notion. The basic Greek word *syneidenai* ("knowing with," namely, with oneself; "being witness of oneself") was used in the popular language long before the philosophers got hold of it. It described the act of observing oneself, often as judging oneself. In the philosophical terminology it received the meaning of "self-consciousness" (for instance, in Stoicism in the derived substantives *syneidesis, synesis*). Philo of

Alexandria, under the influence of the Old Testament, stresses the ethical self-observation in *syneidesis* and attributes to it the function of *elenchos,* that is, accusation and conviction. The Roman language, following the popular Greek usage, unites the theoretical and practical emphasis in the word *conscientia,* while philosophers like Cicero and Seneca admit it to the ethical sphere and interpret it as the trial of oneself, in accusation as well as defense. In modern languages the theoretical and the practical sides are usually expressed by different words. English distinguishes *consciousness* from *conscience,* German *Bewusstsein* from *Gewissen,* French *connaissance* from *conscience*—though the latter word is also used for the theoretical side.

The development of conscience, reality as well as concept, is connected with the breakdown of primitive conformism and a situation in which the individual is thrown upon himself. In the sphere of an unbroken we-consciousness no individual conscience can appeal. Events like the Greek tragedy with its emphasis on personal guilt and personal purification, or like the turn towards personal responsibility before God in later Judaism prepare the rise of conscience by creating a definite *ego*-consciousness. The self, says a modern philosopher, has been discovered by sin. The merely logical self-consciousness does not have such a power. Without the practical knowledge about oneself, produced by the experience of law and guilt, no practical self-consciousness and no conscience could have developed. Predominantly theoretical types are lacking a mature self. Even Nietzsche, who attacks more passionately than anybody else the judging conscience, derives the birth of the "inner man" from its appearance. In pointing to the subpersonal character of guilt and punishment in primitive cultures, he praises the discovery of the conscience as the elevation of mankind to a higher level. The fact that self and conscience are dependent on the experience of personal guilt explains the prevalence of the "bad conscience" in reality, literature, and theory. It gives evidence to the assertion that the uneasy, accusing and judging conscience is the original phenomenon; that the good conscience is only the absence, and that the demanding and warning conscience is only the anticipation of the bad conscience. Since egoself and conscience grow in mutual dependence, and since the self discovers itself in the experience of a split between what it is and what it ought to be, the basic character of the conscience, the consciousness of guilt, is obvious.

Shakespeare, in *King Richard III* (Act V, Scene 3), gives a classic expression to the connection of individual self-consciousness, guilt, and conscience:

> O coward conscience, how dost thou afflict me! . . .
> What! do I fear myself? There's none else by.
> Richard loves Richard; that is, *I am I*.
> Is there a murderer here? No. Yes, I am.
> Then fly. What, from myself? Great reason why,
> Lest I revenge. What, *myself upon myself?*
> Alack, I love myself. Wherefore? For any good
> That I myself have done unto myself?
> O, no! alas, I rather hate myself. . . .
> My conscience hath a thousand several tongues,
> . . . crying all, Guilty! guilty.

In the next moment, however, Richard immerges into the we-consciousness of the battle, dismissing self and conscience:

> . . . conscience is a word that cowards use . . .
> Our strong arms be our conscience, swords our law.
> March on, *join* bravely, let us to't pell-mell;
> If not to heaven, then *hand in hand* to hell.

II
CONSCIENCE IN THE BIBLICAL LITERATURE

While the Old Testament has the experience but not the notion of conscience (Adam, Cain, David, Job), the New Testament, especially Paul, has the word and the reality. Through the influence of Paul—who in this, as in other cases, has introduced elements of hellenistic ethics into Christianity—conscience has become a common concept of the Christian nations, in their religions as well as in their secular periods.

Conscience, in the New Testament, has religious significance only indirectly. It has a primarily ethical meaning. The acceptance of the gospel, for instance, is not a demand of the conscience. It does not give laws, but it accuses and condemns him who has not fulfilled the law. Consequently it is not considered to be a special quality of Christians, but an element of human nature generally. In Rom. 2:14-15 Paul expresses this very strongly: "When Gentiles who have no law obey instinctively the Law's requirements, they are a law to themselves, even though they have no law; they exhibit the effect of the Law written on their hearts, their conscience bears them witness, as their moral convictions accuse or it may be defend them" (Moffatt). According to these words the conscience witnesses to the law (either the Mosaic or the natural law) but it does not contain the law. Therefore its judgment can be wrong. Paul speaks of a "weak conscience," describing the narrow and timid attitude of Christians who are afraid to buy meat in the market because it might have been used for sacrifices in pagan cults. Paul criticizes such an attitude; but he emphasizes that even an erring conscience must be obeyed, and he warns those who are strong in their conscience not to induce by their example those who are weak, to do things which would give them an uneasy conscience. No higher estimation of the conscience as guide is possible. Paul does not say that we must follow it because it is right, but because disobedience to it means the loss of salvation (Rom. 14). You can lose your salvation if you do something which is objectively right with an uneasy conscience. The unity and consistence of the moral personality are more important than its subjection to a truth which endangers this unity. In principle Christianity has always maintained the unconditional moral responsibility of the individual person in the Pauline doctrine of conscience. Aquinas and Luther agree in this point. Aquinas states that he must disobey the command of a superior to whom he has made a vow of obedience, if the superior asks something against his conscience. And Luther's famous words before the emperor in Worms, insisting that it is not right to do something against the conscience— namely, to recant a theological insight—are based on the traditional Christian doctrine of conscience. But neither in Paul nor in Aquinas nor in Luther is the conscience a religious source. They all keep the authority of conscience within the ethical sphere. Luther's refusal to recant his doctrine of justification is an expression of his conscientiousness as a doctor of theology. He declares that he would recant if he were refuted by arguments taken from Scripture or reason, the positive source and the negative criterion of theology. But he does *not* say—as often has been stated by liberal Protestants—that his conscience is the *source* of his doctrine. There is no "religion of conscience" either in the New Testament or in classical Christianity before the sectarian movements of the Reformation period.

In the New Testament the relation of the moral conscience to faith as the foundation of the religious life is dealt with only in two connections. In Hebr. 9:9 the ritual religion is criticized because "gifts and sacrifices . . . cannot possibly make the conscience of the worshipper perfect." Therefore, the writer continues: "Let us draw near with a true heart, in absolute assurance of faith, our hearts sprinkled clean from a bad conscience." Only the perfect salvation can give the moral status from which a good conscience follows. But the "assurance of faith" is not a matter of conscience. The other link between faith and conscience is given in the criticism of heresy. Heresy entails an unclean conscience, because it is connected with a moral distortion. In 1 Tim. 1:19 and 4:2 libertinists and ascetics are rejected, both representatives of pagan dualistic morals. Against them the writer says: "Hold to faith and a good conscience. Certain individuals have scouted the good conscience and thus come to grief over their faith." They are "seared in conscience." The judgment that one cannot be an heretic with a good conscience has been accepted by the church. The moral implications of heresy were always emphasized, though not always rightly. Heresy is not an error in judgment or a difference in experience but a demonic possession, splitting the moral self and producing a bad conscience. On this basis the church waged its fight against the heretics in all periods.

III

THE INTERPRETATION OF CONSCIENCE
IN MEDIÆVAL AND SECTARIAN THEOLOGY

Scholasticism raised the question: According to which norms does the conscience judge and how are these norms recognized by it? The answer was given in terms of the artificial (or distorted) word, *synteresis, i.e.,* a perfection of our reason which leads us towards the recognition of the good. It has immediate and infallible evidence, being a spark of the divine light in us, the uncreated light in the depth of the soul, as the Franciscans asserted; the created light of our intuitive intellect, as the Dominicans said. The basic principles, given by the *synteresis* are: 1. The good must be done; the evil must be avoided. 2. Every being must live according to nature. 3. Every being strives towards happiness. Conscience is the practical judgment, which applies these principles to the concrete situation. It is *syllogismus practicus*. We are obliged to follow our conscience, whether the *syllogismus* is correct or not. We are, of course, responsible for not knowing the good. But we are not allowed to act against our conscience, even if it were objectively correct. So man has an infallible knowledge of the moral principles, the natural law, through synteresis, but he has a conscience which is able to fall into error in every concrete decision. In order to prevent dangerous errors the authorities of the church give advice to the Christian, especially in connection with the confession in the sacrament of penance. *Summæ de Casibus Conscientiæ* (collections about individual cases of conscience) were given to the priests. In this way the conscience became more and more dependent on the authority of the church. The immediate knowledge of the good was denied to the layman. The Jesuits removed the synteresis and with it any direct contact between God and man, replacing it by the ecclesiastical, especially the Jesuitic, adviser. But the adviser has the choice between different authorities since the opinion of each of them is equally probable. Heteronomy and probabilism destroy the autonomous, self-assured conscience.

In spite of these distortions the mediæval development has performed a tremendous task in educating and refining the conscience of the European people generally and the monastic and half-monastic groups especially. The depth and breadth of the bad conscience in the later Middle Ages are the result of this education and the soil for new interpretations of meaning and functions of conscience.

Turning to the "sectarian" understanding of conscience, we find the Franciscan idea of the immediate knowledge of the natural law in the depth of the human soul. But two new elements supported and transformed this tradition, the so-called "German

Mysticism" with its emphasis on the divine spark in the human soul and the "spiritual enthusiasm" awakened by the Reformation with its emphasis on the individual possession of the Spirit. Thomas Muenzer and all his sectarian followers taught that the divine Spirit speaks to us out of the depth of our own soul. Not *we* are speaking to ourselves, but God within us. "Out of the abyss of the heart which is from the living God" (Muenzer) we receive the truth if we are opened to it by suffering. Since the enthusiasts understood this divine voice within us in a very concrete sense, they identified it with the conscience. In this way conscience became a source of religious insight and not simply a judge of moral actions. The concept of conscience as the expression of the inner light has revealing character.

But the question arose immediately: What is the content of such a revelation through conscience? Luther asked Muenzer, and Cromwell asked Fox, What is the difference between practical reason and the inner light? Both of them could answer: The ecstatic character of the divine Spirit! But they could be asked again: What bearing has the ecstatic form of revelation on its content? And then the answer was difficult. Muenzer refers to practical decisions in his daily life, made under the inspiration of the Spirit, and Fox develops ethics of unconditional honesty, bourgeois righteousness and pacifism. It was easy to ask again whether reasonableness and obedience to the natural moral law could not produce the same results. The "revealing conscience" is a union of mysticism with moral rationality. But it does not reveal anything beyond biblical and genuine Christian tradition. The important thing resulting from this transformation of the concept of conscience is the idea of tolerance and its victory in the liberal era. The quest for the "freedom of conscience" does not refer to the concrete ethical decision, but it refers to the religious authority of the "inner light," which expresses itself through the individual conscience. And since the inner light could hardly be distinguished from practical reason, freedom of conscience meant actually the freedom to follow one's autonomous reason, not only in ethics, but also in religion. The "religion of conscience" and the consequent idea of tolerance are not a result of the Reformation but of sectarian spiritualism and mysticism.

IV
MODERN PHILOSOPHICAL DOCTRINES OF THE CONSCIENCE

The modern philosophical interpretation of conscience follows three main lines: an emotional-aesthetic line, an abstract-formalistic line, and a rational-idealistic line. Secularizing the sectarian belief in the revealing power of conscience, Shaftesbury interprets it as the emotional reaction to the harmony between self-relatedness and relatedness to others, in all beings and in the universe as a whole. The principle of ethical action is the balance between the effects of benevolence and the effects of selfishness as indicated by conscience. The conscience works the better and more accurately the more the taste for the universe and its harmony is developed. The educated conscience has a perfect ethical taste. Not harmony with the universe but sympathy with the other man is the basis of conscience, according to Hume and Adam Smith: We identify ourselves with the other one and receive his approval or disapproval of our action as our own judgment. This, of course, presupposes a hidden harmony between the individuals and the possibility of a mutual feeling of identification. It presupposes a universal principle of harmony in which the individuals participate and which reveals itself to their conscience as the divine ground to the conscience of the mystics.

The emotional-harmonistic interpretation of conscience has often led to a replacement of ethical by aesthetic principles. The attitude of late aristocracy, high bourgeoisie, and Bohemianism at the end of the last century was characterized by the elevation of good taste to be the ultimate judge in moral affairs corresponding to the replacement of religion by the arts in these groups. It was an attempt to reach a transmoral conscience, but it did not reach even a moral one, and it was swept away by the revolutionary morality and immorality of the twentieth century.

The second method of interpreting conscience philosophically is the abstract-formalistic one. It was most clearly stated by Kant, and it was introduced into theology by Ritschl. Kant wanted to maintain the unconditional character of the moral demand against all emotional relativism, against fear- and pleasure-motives, as well as against divine and human authorities. But in doing so he was driven to a complete formalism. Conscience is the consciousness of the "categorical (unconditional) imperative," but it is not the consciousness of a special content of this imperative. "Conscience is a consciousness which itself is a duty." It is a duty to have a conscience, to be conscientious. The content, according to Ritschl, is dependent on the special vocation, a special historical time and space. Only conscientiousness is always demanded. This corresponds to the Protestant, especially the Lutheran, valuation of work. It is the expression of the activistic element of the bourgeoisie, for which vocation is identical with adaptation to the technical and psychological demands of the economic system. Duty is what serves bourgeois production. This is the hidden meaning even of the philosophy of the "absolute ego" in Fichte, who describes conscience as the certainty of the pure duty which is independent of anything besides its transcendent freedom: In the moment in which the transcendent freedom comes down to action it is transformed into an immanent obedience to a well-calculated system of economic services. It is understandable that this loss of a concrete direction of conscientiousness paved the way for very immoral contents in the moment in which they were ordered, for instance, by a totalitarian state.

Against the aesthetic-emotional as well as the authoritarian form of determining the conscience, attempts were made in modern philosophy to have rationality and contents united. The most influential of these attempts is the common-sense theory of Thomas Reid and the Scottish school: The moral sense is common to everybody, being a natural endowment of human nature (like the synteresis of the scholastics). Decisive for practical ethics is the sense of benevolence towards the others (Hutcheson). This theory expresses adequately the reality of the British (and to a degree, American) conformism, and the natural benevolence in a society in which the converging tendencies still prevail over the diverging ones, and in which a secularized Christian morality is still dominant. Another attempt to find rational contents for the conscience has been made by Hegel. He distinguishes the formal and the true conscience. About the first he says: "Conscience is the infinite formal certainty of oneself—it expresses the absolute right of the subjective self-consciousness, namely, to know within and out of itself what law and duty are, and to acknowledge nothing except what it knows in this way as the good." But this subjectivity is fallible and may turn into error and guilt. Therefore it needs contents, in order to become the true conscience. These contents are the reality of family, society, and state. In the state as the organization of historical reason the formal conscience is transformed into the true conscience. It is an historical misjudgment to link these ideas to the totalitarian use of the state and the pagan distortion of conscience by National Socialism. Hegel was a rationalist, not a positivist. His idea of the state unites Christian—conservative and bourgeois—liberal elements. His famous, though rarely understood, idea of the state as the "god on earth" is based on the identification of the state with the church as the "body of Christ," expressed in secular terms. The conscience which is determined by the state in this sense is determined not by bureaucratic orders but by the life of a half-religious, half-secular organism—the counterpart to the Christian-rationalistic common sense of the Anglo-Saxon society. While the Scottish solution is largely dependent on the social attitude of Western Christianity and Hegel's solution on Lutheran Protestantism, the spirit of Catholicism has received a new philosophical expression in recent philosophical developments of which I take Max Scheler as a representative. In his doctrine of conscience he fights against the popular conception of conscience as the "voice of God." He calls this, as well as the quest for the "freedom of conscience," principles of chaos. Instead of the freedom of conscience he demands the subjection to authority as the only way of experiencing the intuitive evidence of the moral principles. It is impossible to reach such an evidence without personal experience, and it is impossible to have such an experience without acting under the guidance of an authority which is based on former experience. In this respect, ethical (we could say "existential") experience is different from theoretical (*i.e.*, "detached") experience. Although this fits completely the situation of the Catholic, it is not meant as the establishment of external authority. "All authority is concerned only with the good which is universally evident, never with that which is individually evident." Ethical authority is based on general ethical evidence. But does such a general ethical evidence exist? Or is philosophical ethics bound to be either general and abstract or to be concrete and dependent on changing historical conditions? And if this is the alternative, can the problem of conscience be answered at all in terms of *moral* conscience?

V

THE IDEA OF A TRANSMORAL CONSCIENCE

A conscience may be called *transmoral* which does not judge in obedience to a moral law but according to the participation in a reality which transcends the sphere of moral commands. A transmoral conscience does not deny the moral realm, but it is driven beyond it by the unbearable tensions of the sphere of law.

It is Luther who derives a new concept of conscience from the experience of justification through faith; neither Paul nor Augustine did so. Luther's experience grew out of the monastic scrutiny of conscience and the threat of the ultimate judgment which he felt in its full depth and horror. Experiences like these he called *Anfechtungen,* that is, "tempting attacks," stemming from Satan as the tool of the divine wrath. These attacks are the most terrible thing a human being may experience. They create an incredible *Angst* (dread), a feeling of being enclosed in a narrow place from which there is no escape. (*Angst,* he rightly points out, is derived from *angustiae,* "narrows.") "Thou driveth me from the surface of the earth," he says to God in despair and even hate. Luther describes this situation in many different ways. He compares the horrified conscience which tries to flee and cannot escape with a goose which, pursued by the wolf, does not use its wings, as ordinarily, but its feet and is caught. Or he tells us how the moving of dry leaves frightens him as the expression of the wrath of God. His conscience confirms the divine wrath and judgment. God says to him: "Thou canst not judge differently about thyself." Such experiences are not dependent on special sins. The self, as such, is sinful before any act; it is separated from God, unwilling to love him.

If in this way the bad conscience is deepened into a state of absolute despair, it can be conquered only by the acceptance of God's self-sacrificing love as visible in the picture of Jesus, the Christ. God, so to speak, subjects himself to the consequences of his wrath, taking them upon himself, thus reëstablishing the unity with us. The sinner is accepted as just in spite of his sinfulness. The wrath of God does not frighten us any more; a joyful conscience arises as much *above* the moral realm, as the desperate conscience was *below* the moral realm. "Justification by grace," in Luther's sense, means the creation of a "transmoral" conscience. While in the *Anfechtung* God is the accuser and our heart tries to excuse itself, in the "justification" our heart accuses us and God defends us against ourselves. In psychological terms this means: Inasmuch as we look at ourselves we must get a desperate conscience; inasmuch as we look at the power of a new creation beyond ourselves we can reach a joyful conscience. Not because of our moral perfection, but in spite of our moral imperfection we are fighting and triumphing on the side of God, as in the famous picture of Duerer, "Knight, Death, and Devil," the knight goes through the narrows in the attitude of a victorious defiance of dread and temptation.

An analogy to this "triumphant conscience," as developed by Luther personally as well as theologically, has appeared in the enthusiastic philosophy of Giordano Bruno. The moral conscience is overcome by the "heroic affect" toward the universe and the surrender to its infinity and inexhaustible creativity. Participation in the creativity of life universal liberates from the moral conscience, the bad as well as the good. Man, standing in the centre of being, is bound to transform life as it is into higher life. He takes upon himself the tragic consequences, connected with the destructive side of finite creativity, and must not try to escape them for the sake of a good moral conscience.

While in Bruno the transmoral conscience is based on a mystical naturalism, Nietzsche's transmoralism is a consequence of his dramatic-tragic naturalism. Nietzsche belongs to those empiricists who have tried to analyze the genesis of the moral conscience in such a way that its autonomy is destroyed: Hobbes and Helvetius on the ground of a materialistic metaphysics, Mandeville and Bentham on the ground of a utilitarian psychology, Darwin and Freud on the ground of an evolutionary naturalism—all have denied any objective validity to the voice of conscience, according to their rejection of any universal natural (rational) laws. Nietzsche has carried these ideas further as the title and the content of his *Genealogy of Morals* show. He says: "The bad conscience is a sickness, but it is a sickness as pregnancy is one." It is a creative sickness. Mankind had to be domesticated, and this has been done by their conquerors and ruling classes. It was in the interest of these classes to suppress by severe punishments the natural instincts of aggressiveness, will to power, destruction, cruelty, revolution. They succeeded in suppressing these trends. But they did not succeed in eradicating them. So the aggressive instincts became internalized and transformed into self-destructive tendencies. Man has turned against himself in self-punishment; he is separated from his animal past from which he had derived strength, joy, and creativity. But he cannot prevent his instincts from remaining alive. They require permanent acts of suppression, the result of which is the bad conscience, a great thing in man's evolution, an ugly thing if compared with man's real aim. Nietzsche describes this aim in terms which remind of Luther's descriptions of the transmoral conscience: "Once in a stronger period than our morbid, desperate present, he must appear, the man of the great love and the great contempt, the creative spirit who does not allow his driving strength to be turned to a transcendent world." Nietzsche calls him the man "who is strong through wars and victories, who needs conquest, adventure, danger, even pain." This man is "beyond good and evil" in the moral sense. At the same time, he is good in the metaphysical (or mystical) sense that he is in unity with life universal. He has a transmoral conscience, not on the basis of a paradoxical unity with God (such as Luther has), but on the basis of an enthusiastic unity with life in its creative and destructive power.

Recent "existential" philosophy has developed a doctrine of the transmoral conscience which follows the general lines of Luther, Bruno, and Nietzsche. Heidegger, the main representative of existential philosophy says: "The call of conscience has the character of the demand that man in his finitude actualizes his genuine potentialities, and this means an appeal to become guilty." Conscience summons us to ourselves, calling us back from the talk of the market and the conventional behavior of the masses. It has no special demands; it speaks to us in the "mode of silence." It tells us only to act and to become guilty by acting, for every action is unscrupulous. He who acts experiences the call of conscience and—at the same time—has the experience of contradicting his conscience, of being guilty. "Existence as such is guilty." Only self-deception can give a good moral conscience, since it is impossible *not* to act and since every action implies guilt. We *must* act, and the attitude, in which we *can* act is "resoluteness." Resoluteness transcends the moral conscience, its arguments and prohibitions. It determines a situation instead of being determined by it. *The good, transmoral conscience consists in the acceptance of the bad, moral conscience* which is unavoidable wherever decisions are made and acts are performed. The way from Luther's to Heidegger's idea of a transmoral conscience was a dangerous one. "Transmoral" can mean reëstablishment of morality from a point above morality, and it can mean the destruction of morality from a point below morality. The empiricists, mentioned above, from Hobbes to Freud have analyzed the moral conscience, but they have not destroyed it. Either they were dependent in their concrete ethics on Anglo-Saxon common sense; or they identified utility with the social conventions of a well-established bourgeoisie, or they cultivated a high sense of conscientiousness, in scientific honesty as well as in the fulfilment of duties; or they did not dare, unconsciously or consciously, to draw the radical moral consequences of their dissolution of the conscience. In Nietzsche none of these inhibitions is left, nor is it in Heidegger. But these names are, not without *some* justification, connected with the antimoral movements of Fascism or National Socialism. Even Luther has been linked to them (as in Italy have Machiavelli and Bruno). This raises the question: Is the idea of a transmoral conscience tenable? Or is it so dangerous that it cannot be maintained? But if it had to be dismissed, religion as well as analytic psychotherapy would have to be dismissed also. For in both of them the moral conscience is transcended, in religion by the acceptance of the divine grace which breaks through the realm of law and creates a joyful conscience; in depth psychology by the acceptance of one's own conflicts when looking at them and suffering under their ugliness without an attempt to suppress them and to hide them from oneself. Indeed, it is impossible *not* to transcend the moral conscience, because it is impossible to unite a *sensitive* and a good conscience. Those who have a sensitive conscience cannot escape the question of the transmoral conscience. The moral conscience drives beyond the sphere in which it is valid to the sphere from which it must receive its conditional validity.

4 The Nature of a Liberating Conscience

PAUL TILLICH

After World War I, American anthropologists gave special attention to the total culture of primitive people. These studies showed wide diversity in moral codes so that it became common for social scientists to say, "Anything one thinks is immoral can be shown to be moral in some culture." Tillich replies to this radical relativism by showing that beneath the many moralisms there is a moral imperative.* The modern argument against a morality based on something transcendent is the psychological notion that God is merely a projection of a child's image of his father. Tillich affirms that much religion is indeed such a projection and is demonic. But a deeper examination shows that the need to have a father image and the screen on which it is projected is an essential human condition which indicates a fundamental need for morality.

I am going to ask four central questions under the following four headings: 1. Moralisms Conditioned, Morality Unconditional; 2. Moralisms of Authority and Morality of Risk; 3. Moralisms of Law and Morality of Grace; 4. Moralisms of Justice and Morality of Love.

* From *Ministry and Medicine in Human Relations,* edited by Iago Galdstone (New York: International Universities Press, Inc., 1955), pp. 127-140. Reprinted with permission.

1. *Moralisms Conditioned, Morality Unconditional*

People today are afraid of the term "unconditional." This is understandable if one considers the way in which many rather conditioned ideas and methods have been imposed on individuals and groups in the name of an unconditional truth, authoritatively and through suppression. The destructive consequences of such a demonic absolutism have produced a reaction even against the term unconditional. The mere word provokes passionate resistance. But not everything which is psychologically understandable is for this reason true. Even the most outspoken relativists cannot avoid something absolute. They acknowledge the unconditional quest to follow logical rules in their reasoning, and to act according to the law of scientific honesty in their thinking and speaking. Their character as scientific personalities is dependent on the unconditional acceptance of these principles.

This leads us to a more general understanding of the unconditional character of the moral imperative. What Immanuel Kant has called the "categorical imperative" is nothing more than the unconditional character of the "ought-to-be," the moral commandment. Whatever its content may be, its form is unconditional. One can rightly criticize Kant because he establishes a system of ethical forms without ethical contents. But just this limitation is his greatness. It makes as sharp as possible the distinction between morality which is unconditional, and moralisms which are valid only conditionally and within limits. If this is understood, the relativity of all concrete ethics (moralisms) is accepted and emphasized. The material cited by the sociologist, anthropologist, and psychologist showing the endless differences of ethical ideals is no argument against the unconditional validity of the moral imperative. If we disregard this distinction, we either fall into an absolute skepticism which, in the long run, undermines morality as such, or we fall into an absolutism which attributes unconditional validity to one of the many possible moralisms. Since, however, each of these moralisms has to maintain itself against others, it becomes fanatical. For fanaticism is the attempt to repress elements of one's own being for the sake of others. If the fanatic encounters these elements in somebody else, he fights against them passionately, because they endanger the success of his own repression.

The reason for the unconditional character of the moral imperative is that it puts our essential being as a demand against us. The moral imperative is not a strange law, imposed on us, but it is the law of our own being. In the moral imperative we, ourselves (in our essential being), are put against ourselves (in our actual being). No outside command can be unconditional, whether it comes from a state, or a person, or God—if God is thought of as an outside power, establishing a law for our behavior. A stranger, even if his name were God, who imposes commands upon us must be resisted or, as Nietzsche has expressed it in his symbol of the "ugliest man," he must be killed because nobody can stand him. We cannot be obedient to the commands of a stranger even if he is God. Nor can we take unconditionally the content of the moral imperative from human authorities like traditions, conventions, political or religious authorities. There is no ultimate authority in them. One is largely dependent on them, but none of them is unconditionally valid. The reason for the unconditional character of the moral imperative is that it puts our essential being against what we actually are. The moral command is unconditional because it is we ourselves commanding ourselves. Morality is the self-affirmation of our essential being. This makes it unconditional, whatever its content may be. This is quite different from an affirmation of one's self in terms of one's desires and fears. Such a self-affirmation has no unconditional character; ethics based on it are ethics of calculation, describing the best way of getting fulfillment of desires and protection against fears. There is nothing absolute in technical calculation. But morality as the self-affirmation of one's essential being is unconditional.

The contents, however, of the moral self-affirmation are conditioned, relative, dependent on the social and psychological constellation. While morality as the pure form of essential self-affirmation is absolute, the concrete systems of moral imperatives, the "moralisms" are relative. This is not relativism (which as a philosophical attitude is self-contradictory), but it is the acknowledgment of man's finitude and his dependence on the contingencies of time and space. No conflict between the ethicist, theological or philosophical, and the anthropologist or sociologist is necessary. No theologian should deny the relativity of the moral contents, no ethnologist should deny the absolute character of the ethical demand.

Against the doctrine of the relativity of moral contents, the concept of "natural law" seems to stand. But it is only in the Roman Catholic interpretation of the moral law that a conflict exists. Natural is, according to classical doctrine, the law which is implied in man's essential nature. It has been given in creation, it has been lost by "the fall," it has been restated by Moses and Jesus (there is no difference between natural and revealed law in Bible and classical theology). The restatement of the natural law was, at the same time, its formalization and its concentration into one all-embracing law, the "Great Commandment"; the commandment of love. There is, however, a difference between the Protestant and the Catholic doctrine of the natural law. Catholicism believes that the natural law has definite contents, which are unchangeable and are authoritatively stated by the Church (cf. the fight of the Roman Church against birth control). Protestantism, on the other hand, determines, at least today and in this country, the contents of the natural law largely by ethical traditions and conventions; but this is done without a supporting theory, and therefore Protestantism has the possibility of a dynamic concept of natural law. It can protest against each moral content which claims unconditional character. This whole paper is an attempt to protest in the name of the Protestant principle against the Protestant moralism as it has developed in Protestant countries, and to the existence of which the problem of this meeting is largely due.

2. Moralisms of Authority and Morality of Risk

Systems of ethical rules, that is moralisms, are imposed on the masses by authorities, religious authorities as the Roman Church, quasi-religious authorities as the totalitarian governments, secular authorities as the givers of positive laws, conventional, family and school authorities. "Imposing" in a radical sense means forming a conscience. External imposition is not sufficient for the creation of a moral system. It must be internalized. Only a system which is internalized is safe. Only commands which have become natural will be obeyed in extreme situations. The obedience is complete if it works automatically.

Conscience has been interpreted in different ways. The concept of internalization points to the fact that even conscience is not above the relativity which characterizes all ethical contents. It is neither the infallible voice of God, nor the infallible awareness of the natural law. It is, as the German philosopher Heidegger has said, the call, often the silent call, of man to be himself. But the self to which the conscience calls is the essential, not, as Heidegger believes, the existential self. It calls us to what we essentially are, but it does not tell with certainty what that is. Even the conscience can judge us erroneously. It does not help to a valid moral decision if one says with many theologians and philosophers: Always follow your conscience. This does not say, for example, what to do if the conscience is split. As long as the conscience points unambiguously into the one direction, it is comparatively safe to follow it. Split authority destroys authority, in human relations, as well as in one's conscience.

Authority has a double meaning and a double function in the context of our problem. One is born into a moral universe, produced by the experience of all former generations. It is a mixture of natural interest, especially of the ruling classes and wisdom, acquired by the leading people. A moral universe is not only an ideology, that is, a product of the will to gain and to preserve power. It is also a result of experience and real wisdom. It gives the material in which moral decisions are made. And every single decision adds to the experience and the wisdom of the whole. In this sense, we are all dependent on authority, on factual authority, or, as Erich Fromm has called it, rational authority. Everyone has, in some realm, rational authority above the others. For everyone contributes in a unique way to the life of the whole. And his unique experience gives, even to the least educated man, some authority over the highest educated one.

But besides this factual authority which is mutual and exercised by everybody, there is the established authority which is one-sided and exercised by selected individuals or groups. If they represent the ethical realm, they participate in the unconditional character of the moral imperative. These authorities gain absolute authority because of the absolute character of what they stand for. This analysis contradicts the way in which the idea of God is derived by some philosophers and psychologists from the unconditional impact of the father image on the child. One calls God the projection of the father image. But every projection is not only a projection *of* something, but it is also a projection *upon* something. What is this "something" upon which the image of the father is "projected" so that it becomes divine? The answer can only be: It is projected upon the "screen" of the unconditional! And this screen is not projected. It makes projection possible. So we do not reject the theory of projection (which is as old as philosophical thought), but we try to refine it. It has to be constructed in three steps. The first and basic step is the assertion that man, as man, experiences something unconditional in terms of the unconditional character of the moral imperative.

The second step is the recognition that the early dependence on the father, or on father figures, drives to a projection of the father image upon the screen of the unconditional.

The third step is the insight that this identification of the concrete media of the unconditional with the unconditional itself is, religiously speaking, demonic, psychologically speaking, neurotic. Education and psychotherapy can, and must dissolve this kind of father image, but they cannot dissolve the element of the unconditional itself, for this is essentially human.

Since the ethical authorities are not absolute (in spite of the absolute character of the moral imperative), every moral act includes a risk. The human situation itself is such a risk. In order to become human, man must trespass the "state of innocence"; but when he has trespassed it he finds himself in a state of self-contradiction. This situation, which is a permanent one, is symbolized in the story of the Paradise. Man must always trespass the safety regions which are circumscribed by ethical authorities. He must enter the spheres of unsafety and uncertainty. A morality which plays safe, by subjecting itself to an unconditional authority, is suspect. It has not the courage to take guilt and tragedy upon itself. True morality is a morality of risk. It is a morality which is based on the "courage to be," the dynamic self-affirmation of man as man. (Cf. my *Terry Lectures,* published 1952 under the title: *The*

Courage to Be.) This self-affirmation must take the threat of non-being, death, guilt and meaninglessness into itself. It risks itself, and through the courage of risking itself, it wins itself. Moralisms give safety, morality lives in the unsafety of risk and courage.

3. *Moralisms of Law and Morality of Grace*

Because the moral imperative puts our essential against our actual being, it appears to us as law. A being which lives out of its essential nature is law to itself. It follows its natural structure. But this is not the human situation. Man is estranged from his essential being and, therefore, the moral imperative appears as law to him: Moralism is legalism!

The law is first of all "natural law." In the Stoic tradition this term does not mean the physical laws but the natural laws which constitute our essential nature. These laws are the background of all positive laws in states and other groups. They are also the background of the moral law, which is our problem today. The moral law is more oppressive than the severest positive law, just because it is *internalized*. It creates conscience and the feeling of guilt. So we must ask: Which is the power inducing us to fulfill the law? The power behind the positive laws are rewards and punishments. Which is the power behind the moral law? One could say: the reward of the good and the punishment of the uneasy conscience, often projected as heavenly rewards and punishments in purgatory or hell. (Cf. Hamlet's words about the conscience, which makes cowards of us.) But this answer is not sufficient. It does not explain the insuperable resistance the law provokes against itself, in spite of punishments and rewards. The law is not able to create its own fulfillment.

The reason for this is visible when we consider words of Jesus, Paul, and Luther saying that the law is only fulfilled, if it is fulfilled with joy, and not with resentment and hate. But joy cannot be commanded. The law brings us into a paradoxical situation: It commands, which means that it stands against us. But it commands something which can be done only if it does *not* stand against us, if we are united with what it commands. This is the point where the moral imperative drives towards something which is not command but reality. Only the "good tree" brings "good fruits." Only if being precedes that which ought-to-be, can the ought-to-be be fulfilled. Morality can be maintained only through that which is given and not through that which is demanded, in religious terms, through grace and not through law. Without the reunion of man with his own essential nature no perfect moral act is possible. Legalism drives either to self-complacency (I have kept *all* commandments) or to despair (I cannot keep *any* commandment). Moralism of law makes phariseans or cynics—or it produces, in the majority of people, an indifference which lowers the moral imperative to conventional behavior. Moralism necessarily ends up in the quest for grace.

Grace unites two elements: the overcoming of guilt and the overcoming of estrangement. The first element appears in theology as the "forgiveness of sins," in more recent terminology as "accepting acceptance though being unacceptable." The second element appears in theology as "regeneration" or, in more recent terminology, as the "entering into the new being" which is above the split between what we are and what we ought to be. Every religion, even if seemingly moralistic, has a doctrine of salvation, in which these two elements are present.

And psychotherapy is involved in the same problems. Psychotherapy is definitely antimoralistic. It avoids commandments because it knows that neurotics cannot be healed by moral judgments and moral demands. The only help is to accept him who is unacceptable, to create a communion with him, a sphere of participation in a new reality. Psychotherapy must be a therapy of grace or it cannot be therapy at all. There are striking analogies between the recent methods of mental healing and the traditional ways of personal salvation. But there is also one basic difference. Psychotherapy can liberate from a special difficulty, religion shows to him who is liberated and has to decide about the meaning and aim of his existence a final way. This difference is decisive for the independence as well as for the co-operation of religion and psychotherapy.

4. *Moralisms of Justice and Morality of Love*

The moral imperative expresses itself in laws which are supposed to be just. Justice, in Greek thinking, is the unity of the whole system of morals. Justice, in the Old Testament, is that quality of God which makes Him the Lord of the universe. In Islam, morality and law are not distinguished, and in the philosophy of Hegel, ethics are treated as a section of the philosophy of law (*Recht*). Every system of moral commandments is, at the same time, the basis for a system of laws. In all moralisms the moral imperative has the tendency to become a legal principle. Justice, in Aristotle, is determined by proportionality. Everybody gets what he deserves according to quantitative measurements. This is not the Christian point of view. Justice, in the Old Testament, is the activity of God toward the fulfillment of His promises. And justice, in the New Testament, is the unity of judgment and forgiveness. Justification by grace is the highest form of divine justice. This means that proportional justice is not the answer to the moral problem. Not proportional, but transforming justice has divine character. In other words: Justice is fulfilled in love. The moralisms of justice drive toward the morality of love.

Love, in the sense of this statement, is not an emotion, but a principle of life. If love were primarily emotion it would inescapably conflict with justice, it would add something to justice which is not justice. But love does not add something strange to justice, but it is the ground, the power and the aim of justice. Love is the life which separates itself from itself and drives toward reunion with itself. The norm of justice is reunion of the estranged. Creative justice—justice, creative as love—is the union of love and justice and the ultimate principle of morality.

From this follows that there is a just self-love, namely the desire of reunion of oneself with oneself. One can be loveless toward oneself. But if this is the case, one is not only without love but also without justice toward oneself—and toward the others. One must accept oneself just as one is accepted in spite of being unacceptable. And in doing so one has what is called the right self-love, the opposite of the wrong self-love. In order to avoid many confusions one should replace the word self-love completely. One may call the right self-love self-acceptance, the wrong self-love selfishness and the natural self-love self-affirmation. In all these cases the word "self," as such, has no negative connotations. It is the structure of the most developed form of reality, the most individualized and the most universal being. Self is good, self-affirmation is good, self-acceptance is good, but selfishness is bad, because it prevents both self-affirmation and self-acceptance.

Love is the answer to the problem of moralisms and morality. It answers the questions implied in all four confrontations of moralism and morality. Love is unconditional. There is nothing which could condition it by a higher principle. There is nothing above love. And love conditions itself. It enters every concrete situation and works for the reunion of the separated in a unique way.

Love transforms the moralisms of authority into a morality of risk. Love is creative and creativity includes risk. Love does not destroy factual authority but it liberates from the authority of a special place, from an irrational hypostatized authority. Love participates, and participation overcomes authority.

Love is the source of grace. Love accepts that which is unacceptable and love renews the old being so that it becomes a new being. Medieval theology almost identified love and grace, and rightly so: For that which makes graceful is love. But grace is, at the same time, the love which forgives and accepts.

Nevertheless, love includes justice. Love without justice is a body without a backbone. The justice of love includes that no partner in this relation is asked to annihilate himself. The self which enters a love relation is preserved in its independence. Love includes justice, to the others and to oneself. Love is the solution of the problem: moralisms and morality.

5 How the Bible Speaks to Conscience

N. H. G. ROBINSON

Since it was written over a period of about two thousand years by many authors from different cultures, the Bible cannot be expected to be a handbook for ethical conduct in all kinds of specific situations today. Yet the Bible exerts a tremendous influence for many people and receives respect from multitudes of others who have only a casual knowledge of its content. Somehow the Bible speaks to the human condition or its authority would disappear. How? An answer to this question goes a long way toward helping us to understand conscience. Robinson develops the thesis that the Bible is a means by which God addresses persons today.* Such address is not a narrative but a confrontation with conscience which results in confession, repentance, restitution and change. Conscience is the area where a person experiences the spirit of God; and the experience goes beyond the duty of making only mental moral judgments—as the author shows from the story of Nathan and David.

The Bible is in some sense the Word of God. We do not attempt to prove this. There is no need even if it were possible. It proves itself, for the Bible authenticates itself to heart and conscience as the Word of God. But, when we reflect upon this, we are compelled for the sake of clarity to distinguish two senses in which the Bible is the Word

* From *Christ and Conscience* (London: James Nisbet and Co., Ltd., 1956), pp. 171-178. Used by permission.

of God. It is the record of, and witness to, God's Word spoken to men and women of other times and it is also the vehicle of God's Word spoken to us in our time. Reflection compels us in the interests of clarity to draw this distinction, and the Bible itself illustrates it. Perhaps it does so nowhere more clearly than in the account it gives of a controversy between David the king and Nathan the prophet. It happened that when David was king he fell in love with Bathsheba, the wife of Uriah, one of the king's soldiers; and David arranged that in the heat of battle, at the most dangerous part of the line, Uriah would be killed. Then, with Uriah out of the way, David took Bathsheba as his wife. But, we are told, the thing that David had done displeased the Lord, and Nathan the prophet was sent to him with a message, with a parable, a word from the Lord. There were two men, said Nathan, in one city, the one rich and the other poor. As the king listened attentively, the prophet went on. The rich man had exceeding many flocks and herds, but the poor man had nothing save one little ewe lamb which he had bought and nourished. And it grew up together with him and with his children; it did eat of his own morsel, and drank of his own cup, and lay in his bosom, and was unto him as a daughter. Now there came a traveller to the rich man, but he, as rich men sometimes do, hesitated to take of his own flock and his own herd to prepare for the wayfarer. Instead, he took the poor man's lamb and dressed it for the man that was come to him.

Such was Nathan's message, his word from the Lord to David, spoken in the form of a narrative like the Bible as a whole; and the reader can scarcely miss its point. Behind the figures of those two men who dwelt in one city, the one rich and the other poor, he can plainly discern the shadows of two other people, one a king and the other a soldier in the king's army. And behind the figure of the single ewe lamb in the parable he can detect the shadow of the soldier's wife, Bathsheba. But the important question concerns the understanding and reaction of David. How did he take it? Was he filled with shame? Was he stricken by conscience, and by a higher voice than conscience, the remonstrance of Almighty God? On the contrary, David was angry. His anger was kindled greatly, we are told, against the rich man; and the king said to Nathan, As the Lord liveth, the man that hath done this is worthy to die, and he shall restore the lamb fourfold, because he did this thing and because he had no pity. David was filled and overflowing with indignation against the man. But, said Nathan, *thou* art the man. Thus saith the Lord, the God of Israel, I anointed thee king over Israel, and I delivered thee out of the hand of Saul, and I gave thee thy master's house and thy master's wives and the house of Israel and of Judah; and if that had been too little I would have added unto thee such and such things. Wherefore, then, hast thou despised the word of the Lord to do that which is evil in His sight?

Now this incident clearly necessitates a distinction between two different understandings of Nathan's parable, for, manifestly, David did understand from the beginning what was said to him and yet it is also true that, hearing, he heard but did not at first understand. What is involved in this fact is a distinction between what we shall call a merely narrative understanding of the parable and an understanding of it which can be described as addressive, clamant, literally urgent. The distinction is in some ways similar to, but not identical with, that between indicative and imperative moods. The latter is a distinction between two linguistic forms which are mutually exclusive, in the sense that a sentence which is in the indicative mood is by that very fact not in the imperative mood and *vice versa,* whereas the former distinction is one between two uses and understandings of language, which are not so clearly exclusive of each other. Of course the distinction between language and its understanding must not be pressed too far, for apart from some understanding language is simply a noise or a succession of noises, which would not permit even of the differentiation of verbal moods. On the one hand, there is a formal or abstract understanding of language which takes no account of the particular situation of utterance, which is concerned only with the actual fact of utterance claiming attention. On the other hand, there is a material understanding which does relate it to the particular situation in question. It is within this latter understanding that the distinction arises between a merely narrative and a clamant understanding of language. In other words, we are concerned here with a distinction, not within language merely as an instrument of communication, but within the use of this instrument. The inherent function of all language is to communicate, to convey information, although it cannot be assumed that its original function was that only; and even if a piece of language were to consist as nearly as possible of a bare imperative it would still convey information, for example, about the wishes of the person using it, for unless it did so it could not fulfil any other purpose. If this is true, all language is narrative, in our sense of the word, although it may not all make use of a non-imperative mood. But if all language is narrative it is certainly not all merely narrative; some language is clamant, it is, as we have said, literally urgent; it is used to lay a claim upon the person to whom it is addressed, although, as we have seen, in doing that it does not forsake its inherent function of being narrative and informative, and it may even proceed by means of the indicative mood.

There is, then, a distinction between a narrative and a clamant understanding of language; and this distinction enables us to understand David's encounter with Nathan. David's initial mistake was not simply that he misunderstood the parable. He understood it well enough as narrative, it conveyed a message to his conscience, and, indeed, unless it had done so he could not even have misunderstood it. But he did misunderstand it as merely narrative; he failed to see that he himself was being confronted, addressed, rebuked and claimed by God. That was the very essence of his error, and it was that which distinguished his first understanding of the situation from his last. It was certainly not true that one understanding was a total misunderstanding in comparison with the other; nor was it true that the earlier understanding was spectatorial and dispassionate, for it is clear that it was not so. The difference lay in David's awareness (or lack of it) that a claim was being made upon him and made upon him by a higher Power than man's. The difference, in other words, was exactly that between a merely narrative and a clamant understanding of the message; and to find it elsewhere is to mistake incidentals for essentials.

A similar treatment may be extended to the parables of Jesus, and He Himself seems to invite and suggest it when He warns that those who hear them may indeed hear, but not understand. There are two quite different but not unrelated ways in which these parables may be understood. We may hear in them Jesus talking about God, or God in Christ talking to us—our understanding of them may be merely narrative or clamant and literally urgent. "A certain man had two sons; and the younger of them said to his

father, Father, give me the portion of goods that falleth to me . . .
and the younger son . . . took his journey into a far country." What
do we make of that? Who is this younger son? Is he just a hypothetical figure, a purely imaginary personality introduced to offset
the character of God? Or is he rather a real person, much nearer
home to ourselves? May it be indeed that I am the man? "And
when he came to himself he said . . . I will arise and go to my
Father, and will say unto him, Father, I have sinned against
heaven and before thee, and am no more worthy to be called thy
son. . . ." Once again, it is a hypothetical character who speaks or
someone real? "But when he was yet a great way off, his father saw
him, and had compassion, and ran, and fell on his neck, and kissed
him . . . and . . . said . . . This my son was dead, and is alive again;
he was lost and is found. . . ." What do we make of it now? Is
this a wholly imaginary situation and an entirely fictitious son,
devised by the mind of Christ to display the character of God? Or
is it something more, is it actually our situation, is God Himself
speaking to us?

Plainly, there are two understandings of Christ's parables,
and the difference between them is the one we have already
acknowledged between a merely narrative understanding and one
that is clamant, addressive, literally urgent. Indeed, this distinction
applies to the Bible in its entirety. In one sense it is merely narrative, it tells us about God, about His Word spoken to men and
women of other times, and about those to whom it was spoken. In
this sense it is all narrative, not only the historical books and the
synoptic Gospels, but also its songs, its psalms and its epistles;
and in this sense it requires one type of understanding, a merely
narrative understanding. But the Bible is also the vehicle of God's
Word to us by which He claims us for Himself, by which we ourselves are confronted by His grace and are brought into living fellowship with God; and here it demands a different understanding.
The Bible then, is the Word of God in two senses, in a narrative
sense, for it is *about* God and His Word spoken to others, and in a
clamant sense, for it becomes God's Word spoken *to* us. It is *both*
the record of, and the witness to, God's Word spoken to men and
women long since dead, *and* the vehicle of His present Word to
those now living; and that difference can be expressed as a difference between two understandings of the Bible, a merely narrative

understanding of its language and one that is clamant and literally urgent. Yet, while it is true that the difference is one between these two understandings, it would be error to suppose that it is merely that, for these two understandings themselves correspond to two different uses, a merely narrative and informative use and one that is addressive and clamant. It is only by the action of God Himself, by the use He makes of His own word, by the work of His Spirit, that the Bible can become God's Word to us who read and hear it. It is not a matter of sheer accident that we bring to His Word the one type of understanding or the other, nor is it a matter of our free untrammelled choice. If He did not speak to us we could not hear. It is not the manner of our understanding but His free Spirit that witnesseth with our spirits that we are the children of God. Yet if He speaks to us by His Word, as He is pleased to do, we are wilfully deaf who do not hear, wilfully and sinfully deaf, and fully responsible for our sin. The difference, then, between God's Word as witness and record and God's Word as vehicle and instrument is not *merely* a matter of two different understandings —to say that would be to take for granted His grace which is the last thing any man should take for granted. Yet there is a difference between two understandings involved, and, as we have seen, the difference is not that between a total misunderstanding and a true understanding, nor yet that between a dispassionate understanding and (shall we say?) an existential one, but between a merely narrative understanding and a clamant one, between an understanding that such and such is the case and a similar understanding in which, nevertheless, a personal claim and claimant are present and are acknowledged.

It must be allowed, however, that this new understanding does reveal misunderstanding in the old; and on this aspect of the matter David's reaction to Nathan's parable is again instructive. It is significant that his indignation was righteous indignation, and that in the dispute between the poor man and the rich, David was unreservedly on the side of the former. Similarly the natural man in his narrative and natural understanding of God's Word, as it unfolds the story of God's controversy with His people, unhesitatingly places himself on God's side of the fence. In the same way did the Pharisee, praying with a publican in the temple, place himself, with no thought that this might be a complete distortion of the facts. It is only the new understanding, when God's present voice is heard, that reveals a very different situation and leads to a reinterpretation of the old. For in the light of the new we are universally convicted of sin, of being not only over against God but also against Him, of having turned the narrative of His created world, from the most distant star to our daily bread, the narrative of His law written in our hearts and consciences, and even the narrative of His Word of grace and mercy and atonement, of having turned the narrative of *all* God's dealings with us into *mere* narrative, and of having turned His world into ours. We see that in the light of this revelation, sin cannot be defined or adequately described in relation to what is only a part of ourselves; it is an alienation of the whole man from God, in his reason as well as his will, in his understanding no less than in his conduct of life. Moreover, so far as reason is concerned, it is not simply a matter of putting error in place of the truth, but of taking half-truths for the whole, mixing understanding with misunderstanding, and reducing to narrative and information the clamant language of life in which deep calls unto deep, so that seeing we see but do not perceive, and hearing we hear but do not understand. In similar fashion, as far as will is concerned, God, as living Person and sovereign Will, is driven out and man takes His place, so that God's law is reduced, even in its imperative form, to a mere narrative, to a human and humanly manageable code; and even the Word of God's grace may be drawn into the circle of man's life as no more than a satellite in a man-centred universe. By God's living Word, spoken and addressed to us, we are convicted of sin in being redeemed from it and claimed for God and God alone; and it is because He speaks, it is because He is pleased to speak, that we can hear and respond. But in hearing we know that He has spoken all along, in the things that gave us birth, in home and kin and country, in law, civilisation and conscience, in the Word made flesh and in the record thereof.

6 Protestant Problems with Conscience

HANS SCHÄR

The average Protestant thinks of conscience in terms of the heroic figure of Martin Luther at the Diet of Worms. There he sees the image of a lonely, courageous individual confronting the authority of the established church and the power of the state. He identifies himself with Luther, who, through his freshly discovered "New Testament faith," endured rejection and imprisonment but triumphed in the end. After correcting the historical data on which this image is built, Schär shows that what Luther actually said on that occasion is more profound and perplexing than the popular image suggests.* Luther did not make conscience an important element in his theology, nor did the churches of the Reformation. Rather, Protestants—by freeing conscience from church authority—have created a problem to which they have found no satisfactory solution.

At the turn of the nineteenth century it was popularly believed that religious freedom and freedom of conscience were one of the great blessings of humanity and that freedom of conscience began with the Reformation. Martin Luther's stand at the Diet of Worms seemed to mark the breakthrough for freedom of conscience, when, upholding his point of view against state and church, he is said to have declared:

* From *Conscience,* edited by the Curatorium of the Jung Institute, Zurich (Evanston, Illinois, Northwestern University Press, 1970). This article found on pp. 113-130, was translated by R. F. C. Hull and Ruth Horine. Reprinted by permission.

"Here I stand, I can no other!" At that moment, Luther broke with the authorities of his time, state and church, which are still considered authorities today. He had nothing to back him but his own conscience. Thus the Diet of Worms witnessed the advent of the man who knew he was committed solely to his conscience and who mobilized freedom of conscience against all secular and spiritual authorities,

This conception of Luther's Reformation had to be revised at several essential points during the early part of the twentieth century. For one thing, critical research into the history of the Diet of Worms established that there is no definite historical evidence for Luther's words, which for a long time had been a banner for a sort of jingoistic Protestantism. However, it transpired that Luther did in fact maintain his position—even if somewhat hesitantly—and did assert that no one should be compelled to accept a faith against his own conscience and conviction. The appeal to commitment to conscience was certainly made, though not in the dramatic and theatrical style so dear to the nineteenth century, as though Luther were writing his own epitaph. What he actually said was something like this: "If I were not convinced by the testimonies of the Holy Scriptures or on obvious grounds—for I do not believe the pope and the synods alone, since it is certain that they have frequently erred and contradicted themselves—I am bound by the Scriptural texts I have cited, and my conscience is a prisoner of God's word. I cannot, and I will not, recant, for to act contrary to conscience is neither safe nor honorable. So help me God, Amen." [1]

But now we come to another point, which is of crucial importance. While it is true that Luther did act from the compulsion and commitment of his own conscience at the Diet of Worms, he expressly refrained from putting freedom of conscience into effect later on. In the first place, he did not enlist freedom of conscience in his own work of reforming theology and founding the Protestant church. Also, he did not appeal to his own conscience any more but wanted his actions to be determined solely by the Bible. He intended to carry out a reform of the church according to the clear and definite precepts of the Scriptures and not according to the dictates of his own conscience or that of his supporters. The purpose of his reform was a restoration of the true Christian faith, and the church he founded, when reform of the Catholic church proved impossible, was to be the original and now restored Christian church and community. He did not appeal to conscience to justify this reform, unmindful of the fact that by appealing to his own conscience he had launched the Reformation.

There is a second important reason why the further course of the Reformation left little room for freedom of conscience. The struggle with the Counter Reformation launched by the Catholic church resulted in a Protestant orthodoxy, increasingly rigid and sternly committed to established principles. Even later, the Reformation did not allow believers freedom of decision in matters of faith but adopted the principle of *cuius regio, eius religio,* which meant that, both by law and in practice, the confessional allegiance of the ruler determined that of his subjects and of the entire region. In Protestant and Catholic territories alike, the ruler ensured the uniformity of religious belief. Consequently, not only Catholicism was attacked in the Protestant countries but various sects as well, such as the Baptists, and—strangest of all—a campaign was even waged against other Protestant denominations. Protestants with a Lutheran bent were expelled from Switzerland, and it remains a thoroughly unsettling fact that Lutherans did not tolerate Zwinglians and Calvinists and even punished them with death. For a long time a sword was kept in Saxony with which crypto-Calvinists were executed. It bore the appropriate inscription *cave Calviniste* ("Calvinist, beware!"). Obviously, this internecine religious intolerance abolished the very idea of freedom of conscience.

From this brief review of the development of the Reformation some important inferences may be drawn which are relevant to our theme. First, conscience is a reality that continually makes its presence felt in practical life. Second, the precise definition of the essence of conscience proves to be extraordinarily difficult. Third, it is evident that in the sphere of religion conscience does not always have a constant, uniform function but subsists in a relation of reciprocal influence with other psychic and spiritual factors by which it is continually modified.

Hence we are obliged to reflect upon what conscience really is from the Protestant point of view, how it is evaluated, and what its function is in the general context of human behavior.

The concept of conscience in German occurs for the first time

in the writings of Notker [2] as *gewizzide* or *gewizzani,* a literal
translation of the Latin *conscientia,* which in turn was derived from
the Greek *syneidēsis.* The concept is pre-Christian; indeed the very
term was coined by the Greeks and Romans. There are, however,
indications that the phenomenon itself, conscience as psychospiri-
tual function, had already developed among the ancient Egyptians.
For them a functioning conscience was inherent in the nature of
man, though the concept as such did not yet exist. According to
the histories of philosophy, it played but a minor role in Greek
thought too, for Greek writers mostly mention only that people can
have a bad conscience that torments them, perhaps even more
severely than social censure and punishment. It was Cicero, Livy,
and Pliny the Younger who elaborated the concept by speaking
not only of a bad but also of a good conscience.

Passing on to the Christian era, we must ask what is said about
conscience in the Bible. In Hebrew and thus in the Old Testament
there is no word for conscience. In the Septuagint, the Greek translation of the Old Testament, the Greek term for conscience is used
only once as the translation of a Hebrew word (Eccles. 10:20).[3]
Conscience is also mentioned once in The Wisdom of Solomon
17:11, but this is part of the Apocrypha and not a canonical book.
Although the concept of conscience does not occur in the Old
Testament, the phenomenon itself emerges very clearly, for instance in the story of Cain and Abel and, more particularly, of the
Fall. Cain's defiant question, "Am I my brother's keeper?" (Gen.
4:9) clearly expresses a bad conscience. But the story of the Fall
is even more interesting and instructive. Adam and Eve are
seduced into eating the apple by the serpent's promise "ye shall be
as gods, knowing good and evil" (Gen. 3:5). Taken literally, this
implies that the purpose of the Fall was what we commonly suppose to be the function of conscience: discrimination between good
and evil. This raises the question whether the Fall was really so bad,
so sinful. However, the seduction includes the rider "ye shall be as
gods" and hence also the element of *hybris.* The consequence of the
Fall is shame, and it is a sexual shame, for Adam and Eve cover
their sexual parts. Whether they reached the promised goal as a
result of the Fall is not made very clear, but the fact that they are
ashamed is evidence enough of their bad conscience. They hide
from God.

Another feature of this story is that although God punished man for transgressing his commandment, he apparently allowed him to keep his knowledge of good and evil (Gen. 3:22). And in the story of the Flood, which follows, it is noteworthy that God did not restore the paradisal *status quo ante* but left man also with his knowledge of shame (Gen. 9:21-23). We are left in the dark as to whether the consequence of the Fall was the awakening of conscience as a vital function or whether it was merely the first awakening of a bad conscience. Should the latter interpretation be accepted, the promise of the serpent would be superbly ironical, for in effect it would be saying: "After eating of the Tree of Knowledge, you shall know good and evil by having a bad conscience." But the story can be given yet another twist: only through sin, through violating a divine commandment, does man realize that he has a conscience. The only way of knowing that we have a conscience is in the experience of personal guilt. At all events, it is plain that more is known about conscience in the Old Testament than the purely philological evidence allows, according to which there is no word for conscience in Hebrew.

In the New Testament the philological picture is quite different. Here we find two Greek terms, *synoida* and *syneidēsis,* both taken from common usage and of long standing. The literal meaning of *syneidēsis* is "knowledge with," which was later interpreted as "knowledge with God." But at the time of the New Testament it is certain that it had not yet been construed in this way. The prefix *syn-,* or Latin *con-,* implies connection, combination, union. Hence *syneidēsis,* derived from *syneidos* (literally, "seeing with or together"), is a synthesizing kind of knowledge or understanding, unifying the multiplicity of perceptions into a spiritual awareness or self-awareness. The term can also be applied to moral consciousness, or man's evaluation of himself by means of his self-awareness. In Christian usage *syneidēsis* is the inner awareness of God and his order, awareness of sin as a violation of this order for which no outer acts can atone. Man's *con-scientia* bears joint witness to the law of God that is written in the heart, even though his thoughts may be in profound conflict with one another. Conscience is thus the expression of man's inner awareness, with special reference to ethical conduct. With these conceptions of conscience Christianity hardly contributed anything new to the times. More important was the Christian insistence on a good conscience, which in the New Testament is often described as Christianity's essential gift to man, along with faith. Attention is paid not only to bad conscience resulting from the commission of an evil deed but also to good conscience as our awareness of having done good and eschewed evil.

In this connection it may be of interest to cite some further references in the New Testament. A text that lays particular emphasis on the function of conscience is the parable of the Prodigal Son (Luke 15:11ff.). Actually, the son does not break any specific commandment, except possibly the general one of filial piety. When the son asks for his inheritance, his father gives it to him without protest or reprimand. His insight, or bad conscience, is awakened only after he has squandered his fortune and has found himself in difficult straits, owing partly to his evil ways and partly to the hard times (widespread famine). Here the transgression is not so much the breaking of a commandment as the son's selfish and disrespectful behavior toward his father, who stands for God. To us this would probably seem less striking and indeed revolutionary than it did to the Jews at that time, who were brought up in fidelity to the Law and for whom disobedience to the Law was synonymous with sin.

To grasp the full significance of the New Testament statements about conscience we must also take baptism into account. Baptism, as the bath of rebirth, signified the death of the old man and the resurrection of the new. Among other rewards, it brought forgiveness of sins. Before being baptized, the candidate made a full confession of sin and promised to lead a sinless life from then on. He was then accepted into the community of the saints. This conception of baptism arose in connection with the anticipation of an imminent end of the world, for in the first centuries of our era the coming of the Kingdom of God was expected daily. The obligation to lead a sinless life was taken very seriously by the early Christians. They were also convinced that sinless life and the assurance of forgiveness were possible only through faith. Faith brought trust in, and participation in, the coming Kingdom of God, as well as the infusion of the Holy Spirit, who would lend them moral strength and enable them to overcome sin as the temptation of Satan and the Antichrist. Thus a good conscience was possible in the context of a given historical situation and under the impact of experiences which were connected with baptism and the early Christians' experience of the spirit. But these experiences had by then reached a climax and could not long be maintained at that level of intensity.

Baptism brought forgiveness of sins but was possible only once in a lifetime. Then two things happened—or rather, did not happen. The imminently expected Kingdom of God failed to appear, and, instead of being strengthened, spiritual experiences took a different turn and became less intense. A crucial change was obviously in the making, because the sinless life originally demanded of the baptized was turning out to be impossible. Before long, the Christian communities had to face the question of what to do with people who had been baptized and yet continued to sin. At first, the demands for a sinless life were mitigated by making a distinction between forgivable and unforgivable, or venial and mortal, sins. As time went on, this led to the institution of penitence, or confession. Thus the church became a veritable therapeutic institute, since it controlled the door to salvation. The striking thing about the institution of confession is not only that the connection between the gift of faith and the forgiveness of sins through baptism was broken but that, above all, the authority of the church increasingly took the place of conscience. It was the church that decided, more and more obviously and explicitly, what was good and evil and what was merit and sin. Regard for conscience was pushed into the background.

While it is not possible for us to outline here the whole development of conscience throughout the history of Christianity, we should at least like to draw attention to two contributions made by Saint Augustine. First of all, he had a strong sense of his personal guilt, which he acknowledged to the full. In his *Confessions* he made a matchless confession of it in the form of a prayer. Even as a bishop, the head of a community with great authority, he frankly and openly revealed his entire personal life and his sinful inclinations. The judgment he pronounced on himself was in fact clear judgment of conscience, and he acknowledged it as such without reservation. His procedure marks an advance in the recognition of conscience.

Saint Augustine's second contribution is the doctrine of

original sin. Rigorously elaborated under the influence of Man-
ichaeism, it states that man is incapable of good. Fallen man
cannot avoid sinning (*non potest non peccare*). Original sin is
automatically transmitted to every man by heredity, through
physical procreation and his physical nature in general. Therefore,
everything the natural man does is sin and only sin. Saint Augustine did not even ask himself whether recognition of sin does not
presume at least a good insight and some capacity for good. He
obviously used the doctrine of original sin to bind man even more
closely to the church. Only baptism can deliver man from original
sin, and only the church can administer baptism. In order to avoid
being an eternal prisoner of evil, man has to submit to the authority
of the church. Coupled with this is the demand for an ascetic life,
which Saint Augustine valued above any other,

Saint Augustine's attitude to conscience thus contains a contradiction. On the one hand, more than anyone at that time he
sharpened the emphasis on conscience, but on the other hand he
demanded man's submission to the authority of the church so
emphatically that conscience became practically superfluous, if not
ruled out altogether. So it is hardly surprising that the dictum is
attributed to Saint Augustine: *Roma locuta, causa finita* ("Rome
having spoken, the case is closed"). Actually, he applied this dictum only to one particular case and did not recognize at the outset the authority of the bishop of Rome in all matters. Nevertheless,
his thinking and his whole attitude tended in that direction.

Among the various steps in the historical development of
conscience during the Middle Ages, we should like to single out
only the distinction which the Schoolmen made between *synterēsis*
and *conscientia*. The word *synterēsis* appears to derive from a
scribal error in Saint Jerome's *Commentary on Ezekiel* (1:7),
where it occurs as a corruption of *syneidēsis*. According to the
Scholastic view, *conscientia* is the scrutinizing and regulating conscience, while *synterēsis* represents the rational principles of moral
action which are inborn in man as the "natural law" by which he
should regulate his whole conduct. Accordingly, *synterēsis* would
be the general theoretical conscience, while *conscientia* is its practical application in individual cases.

The beginning of the Reformation was marked by a conflict of
conscience which Luther experienced while he was in the monas-

tery at Erfurt. Today it is assumed that this conflict arose as a result of Luther's decision to enter the monastery, though his reasons for doing so are not altogether clear. At any rate, he reached this decision without securing the consent of his father, who had entirely different plans for his son. Luther himself claimed that he entered the monastery because of a vow he had made to Saint Anne during a violent thunderstorm near Stotternheim which had endangered his life. The thunderstorm occurred during a journey that was probably connected with his departure, at mid-semester, from the University of Erfurt, when he went home to announce that he no longer intended to study jurisprudence, as his father wished. His father did not agree with this change of plan. It was during this journey that Luther, in real or imaginary danger, suddenly made his vow, probably expressing a long-standing or unconscious wish which he now fulfilled by entering the Augustinian monastery at Erfurt. Luther took this step in the conviction that the storm was a clear sign from God that he should carry out his plan. His novitiate passed without difficulties or temptations; these came only after he had taken his vows and celebrated his first Mass. Something must have happened then that troubled Luther deeply. It may have been the presence of his father, who, on that solemn occasion, had expressed his displeasure at his son's monkishness. When Luther, in self-defense, pointed out that his thunderstorm experience was an act of divine providence and that he was bound by the vow he had made to the saint, his father riposted that obedience to parents also figured among the divine commandments and furthermore that there was no evidence at all that divine providence had been at work—the thunderstorm experience might equally well have been the work of evil spirits or demons. With that Luther was plunged into a profound inner conflict which reduced him to utter despair. In the end he could only suppose that he was completely damned by God.

As a result, Luther was tormented by a conflict of conscience, being confronted with two contradictory obligations both of which he felt duty-bound to fulfill. He also had to admit that decisions of conscience might be precarious; we may think we are obeying our conscience, yet we cannot avoid falling into sin. On top of all that, in the period that followed he was plagued by further difficulties. In his depressed state, he accused himself of every conceivable sin but could find no relief in confession. He was in fact unable to confess anything that would have been sufficient reason for such an abysmal feeling of guilt. His friend and superior, Father Staupitz, is said to have told him that he was confessing the merest trifles. Unless he was able to accuse himself of some really outsize fault, he should put away his guilt feelings. At this time Luther turned into a regular scruple-monger, continually running to the confessional yet unable to unbosom himself of his guilt.

Luther finally regained his peace of mind in the so-called theology of the Cross. This consists in man's humble submission to God's decrees, even though God should reject him. In Luther's view, man's attitude is thus brought into harmony with that of Jesus Christ, who in all humility accepted the Cross and bore it to the end. From the mystic Johann Tauler (d. 1361), Luther took over the similar idea that man, out of love for God, must submit to every divine decree no matter how harsh and damning. If man out of love for God could accept every divine decree, and if out of such love he is even able to resign himself to total rejection and to Hell (se resignare ad infernum), then, despite everything, he is not wholly separated from God. In this way Luther arrived at an extremely irrational formula which affirmed at the same time both guilt and bond with God, both distance from God and nearness to him.

Luther's inner development is relevant to our problem, because it shows that conscience and the feeling of guilt operating within it together constitute an important agent in the evolution of his reformatory ideas. It also clarifies the inner reason for his gradual breaking-away from the Catholic church, since in his case confession, offered by the church as a relief from a bad conscience, did not work. It was because the church was unable to cope with conscience that he put his trust in conscience rather than in the church.

But conscience alone did not provide Luther with an answer to his problem. He learned that conscience is a tough prosecutor and that against the verdict of conscience man cannot justify himself even by his ethical behavior. Here faith provides the only answer. For this reason, Luther insisted that man must acknowledge the reality of his bad conscience and guilt feelings. Man is a sinner, and his behavior remains sinful. Saint Augustine had already established this fact, but his solution—an ascetic life and submission to the church as a divine therapeutic institute—was no longer valid for Luther in overcoming sin, for even the ascetic life remains sinful. Torn between two duties, he had personally experienced a conflict of conscience, and he knew that we may become guilty not only through our sins of commission but also through our sins of omission. The ascetic may deny himself as much as is humanly possible, but he still does not escape his guilt. Therefore asceticism is no guarantee of a good conscience. Conscience accuses and must accuse because its accusations are true.

Luther found his answer in faith alone. In love of God, and by accepting himself as he really is, man submits to God's judgment and providence. He does not achieve a good conscience, but at least he recognizes that God's love is stronger than his own guilt and the verdict of his own conscience. Later, as we know, Luther did not stick to the theology of the Cross, but, influenced by the Pauline epistles and by the need to have an authoritative backing for his views, he focused on the doctrine of justification by faith. The theology of the Cross cannot be found either in Paul's letters or in the Gospels. The doctrine of justification by faith does, however, occur in Paul, though in a context very different from the one Luther thought it did. But that was immaterial to Luther; it was enough for him that it occurred in the New Testament. He interpreted it in accordance with Anselm's doctrine of satisfaction, namely, that God through Christ had made sufficient atonement for human sin and that those who believed in Christ would therefore be forgiven. However, Luther modified the effect of God's work of reconciliation at one point: although man may be *declared* righteous through faith, he is not thereby *made* righteous, as was taught by Anselm and the Catholic church. An essential part of the theology of the Cross is thus preserved, the irrational combination of opposites: before his conscience man remains a sinner and is forever unable to satisfy God's law, but before God he is accepted through God's grace. Thus, according to Luther's irrational formula, man is at the same time sinful and righteous (*simul iustus et peccator*). In other words, Luther accepted the judgment of conscience and rejected any appeasement of it. The function of conscience is to measure man against God's law and continually to make clear to him how far he is removed from any perfection and how much he remains guilty before God in all his doings. For Luther it is not the function of conscience to pronounce the final judgment on man. That is left to God. Man has access to God's judgment through faith.

So it all depends on the context in which Luther spoke about conscience. He had more faith in conscience than in absolution by the Catholic church. At the Diet of Worms he declared that no man should be compelled to accept a belief contrary to his conscience. Yet he seemed almost to make light of the *terrores conscientiae*. He says in effect: if conscience so persecutes you with hair-splittings and guilt feelings that you cannot live any more, then have a good laugh at it and sin boldly. For—so Luther reasoned —Satan or other evil spirits might well be lurking behind the insinuations of conscience. Like Ignatius of Loyola, he had come to the conclusion that a hair-splitting and overscrupulous conscience might well not be the voice of God but the work of the devil. But the essential point for Luther was always man's relation to God. Employing a word which Luther used in a different context, one could say that he judged conscience in every situation according to whether it "promotes" (*treibet*) Christ or not. Whenever conscience served to clarify man's relation to God, Luther wanted it taken carefully and unreservedly into account. But conscience must not come between man and God in a manner calculated to disturb or actually destroy his trust in God and his firm foothold in faith.

Luther's assertion went further than this since he also recognized a good conscience. According to him and other reformers, a good conscience is possible only through God's grace. Grace grants remission of sins, and thus the sinner who admits his guilt overcomes fear. The resulting state of inner peace brings about a good conscience. For Luther a good conscience may be achieved in another way too. The believer who has received God's grace is delivered from fear of sin and possesses the capacity for real love. Whatever comes from love is ethically good. To a certain extent, the believer is capable of doing good, not because of personal merit but because of grace and in gratitude for this grace; and that kind of good action is combined with a good conscience.

We may thus discern in Luther two conceptions of conscience. First, conscience is the faculty of ethical judgment; second, it is a form of awareness, common to all men, that is directly related to religious experience and faith.

Luther's statements concerning the function of conscience clarify much that came to light in the subsequent development of Protestantism. Protestantism has always recognized conscience as a paramount authority. Although Luther's Protestantism created no new conception of conscience, his inner self-reliance and his guidance by the decisions of conscience did succeed in preventing freedom of conscience from disappearing altogether, in spite of increasing orthodoxy. Conscience preserved both of the above-mentioned meanings: the faculty of ethical judgment and the totality of religious knowledge and judgments. It is, of course, possible to interpret Luther as meaning that conscience alone is empowered to judge good and evil, the criterion lying not in man but in the Bible. Conscience thus becomes a purely formal faculty of judgment, intrinsically bound to the Bible and its divine commandments. This is the Bible-bound conscience of the orthodox period, when conscience was directed just as authoritatively as in Catholicism. The Catholic direction of conscience is more accommodating in that the Catholic church recognizes not only the biblical revelation but, in addition, the teaching office, which, by the application of casuistics,[4] largely relieves conscience of its directing role in matters of ethical decision. In time, the orthodox sanction of conscience by the sole authority of the Bible was bound to become questionable, for even the most consistently orthodox person had to choose between the various biblical commandments, and do so moreover on the basis of a personal decision. The Old Testament laws concerning worship and purification were simply impossible to carry out, although in the Old Testament they were considered to be just as important as the ethical commandments. In consequence, the casuistic use of the Bible as a moral authority for conscience was put in question. Pietism and the Enlightenment brought about a turning point. The Enlightenment applied the criterion of reason to biblical pronouncements and commandments and so did not permit the solitary word of the Bible to be the ultimate authority for conscience. For the Pietists, conversion, the living experience of faith, was more important than the usurpation of the biblical word for one's own use.

These developments led to an unshackling of conscience from

its bondage to the Bible and the church, and the problem of freedom of conscience emerged once again. In its entry for *Gewissen*
(conscience) the new Brockhaus dictionary says that Protestantism
began by deriving conscience from the Bible and building it up
into a philosophical doctrine but then laid the emphasis on personal responsibility and freedom of conscience. This is also true
of Neo-Protestantism. As we have seen, the beginnings of Luther's
Reformation fitted this definition, but its continuation was different.
Seen in the broad historical and cultural perspective, the Reformation was closely associated with Humanism and the Renaissance.
Both defended the cause of freedom of conscience far more energet-
ically and persistently than did the orthodoxy that followed the Reformation. Concern for freedom of conscience reemerged only in
Neo-Protestant times, conscience being defined as the totality of
man's cognitive and judging faculties. In that case, the goal of
freedom of conscience is that man should be able to stand by a
particular point of view without qualification, doubt, or *reservatio
mentalis*. The oath of office for Protestant ministers in Bern includes an obligation to preach the Gospel purely and honestly,
according to their best knowledge and conscience. In other words,
no one should preach anything he cannot wholly subscribe to or
which would bring him into conflict with his ethical duty to be
truthful. Man must have this freedom, since freedom is a necessary
condition of truthfulness. This means that the individual must preserve his freedom vis-à-vis all authority. Naturally he can bow to
authority if impelled by an insight or conviction of conscience,
but that does not absolve him from the obligation to preserve a
measure of inner freedom from this authority, nor may he obey
at the cost of his individual truthfulness. In the Neo-Protestant view,
there is only one absolute authority, God. If an experience is felt
to be absolute, we must bow to it. The ethical requirements of the
Bible, especially those of Jesus Christ, may be, and often are, experienced as absolutes by Protestants. But these are only guidelines
for conscience, and it is not required that truthfulness bow to them.
Furthermore, the ethical commandments of the Bible are requirements, not experiences. Absolute experiences occur very rarely,
and, such experiences apart, Protestants have the duty to search
their conscience scrupulously and take its decisions with the utmost
seriousness.

Conscience as a moral judge gave Neo-Protestants considerable cause for reflection. One thing was certain: there could be no room for the method of casuistics. By his commandment to love —a commandment that for him summed up all others—Jesus Christ provided a guideline by which conscience had to decide in each individual case. The question of a good and a bad conscience also arose. Can Christians have a good conscience, or are they always under the pressure of a bad conscience, which they need time and again as a salutary stimulus? Both views have been defended in Protestantism. In his short story "Meretlein," [5] Gottfried Keller denounced the kind of Christianity that is entirely motivated by a bad conscience, which, it is alleged, is indispensable for subjugating man's nature and preparing him for acceptance of the true faith. Another trend in Protestantism lays particular emphasis on the acquisition of a good conscience. Anyone who has the right kind of faith must have a good conscience, as he is on the right road. Conversely, a good conscience is an infallible sign that one possesses the right faith. The doctrine of justification by faith is apt to lead to this emphasis on a good conscience. Revivalist movements usually arouse a bad conscience to begin with; later the time may come when a good conscience and an optimistic view of human behavior get into the running. Fundamentally, though, the same tension which Luther experienced must be held fast and endured: a recognition of the moral insufficiency of all human behavior in the face of an absolute ethical demand. Yet conscience must not be used to abandon man completely to the *terrores conscientiae* and to rob him of all courage and of the very possibility of ethical action. The *terrores conscientiae,* the temptations of conscience, may easily lead to paralysis of the moral will. That is the exact opposite of the true purpose of a bad conscience. On the one hand, the tension is necessary because in many cases ethical action means acting contrary to our natural impulses and strivings. On the other hand, we must always find the courage and strength to dare to do good. Luther knew that the *terrores conscientiae* may be the work of the devil, but Albert Schweitzer was equally justified in postulating that a good conscience may be an invention of the devil too.

In summoning up the Protestant view of conscience, the first conclusion we must come to is that conscience is a primordial phenomenon, present in man from the beginning. Yet the phenomenon is a puzzling one, for the fact that there is something in man which can oppose his natural behavior is far from self-evident and is rather a matter for continual amazement. The second conclusion is that conscience, as a human function, has certain specific tasks to perform. It must therefore be recognized and heeded, as well as being meaningfully integrated into the total personality. Conscience also has a religious function, but it is not the only religious function and must always be coordinated meaningfully with other functions. This coordination must take into account the nature of conscience and what it can give to man but must also consider his inner constellation and the outer circumstances in which he lives. It is the duty of every epoch, indeed of every individual, constantly to reflect anew on the nature, the significance, and the tasks of conscience.

NOTES

1. Quoted from R. Huch, *Das Zeitalter der Glaubensspaltung* (Zurich, 1937), p. 115.

2. [Notker the Biglipped (Labeo), also called the German (Teutonicus), *ca.* 950-1022, of the monastery of St. Gall, Switzerland. He translated a large number of Latin writers into Old High German and is therefore a source for many philosophical and theological terms in German. His use of "conscience" first appears in OHG in his translation of the Psalms, Cf. *Die Religion in Geschichte und Gegenwart,* 3d rev. ed., ed. K. Galling *et al.* (Tübingen: J. C. B. Mohr [Paul Siebeck], 1957-65), articles on Notker, Vol. IV, p. 1532, by H. Beumann, and on "Gewissen," Vol. II, p. 1551, by E. Wolff.—EDITOR.]

3. ["Curse not the king, no not in thy thought" (Authorized Version). "Thought" also in Douai and Revised Standard and Soncino versions. Cf. note 25a in the preceding essay.—TRANSLATOR.]

4. [The word "casuistics" is used here instead of the theological term "casuistry" to avoid confusion with its other, and more general, connotation: "sophistical, equivocal, or specious reasoning" (Webster). Casuistry in the theological sense is defined as "The art or science of bringing general moral principles to bear upon particular cases. Its exercise is always called for in moral issues, whether the particular decision is made by individual judgment or in accordance with an established code" (*Oxford Dictionary of the Christian Church*).—TRANSLATOR.]

5. "Little Meret," in *Green Henry,* trans. A. M. Holt (London, 1960).

7 A Catholic View of Conscience

JOSEF RUDIN

In the long history of the Roman Catholic church a variety of views about conscience has been held, so that a brief reconciliation of these views into a systematic statement is exceedingly difficult. Rudin has accomplished this task by using the theology of the church rather than the personal conceptions of conscience held by individual Catholic philosophers.* He assumes that conscience is a given human reality, not unique to the Christian faith; therefore, his discussion centers on what the church must do to incorporate conscience within its belief system. The paradox of the individual following his conscience, yet making wrong decisions, is clearly described. The church's limitation on freedom of conscience in past historical epochs is faced, as well as the church's dilemma in dealing with some believers who insist that conscience is wholly a private matter.

For Catholic thinking, conscience is characterized by two very different aspects which must be clearly differentiated if it is to be understood from the Catholic point of view. First, we encounter it as a disposition ingrained in man's whole nature, and to this extent conscience is

* From *Conscience,* edited by the Curatorium of the Jung Institute, Zurich (Evanston, Illinois, Northwestern University Press, 1970). This article, found on pp. 137-158, was translated by R. F. C. Hull and Ruth Horine. Reprinted by permission.

firmly established, binding, mandatory, and without freedom for the Catholic. Second, it manifests itself conclusively as a personal decision arrived at by an act of judgment, and in this sense the conscience of the Catholic is free, profoundly his own, and a matter of individual responsibility.

I
CONSCIENCE AS A DISPOSITION OF MAN'S WHOLE NATURE

The ultimate foundation of conscience does not come from outside but is inherent in man's innermost being as a structural ground plan and a permanent pattern of order. It is his nature itself, struggling toward the goals of wholeness and harmony and conscious of its obligation to do so. The Schoolmen called it *synderēsis* or, even better, *syneidēsis,* which we may paraphrase as the "natural disposition for conscience." As a result, man feels and knows himself "in the deepest and higher reaches of his soul to be so bound by value that fulfilling the demands of *syneidēsis* gives him strength, health, joy, and peace, but nonfulfillment brings disruption, anxiety, torment, and guilt." [1] What is this natural disposition, looked at more closely? We can hardly imagine anything more comprehensive and all-embracing. In a lengthy address to the Congress of Catholic Psychotherapists in April, 1953, Pope Pius XII dealt exhaustively with this natural disposition as the natural image of man. We cannot reproduce his ideas *in extenso* but shall refer only to those having particular significance for our discussion. Essentially, the natural disposition is characterized by three dimensions: (1) the dimension of the intra-individual, (2) the dimension of social commitment and orientation, and (3) the dimension of transcendental relationship.

1. *The Dimension of the Intra-Individual*

This includes, first of all, everything relating to what is currently designated the "conscience of biological fitness" [2]—the innate drive of the somatic organism to develop, its various warning signals, its need for a healthy state of equilibrium. The "psychic conscience" penetrates much deeper and legitimately demands the development of all psychic forces and functions, on the conscious as well as the unconscious level, in accordance with their nature. The investigations of depth psychology into the various determinisms, mechanisms, and the whole dynamism of the psyche were highly appreciated by Pius XII. However, the prime requisite which the ecclesiastical authorities stress and insist on is the quite specific recognition of the spiritual disposition as well. This cannot be considered a mere *quantité négligéable* in the intrapsychic structure but must be acknowledged as the guiding and orienting organ of the psyche itself. While no elementary instinctual drive can lay legitimate claim to this leading role, the spiritual organ is normally in a position to exercise this inner guidance. We must not assume that psychic disturbances are the norm. Panpsychologism is just as one-sided and therefore just as erroneous as its opposite, Rousseau-esque naturalistic optimism.

The intrapsychic dimension of man's natural disposition therefore presents a very complex picture, and one can well understand why this disposition has been given so many names, most of which express only one of its aspects. At times it is called an inner instinct; at others, an inner feeling of wholeness, Some speak of deep inner knowledge; others have declared that man, "out of some dark urge, is conscious of the right path." [3] Von Monakow speaks of *hormē* (impulse, driving force), while some, like C. G. Jung, lay stress on archetypal images, recognizing an inner entelechy and thus coming quite close to what medieval philosophy designated as *syneidēsis,* the innermost "focus" and balanced interplay of all natural forces.[4]

The intra-individual dimension shows a typical dual aspect: it is as strongly ego-related as it is value-related. Its ego-relatedness becomes particularly clear when we remember that it is from the depths of the psyche that we receive those alarm signals which register danger, loss, injury, inner discord. Yet from these same depths come feelings of joy and inner satisfaction when the psyche is able to develop naturally. Thus the ego experiences itself either as well balanced, whole and healthy, or as threatened and disunited. The quality of value-relatedness is expressed in the fact that the ego cannot remain indifferent to the voice of the natural disposition but feels itself summoned because it senses value, which it experiences as its own value. This is where obligation and involvement come into play. The intra-individual dimension strives for self-realization, and unless it can accomplish this it is cheated of its meaning and value. On this level, living according to one's conscience simply means letting one's individual potential develop according to its own laws.

2. The Dimension of Social Commitment and Orientation

We come now to a crucial point. Is it permissible to speak of a social dimension of man's natural disposition, or does everything social belong at the start to the environment? Two things depend on the answer to this question: whether we should condemn all outside influence as a foreign determinant, an artificial interference, and whether we should speak of a "spurious" conscience when social viewpoints are accepted as a criterion. The danger should not be minimized. The personal center is only too often falsified by outside influences, and the individual begins to live by the judgments and expectations of others. Man becomes alienated from himself, and what alone would constitute dignity and truly human behavior soon becomes illusory. The typical mass man lives by the standards of an alien conscience in a state of nonconscience, though usually he is unaware of this because most of his fellow men are exactly like him. For him a "good conscience" simply means conforming with the current moral views. This conception of conscience extends even to the ethics of comradeship found among gangs of criminals. In reality, an alien conscience is not a form of conscience at all but is a counterforce acting against conscience, depersonalizing and deeply dehumanizing man.

Equally uncritical and naïve, however, is the conception which grants conscience complete sovereignty and autonomy, placing the natural disposition in a vacuum, in an autistic, imaginary, solipsistic world of illusions far removed from any concrete reality. Here conscience assumes the role of an autocratic authority, issuing directives and commands without regard to the hierarchy of values in human nature.

The question we must ask, therefore, is a different one: Is human nature not essentially dependent on and oriented toward a social sphere in which alone it can develop naturally? We would misjudge man's nature if we failed to recognize how intimately it is involved and coordinated with the authority of parents and educators as well as with the human community as a whole. Aristotle included the social factor in his well-known definition of man. For him social commitment and orientation are constituent elements in man's makeup, and Catholic philosophy has taken over this view and held it fast. This is as much as to say that conscience as a natural disposition is partially molded by man's social nature. We know that the plasticity of man's instincts and aptitudes is greater than in the animal organism, hence they are more elastic, more variable, more easily molded. Man is not a self-contained monad; he is open in all directions. He can realize his best self only as a member of a community. This is not to deny that an artificial superego may be constructed if the educational influences are not consonant with the inner social nature of man but assume the form of outer coercion masking the educator's self-assertiveness and lust for power. Conscience as a function of man's whole natural disposition is an expression also of the social aspect of his nature. Because of that it can warn him against the worst excesses of the aggressive drive and cruelty which are given him along with the instinct for self-preservation,

Conscience is not only socially conditioned but also socially oriented. A very extensive and—in a highly civilized society—exceedingly costly apparatus of educational influences and guidance is therefore required for its optimal development. If we squander the vast sums appropriated for our highly complex educational systems only on the perfecting of technology, it will be difficult to escape the destructive tendencies of the atomic age. The dimension of social commitment and orientation which also speaks as the voice of conscience must be respected.

Today, however, there is a tendency to overemphasize the social aspect of human nature, which would lead to a cramping of man's individuality. Disapproval of this trend is expressed in the papal address mentioned above:

Protection, respect, love, and service of oneself are not only justified but are direct requirements of both psychology and moral law. That is at once a self-evident fact of nature and an article of Christian faith. The Lord taught, "Thou shalt love thy neighbor as thyself" (Mark

12:31). Christ therefore considered love of oneself to be the criterion of neighborly love and not the reverse. . . . We should fail to do justice to this reality if we dismissed all regard for the ego as psychological imprisonment, as an aberration or a return to a more primitive stage of development, on the pretext that it is opposed to the natural altruism of the psyche.[5]

The social nature of man is only one of his many dimensions and must not overshadow any of the others. The voice of conscience arising from this dimension goes against the true and natural conscience of the individual unless it rings out in unison with the other dimensions, and only then should it be heard and obeyed.

3. *The Dimension of Transcendental Relationship*

From the center of man's nature, conscience strives for the fulfillment of all his potentialities, yet at the same time it feels this process of self-realization as a challenge by a higher authority which man has to recognize. We can therefore understand why he has the impression of being in the presence of something divine. Is it only a rigid, abstract principle which is trying to gain recognition, or is it a dynamic, concrete power through which a divine will issues its summons to man? Ovid described conscience as *Deus in nobis,* and Seneca called it the "God who is near you, with you, and in you," adding that "a holy spirit dwells in us, observing our good and evil." [6] Whereas it is difficult to conceive that a rigid impersonal principle—an iron *anankē*—rules over our personal freedom and dignity, it is relatively easy to accept the idea that the voice of a personal God speaks directly to us in the dictates of conscience and that conscience illuminates a third dimension of human nature: the relation of the image to the prototype.

All this seems fairly unproblematical and self-evident. But are we really so naïvely uncritical and optimistic in our judgment of human nature? Or are we—unlike Rousseau—aware of its somber and abysmal aspects, its tendency to fragmentation and ambivalence? The presence of evil is such an elementary fact of human history that we can hardly overlook it. There is that other fascinating voice, likewise resounding from the depths of our being and holding out possibilities of development and self-realization, of richer and lusher experiences far removed from the divine prototype and which, it seems, are likewise deeply embedded in our nature.

Christianity explains this ambivalence by the doctrine of original sin, which has, however, been variously interpreted. According to the Catholic conception, original sin has not in any way inwardly corrupted and poisoned man's nature. The Fall is viewed rather as a breaking-away from friendship with God, resulting in the loss of man's alleged supernatural endowments and in a fatal weakening of his nature as well as a confounding of instinct and spirit. Redemption through Christ must therefore be understood as a summons to man for a resumption of the supernatural filial relationship with God and for the gradual restoration of his weakened nature. According to Catholic doctrine, baptism effectively places Christians within reach of God's love: "We should be called children of God; and so we are" (1 John 3:1, RSV). An actual exaltation and transformation of human nature has been effected, a participation in the divine. But even in this redeemed and blessed nature conscience remains active. It would be inconceivable if only man's biological and sociopsychological nature, and not his exalted nature, should possess in conscience an organ of moral conduct. Through the Holy Spirit, the inner principle of a Christian's life, conscience acquires a new strength, which shall "guide you into all truth" (John 16:8). Conscience is thus the *organon* (tool) of God, "who in a wonderful manner didst create and ennoble human nature, and still more wonderfully hast renewed it," as is said in the Offertory of the Mass.

This increment to our human nature is not forced upon man from outside, by a higher order. He is not urged, still less compelled, by an alien power into a form of behavior fundamentally contrary to the laws of his inner being. Rather, the voice of the spirit strikes a note in accord with the natural spiritual level of the individual and the new level of Christianity he has attained. The extremely difficult and complex problem of the relationship between the natural and the supernatural can only be hinted at in the limited space of this essay.

It takes a considerably deepened theological insight into the church to understand how, for the Catholic, the voice of God can also make itself heard outwardly, through the teaching office. For the Catholic, the church is not just an external organization, like a club you can join or leave at will. It is the outward and visible expression of that invisible community which, as the *corpus Christ mysticum,* embraces all those who have received the new life. It is obvious that this new, living community also entails new forms, new laws, and a new kind of freedom as well as new obligations. Conscience thus acquires a new function. Both the intra-individual and the social dimension of *syneidēsis* are deepened and expanded by the transcendental dimension. Through his participation in the divine, man enters into communion with the *corpus Christi mysticum.* While the church should not be identified with Christ in all its organizational forms and institutions, it should not be understood either as separate from Christ, its central life-giving principle. Furthermore, we should have to reject as altogether too primitive any attempt to explain the difference between Catholicism and Protestantism simply by contrasting the church and Christ. The antithesis "Catholics are church-bound whereas Protestants affirm that salvation can be found only in Christ," or "Catholics remain dependent on the authority of the church whereas Protestants recognize in Christ alone the direct road to God," does not show even a superficial understanding of Catholic theology. The way in which the early church bore witness to the social dimension of Christian conscience is too overwhelming to be passed over in silence.

None other than Paul himself took great pains to indoctrinate the Christians of his time with this new concept. As a former Pharisee, he was well aware of the practical importance and sublime grandeur of moral law, and his conversion to the new morality of Christian freedom was an experience that cut to the core of his being. Nowhere do we encounter a more soul-stirring debate than in his Epistle to the Galatians, which is the greatest proclamation of freedom in Christianity. The sentences ring out like a fanfare of trumpets: "Stand fast therefore in the liberty wherewith Christ hath made us free, and be not entangled again with the yoke of bondage" (5:1). "For, brethren, ye have been called unto liberty" (5:13). And then, when the epoch-making articles of liberation stood there as if hewn in rock, he himself came to experience the paradox of Christian conscience: the new, overwhelming freedom of conscience turned out to be a yet mightier bondage to this same conscience. The highest and truest criterion of the Christian attitude had to be hammered out in the debate with Gnostic ideology, and here the bond of love proved more decisive and more powerful than freedom. The most important passages can be found in 1 Corinthians, chapters 8-13. Paul's thinking circles in spirals around the central problem of freedom and bondage. Actually, he says, the Christian is free to eat of "those things that are offered in sacrifice unto idols" (8:4); actually, in Christ, woman has equal rights with man (11:11-12); actually, all gifts of the spirit are important and great (chap. 12). *But* Christianity has to employ a wholly different and new criterion, a new norm of conscience: the norm and criterion of love (chap. 13). This love is so far-reaching that a man will surrender his freedom if it happens to be harmful to a fellow Christian who lacks the courage and inner freedom of the stronger one. The Christian conscience grants freedom but it also binds anew through that freely expressed love for the community of those sharing the new life wrought in the depths of their being by the Holy Spirit (12:12-14, 25-28).

Three dimensions are thus conferred on us by *syneidēsis:* the intra-individual, the social, and the transcendental, which interpenetrate and complement one another. *Syneidēsis* might be considered as a function of that image of man which dwells deep in the psyche and strives for progressive development and realization. But this image is seldom seen whole and complete in any given age. Each period tends to stress new or hitherto neglected aspects, while previous ones are pushed aside with equal bias. Thus every epoch is called upon to acquire an ever more comprehensive and penetrating knowledge of human nature. Today we may acknowledge with particular gratitude the findings of anthropological psychology since they afford us a more refined and effective understanding of *syneidēsis* and its significance for our time. The disposition for conscience will, of course, always be fundamental in all decisions which are of universal importance to human life. Its peculiar dynamism will always assert itself, provided that the somatic, psychological, and spiritual functions are relatively sound, that the social organism is reasonably well ordered, and that the individual does not deliberately cut himself off from the gift of

Christian grace. In other words, conscience is not a free-floating entity but rests on a normative and natural foundation.

The stage is thus set on which the drama of decision by conscience is enacted. We have established the point of departure from which the conscience of the Catholic summons him to responsible and ethical action. To *syneidēsis* we might apply the oracle: *Vocatus atque non vocatus, deus aderit* ("summoned or not summoned, God will be present").[7] It is the immanent God who abides within us and summons us, the God whose image awaits realization in the depths of the psyche: "Let us make man in our image, after our likeness" (Gen. 1:26). For concrete application in life, the practical judgments and verdicts of conscience must be formed on the foundation of *syneidēsis*.

II
CONSCIENCE AS AN ACT OF FREE DECISION

Although conscience, as integral to the structure of our human nature, presents itself to us as a binding and determining factor, the authentic act of conscience is the result of a wholly free and personal decision. This state of affairs sounds relatively simple, but it is very difficult to describe more precisely, because here we touch on the mystery of human freedom. The mystery resides in the fact that human freedom can never be absolute. It must continually reconstitute and realize itself anew because of the multiplicity of determinisms which are at work in nature. To begin with, it can be established that authentic and well-considered judgments of conscience are not very common. In many situations of life, *syneidēsis* as the foundation of judgments of conscience functions almost automatically, so that it is relatively easy for a man to act in accordance with his natural disposition. But, in the life of every human being, situations arise and decisions must be made which confront him with more complex problems. The different dimensions of *syneidēsis* then seem to conflict with one another, and careful reflection is required before conscience can exercise judgment and arrive at a straightforward decision. There are people who are faced again and again with such decisions, indeed their whole life seems to consist of endless decision-making.

Others, more matter of fact and more integrated, allow themselves to be guided quietly and surely by their natural disposition. People who are burdened with problems, who are less integrated, are more intensely aware of the divergent possibilities, the dissonances, the polarities of their being and for this reason must make conscious decisions more frequently. They continually experience conscience in its executive function, as taking up a personal position, as an act of spiritual freedom.

In order to demonstrate the full significance of the act of decision, we shall discuss it under three headings which are especially important from the Catholic point of view: (1) the act of free decision proper, (2) the right of the erring conscience, and (3) the church and freedom of conscience.

1. The Act of Free Decision Proper

Correctly understood, this act is carried out in three phases. The first and the third are well known, while the second seems to elude phenomenological description.

Catholic moralists have described the first phase as *conscientia antecedens* (antecedent conscience). In this phase conscience again appears as a natural disposition, but this time before the forum of intellectual reflection, stating its case in the form of a practical judgment and demanding attention. The cogent arguments for or against a particular mode of conduct are there deliberated. In this phase the appellant hears the voice that warns him against evading the issue or admonishes him not to repress *syneidēsis*, while at the same time encouraging him to act correctly.

In the third phase, *conscientia consequens* (subsequent conscience) raises its voice as the incorruptible prosecutor, if a mistake has been committed, or as the corroborative witness of right behavior and action. Remorse or peace of mind are the outcome of this phase. In both these phases man experiences an inner tension —perhaps a disturbing gap or even a conflict—between his ego and the dictates of conscience. Conscience appears here clearly as a nonego, as a higher self.

Between these two phases lies the second phase, where conscience makes the decision proper. This decision seems to be carried out by the innermost psychic center, which pronounces judgment in full freedom and accepts the responsibility. In this act the ego experiences the potential identity of conscience with the self or else its own infinite detachment from it. The Schoolmen were much given to elaborate and deep speculation about this act, and each school of thought evolved different theories concerning the psychic function that makes the decision. Albertus Magnus and Thomas Aquinas defended the intellectualistic, and Alexander of Hales, Bonaventure, and Henry of Ghent the voluntaristic theory. Nowadays we are inclined to accept the so-called holistic theory, which postulates the interplay of all psychic faculties in this act. Here we come face to face with the mystery of the individual; here he experiences his highest and strongest potentialities, but also his inalienable personal responsibility. The act of decision cannot be performed in an atmosphere of willful, arbitrary, or frivolous freedom. It requires the utmost seriousness of purpose.

It is on this freedom that morality of action is founded. Through it the objective demands of man as a microcosm, an image of totality, are subjectivized and recast into a personal confession of faith—or are rejected and excluded from this innermost sphere.

In this realm of personal freedom there are no longer any determining influences from outside. Here even the Catholic has to make the judgments of conscience entirely by himself, and in this respect his position is in no way different from that of the Protestant or the true humanist, unbeliever though he may be. The Catholic has to follow the judgment of conscience even if, objectively speaking, it is erroneous, and even if it should separate him from his church. The judgment of conscience is absolutely binding: it commits man to himself and to God. No excuses and no appeals to the commands of military or ecclesiastical authorities are of avail here. There is no replacement or substitute for personal conscience. Authority is valid only to the extent that it can justify itself as competent and binding before the bar of a mature and serene conscience.

Man cannot abstain from these judgments since they are not subjective, arbitrary opinions or expressions of momentary experiences but grow out of the inner bond with *syneidēsis,* thus indirectly revealing God's will. Subjective caprice can give in, conform, or bow to totalitarian pressure any time it seems opportune to do so. But conscience can win the struggle for freedom in the face of all the arbitrary demands of human institutions precisely because it is bound by the true and unconditional demands of nature herself.

Are we now affirming, after all, that conscience is *absolutely* autonomous and sovereign? By no means. Our discussion of *syneidēsis* has shown how closely conscience is tied to the objective order of its own multifaceted nature. Within the many dimensions of this moral order, wherein is expressed the will of God the creator and redeemer, there is no freedom of conscience. The freedom that remains to it consists in its opening itself to demands that are in accord with its highest nature and in striving, by this inner assent, to do them justice. Only in this sense is the phrase "freedom of conscience" meaningful and attuned to the nature and dignity of man. And this is also the position we must adopt in elucidating the seeming contradictions in the attitude of the church and its official pronouncements.

2. *The Right of the Erring Conscience*

Conscience would be an effective guarantor of moral order if we could assume that its decisions and judgments were ordinarily based on *syneidēsis* and were followed by actions not subject to outside interference. The sole reason for the failure of conscience would then lie in the second phase of the act of free decision. Freedom to decide would carry the entire responsibility for any deviations and for all behavior running counter to *syneidēsis*. We would then be entitled to a certain amount of optimism regarding the morality of individual conduct and of society at large. But world history, as well as the public and private lives of individuals, has taught us a different lesson: injustices great and small, intrigues, egotism and self-assertiveness, brutal jockeying for position, and downright criminality cannot be considered rare exceptions. Are they indicative of a blatant failure of the freedom of conscience? Are injustice and evil always only the product of a free decision against the better knowledge of *conscientia?* Or is it conceivable that logical and, perhaps more often, emotionally conditioned errors have already crept in at the very moment when conscience forms its judgment? As a matter of fact, dynamic psychology is engaged in investigating the gradual evolution of psychic modes of behavior, and it attempts to explain the formation of emotionally or intellectually conditioned attitudes and judgments in terms of educational influences, collective opinions, and individual moral prejudices. *Syneidēsis* does indeed provide the ground plan and the most elementary, primary requirements for a truly human existence. But in the derivation of secondary ethical standards conflicts between two or more basic principles may arise, leading to erroneous conclusions or furnishing pretexts for falsifications based on affect. Errors may then not only seem permissible but may even appear as dictates of conscience, although deeper insight and more careful, disinterested consideration and judgment would show them to be contrary to the moral order. There is, evidently, an erring conscience, and we must ask ourselves whether such a conscience should be entitled to the same freedom as an incorruptible conscience which much practical experience has rendered capable of great objectivity of judgment.

Are the head-hunters of Borneo entitled to their trophies and to this grisly ritual which promises them increased magical powers? Should the burning of widows in India be considered the legitimate right of a free conscience, since it gives expression to a lofty conception of marital union? And is temple prostitution in India acceptable because it is practiced in the name of the god of fertility? Are we compelled to acknowledge the right of communism to exist and to spread propaganda, knowing as we do that it undermines the foundations of true democracy and works systematically for its overthrow? Can conscience absolve people who refuse to pay taxes because of their conviction that the money would be squandered by the government anyway?

To formulate the question theoretically, are all convictions based on conscience *equally* entitled to freedom because each is the expression of personal conscience, even though they may be contrary to the generally accepted convictions of the day? The topicality of this question is felt again and again, as when we learn that the Skoptsy, a Russian religious sect, practice self-mutilation and that the Chlystes, another Russian sect, indulge in sexual orgies as part of their ritual; that, in 1948, the Oldenburg police were barely able to prevent the human sacrifice of two refugee children from eastern Europe by members of a nonstop prayer group who sought in this manner to forestall the imminent end of the world; and that, in 1954, members of a religious sect in Marseilles allowed their children to die because its teachings forbade them to call a doctor.

The question of divergent opinions in the matter of an objective moral order or the possibility of recognizing objective, ultimate, and absolute truths is not peculiar to our time. Thomas Aquinas was familiar with it in another form and gave his own answer: "Belief in Christ is good in itself and necessary for salvation. But if a Christian who held it wrong to believe in Christ were to do so, he would commit a sin." [8]

Thus the right of the erring conscience was recognized in the Catholic Middle Ages too. Those who err innocently, having acted according to their best knowledge and conscience, cannot be morally condemned even if they have acted immorally according to the general consensus. Whether or not they should be punished nonetheless is another question altogether. A delinquent acting from conviction may be able to justify himself before his own conscience, but the state has to consider the welfare of society as a whole. It must defend law and order by making the delinquent aware of the fact that his conscience is at odds with the existing order.

We might go a step further and declare that those who commit an error of conscience should not be forced to act against their conscience. It is their moral right not to be obliged to act contrary to their conscience even if it is in error. Thus a conscientious objector may be employed in some civilian occupation, and one may try to persuade him that he is acting in error, but on no account should he be forced to take up arms if he considers it to be a sin against his conscience.

On the other hand, we believe there is an essential difference between not having the right to force people into certain actions against their conscience and actually giving them the right to live publicly by the convictions of their conscience if this would violate the rights of others. Anyone preparing and promoting the overthrow of the existing order may, of course, justify himself in the name of his convictions, but we cannot oblige the representatives of that order to allow these convictions to take positive effect. While he is thus prevented from carrying out his presumed duty to his conscience, he is not required to violate it. Duty to one's conscience ceases, however, when it becomes impossible to carry it out. The erring conscience as such remains inviolate, but its consequences may be prevented.

3. *The Church and Freedom of Conscience*

For the Catholic, conscience is the supreme authority even in matters relating to his faith and his membership in the Catholic church. The pronouncement of Lactantius in the third century against the Roman law enforcing religious sacrifice should never be forgotten: "Nisi enim sponte et ex animo fiat, execratio est" ("Unless the act is done freely and from the heart, it is an abomination accursed").[9] In the same spirit, Thomas Aquinas teaches that "anyone upon whom the ecclesiastical authorities, in ignorance of the true facts, impose a demand that offends against his clear conscience, should perish in excommunication rather than violate his conscience."[10] The doctrine and the fundamental attitude of the church are thus quite unequivocal and cannot give rise to any doubts.

On the other hand, we cannot deny the facts of history. The Inquisition, which became in effect an institution for the mass violation of conscience, and individual cases, of which Galileo's is only the best known, are no light mortgage for a church that considers itself the advocate of human dignity. For centuries the church had to fight for its own freedom of conscience. To this day the names of those witnesses who paid for it with their lives are recorded in the church martyrology and are continually being recited. It is indeed inconceivable how the church was able to change its attitude so quickly—not in doctrine but in practice. We cannot and do not wish to defend this *volte face*. Today it is possible to say this in public and to write about it. Albert Hartmann, a Jesuit, exposed the facts as follows in his book *Toleranz und christlicher Glaube:* "By means of bloody martyrdom the church fought for the freedom of conscience against the pagan state, until it was proclaimed for the first time in the historic Edict of Tolerance at Milan in 311. But later this same church denied others that freedom and persecuted people for the sake of their faith."[11] Only the honest admission of past errors can offer some slight guarantee against easy repetition of similar abuses of power in the future. Justice demands, however, that in judging the church we should consider as extenuating circumstances the conditions of the time, such as the absence of psychological insight and the close ties of the church with the existing social and political order.

Nevertheless, certain doctrinal statements made by the church in the nineteenth century, though apparently directed against the freedom of conscience, must be viewed in a different light. It is easy to misconstrue them. In 1832 Gregory XVI condemned as "absurd and erroneous and even as *deliramentum*"—folly—the idea that "freedom of conscience should be proclaimed and secured for all." [12] In 1864 Pius IX took Gregory's statement as a precedent and confirmed it.[13] The freedom of conscience attacked here is that arbitrary freedom which recognizes none of the binding values of truth and the moral order. Its advocates ignore the foundations of conscience in human nature in order to defend the sovereignty and autonomy necessary to them for making decisions as and when they please. Gregory's words were directed against the idea that anyone may consider right what seems to him so at any given moment and without paying his due to the standards set by nature and divine revelation. Freedom of conscience must not become a *carte blanche* for a specious, worldly morality.

But, is there not after all a coercive aspect of dogma, compelling the Catholic to adhere to the tenets of the faith which are proclaimed as universally binding revealed truths? For many people this is the greatest stumbling block as far as their attitude to the church is concerned. Where, then, is there any room for freedom of conscience? Within the space of this essay it would be quite impossible to make anything like an exhaustive study of these problems, which raise so many difficult questions. We can only hint at an answer, without substantiating it in detail.

The Catholic church believes that in the exercise of its infallible teaching office it has the support of the Holy Scriptures. It insists that it was founded by Christ himself, together with the institution of this teaching office and also its pastoral function. "He that heareth you heareth me" (Luke 10:16). It insists equally on the institution of primacy in the church: "Thou art Peter, and upon this rock I will build my church" (Matt. 16:18). We know, of course, that outside the Catholic church these texts have been interpreted differently and that in the past two centuries new interpretations have been continually put forward which are in part

diametrically opposed to the Catholic one. Which of these interpretations is the correct one to which Christians can look for
guidance? Does the level of exegetical knowledge at a given time
determine what constitutes the body of faith for the Christian, or
can he choose from among the many different viewpoints the one
that seems most plausible to him? Or should he follow the zigzag
path of continually changing interpretations? We are in no way
blind to the fact that in individual cases the coercive aspect of
dogma may lead to very serious spiritual conflicts. This is particularly true, for instance, when an eminent theologian has doubts
about the conclusiveness of a certain dogma or even feels that he
must reject it altogether.

We are fully aware of the tremendous significance which the
mere existence of an infallible teaching office has. Although the
formal assent of faith is required only for tenets solemnly pronounced *ex cathedra,* in many other matters of faith and morals
decisions which are not solemnly pronounced are also relatively
binding. It would be unrealistic and dishonest not to admit that
very often this is the crucial point which determines whether the
Catholic will profess his allegiance to the church's view or
whether he will hold it incompatible with his personal freedom of
conscience. But very often this is also the point at which considerable confusion arises, because some Catholics make adherence to
the dogma and moral teachings of the church responsible for their
own lack of spiritual freedom, for their neurotic inhibitions and
frustrations. Closer examination of these neurotic symptoms and
careful analysis of the psychic background shows, however, that
in most cases the lack of spiritual freedom is due rather to an overstrict and harsh upbringing or to a false understanding of the
church's precepts. We are in entire agreement with John B.
Hirschmann, a Jesuit, when he writes: "We should neither deny
nor minimize nor peremptorily dismiss the impression which some,
perhaps too many, of its members have today of a certain lack of
freedom within the church." [14] But we should do well to make a
clear distinction between lack of spiritual freedom and spiritual
commitment. Too often lack of spiritual freedom is caused by
spiritual confusion and lack of insight into the coherence of
Catholic doctrine. The spirit is oriented toward and committed
to truth. Noncommitment does not make free, but truth which is

assimilated to reality does. The reality principle so much emphasized by depth psychology is all-embracing and has universal validity. We are not the creators of reality. We must learn to recognize and accept it as completely as possible, even when we meet it as spiritual and supernatural reality. Both the teaching and pastoral offices of the church serve this great reality and thereby the truth which makes free the children of God. This is why the church was promised the Paraclete, "the Spirit of truth" (John 16:13). Through him the competence and scope of this service are firmly established, but also its limitations, because only voluntary obedience, and not the outward performance of duty, constitutes a moral achievement for free and emancipated human beings.

For this reason it is very important that no one should ever be forced into this faith and into membership in the church. Canon 1351 of the Canon Law puts it succinctly: "No one may be forced to accept the Catholic faith against his will." In 1943 and again in 1946 Pius XII quoted this canon, adding: "For faith, without which it is impossible to please God, must be an entirely free homage of the intellect and will. Hence, if it should happen that, contrary to the constant teaching of this Apostolic See, anyone should be brought against his will to embrace the Catholic faith, we cannot do otherwise, in the realization of our duty, than disavow such an action." [15]

On this basis the personal freedom of the act of decision is ensured and the personal responsibility of conscience recognized. Hence even for Catholics conscience is the ultimate authority from which there can be no appeal to a higher one. Here again there is a broad consensus, at least among civilized peoples.

In the light of these considerations we can understand why the Catholic church is so vitally interested in the education of conscience. It cannot remain indifferent, since it regards not only the teaching office but also the pastoral office as its allotted task. Obviously, this task is of such magnitude and reaches so far into all realms of life that it would be necessary to devote an entire essay to this topic alone. The education of conscience is probably the most difficult task all educators have to face, and it is one that continually presents itself in new form. We are fully aware of the extent to which the Catholic education of conscience again and again falls short of what it should accomplish, and how great—and almost inevitable—is this failure.

While we may have succeeded in sketching a Catholic view of conscience in broad outline, most of the ideas touched on here would have to be studied in much greater depth in order to do it full justice. Conscience is the focal point on which all problems concerning the image of man and of God, the individual and the collective, the subjectivity and objectivity of our knowledge, converge. This shows with particular clarity that conscience is the battleground where our spiritual forces must carry out their true struggle for decisions.

NOTES

1. B. Häring, *Das Gesetz Christi: Moraltheologie* (Freiburg i.B., 1954), p. 187.

2. [Cf. below, Blum's essay, n. 4, relating to Monakow's definition of *hormē.*—TRANSLATOR.]

3. Goethe, *Faust,* Part I, "Prologue in Heaven."

4. [*Syneidēsis,* amplified in the author's German text as *Zusammenschau.* English: "view together" or "focus."—TRANSLATOR.]

5. *Acta Apostolica Sedis,* Annus XXXXV, Series II, Vol. XX (1953), p. 283.

6. [Seneca, Epistle XLI, trans. R. W. Gummere, Loeb Classical Library edition of Seneca's *Epistulae morales,* Vol. I (Cambridge, Mass.; and London, 1917; reprinted 1953).—TRANSLATOR.]

7. [Delphic oracle given to the Lacedaemonians when they asked whether they should make war against the Athenians. The oracle is carved over the front door of C. G. Jung's house in Küsnacht.—TRANSLATOR.]

8. *Summa Theologica,* I/II, 19.5.

9. Lactantius *Divinarum Institutionum* V. 19 [*Patr. Lat.* (Migne), VI. 20, 614-16].

10. IV, *Sent., dist.* 38, art. 4, expos. text.

11. Albert Hartmann, *Toleranz und christlicher Glaube* (Frankfurt a.M., 1955), p. 172.

12. *Mirari Vos* (1832) (Sammlung Marmy, 1945, No. 16). [See *Papal Teachings* (Boston: Daughters of St. Paul, 1962), pp. 124ff.—EDITOR.]

13. *Quanta Cura* (1864).

14. "Die Freiheit in der Kirche," *Stimmen der Zeit* (1957/58), Heft 2, p. 86.

15. *Mystici corporis* (1943) (Sammlung Marmy, No. 1441). [See *The Documents of Vatican II,* ed. Walter M. Abbott (New York: America Press, Association Press, 1966), p. 689; see also *Acta Apostolica Sedis,* No. 38 (1946), p. 394.—EDITOR.]

8 Conscience and Church Authority

Avery R. Dulles, S.J.

Most of our discussion about conscience has to do with moral behavior and ethical responsibility. There is another facet of conscience that must also be considered—a person's right to think through his religious beliefs in order to accept and follow the prompting of his conscience. In this sense, conscience is the conscious, deliberate commitment of the self and cannot be forced by an external authority. How can there be such a zone of intellectual freedom if the church claims that its teachings are true? This dilemma is acute and cannot be resolved by saying that those who void or avoid the church's teachings are sub-Christian in outlook. Dulles suggests, rather, that a reconsideration of the nature of church authority will be a more useful way to treat the dilemma.*

From my own area of specialization, I intend to address this topic not from the point of view of the moralist but from that of the systematic theologian. Accordingly, I shall understand the term "conscience" not as a judgment regarding the rightness or wrongness of a particular course of external behavior but as a man's personal judgment regarding what he should believe. Freedom of conscience obtains when a man is able to make this decision sincerely and spontaneously, without undue moral or psychological pressures. By "authority" I

* From *Conscience, Its Freedom and Limitations,* edited by William C. Bier, S.J. (New York: Fordham University Press, 1971), pp. 251-257. Reprinted by permission.

shall understand not the Church's power to command or to forbid certain external actions but rather its claim to teach in a way that calls for internal assent. Limiting my topic yet further, I shall omit all consideration of the unofficial authority of the scholar, the man of experience, and the charismatic, important though their role in the Church is. I shall confine my attention to the official magisterium, which claims to issue binding doctrinal pronouncements. How can the imposition of official doctrine be reconciled with the freedom of the individual believer?

The Freedom of Christian Faith

The conflict between freedom and authority, which arises in one form or another in all societies, is particularly poignant in the Church. For the Church is a society of faith, and faith, by its nature, is a free act. According to Vatican Council II, in its Declaration on Religious Freedom, "it is one of the major tenets of Catholic doctrine that man's response to God in faith must be free" (Vatican Council II, 1966, n. 9, p. 689). Christian faith, moreover, claims to enhance man's freedom. In the New Testament, Paul exultantly declares that Christ has set us free "from the law of sin and death" (Rom 8:2). "For freedom," he declares, "Christ has set us free. . . . Do not submit again to a yoke of slavery" (Gal 5:1). Christian freedom rests upon the gift of the Holy Spirit. "For you did not receive the spirit of slavery to fall back into fear, but you have received the spirit of sonship" (Rom 8:21). The faithful are called to "the glorious liberty of the children of God" (Rom 8:21), for, as Paul declares elsewhere, "where the Spirit of the Lord is, there is freedom" (2 Cor 3:17). The fourth Gospel likewise stresses freedom as one of the most precious fruits of Christian faith. "If you continue in my word," says Jesus, "you are truly my disciples, and you will know the truth, and the truth will make you free" (Jn 8:32). "If the Son makes you free you will be free indeed" (Jn 8:36).

That these assertions are not empty words is verified by the experience of countless Christians. Those who take the gospel seriously, and commit themselves to it, are wonderfully liberated from servitude to passion in its various forms and are emancipated from earthly attachments which could inhibit their self-mastery. Faith gives men courage to renounce all things, and to stand up unflinchingly against the threats of persecutors.

The Church's Failure To Liberate

In our own day, however, many Catholics complain that their faith seems to subject them to a new legalism of doctrine, not less burdensome in its way than the Old Law had been to Paul before his conversion. This malaise is clearly articulated by Charles Davis in his thoughtful testament, *A Question of Conscience*. After referring to some of the New Testament texts just quoted, he remarks that, whereas the early Christians experienced their entry into the Church as a liberation, today the reverse is true.

A sense of narrowness and restriction pervades the Church. We meet with a suspicion of individual initiative, an anxious fear of new ideas even before they have been examined, a reluctance to discuss reasonably and a pressure to conform. Where is the joy and confidence in the truth which should be the mark of those freed by Christ? . . . Is it surprising that men have thrown off the yoke of the Church as an unbearable oppression? They are looking for freedom; they want to be themselves. They find no signs of a liberation in a life within the Church [Davis, 1967, p. 106].

Many Catholics would reply that the teaching of the Church is in no way contrary to true freedom, but that it fosters this by rescuing men from the slavery of error. Set up by Christ as teacher of all nations, the Church must staunchly adhere to its deposit of faith. Far from changing its doctrine in the light of shifting human opinions, the Church should judge the wisdom of the world in the light of God's revelation. Relying on Christ's assurance "he who hears you hears me" (Lk 10:16), Church authorities may rightfully exact a religious submission of mind and heart, even though there will always be some who "will not endure sound doctrine" (2 Tim 4:3).

This argument, however, is too authoritarian in character to meet the objections of theologians such as Davis. If we think of the magisterium as if it functioned automatically without dependence on human inquiry and debate, we can easily become victims of a myth of our own making. Modern psychology and theology are at one in pointing out that man likes to prostrate himself masochistically before an imaginary omniscient Church, thereby relieving himself of responsibility for his own religious convictions. With reference to such believers, Hans Küng rightly asks: "Do we not very often find hidden here a flight from personal responsibility disguising itself as loyalty to the Church, a timid lack of self-reliance pretending to be subordination, a misplaced waiting for ecclesiastical direction masked as obedience?" (Küng, 1966, p. 60). Where this mentality prevails, the Church becomes a haven for persons who cannot endure the strains of freedom rather than a place where freedom is achieved. Dostoevsky's parable of the Grand Inquisitor gives classical expression to the Church's perennial temptation to become the enemy of human freedom.

The Magisterium Is Not Omniscient

The myth of an omniscient magisterium with a "direct wire" to heaven is an illusion based on dark psychological tendencies. Certain pastors and religion teachers foster this illusion by exaggerating the authority of ecclesiastical documents and by acting as though conformity with the pope were the essence of religion. Vatican II, in several of its finest documents, cautioned against such extreme authoritarianism, and sought to emphasize the responsibility of the faithful for forming the mind of the Church. The Pastoral Constitution on the Church in the Modern World, for example, declares frankly that the pastors of the Church do not always have solutions to every problem which arises, and acknowledges that, in the complicated and rapidly changing world of our day, the Church needs special help from experts in various sciences in order to "hear, distinguish and interpret the many voices of our age, and to judge them in the light of the divine Word" (Vatican Council II, 1966, nn. 43-44, pp. 243-247). In general, the Pastoral Constitution, following sound theological principles, greatly helped to dealienate and humanize the Catholic understanding of religious knowledge.

To make further progress in overcoming the dilemma of freedom *vs.* conformity in the Church, several practical steps may be proposed. For one thing, we need a more realistic theology of the magisterium. As already noted, the magisterium is not omniscient; it has no power to pass judgment on questions that belong properly to human sciences such as history, physics, and philosophy. Even in the religious area, its task can be little more than to find new ways of expressing the gospel of Jesus Christ. In working out new formulas of faith, the magisterium has to cooperate closely with the theologians and the faithful. In so doing it will not avoid all error, but it will minimize the number and seriousness of its mistakes.

In this connection, there is need of a theology of the Church's fallibility. While everyone knows that the Church sometimes makes mistakes, we *still* treat this too much as a theologically embarrassing anomaly, thus betraying our own failure to grasp the consequences of the Church's pilgrim state. Connected with this is an all-too-common concept of faith as a "blank check" by which we commit ourselves to whatever the Church teaches—as though the content really made no difference. In some juridicizing theories, the motive for the assent of faith would seem to be the will of the magisterium rather than God Himself in His truthfulness. Once we eliminate this confusion between God's authority and that of the Church, we can begin to develop a theology of conscientious dissent within the Church. Assent should never be automatic. Every Christian has the right and duty to use critical good sense. The authority of the magisterium should be prudently weighed against the evidence of reason and against other authorities, such as the consent of the theologians and the sense of the faithful.

Improved Atmosphere of Freedom Needed in the Church

Occasionally, of course, the Church claims to make use of its power to teach infallibly the revelation committed to it by Christ. Assuming that he has satisfied himself that the magisterium has not exceeded its mandate, the Catholic will of course wish to assent to such teaching. But even here, one should be on guard against feeling obligated to believe too many things. The Decree on Ecumenism acknowledged a hierarchical order of doctrines, varying in their relationship to the fundamental Christian faith (Vatican Council II, 1966, n. 11, 356). Primary emphasis should always be given to the gospel, the good news of God's saving action in Jesus Christ. Some secondary doctrines, even though they may once have been defined, are today of only peripheral significance, and need not be urged as if they were still crucial. Perhaps one may apply to dogmatic theology the principle which, in moral theology, has been called "parvitas materiae." Matters of trivial moment should not be treated as if they were all-important.

To draw a sharp line between fundamental and non-fundamental truths of faith is of course impossible, as the Fundamentalists of every generation have discovered. But for men of a given era living in a given sociocultural situation, we can sometimes say that a certain doctrine is clearly not decisive. For most of our contemporaries, for example, it is inconsequential what the shape of the glorified body is to be. For this reason I believe they should not be anathematized, as the Origenists were, for holding that the risen body would be spherical (Denzinger-Schönmetzer, 1963, n. 407). To give another example, I might add that I see no reason for demanding that men of our day should affirm that Cornelius Jansen understood his condemned propositions in the very same sense in which they have been condemned. If the Jansenists in the seventeenth century were required to accept this view, that is no reason why men of the twentieth century should be similarly obliged (cf. Denzinger-Schönmetzer, 1963, n. 2012). One might even ask whether the doctrine of indulgences, as defined against Luther, is so central in our day that anyone should be ejected from the Church for denying it (cf. Denzinger-Schönmetzer, 1963, n. 1449). Just as new anathemas can from time to time be imposed, as circumstances require, so too, it would seem, old anathemas can, in principle, be lifted.

To avoid misunderstanding, let me hasten to add that I am not advocating indifference to truth or historical relativism. I recognize that truth is a value in itself, and that what was once true remains true. But propositional truth assumes its true meaning and importance within a historical and spiritual context, and as the context changes, there may be reasons for relaxing certain prescriptions. To deny matters that are no longer central to anyone's concerns should not be considered tantamount to making "shipwreck of the faith" (cf. Denzinger-Schönmetzer, 1963, n. 2804).

I should like to mention just one more measure which I think might improve the atmosphere of freedom in the Church. In the present situation of doctrinal fluidity, the magisterium should be very reluctant to issue definitive pronouncements which purport to settle controverted questions. Vatican II, guided by the sure instinct of Pope John XXIII, already followed this policy. It recognized that doctrinal leadership for today must consist in giving light and in persuading, rather than in demanding submission under pain of canonical or other penalties. As a matter of fact, any attempt to settle controversies by decree is almost foredoomed to failure in the pluralistic Church of our time. The response given to recent papal pronouncements on transubstantiation, on clerical celibacy, and on artificial contraception proves that the attempt to use the authority of office to terminate the discussion often merely fans the flames of controversy.

The Church Remains a Voluntary Society

I recognize, of course, that the Church must draw the line somewhere. Being essentially a community of faith and witness, it must stand by its original commitment to the gospel and firmly reject positions evidently incompatible with this commitment. But the obligation to belong to a voluntary society, such as the Church, is not unconditional. If anyone feels in conscience that he cannot accept the Church's basic stance, he should not be made to feel guilty about leaving. Catholic pastors and educators should not so inhibit the psychological freedom of the faithful that they can no longer take any responsible attitude, either for or against the Church. At such a price, it would not be worth while trying to keep people within the fold. We must have enough faith to believe that in the long run it is better for mature people to follow their conscience in full freedom than to be kept in servile dependence, even though we may regret the immediate consequences of a particular conscientious decision.

The tragedy today is that so many leave the Church not because they reject Christ but because the Church does not seem to be Christian enough. Perhaps if we can make the Church appear once more as a place of freedom, this phenomenon will be less widespread. In any case, the power of Christian witness never came chiefly from numbers. A few thousand free and committed believers, enthusiastic for the faith, can do more than many millions, if the majority of these millions are sullen, bored, unhappy, and oppressed. The more vividly the Church can recapture the exhilarating sense of freedom that characterized it in New Testament times, the more effectively it will bear witness to Christ in the world, and the more powerfully it will attract those who are drawn by the grace of Christ.

REFERENCES

Davis, C. *A Question of Conscience*. New York: Harper & Row, 1967.

Denzinger, H., & Schönmetzer, A. (S.J.) *Enchiridion Symbolorum Definitionum et Declarationum de Rebus Fidei et Morum*. (32nd ed.) Freiburg: Herder, 1963.

Küng, H. *Freedom Today* (trans. by C. Hastings). New York: Sheed & Ward, 1966.

Vatican Council II. W. M. Abbott (S.J) (Ed.) *The Documents of Vatican II*. New York: Herder & Herder, 1966.

9 An Anglo-Catholic View of Conscience

R. C. MORTIMER

Anglo-Catholic views of conscience differ very little
from classical Catholic doctrines, as they are all indebted to St. Thomas. In this selection,* Mortimer
gives a straightforward account of conscience as the
subjective aspect of the will of God and therefore to
be obeyed. The problem, of course, is knowing what
the will of God is; and attention must be given to
the kind of knowledge a person has of the laws of
God. Distinctions have to be made between vincible
and invincible ignorance of morality in order to judge
the rightness of any act, and the Christian has the
"clear duty to keep his conscience alert and informed." The strength of this position is its clarity.
Whether such clarity might tend to produce a moralistic stance depends mainly on the quality of love
a person has, yet love is not a major feature of this
understanding of conscience.

As the objective standard or norm of morality
is the will of God, as that is perceived by
right reason, so the subjective norm for each individual is his own
conscience. In the last resort each man must decide for himself
what is right or wrong. This decision is called conscience. Conscience is an act of practical judgement of the rightness or wrongness of particular actions. In this it is distinguished from synderesis
on the one hand and moral wisdom or prudence on the other.

* From *The Elements of Moral Theology* (New York: Harper and
Brothers, 1947), pp. 75-83. Reprinted by permission.

Synderesis is the name given to that faculty whereby we make the broadest judgements on the most general moral issues. It is little more than our awareness of the distinction between right and wrong, which may be called our moral sense. The kind of judgment which is made by synderesis is "Good should be done, evil avoided", "One ought to be just, and not unjust". This very general awareness that one ought to do what is right and avoid what is wrong, is the spark which fires conscience to order right action in the future, and the "worm" of remorse which gives sting to the condemnation which conscience pronounces against a past wrong action. Moral wisdom or prudence is speculative and not practical. That is to say, it is not necessarily concerned with my actions past or future, but with moral problems; it considers and determines the morality of different classes of actions, or even of particular actions, solely from the point of view of their objective rightness or wrongness, without reference to their performance by any particular person at any particular time. It is the quality of the "expert in morals" or the good moral theologian.

But conscience is the act of determining that I ought to do or not do this action now, or that I was right or wrong in performing that action then. It is a determining, an act of judgement, for it is my reason making a moral judgement. It is practical, that is, it is not the abstract question of morality with which it is concerned, but this action here and now, as something to be done or not done. From this dictate or judgement of conscience the individual has no appeal. For it is his own reason declaring to him what is, here and now, the will of God. This being so, it is everyone's paramount duty to obey his conscience, for in so doing he is obeying what he holds to be the will of God, and in disobeying he is going against what he holds to be the will of God. It is in this sense that conscience is said to be the subjective standard of morality and to be always binding. For to disobey conscience is deliberately to choose what is recognised as wrong, and to obey is to choose what is recognised as right. We praise those who obey their consciences, we blame those who do not. Indeed, praise and blame are confined to this single point. We praise the will which chooses what is presented to it as right, i.e. obeys conscience; we blame the will which chooses what is presented to it as wrong. All else, tempers, dispositions, feelings, we may approve or disapprove, but because, or in so far as they are involuntary, we neither blame nor praise. Only conscience, the deliberate obedience of conscience, is the proper object of praise.

Since, then, conscience is the standard for each man of morality, and every man merits praise only for obeying his conscience, it is of the utmost importance that the dictates of conscience be true. For it is clear, and only too often proved by experience, that conscience may err, and pronounce this action to be right, when in fact it is wrong. Every man, therefore, has a clear duty to keep his conscience alert and informed. This he does by refraining from adopting any attitude of indifference to moral questions, or from acting as though it were a small matter whether his actions are right or wrong. Again, he takes reasonable care to learn the rules of morality; among Christian families the general and necessary knowledge is gained from parents and school teachers in the course of growing-up, but this should be supplemented by reflection on the principles which underlie the moral rules which have been taught. Further, each man, when he finds himself in doubt, should take advice and learn, either from books or from persons whose opinions he has ground to respect. Prayer also is the great instrument for the enlightenment of conscience. "Blessed are the pure in heart, for they shall see God." He who waits on God, and asks for wisdom, will not go unrewarded. Lastly, a man must, so far as possible, avoid the temptations and the consequent darkening of counsel which arise from strong passions, evil habits and bad companions.

That it is a man's duty to obey his conscience when it is true, and that he merits praise for doing so, is clear enough. But what if his conscience be false? Here also it is binding. For in obeying his conscience a man chooses to do what he holds to be right: if he were to disobey his conscience, he would be choosing to do what, at the moment, he holds to be wrong. The resultant action would, in the circumstances, be materially right, i.e. would produce the change in the situation which is objectively right and what God desires, but would be formally wrong, for it would be the result of an act of the will choosing what was presented to it as bad. We must therefore hold that a man is always bound to obey his conscience, whether his conscience be true or false, and that, in consequence, he is always to be blamed if he disobeys his conscience.

This is the meaning of St. Paul's phrase "whatsoever is not of faith is sin", i.e. whatever is done against conscience, against a belief or conviction of right, is sin.

At this point a further question arises. Granted that it is always blameworthy to disobey one's conscience, even when one's conscience is in error, is it always praiseworthy to obey one's conscience, even when it is in error? Or, in other words, does the sentence "a man is always bound to obey his conscience" mean that a man can never be rightly blamed if he obeys conscience? This raises once more the question of ignorance, for error is a form of ignorance. The classical answer to this question is given by St. Thomas (I, II, quaest. xix, art. 6). It turns on the distinction between vincible and invincible ignorance. Where the error is in any way voluntary, directly or indirectly—that is to say, when the individual either deliberately refrained from learning better, or carelessly omitted to do so—there the error is no excuse for the wrong act. So that he who is thus in a state of vincible ignorance is to be blamed, whether he obeys his conscience or disobeys it. Normally we should find it difficult to accept a position which makes it necessary for a man to be in the wrong, whatever he does. Where a man is thus "perplexed", i.e. convinced that either of two actions, one of which he must do, is wrong, we generally say that in these circumstances one of the two actions is in fact right, or else that he who chooses what he believes to be the less of the two evils is not to be blamed. But in this case of a vincibly erroneous conscience, a man is not genuinely "perplexed", as St. Thomas points out, because he can get rid of his error. This, it must be remembered, is the case of the man who "neither knows nor cares". Sometimes he is actually doubtful, but will not bother to find out; sometimes he is, indeed, in no doubt about his course of action, but a little reflection would have been enough to show him either that the matter was not so clear as he thought or that he was definitely wrong. And this degree of reflection is a duty for him. Thus in acting under the influence of an error for which he is himself responsible, he is to blame, He would be likewise to blame if he acted against his erroneous conscience. But where the conscience is invincible, i.e. caused by no fault or negligence on the part of the individual, there no blame is to be attached.

St. Thomas in his discussion clearly supposes that such invincible ignorance can only be of some accidental circumstance; it cannot be of a moral rule itself. To be ignorant, he says, of something which one ought to know—*quod scire tenetur*—is always to be vincibly ignorant, for the ordinary rules of morality are so plain and easily learnt that one can only be ignorant of them wilfully or by gross negligence. The two examples which he gives make his point of view clear. If a man's conscience tells him that he ought to commit adultery, then he sins, i.e. is to be blamed, if he obeys his conscience, because the error arises from an ignorance of the divine law of which he ought not to be ignorant. But if a man thinks he ought to have intercourse with this woman, because he thinks that she is his wife and that therefore he owes it to her to accede to her request, then he does not sin, although, in fact, the woman is not his wife, because the ignorance arises through no fault of his. It is clear from this that St. Thomas is only thinking of an ordinary case of ignorance, and not of one of conscientious conviction. This invincible error is one which is indeed invincible at the moment, but one which subsequent enlightenment and information as to the actual facts will always immediately dispel.

A much greater problem is raised by the condition of error about a moral question even after long discussion and reflection; is it possible, for example, for a man to be invincibly ignorant that adultery is wrong, to take the case which St. Thomas himself instances? We have already glanced at this problem, when speaking of the precepts of the natural law and of the possibility of ignorance in regard to them. For St. Thomas, fornication was a thing so obviously wrong that no one could think it right, unless he were wilfully blind to facts and deliberately negligent in considering what is his duty. In the case of polygamy, he did apparently recognise that backward peoples might fail to see the reasons for its condemnation, and might conscientiously approve its practice. In other words, the wrongness of polygamy is not immediately obvious as that of fornication is. In general, traditional moral theology has assumed that invincible ignorance is possible where the matter in question is obscure or doubtful, but impossible in regard to actions which are obviously wrong. Yet even here it is recognised that exceptions are possible. St. Alphonsus, in discussing the matter (Lib. I, Tract II, cap. 4, sub. i, no. 171), quotes Gerson as saying that on occasion there may be invincible ignorance of even the primary principles of the natural law, as when someone is convinced that he ought to tell a lie in order to save his friend's life. And he gives his own opinion in these words, "I have never been able to understand how a man sins, when, after taking all proper steps to inform himself, he still labours under invincible ignorance" (no. 173). He therefore recognises, it would seem, that, even after long investigation and reflection, a man may arrive at and hold an opinion about the morality of an action which is at variance with the truth. When this happens, the ignorance is invincible, and that not only when there is ignorance that there is any other point of view, as in the cases imagined by St. Thomas, but also in the full face of all arguments; and such obedience to conscience then merits no blame.

It is of the greatest importance, however, to know whether the ignorance is truly invincible or not. The first and most revealing test is given by the question "Did any doubt, at any time, arise?" If the answer is truthfully "No", it is probable that the ignorance is invincible. This is the case of those brought up in a closed environment where certain moral rules are taken for granted and never questioned. If the answer is "Yes", all depends on what steps were then taken. For the ignorance is clearly vincible through negligence if, in spite of a recognised doubt, nothing was done to arrive at the truth, The easy suppression of a doubt by reference to the practice of many contemporaries, and the refusal to enquire further, is evidence of moral levity. If, on the other hand, anxious enquiry followed, books were read, due care and attention was given to the opinions of authoritative persons, due respect was paid to traditional Christian teaching, and a certain, though wrong conclusion finally reached, then the ignorance may be judged invincible. Though any individual must hesitate long before he can assure himself that he is right and the world is wrong, yet it is possible for him to arrive at that conclusion in all honesty. I may, after anxious thought and consultation, decide that it is my duty to commit a murder (others, that is, call it a murder, I do not. For murder is *ex hypothesi* wrong, but I adjudge this act in these circumstances to be right, a justifiable homicide), and in that case my error, if it be an error, is invincible, and I am not to blame if I proceed to action; on the contrary, I deserve blame if I refrain from action.

Such conscientious divergence from an accepted rule of morality raises a special problem for those in authority. On the one hand, the facts of the case forbid them to condemn one who is, in good faith, obedient to his conscience. On the other hand, it is their duty to prevent the spread of error, and to put down wrong-doing. If they take no action against the conscientious dissident—if, for example, they do not arrest and hang him whom they and their subjects alike hold to be guilty of murder—they give ground for the opinion that they do not hold the act in question to be wrong, and others will come to regard it as legitimate. In this way the authorities fail in their duty to conserve society. If, however, they take action, they punish a man as a criminal who is in fact an honest man of good-will; one who has obeyed his conscience and who would have been blameworthy if he had not performed this action for which it is proposed to punish him. Yet the good of the whole is superior to the good of the individual. In the interests of society the authorities must take action. Yet any action which they take is not rightly regarded, in these circumstances, as a condemnation or punishment of the individual. He, indeed, merits nothing but honour for his conscientiousness. It is purely and simply a condemnation of the action. It is declaratory that the action was wrong, unlawful, injurious to society. It is a warning to others not to suppose that this action is right and may be done with impunity. It is a forceful, dramatic and public reaffirmation that the traditional moral judgement in this matter is the true one, and that of the individual false.

This distinction between a condemnation of the individual and a condemnation of his action underlies and justifies many acts of excommunication pronounced by ecclesiastical authorities. A sentence of excommunication may mean that, by reason of his persistent wrong-doing and obstinate refusal to make amends for actions which he knows to be wrong, a person is adjudged unfit to receive the sacraments, or to enjoy the fellowship of his fellow Christians. It is hoped that by being thus excommunicated he may be brought to realise the heinousness of his conduct and be moved to repentance and amendment of life. This is the aim and meaning of the excommunication of a man in bad faith. But a sentence of excommunication may also be pronounced against a person in good faith. In this case it carries with it no stigma whatever. It does not imply that the Church thinks the person thus excommunicated to be a man of evil living, a sinner, and guilty before God. Being in good faith, obeying his conscience, the Church has no doubt that such a man is guiltless, and merits only praise for his loyalty to his duty as he sees it. But his conduct in some particular respect is such that if the Church were to take no action it must appear that she approved it, whereas in fact she is certain that his conscience in this matter is in error. She has her duty to make it clear to her members and to the world at large that the true will of God in this matter is other than that which the person excommunicated thinks it to be. She excommunicates as part of her duty to bear witness to the truth. The excommunication carries with it, in these circumstances, no stigma, because it is only the proclamation that there is here an honest difference of opinion about a moral truth between two parties, both of which are equally devoted to the truth and loyal to conscience. It does not rule out the possibility that, of the two parties, it is the ecclesiastical authorities who in fact are in the wrong.

It should not, however, be inferred from all this that it is the duty of the ecclesiastical authorities to excommunicate in every case of conscientious disagreement, nor yet that, in every case, deference should be paid to good faith and invincible ignorance, and no action be taken. Every case must be judged on its own merits. In general, persons in good faith should be left in undisturbed possession of all their rights as members of the Church, for they are conscientious and obedient to God. But in particular cases scandal, offence to other Christians, and the need to witness against a growing error, justify the excommunication of such meritorious members.

They are meritorious because, as has been said, they are but obeying their consciences, which it is their duty to do, and which if they did not do, they would sin. The gravity of their sin, the degree of their guilt if they had not obeyed conscience, is in proportion to the gravity of the sin which they think they are committing. For example, if the conscientious total abstainer who thinks that to drink a drop of alcoholic liquor is a grievous sin, nevertheless on some occasion drinks a glass of beer, he is guilty of a grievous sin, because he has consented to an action represented to his conscience as grievously wrong. Or again, a man who is honestly convinced that on this occasion it is his duty to steal, sins as gravely in not stealing as the man who steals knowing stealing to be wrong. It is therefore important that actions should not be represented as being more wrong than in fact they are; that people should not be told that things which are trivial or even indifferent are "mortal" sins. It is often a temptation to preachers to magnify the wrongness of certain approaches to sin, in order to prevent people from committing those sins. This is to "set a hedge about the law". Thus we are sometimes told that it is "a sin to go to the pictures" or to the theatre, because of the danger that cinemas and theatres may corrupt our morals. Or, in order to build up that habit of regular constant prayer which is so vital to the Christian life, we may be told that it is a "mortal" sin to omit our prayers on even one occasion. But this practice is dangerous and defeats its own end. It lays on people an unnecessary burden, and exposes them to unnecessary risk of grave sin. For persons who have taken this teaching to heart, and are convinced in their consciences that the actions prohibited are indeed all of them grave sins, are guilty of grave sin if they commit one of them.

We may sum up this section thus. Conscience is each man's guide to morals. He must always obey it, even if it is in error. If the error is invincible, not due to gross or deliberate negligence, he is in no way to blame, but is rather praiseworthy. If the error is vincible, it is a man's duty to get rid of the error by taking the appropriate measures. Though the invincibility of the error is always suspect where it concerns a matter of ordinary morality, and the error in such cases more probably arises from indifference or bad habits, yet in particular, difficult, circumstances such error may indeed be invincible. Invincible error, or conscientious nonconformity, is not sinful, and although authority may take steps to make clear its own disapproval of the particular action dictated by the erroneous conscience, such disapproval implies no condemnation of the agent himself, and carries with it no stigma. The duty of obeying an erroneous conscience is such that he who disobeys sins as gravely as he who disobeys a true conscience and incurs the guilt which he thinks he is incurring.

10 The Christian Conscience Today

CHARLES E. CURRAN

A theology of conscience must conclude with some guidance about practical affairs or it fails to treat the nature of the subject. Thus, the discussion of conscience in each historical period reflects the central ideas about mankind's relation to God which were in vogue at that time. Using this historical method of analysis, Curran relates conscience to the general cultural situation in the past without giving up the central affirmation that conscience is a natural power within the soul.* Then, taking the present situation seriously, he describes how conscience should be motivated by love and used creatively to build human community.

E ven a superficial reflection shows the existence of moral conscience. Man experiences the joy of having done good or the remorse of having done evil. He recognizes an imperative to do this or avoid that. A more profound analysis distinguishes moral conscience from social pressure or even a religious imperative.[1]

Moral conscience has many meanings. St. Paul describes conscience as a witness or judge of past activity, a director of future action, the habitual quality of a man's Christianity, and even as the Christian ego or personality.[2] This chapter will discuss the problem of antecedent conscience; that is, conscience as pointing

* From *Christian Morality Today* (Notre Dame, Indiana: Fides Publishers, Inc., 1966), pp. 13-25. Reprinted by permission.

out to the Christian what he should do in the particular circumstances of his life.

Historical Summary

Scripture reveals Christianity as a dialogue or covenant relationship between God and his people. Christian tradition frequently refers to conscience as the voice of God telling man how to respond to the divine gift of salvation. Both the reality and the concept of moral conscience have evolved in the course of salvation history. Two reasons explain the evolution. First, God speaks to primitive man in one way and to more mature man in another way. Second, only when man has acquired a certain degree of maturity can he reflect on his own subjective states.[3]

In the beginning of salvation history, conscience (the reality, not the word) appears as extrinsic, objective, and collective.[4] Theophany, however, gives way to angelophany, and finally to human prophets who speak in the name of God.[5] The prophets, the conscience of Israel, stress interior dispositions and begin to mention individual responsibility (Jer 31:29-30; Ez 14:1-8). They look forward to the day when God will plant his law in the innermost part of man (Jer 31:33-34; Ez 36:26-27; Psalm 50:12). Since the prophets insist on God as the first cause, conscience is not the voice of man but the voice of God who speaks to man.

St. Paul, with his emphasis on the internal and subjective dispositions of man, brings into Christian thought the term conscience ($\sigma \upsilon \nu \epsilon i \delta \eta \sigma \iota \varsigma$), which originally appeared in Democritus and was developed by stoic philosophy.[6] Paul, while adopting the uses of the term in pagan philosophy, introduces the notion of conscience as the director of human activity—antecedent conscience.[7] Commenting on the different Pauline uses of the term conscience, the Fathers of the church explicitly make the last step in the interiorization of conscience. Conscience now becomes the voice of the human person himself and only mediately and indirectly the voice of God.[8]

Scholastic theology of the thirteenth century first considered scientifically, as opposed to the pastoral approach of the Fathers, the nature of moral conscience. Is it a faculty? A habit? An act?

The Thomistic school distinguished conscience, the judgment of the practical reason about a particular act, from synteresis, the quasi-innate habit of the first principles of the moral order. St. Bonaventure placed more emphasis on the will, especially with regard to synteresis. The subjective voice of reason was open to God through the mediation of law.[9]

Unfortunately, the scholastic synthesis succumbed to the dangers of sterile intellectualism, the nominalistic tendency to extrinsicism, and the increasing influence of positive juridic sciences. The decree of the Council of Trent again legislating the necessity of annual confession of sins according to their number and species orientated moral theology (and the question of conscience) toward the judgment seat of the confessional rather than toward the living of the Christian life.[10]

In this light one can better understand the famous controversy of the seventeenth and eighteenth centuries about the question of a probable conscience. When I am not certain about the existence of a law, am I obliged to follow the doubtful law? Today the vast majority of moral theologians accept some form of a mitigated probabilism, which maintains that only a law which is certain can oblige a subject.[11] As a result of the controversy, De Conscientia became a separate and well-developed treatise in the manuals of moral theology. Among the benefits accruing to moral theology from such a development are the balance and equilibrium finally attained, the precise terminology acquired, and the realization that conscience must consider the many problems of daily living.

However, the defects of the manualistic treatises on conscience are great. Briefly, legalism, extrinsicism, impersonalism, and an ethic of obligation characterize such considerations of conscience. Positive law and objective considerations are greatly exaggerated. Conscience becomes negative, oppressive, and sin-orientated.[12] The dire consequences are not restricted merely to the intellectual and theoretical plane. History and empirical studies show that the linking of introspection with a legalistic approach to morality provides fertile ground for the formation of the scrupulous conscience.[13] Unfortunately, in everyday Catholic life, the average Catholic equates Christian morality with Mass on Sunday, no meat on Friday, and the need to obey what the Church teaches about sex.

In the last few decades theologians have begun to react

against the manualistic treatment of conscience. Under the influence of the Thomistic renewal, authors now stress the virtue of prudence and the subjective element which cannot be found in any of the books on cases of conscience.[14] In keeping with the return to the primitive sources of scripture and the Fathers, which is characterizing all theological investigation today, theologians consider conscience in the light of charity, or the responsibility of the Christian before the call of God, or as an anticipation of the eschatological judgment.[15]

Outside the pale of theology, two divergent tendencies—exaggerated interiorization and over-objectivization—have destroyed the true notion of conscience. Ever since Descartes, philosophers like Montaigne, Rousseau, and Kant have overemphasized the subjective element. Existentialism, the last step in the tendency, makes subjective conscience the center of the whole world completely cut off from God or any other subject. At the other extreme, conscience is considered merely a function of physiological factors (Chauchard), psychological factors (Freud), or sociological factors (Durkheim).[16]

The Nature of Conscience

Guided by the lessons of history, one can better understand the nature of conscience, its function, and its formation. Catholic theologians generally distinguish synteresis, moral science, and conscience. Adopting a synthetic approach, we can define synteresis as the power of conscience situated in the inmost part of the soul (*scintilla animae*). In its rational aspect, synteresis tends to the truth so that man almost intuitively knows the fundamental principle of the moral order—good is to be done and evil is to be avoided. In its volitional aspect, synteresis tends toward the good and the expression of such a tendency in action.

Moral science is the knowledge of the less general principles of the moral law which man deduces from the primary principles. The category of moral knowledge also includes whatever man knows from revelation or authority. It pertains to the objective, the conceptual, the essential order.

Conscience is the concrete judgment of the practical reason, made under the twofold influence of synteresis, about the moral goodness of a particular act. Conscience forms its judgment discursively from the objective principles of the moral order; but at the same time, there is also a direct connatural knowing process. The dictate of conscience is concrete, subjective, individual, and existential.

Conscience tells man what he should do. Man's "ought" follows from his "is." Man's actions must affirm his being. St. Paul makes Christian existence the foundation of Christian morality. The Christian is baptized into the death and resurrection of Christ. Consequently, he must die to self and walk in the newness of life (Rom 6). Man's existence is a loving dependence on his God and a communion with his fellow men. Human endeavor must express this twofold personal relationship.

Conscience and human freedom are not completely autonomous. In practice man rejects the complete autonomy of conscience. In the eyes of the world Adolf Eichmann and the Nazis were guilty of crimes against humanity despite the plea of a clear conscience. Conscience must act in accord with the nature and person of man. The greatest possible freedom and the greatest possible happiness for man consist in the fulfillment of his own being.

The judgment of conscience expresses with regard to a particular act the fundamental tendency of man to truth and good. The basis of Christian morality, however, is not man's relation to an abstract principle, but to a person, *the* person, God. Since he first loved us, God has freely given us his love, his friendship, our salvation. Scripture uses the words faith and love ($\pi\iota\sigma\tau\iota\varsigma$, $\dot{\alpha}\gamma\dot{\alpha}\pi\eta$) to express man's acceptance and response to God's gift. Like Christ himself, man's external actions must manifest this love. At the same time man's actions dispose him to enter more intimately into the mystery of divine love. The ultimate norm of Christian conduct is this: what does the love of God demand of me in these concrete circumstances? Love, as a complete giving of self and not a mere emotion, seeks always the will of the beloved.

The Formation of Conscience

God speaks to us through the very existence he has given us —creation, salvation, our talents, abilities and even weaknesses, and the existential circumstances of our situation. In other words, the will of the beloved is made known to us through his "laws"— the law of the Spirit, the natural law, positive law, and the law of the situation.[17]

The primary law of the new covenant is the internal law of the Spirit, the law of Christ, the law of love. Even Christ, however, found it necessary to express his law in external rules; but the demands are comparatively general; e.g., the beatitudes.[18]

God also speaks to man through the human nature he has given him. The natural law, as theologians call it, is primarily a dynamic, internal law. Since it is the very law of man's existence and being, it has an absolute character.[19] Christ, at least implicitly, affirmed the value of the natural law within the framework of the new covenant.[20] The law of nature is assumed into the law of Christ, for all nature was created according to the image of Christ and all nature exists for Christ.[21] From the first principle of the natural law, more objective, detailed rules of conduct are formulated.

Unfortunately, many Catholic theologians have exaggerated the natural law. It is not the primary law for the Christian. Some have succumbed to the temptation of using the natural law as a club. Others have overextended it in attempting to prove the moral certitude of mere hypotheses. Many still tend to codify completely the natural law and thus rob the natural law of its dynamic character.

Living in human society, the Christian is also the subject of human law, both civil and ecclesiastical. Such law is purely external and consequently seen as an infringement on human liberty. Since positive legislation is not absolute, it does not oblige when in conflict with the interest of the higher laws.

God has called each person by his own name. In one sense, every individual is unique; every concrete situation is unique. The Christian's answer to the divine call must correspond to his individual circumstances.

Conscience is a supernaturally elevated subjective power of man. The law of Christ and the natural law are primarily internal laws. Why then is it necessary to have detailed, particular, external expressions of these laws? Why a code? Man's love of God is not yet perfect. Fallen human nature still experiences the

tendency to self and not to God. Spiritual schizophrenia is a necessary characteristic of earthly Christianity. Even the impulsive
reaction of the human will of Christ was to avoid the sacrifice
willed by his father.[22] Love of God is by its nature a self-sacrificing love. Man in his present state cannot know perfectly what the
demands of love of God are. Particular, external expressions of
the law of love and natural law have a value only insofar as they
point out the minimum and basic demands of the law of love.
Code morality is not opposed to an ethic of love.[23]

External law, if considered without any relation to the internal law, can be even an occasion of sin (Gal. 3:19, Rom 5:20-
21; 7:523). The external law is static and very incomplete. It does
not and cannot express the totality of man's relationship to God.
The vast majority of the decisions of conscience pertains to matters
where there are no determined external expressions of law. Thus
far we have not been speaking of the positive human laws which
are primarily external. Here, too, self-sacrificing love of God and
respect for the common good move man to obey positive law
despite its inherent imperfections, unless such positive law runs
counter to a higher law.

The formation and training of conscience include much more
than the mere knowledge of external formulas of law. Insistence
on external law is the haven of the insecure (neuroticism, scrupulosity) or the shallow (legalism, Phariseeism). Christian morality
is ultimately love, an "I-thou" relationship between God and man.
By meditating on true values, the Christian grows in wisdom and
age and grace. Likewise, the formation of conscience must take
into consideration the findings of many of the positive sciences.
For example, what purports to be religious obedience might in reality be the manifestation of an inferiority complex. A proper
formation, joined with the virtue of prudence acquired in daily
Christian experiences, prepares the conscience to hear the call of
God's love.

Space permits the mention of only two important characteristics of Christian conscience: communitarian and creative. A
communitarian conscience recognizes man's relationship with his
fellow men in the kingdom of God. A communitarian conscience
avoids excessive individualism and the opposite extreme of mass
hypnosis. A creative conscience, attuned to the Spirit, throws

off the shackles of stultifying legalism. A true Christian conscience leads man to make Christianity and Christian love "the light of the world and the salt of the earth"—a positive commitment to the kingdom of God in its reality both as the city of God and the city of man.

Reality is complex. The problems of conscience are complex. Frequently, there are no easy solutions. After prayerful consideration of all values involved, the Christian chooses what he believes to be the demands of love in the present situation. The Christian can never expect to have perfect, mathematical certitude about his actions. The virtue of humility preserves him from falling into the opposed extremes of introspective anxiety and mere formalism. Neurotic anxiety has no place in Christianity. Christianity is fundamentally a religion of joy—of man's participation in the joy and triumph of the resurrection. The paradox of Christianity is that joy comes through self-sacrificing love.

For the Christian who has made a commensurate effort to form his conscience correctly, the dictate of conscience is an infallible norm of conduct. Even though the action itself is not in objective conformity with the divine will, the Christian's conduct is pleasing to God, for it stems from a pure heart.[24]

The opposition that conscience experiences between Christian law and Christian freedom, between love and code morality, stems from man's imperfect love of God and wounded human nature. In reality, there is no dichotomy. The Christian law is the law of love—"the law of the Spirit, [giving] life in Christ Jesus, has delivered me from the law of sin and death" (Rom 8:2). Conscience leads man to participate ever more deeply in Christian love and freedom until the Christian reaches his final destiny where love, joy, freedom, and conformity with God's will are one.

NOTES

1. Jacques Leclercq, *Les grandes lignes de la philosophie morale* (Louvain, 1953), pp. 7-13.

2. C. Spicq, "La conscience dans le Nouveau Testament," *Revue Biblique* 47 (1938), pp. 55-76. Cf., C. A. Pierce, *Conscience in the New Testament* (London, 1955).

3. For the general lines of the evolution by which God brought his people in the Old Testament to both self-knowledge and a knowledge of

the true God, see Marc Oraison, *Love or Constraint?* (New York, 1959), pp. 152-163.

4. The characteristics of a primitive conscience in general are aptly described by Richard Mohr, *Die Christliche Ethik im Lichte der Ethnologie* (München, 1954).

5. Theophany abounds in the first chapters of Genesis. There is some dispute among scripture scholars on the exact nature of the "Angel of Yahweh" which appears in Genesis 16:7; 22:11; Exodus 3:2; Judges 2:1. Even if the expression here refers merely to God in a visible form, such an expression indicates a "sophisticated" reluctance to speak of a pure theophany. In the Old Testament, angels exercise the same twofold function as conscience; namely, they make known the will of God and serve as guides both for individuals and the whole people of God.

6. Spicq, pp. 51-55; Pierce, pp. 13-53. Also Th. Deman, *La Prudence* (Paris, 1949), pp. 479-487.

7. Eric D'Arcy, *Conscience and its Right to Freedom* (New York, 1961), pp. 8-12; Pietro Palazzini, *La Coscienza* (Rome, 1961), pp. 63-71; Deman, pp. 488-489. Spicq maintains that the concept of an antecedent conscience was known by Paul's contemporaries, but it is certain that Paul contributed the most to its development (pp. 63-67). Among the texts cited as instances of Paul's referring to antecedent conscience are: 1 Cor 8; 10:25-33; Rom 13:5.

8. The affirmation is made by Antonio Hortelano in unpublished notes. Hortelano refers to the following citations from *Cursus Completus Patrologiae,* ed. J. P. Migne (Paris). Augustinus, "Tractatus in Joannem," *Pat. Latina* 35, col. 1382; Origines, "Commentarium in Epistolam ad Romanos," *Pat. Graeca* 14, col. 895; Basilius, "Homilia XIII," *Pat. Graeca* 31, col. 432.

9. Odon Lottin, *Morale Fondamentale* (Tournai, 1954), pp. 163-165; 221-228. The author summarizes here the conclusions derived from his multi-volumed historical study, *Psychologie et Morale aux XIIe et XIIIe siècles* (Gembloux).

10. There is no complete and authentic history of moral theology. Nor can there be until more particular studies are made. For the best available study of the development of moral theology of this time, see Bernard Häring–Lois Vereecke, "La Théologie Morale de S. Thomas d'Aquin à S. Alphonse de Liguori," *Nouvelle Revue Théologique 77* (1955), pp. 673-692. Also Louis Vereecke, "Le Council de Trente et l'enseignement de la Théologie Morale," *Divinitas* 5 (1961), pp. 361-374.

11. Most of the manuals of moral theology accept such a probabilism. In practice, the antiprobabilists do not differ much from those who espouse simple probabilism. Outside the manuals, there is a reaction against the legalistic mentality of probabilism which has taken different forms. Cf., Th. Deman, "Probabilisme," *Dictionnaire de Théologie Catholique* 13 (Paris, 1936), col. 417-619; also Deman, *La Prudence;* Georges Leclercq, *La Conscience du Chrétien* (Paris, 1947), pp. 127-197; P. Rousselot, *Quaestoines de Conscientia* (Paris, 1947), pp. 51-80.

12. The increasing awareness of the need for a renewal of moral theology in the last few years stems from these negative characteristics present today in most manuals. For a brief review of the recent literature

on the subject of renewing moral theology, see John C. Ford and Gerald Kelly, *Contemporary Moral Theology* (Westminster, Md., 1958), pp. 42-103. It is my personal belief that the authors have not paid sufficient attention to the part played by the Tübingen school of theology, nor do they seem to fully appreciate the need for a life-centered and not confessional-orientated moral theology.

13. Juan Garcia-Vicente, "Dirección pastoral de la escrupulosidad," *Revista de Espiritualidad* 19 (1960), pp. 514-529. Also *Cathiers Laënnec* 20 (June 1960) which is totally concerned with the question of scrupulosity.

14. Deman, *La Prudence,* especially pp. 496-514. Perhaps Deman overemphasizes prudence at the expense of conscience. For a very satisfying discussion of the relationship between prudence and conscience, see Domenico Capone, *Intorno alla verità morale* (Naples, 1951). A fuller bibliography on the relationship between prudence and conscience is given by Josephus Fuchs, *Theologia Moralis Generalis* (Rome, 1960), p. 169.

15. Bernard Häring, *The Law of Christ I* (Westminster, Md., 1961), pp. 91-213; René Carpentier, "Conscience," *Dictionnaire de Spiritualité* 2 (Paris, 1953), col. 1548-1575; Gérard Gilleman, "Eros ou agapè, Comment centrer la conscience chrétienne," *Nouvelle Revue Théologique* 72 (1950), pp. 326; 113-135.

16. For a critique of such opinions based on theological principles, see Palazzini, pp. 217-275. Also, Jacques Leclercq, *Christ and the Modern Conscience* (New York, 1962), pp. 7-104.

17. The word law is not a univocal term. Unfortunately, the coercive characteristic which essentially belongs to external positive law has been illegitimately transferred to the law of the Spirit and the natural law.

18. Some of Christ's laws are materially determined and particular; e.g., with regard to divorce, adultery, or even the thought of adultery. For an explanation of the general and more formal demands of Christ as the expression of a mentality or tendency rather than a determined material command, see C. H. Dodd, *Gospel and Law* (Cambridge, 1951), pp. 73-83.

19. A good description of the natural law with regard to its internal and historical character as well as its relationship to the law of Christ is given by J. Fuchs, *Le Droit Naturel: Essai Théologique* (Tournai, 1960).

20. Matt 5:27-48; 19:3-12, 17-20; Mark 7:20-23; Luke 12:57.

21. For Christ as the exemplar of all creation and nature, see Col 1:15-20; 1 Cor 8:6; Eph 1:3-10. Theologians speak of Christ as the final cause of all creation because of the same texts as well as John 1:1-14 and 1 Cor 3:22-23.

22. Matt 26:39. Theologians, interpreting the different acts of the will of Christ in this passage, distinguish between the *voluntas ut natura* and the *voluntas ut ratio.* Christ's human will impulsively shrank from suffering. He could accept suffering only insofar as he saw it as the will of his Father.

23. For the Catholic, the magisterium or teaching function of the Church gives an authentic interpretation of Christian morality. Doctrinal and moral pronouncements constitute just one aspect of the teaching office of the Church. The whole Church in the lives of all members must bear living witness to the truth.

24. During the probabilism controversy, anti-probabilists frequently cited the opinion of St. Bernard that a person following an erroneous conscience in good faith commits sin. Bernard's opinion stems from his mystical insistence on conscience as the voice of God. Consequently, any error or deviation can be attributed only to the bad will of man. Philippe Delhaye, *Le problème de la conscience morale chez S. Bernard* (Namur 1957), especially pp. 44-45.

11 The Mature Christian Conscience

EWERT H. COUSINS

A theology of conscience must deal with contemporary human experience in the light of revelation and the teachings of the church. Reason, the tool of theology, explores and relates these elements in order to provide a perspective by which Christians can judge their moral responsibility. Cousins—using this theological method—finds morality is not imposed by any kind of external authority but is a subjective realization that good and God are united in one's self.* This union, properly understood and led by the spirit, makes for a mature conscience that is open to whatever changes the future may require.

A mature person is one who faces reality and faces it in its deepest dimension. The child grows to maturity by opening himself to reality—to its limits, its crises, its possibilities, and its fullness. If one achieves maturity by opening himself to the depths and complexity of reality, then the Christian has a special task. For the Christian reaches maturity not only by opening himself to personal, social, and political reality, but by becoming increasingly aware of that level of reality from which revelation has removed the veil of darkness. Illumined by faith, the Christian must penetrate the mysteries of revelation and allow them to transform every facet of his life and bring him to spiritual maturity. For the Christian, then, conscience

* From *Conscience, Its Freedom and Limitations,* edited by William C. Bier, S.J. (New York: Fordham University Press, 1971), pp. 369-378. Reprinted by permission.

is not merely a matter of a personal ideal or of social norms. The Christian's conscience and his moral decisions are bound up with the mystery of Christ and the life of the Spirit. His conscience has its ontological roots and its ultimate meaning in the Trinitarian life; and his concrete moral decisions are caught up in the mystery of the fall, the incarnation, and redemption, and the eschatological fulfillment of the kingdom. The Christian, then, grows to maturity not merely by reaching adulthood in the family and state, but by reaching spiritual adulthood in the Church and the life of the Spirit. For the Christian, the mature conscience is one that is illumined by the Spirit and conformed to Christ, and through Christ is united to the Father. In this context we will explore the Christian's conscience in its theological perspective and attempt to draw into relief those qualities that are a mark of its maturity.

Theological Method

The theologian's task is complicated, for he must examine human experience in the light of revelation and in the life of the Church. Although he knows that revelation illumines human experience and that grace transforms human possibilities, he can never grasp the extent of that transformation nor comprehend the ultimate dimension of the mysteries. Yet he is assured by the statement of Vatican Council I that "if human reason, with faith as its guiding light, inquires earnestly, devoutly, and circumspectly, it does reach, by God's generosity, some understanding of mysteries, and that a most profitable one" (Denzinger & Schönmetzer, 1965, #3016 [#1796]). The Council goes on to say that human reason can do this by exploring "the similarity with truths which it knows naturally and also from the interrelationship of mysteries with one another and with the final end of man" (Denzinger & Schönmetzer, 1965, #3016 [#1796]). Following the method outlined by the Council, we shall examine the mature conscience by bringing it in contact with the mysteries of Christian revelation. In this way we enter into a dialogue between revelation and human experience. We will examine human experience in the light of revelation and revelation in the light of human experience. By correlating these two poles, we hope to clarify each in the light of the other. Thus by viewing the mature conscience in the light of the Christian mysteries, we can bring to the fore new dimensions of its richness and complexity.

We shall begin by examining the mature conscience in its personal and social dimensions and then view it in the light of the mystery of Christ, seen primarily through the Pauline and Johannine writings. Secondly, we shall view the mature conscience in the light of the mystery of the Spirit working in the processes of history. For maturity involves not only growth toward the ideal of Christ, but also the anguish of growing in history as an individual, a nation, and a world community. Only by situating the mature conscience in the mystery of Christ and the Spirit can we view its ideal possibilities and its tragic and problematic historicity—as the Spirit works to bring man to the full stature of his identity in Christ.

Interior Morality

If we examine human experience, we observe that the mature person does not look upon the moral law as something merely outside himself: as a command of his parents, a decree of his Church or government, a taboo of his culture, an impersonal law of nature, or an edict of God. If he looked upon law as something merely extrinsic to himself, he might respond to situations like a child who submits slavishly to the voice of his parents. Or like a rebellious child, he might reject the law as an infringement on his freedom. Or he might submit to the law out of a sense of abstract duty or helplessness, yet with rancor within, crying out in the depths of his soul like Prometheus against the injustice of a tyrannical Zeus. Unlike the submissive or rebellious child, the mature person realizes that the moral order, while extrinsic to himself, is also most intimate to his subjectivity. Like Socrates he believes that doing evil destroys what is noblest within us; therefore it is better to suffer injustice than to commit it (Plato, *Gorgias*). Finally, like Socrates he would be willing to face death rather than go counter to his deepest moral convictions (Plato, *Crito, Phaedo*). In his authentic moral decisions, he knows that his own deepest self is at stake.

When the mature person discovers the moral law at the heart

of his subjectivity, he does not fall into subjectivism or relativism—that is, into a type of moral solipsism in which his own autonomous will determines the law. This would be to reduce maturity to the state of a childish tantrum in which willfulness prevails. The mature discovery of the moral self is much more profound and paradoxical than that. At the very moment when autonomous subjectivity is touched, the moral self is most universalized. At the moment one realizes that an absolute moral demand touches his deepest subjectivity, he becomes aware that this demand is capable of being universalized to all subjectivities. Thus in discovering his moral self, the mature person grasps finite subjectivity as such. Hence he realizes that any man in these circumstances should feel the absolute demand of the moral ought. At the same time his moral awareness becomes most personal, it becomes most social and universal. It is this convergence of the deepest subjectivity with the greatest universality that Kant expressed in his dictum: So act that your maxim can be made a universal law (Kant, 1923, pp. 38-39). However, this universalizing property of the moral law should not be read primarily with the logic of classification, but with the logic of the coincidence of opposites. The important point here is not that we can easily specify or classify the circumstances in which an action would be right or wrong, for the circumstances are not easily universalized. The important point is that at man's moral center an absolute moral demand converges with the relativity of circumstances, so that in the depths of the moral decision each man becomes universal man. In the moral decision, particular man rises above the endless qualities of classification—above the relativity of circumstances—and becomes his true self, and at that moment reaches the point where his autonomous subjectivity coincides with that of all men.

The reason why one's deepest individuality coincides with the greatest universality is that in their moral centers all men coincide before the absolute call of God. According to Christian theology, each man is an image of God (Ladner, 1959), with God's light shining in the depths of his soul. This divine light touches man profoundly in his moral decision, confronting him with an absolute call at the center of his freedom where he is most unique and at one with all men. Here in the moral decision, where man touches God, the opposites coincide: what is most individual with what is most universal; what is most immanent with what is most transcendent. At this point of convergence moral maturity is reached. The morally mature man is at one with himself, with God, and with the universe. He stands at the farthest remove from the submissiveness or the autonomous willfulness of the child. At this point of convergence he is beyond conflict, for in pursuing his true self he is pursuing God and in pursuing God he is pursuing all things.

Maturity through Christ

To achieve this maturity is a difficult task. Man is caught in the mystery of evil: he is a soaring spirit entrapped in finitude; he is split off from his true self—the slave of his own desires, imprisoned in a maze of self-deception, and overpowered by the forces of evil (Dubarle, 1964). In a classic passage in the Epistle to the Romans, Paul describes man's moral helplessness in the face of evil. Overcome by the burden of extrinsicism, Paul cries out against the letter of the Mosaic Law. But it is not merely the extrinsicism of the Mosaic Law or its ritualistic prescriptions that Paul inveighs against, but moral consciousness itself. "If it had not been for the law," Paul says, "I should not have known sin. I should not have known what it is to covet if the law had not said, 'You shall not covet' " (Rom 7:7). Moral consciousness is indeed ambiguous. At the same time that it awakens man to his highest ideals, it stirs the law of sin within his members. "The very commandment," Paul says, "which promised life proved to be death to me" (Rom 7:10). Paul describes the warfare within: "For I delight in the law of God, in my inmost self, but I see in my members another law at war with the law of my mind and making me captive to the law of sin which dwells in my members" (Rom 7:22-23). Paul cries out against the intolerable demand of the moral ought and the burden of guilt it imparts: "Wretched man that I am! Who will deliver me from this body of death?" (Rom 7:24). Paul answers that it is Jesus Christ:

For God has done what the law, weakened by the flesh, could not do: sending his own Son in the likeness of sinful flesh and for sin, he condemned sin in the flesh, in order that the just requirement of the law might be fulfilled in us, who walk not according to the flesh but according to the Spirit [Rom 8:3-4].

It is Christ who overcomes the forces of evil and liberates man to become his true self. Christ removes the extrinsicism of morality and touches man's deepest subjectivity. As Image of the invisible God, He awakens the image of God in man. As Son of the Father, He draws man into adoptive sonship:

For you do not receive the spirit of slavery to fall back into fear, but you have received the spirit of sonship. When we cry, "Abba! Father!" it is the Spirit himself bearing witness with our spirit that we are children of God, and if children, then heirs, heirs of God and fellow heirs with Christ, provided we suffer with him in order that we may also be glorified with him [Rom 8:15-17].

In the Spirit we are united to Christ. The mature Christian is one who in the depths of his moral self has "put on Christ" (Gal 3:27), who with Paul can say: "It is no longer I who live, but Christ who lives in me" (Gal 2:20).

Throughout the centuries, Christians have reached moral maturity by meditating on the life of Christ, by imitating His virtues, and by adopting His fundamental moral attitudes (Häring, 1963, pp. 51-53). This does not result in a moralism or a mere surface copying of his virtues, but involves a total transformation of the personality, resulting in a new spiritual identity and attitude toward the world. In the Johannine writings this attitude is described in terms of love and the Trinitarian life. In the discourse at the Last Supper, Christ tells His disciples:

As the Father has loved me, so have I loved you; abide in my love. If you keep my commandments, you will abide in my love, just as I have kept my Father's commandments and abide in his love. These things I have spoken to you, that my joy may be in you, and that your joy may be full. This is my commandment, that you love one another as I have loved you [Jn 15:9-12].

This is the mature Christian attitude: law has been subsumed into love (Gilleman, 1959, pp. 253-279). The commandments have been completely interiorized and lifted up to the divine level, for Christ has drawn the Christian into the intimate love of the Trinitarian life. Christ prays that "they may all be one; even as thou, Father, art in me, and I in thee" (Jn 17:21). Christ promises to send the Spirit, who will draw men into the Trinitarian life because, as theologians will explain later, the Spirit Himself is the love of the Father and the Son.

Having been drawn into the Trinitarian life of love, the mature Christian is assimilated in his moral self to the Trinity. He realizes himself as image of the Trinity and shares in a special way in the mystery of creation and the incarnation. In the technical terms of moral theology, conscience "is a judgment of the practical reason on the moral goodness or sinfulness of an action" (Jone, 1953, p. 38). As incarnate spirit, man must express himself in his actions in space and time. His conscience is his guide, the faculty that directs this expression so that his actions will be the adequate expression of his moral self as image of God. Having united himself to Christ, the Christian is swept up into the mystery of the generation of the Son from the Father. As perfect image of the Father, the Son adequately expresses the reality of the Father; and as the Word of the Father, He is the vehicle for all expression in creation and ultimately in the incarnation. The Trinity is the mystery of perfect expressionism—both internally in the processions and externally in creation and the incarnation. Through union with Christ, the Christian strives to approximate the perfect expressionism of the Trinity. Through the guidance of his conscience in the incarnate moral decisions of his life, the Christian grows toward the maturity of the ideal expressionism revealed in the Trinity.

The Spirit in History

Although Christ has given us the ideal of maturity and has inaugurated the era of the resurrection, we have not yet reached the goal. We are a pilgrim Church, involved in the processes of history. The Spirit has been promised and has been sent, but He works slowly through human institutions and human culture. Although Christ has revealed the ideal, we do not know how the fullness of the ideal will be incarnated in history. Yet because of the power of the Christian ideal, we may fall into a moral triumphalism and take on the attitude of the idealistic adolescent who feels that he has the fullness of truth and must convert the world overnight. The mature adult, on the other hand, faces up to the ambiguity and complexity of living in history. And the Christian realizes that history in its ultimate dimension is the work of the Spirit.

What are the marks of maturity for the Christian who is open to history and the Spirit? The first quality of the mature conscience is a sense of ambiguity and limitation. Although the absolute ideal of the moral ought presses heavily upon him, the Christian realizes that there is much he cannot achieve. He is not at the ἔσχατον, but *in via*. He realizes that his own finitude, the powers of evil, and his historicity set limits to his moral achievement (Schoonenberg, 1965, pp. 63-123), and that success is ultimately not his, but the work of the Spirit. Although he bears within himself the remembrance of paradise, he will acknowledge that he now lives east of Eden and after Cain. He will strive earnestly to reinstate paradise; but he realizes that after the fall this is an arduous and complex task, for life is ambiguous, and before the final judgment we cannot neatly divide the sheep from the goats. Hence he will not be disillusioned, like the adolescent, when he discovers that his idols have clay feet. Nor will he rail in outraged indignation against the evil forces in the universe. For, even in his most inspired prophetic moments, when he calls divine judgment on society, he will realize that he himself is not innocent and at that very moment may be the victim of illusion and the pawn of evil. But he will not be discouraged, for he has confidence in the redemptive work of Christ and the power of the Spirit.

The second quality of the mature conscience is a certain tragic sense—an awareness that maturity involves suffering and that true spiritual growth takes place through the mystery of death and resurrection. Although the mature Christian knows that the good will triumph in the end, he realizes that this does not follow the neat formula of a Western movie. Like the dreamy adolescent, one might believe that spiritual maturity or moral reform happens automatically or is easily bought. But as the Christian begins to mature and becomes aware of ambiguity, one thing becomes increasingly clear to him: that profound moral growth, both personal and collective, follows the way of the cross. Christ's victory over evil did not liberate Christians from suffering and death. To live in history and to be led by the Spirit toward the Christian ideal is to become increasingly involved in the mystery of Christ's death and resurrection. If, for example, a Christian feels constrained to protest against unjust institutions or warfare, he will not expect to be rewarded like the good little boy by his parents or like the adolescent who has won honors in school. He will rather expect to be persecuted—especially by those who represent justice. He will anticipate being rejected, reviled, and punished. He realizes that his efforts may fail or that they will bear fruit only in the next generation when his contribution is forgotten. He will accept all this gladly, for he knows that this is the way the Spirit works in history.

The third mark of the mature conscience is a sense of responsibility. As one matures, his sense of responsibility enlarges. As a child, he is expected to respond to the rules of the family, but when he passes through adolescence, he takes responsibility for himself, his life, his destiny; as an adult he shares the responsibility for other lives—his own family and to a varying extent the community. At the present time, man's responsibility is enlarging in a remarkable way. Through communications, he is breaking out of his tribal consciousness into a global community. Through science and technology he is moving into space and shaping his environment, even the forms of life of the future. As horizons enlarge, new moral issues emerge and a new dimension of moral consciousness is called for. Man must begin to think of morality in a new perspective, for he is gradually becoming responsible for his future and for history itself (Lepp, 1965, p. 85; Monden, 1965, pp. 168-69).

At one time man could enjoy the moral security of the child in the family. He could learn the moral demands of his social relations in a closed society, as expressed in the ten commandments, and live up to these. But the world is much more complex than the desert tribal culture in which the ten commandments were formulated. The man of the future must enlarge his sense of moral responsibility from the tribal circle to the world community and the community that is in an historical process. His most urgent moral question should not be merely "What should I do here and now?" but "What contribution can I make to the expansion of human freedom and moral consciousness in history?" To move into the larger world of moral responsibility is both challenging and frightening. If we have no place to ground our hope, we may hesitate to step into this larger world and turn from the responsibility of the future. It is here that the theology of the Spirit can come to the Christian's aid. If the Christian can enlarge his concept of the Spirit from the one who gives individuals strength to perform good moral actions to the one who guides history itself, then he will have the hope and the courage to accept the responsibility of his new moral position in the world (Cousins, 1969, pp. 171-176).

The Catholic and History

At the present time the Catholic community is in a state of transition, since Vatican II has ushered in the age of the Spirit and plunged the Church into the world. Many Catholics are learning for the first time what it means to live without childhood security or adolescent triumphalism. They are discovering a deeper security and a more realistic vision in the mystery of the Spirit as that mystery unfolds in the processes of history. Coming out of their closed world, they have learned to accept the consciences of other men and to acknowledge the ambiguity of the moral sphere. They have enlarged their moral sensitivities from the personal to the social sphere and have abandoned their conservatism to raise a prophetic voice against institutions. While many are disturbed by the changes, and fear that they have been thrown into a moral relativism, others are beginning to sense that under this loss of bearings is the mystery of the Spirit working in the world.

As the Catholic is entering more deeply into the present and the future, he is beginning to read his past history with more sophistication. Instead of seeing the Church as providing moral security in each age by giving definitive solutions to all problems of conscience, he can read history more dialectically. He can see the Spirit working through the Church and the structures of society—often in struggle and ambiguity—to bring moral consciousness into concrete reality. He can accept the fact that it is not always easy to form one's conscience in a given age. For each period of history seems to have a problem area where the moral values are so bound up with change in the structures of society that a simple solution seems impossible. When Europe was changing from a feudal to a capitalistic society, the moral status of usury was clouded. At the time of the Reformation, when Europe was being torn into new religious and political divisions, issues of personal loyalty became excruciatingly complex. In our age the issue of birth control has become such a storm center that one is impelled to see behind it some radical change taking place—not merely in economic, political, or religious structures, but in man's basic relation to nature. Man's power over nature and life has reached a critical point in the twentieth century; for man is on the verge of changing his basic attitude from passive observer to active creator. How far and in what ways should this power extend so that he can maintain human dignity and the moral value of life? The ultimate solution to questions of this kind, and the moral dilemmas they create, usually lies in the future. The new economic form of capitalism emerged so that the moral issue of money-lending could be seen clearly; the religious and political divisions of Europe have settled to the point where a mood of ecumenism prevails at the present. Perhaps the solution to the birth-control issue will be seen only when man develops more fully the very scientific and economic resources that brought the issue into the fore. But in the meantime our age may have to endure the moral anguish of bearing the cross of history so that the next age will be able to reach a satisfying moral solution. It is a sign of maturity for a given age to bear courageously uncertainty and confusion so that the next age may have, through the help of the Spirit, an enlarged moral consciousness.

The chief need of our times, then, is for the virtues of the Spirit, especially for the gift of the discernment of spirits so that the Christian can penetrate beyond his personal moral dilemmas to see the larger historical issues at stake. At this time, the Christian must not be entrapped in the childish security or the adolescent triumphalism of a closed moral world. He must not only accept change, but through confidence in the Spirit he must be in the advance of the development of moral consciousness. But this requires that he accept the marks of a mature conscience—its responsibility, its tragic sense, its awareness of ambiguity and limitation—so that he can have the courage to bear his cross of his-

154 top.

toricity and the confident joy to make a positive contribution to the development of the kingdom as the Spirit transforms the universe in the image of Christ.

REFERENCES

Cousins, E. "Teilhard and the Theology of the Spirit," *Cross Currents,* 1969, *19,* 159-177.

Denzinger, H., & Schönmetzer, A. (S.J.) (Eds.) *Enchiridion Symbolorum.* (33rd cd.); Barcelona: Herder, 1965. English translation from: Clarkson, J. (S.J.), *et al. The Church Teaches.* St. Louis: Herder, 1955.

Dubarle, A. M. (O.P.), *The Biblical Doctrine of Original Sin* (trans. by E. M. Stewart). New York: Herder & Herder, 1964.

Gilleman, G. (S.J.) *The Primacy of Charity in Moral Theology* (trans. by W. Ryan [S.J.] & A. Vachon [S.J.]). Westminster, Md.: Newman, 1959.

Häring, B. (C.SS.R.) *The Law of Christ* Vol. I (trans. by E. Kaiser [C.PP.S.]), Westminster, Md.: Newman, 1963.

Jone, H. (O.E.M., Cap.) *Moral Theology* (trans. by U. Adelman [O.F.M., Cap.]). Westminster, Md.: Newman, 1953.

Kant, I. Fundamental Principles of the Metaphysic of Morals. In *Kant's Critique of Practical Reason and Other Works on the Theory of Ethics* (trans. by T. K. Abbott). (6th ed.) London: Longmans, Green, 1923.

Ladner, G. *The Idea of Reform: Its Impact on Christian Thought in the Age of the Fathers.* Cambridge: Harvard University Press, 1959.

Lepp, I. *The Authentic Morality* (trans. by B. Murchland [C.S.C.]). New York: Macmillan, 1965.

Monden, L. (S.J.) *Sin, Liberty and Law* (trans. by J. Donceel [S.J.]). New York: Sheed & Ward, 1965.

Plato. *The Dialogues of Plato* (trans. by B. Jowett). 2 vols. New York: Random House, 1937.

Schoonenberg, P. (S.J.) *Man and Sin* (trans. by J. Donceel [S.J.]). Notre Dame: University of Notre Dame Press, 1965.

12 The Struggle of Conscience for Authentic Selfhood

JOHN MACQUARRIE

The two traditional distinctions in conscience—the practical regulator of behavior and the generalized knowledge of moral principles—are acknowledged by Macquarrie in this selection.* But he explains and elaborates a third level of conscience as "a special and very fundamental mode of self-awareness, of how it is with oneself." This deeper level of conscience has the function of disclosing one's self to his deeper self so that a true self may emerge. Such a life-long struggle is against conventional conscience as formed by society and parents (Superego): it is a struggle for authentic selfhood that will make possible moral decisions and a style of life which opens up new possibilities for the primordial goodness of mankind.

As it is usually understood, conscience is a kind of built-in monitor of moral action, an interiorized law, as it were. But just as we have found it necessary to distinguish between actual codes of law and a "natural law" which underlies them, so it is possible to distinguish several levels of conscience. At its most concrete, conscience wrestles with some particular occasion of choice and decides on the right course of action in that situation. We can also think of conscience in a broader way as a more generalized knowledge of right and wrong, of good and bad. Moral theologians have sometimes used the ex-

* From *Three Issues in Ethics* (London: SCM Press, 1970), pp. 111-123. Reprinted with permission.

pression "synderesis," or "synteresis," for this knowledge of general moral principles, but while it has been useful to distinguish it from the concrete exercise of conscience, there seems to be little point in retaining such an archaic and uncertain term, and it should probably be dropped from use. There is, I believe, still another level of conscience. It can be understood as a special and very fundamental mode of self-awareness—the awareness of "how it is with oneself," if we may use the expression. It is with this third level of conscience that we shall be mainly concerned.

However, the three levels should not be too sharply marked off from each other, for there is obviously continuity among them. This means also that the scheme could be further complicated if we were to take note of intermediate levels among the three that have been mentioned; for instance, between the knowledge of general moral principles and concrete conscientious deliberation over a particular question, there will be the intermediate knowledge of a particular code or set of rules. In this, the general principles are not only broken up into more specific prescriptions but are colored and interpreted by social and historical conditions.

St. Paul acknowledged a basic universal knowledge of moral principles when he wrote: "When Gentiles who have not the law do by nature what the law requires, they are a law to themselves, even though they do not have the law. They show that what the law requires is written on their hearts, while their conscience also bears witness and their conflicting thoughts accuse or perhaps excuse them." [1] Paul seems to be arguing here that even when there is no knowledge of the actual formulations of the law of Moses, there is a knowledge of moral principles (a law "written on their hearts") which may well issue in the same kind of conduct as is required by the law of the Old Testament, supposedly a law revealed directly by God. When Paul speaks explicitly of conscience in the passage quoted, it seems to me that he is thinking not just of a knowledge of general moral principles but of that further level of conscience, that fundamental mode of self-awareness that belongs to man's existential constitution and that "bears witness" as to how it is with him. Conscience is more likely to "accuse" than to "excuse." Yet the fact that we can be accused from the depth of our own being points to the presence there of an image or self-understanding that is being violated by our actual condition and demands that another condition ought to be realized.

Although Paul no doubt believed that the actual detailed precepts of the Jewish law were divinely given, nowadays we would be more likely to think of this complicated system of laws and rules as very much historically and socially conditioned; and if we recognized any law as having a claim to be considered "divine," it would consist in the underlying general moral principles. On one of its levels, however, conscience is formed by actual codes that bear all the marks of a particular historical and social context. These codes, moreover, are taught by parents, teachers, clergy, and others, who stamp them with still further idiosyncrasies of emphasis and interpretation. The kind of conscience that is formed by the inculcation of some particular code would seem to be the phenomenon that Sigmund Freud had in mind when he described the superego: "The long period of childhood during which the growing human being lives in dependence on his parents leaves behind it a precipitate, which forms within his ego a special agency in which this parental influence is prolonged. It has received the name of 'superego.' . . . The parents' influence naturally includes not only the personalities of the parents themselves but also the racial, national and family traditions handed on through them, as well as the demands of the immediate social *milieu* which they represent." [2] Conscience, then, understood as the superego, reflects the standards of a particular society or even a segment of a society, and conformity to these standards is required if one is to be acceptable in that society. So conscience in this sense would seem to have a considerable admixture of more or less narrow social conventions along with its basic moral insights, and it is presumably these conventions that people have in view when they speak disparagingly of "bourgeois morality," "Victorian taboos," the "Protestant work ethic," and the like.

Of course, the superego is a real and important phenomenon. But it does not account for more than some aspects of the complex phenomenon of conscience, and certainly not for the more important aspects. Actually, more recent psychoanalytic theory has recognized the importance for conscience of the so-called "ego-ideal"—a positive image toward which man transcends himself, in the manner we have earlier described.

We must therefore try to understand better those deeper levels of conscience which will sometimes sit in judgment on the pronouncements of a person's own superego (that is to say, the standards of his own society or social group) and may decide that they are inadequate or regressive. He may experience a lot of pain and guilt feeling before he can break away from them, but the fact is that some people do break away. Their very consciences, shall we say, are accused by a deeper level of conscience.

We have already entertained the suggestion that conscience is most radically understood as a fundamental mode of self-awareness. The Latin *conscientia* and the Greek *syneidesis* both signified "consciousness" in a general sense before they came to indicate specifically the moral consciousness. The basic function of conscience is to disclose us to ourselves. Specifically, conscience discloses the gap between our actual selves and that image of ourselves that we already have in virtue of the "natural inclination" toward the fulfillment of man's end.

Thus, conscience is not merely a disclosure; it is also, as Heidegger insists,[3] a call or summons. It is a call to that full humanity of which we already have some idea or image because of the very fact that we are human at all, and that our nature is to exist, to go out beyond where we are at any given moment. Although we commonly think of conscience as commanding us to *do* certain things, the fundamental command of conscience is to *be*. What we do in any particular situation depends on what we seek to be, and, to this extent, ethical questions are dependent on ontological questions.

It will sometimes be the case that the summons of the authentic conscience will conflict with the standards of the conventional conscience, that is to say, the superego of Freudian analysis. We may think of this conflict as standing in analogy to the way in which the natural law may clash with some particular code of law. But, especially when the clash takes place on the level of the individual conscience, there is always grave danger of self-deception and perversion of conscience. There is a tendency nowadays to speak always disparagingly of "conventional morality" and of the "overstrict superego." But one has to be careful to inquire whether the criticism or rejection of the conventional standards is really based on a clearer conscientious insight or whether it flows simply from individual preference or veiled self-interest.

While undoubtedly there are occasions when the individual must heed his own conscientious convictions, no individual is a superman (*Übermensch*) so that he may lightly overrule the commonly accepted moral standards of his society. We have again to remind ourselves that the Nazis did this, with disastrous results. Friedrich Nietzsche offered a number of reasons for setting aside conventional morality, but the said reasons are frighteningly inadequate. According to him, ordinary morality derives its power from three factors: "the instinct of the *herd,* opposed to the strong and the independent; the instinct of all *sufferers* and *abortions,* opposed to the happy and well-constituted; the instinct of the *mediocre,* opposed to the exceptions." [4] Nietzsche's criticisms of conventional morality may be correct, but they set aside compassion and open the door to the possibility of ruthless exploitation and inhumanity.

At this point we come up against a very serious difficulty. On the one hand, conflict between the existential conscience and the conventional conscience would seem to be inevitable in all who are not content to be mere conformists. Only because there are such conflicts can moral progress take place, and the accepted codes of morality become modified as some members of the society gain deeper insights and protest against the accepted standards. But how are they to guard against claiming as "deeper insights" what may in fact be only personal prejudices? No conscience is infallible, and perhaps in this area self-deception is harder to detect and overcome than anywhere else. No moral philosopher has shown more respect for conscience or assigned it a more important role than has Bishop Butler. Yet this same thinker, in his brilliant sermon "Upon the Character of Balaam," [5] has also shown how subtly the conscience of a good man can be influenced and distorted by self-deception.

But the fact that conscience is fallible cannot be taken to mean that the commonly accepted moral standards must never be challenged. The difficulty is to be met by insisting again on the essential social dimension that enters into all human existence, so that the existent can be truly described as a being-with-others.[6] There can be no self-fulfillment for such an existent apart from the fulfillment of the community in which his existence is set. Thus, if his conscience ever leads him into conflict with the commonly accepted standards, he must first of all open his conscience to the judgment and counsel of his fellows. If he is a Christian, he will also open it to any teachings of the Bible and the church on the matter in question. Only when he has endeavored, to the utmost of his ability, to make allowance for his own tendencies toward distortion and egocentricity can a person justifiably set up his own conscience in opposition to the commonly accepted code. Even then, it is possible that he may be mistaken. But unless some individuals were prepared sometimes to take this risk, it is hard to see how any moral progress could take place.

But now we strike upon a new and greater difficulty. If we allow that conscience is a kind of interiorized law by which man is disclosed to himself and summoned to authentic selfhood, it does not follow that he will in fact obey the summons. It is hard to know whether anyone ever acts deliberately and directly against his conscience—he is much more likely to manipulate his conscience and to justify his action. This is to be expected, for if conscience directs us to authentic selfhood, then to go deliberately against it would seem to be equivalent to deciding to destroy oneself. But there are times when conscience has been clarified as far as possible and the direction which it indicates cannot be doubted or evaded, and yet it is not obeyed; for the agent may at such times experience a kind of moral impotence which prevents him from responding to conscience's demand. It is partly for this reason that conscience is more often experienced as "accusing" than as "excusing," to use St. Paul's terminology. It is Paul himself who furnishes a classic description of the situation that we have in mind: "I do not understand my own actions. For I do not do what I want, but I do the very thing I hate. . . . I can will what is right, but I cannot do it. For I do not do the good I want, but the evil I do not want is what I do." [7]

Paul's words are a useful reminder that the moral life is neither so simple nor so easy as it is sometimes represented to be. But, more than that, the description of his experience brings us to face a crucial paradox of the moral life—a paradox so sharp that unless we can offer some solution to it, it threatens to reduce morality to absurdity. For what is the point of all our talk about law and conscience if in fact men cannot follow them? If conscience directs someone to a particular course of action, and if this person assents to his conscience and desires to follow its bidding, but in fact he finds himself doing something else, how can we talk of moral action at all, or what sense does it make to recommend one course of action rather than another?

There is universal agreement among moral philosophers that a moral act, as distinct from a mere occurrence like the falling of a snowflake, is characterized by both freedom and knowledge on the part of the agent. The agent is free, in the sense that he is not completely determined to act in the way he does, either by external circumstances or by internal drives. He acts with knowledge, both moral knowledge of what is right and wrong, and factual knowledge of what he is doing and the circumstances under which he is doing it. But if one can say, "I do not understand my actions," or, "I meant to do one thing and found myself doing another," as we find Paul saying, then how can we talk of moral action? Yet Paul clearly supposes that his actions did have moral quality— they were his own actions and he apparently felt guilty about them.

There can be no doubt that he does describe a state of affairs by no means uncommon. Conscience summons with its ultimate demand, yet in the face of this demand there is an impotence to act, a kind of inertia or pull in another direction, stultifying the good intention. This frustrating possibility drives us to ask whether man's moral strivings and aspirations make sense or are finally absurd, as so many "useless passions," in Sartre's language. If morality is to be taken seriously, then, in Kantian terms, "ought implies can." It makes no sense to say people ought to act in a certain way if they cannot. Yet, often enough, it seems to be just the case that they cannot.

The problem of whether and how one can make sense of the moral life brings us once more to the border of theology and ethics. The paradox can be resolved only if it can be shown that the moral life has a more complex and dialectical structure than is often supposed. I am going to suggest that such a structure is brought into view by a consideration of the theological notions of sin and grace. Although these notions have frequently been criticized by secular moralists, I think they can be expounded in ways that are not inimical to the integrity of secular morals, and one can even show that what the theologian calls "sin" and "grace" have parallels in nonreligious experience.

However, it must frankly be admitted that sin and grace are religious or theological ideas, and that the suspicion of the secular moral philosopher about the introduction of such ideas into ethical discussion has some justification. Yet, although sin and grace have primarily a theological import, they can be interpreted in a broader fashion. In relation to the moral situation and its demand, "sin" may be understood as the *disabling* factor that sometimes prevents the appropriate response to the demand; while "grace" is the *enabling* factor that sometimes permits the response to take place. I shall try to show that when we allow for the complexities introduced by these ideas, we shall be able to make sense of those perplexing situations in which, as it seems, ought no longer implies can, and the whole moral enterprise is threatened with a breakdown into absurdity.

However, we must first of all pause to consider the objections which moral philosophers might make to bringing such theological ideas as sin and grace into a discussion about ethics. Both of these ideas seem, in some way, to imply that man is not completely the master of his actions and that his moral life is not fully autonomous. But how can there be moral action, properly so called, unless it is free? And how can it be free if man's capacity to act is either disabled, so that he cannot do the good, or else must be enabled, so that the act would then seem to be not really his own? The moral philosopher could argue that the notions of sin and grace are so far from making sense of the moral life that they finally destroy it. They seek to alleviate one contradiction by introducing an even more monstrous contradiction.

A powerful defense of the autonomy of ethics against theological encroachments has been made in recent years by W. G. Maclagan.[8] He points out that many theologians of our time (Barth, Brunner, and Niebuhr are mentioned in particular) have held that man is rendered incapable through sin of either right action or even right thinking; and that, conversely, they have argued that whatever morally good action a man does must be accounted a work of grace. Such views, Maclagan believes, are destructive of the very meaning of morality. "The heart of the theology to which I am objecting is, as I understand it, the doctrine of *sola gratia,* the doctrine that what may be called 'natural man,' man apart from the work of grace, lacks the capacity to live as he should." [9] Maclagan's point is that if we accept such views, then there is no responsible human action—and therefore no morality—at all. "It is surely the case that, unless an act of will is in a quite unqualified sense a man's own work, there is nothing that can be his work even in a qualified sense and in some degree." [10]

Maclagan's objections are undoubtedly valid against some extreme views that have been put forward by Christian theologians, especially those working in the traditions of St. Augustine and John Calvin. If anyone gives credence to doctrines of either "total depravity" or "irresistible grace," then he does appear to deny the possibility of free responsible action, and he takes away any grounds for making a moral judgment on human conduct. Indeed, more than this, he really denies that man's being is truly personal. A man whose actions are already determined for him through his total subjection to sin or through his total possession by grace is a puppet, and so not a moral agent, for a puppet's activities are neither right nor wrong.

Christians ought also to consider how offensive the statements of some theologians must be to honest secularists who are striving hard to achieve an authentic human community. Who is going to have the effrontery to say that all their efforts are rendered nugatory by sin and that they will get nowhere without the grace that comes with Christian faith? It must be added that there is no convincing empirical evidence that would support these Christian—or supposedly Christian—assertions.

But if we allow that Maclagan has a valid case, are we then to accept a Pelagian view of the matter and say that man is always free to make a choice between good and evil or, at least, a choice between better and worse? I do not think we can say this either, for in fact our freedom is usually limited, and sometimes is reduced almost to the vanishing point. Our own past actions and the habits we have built up, the pressures and prejudices of society, and a great many other factors combine to push us toward actions that we would not really choose to do. Sin may be reckoned among these factors, or it may be the inclusive name for all of them taken together. It is not absolutely determinative of our action, but it pushes us one way rather than another. Moral realism has to recognize that in spite of high moral aspirations and the determination to follow them, there may be impotence to carry out the policies that are inwardly approved. So we seem to be driven back from the untenable position in which sin and grace are so interpreted that man is reduced to a puppet to the equally untenable, because self-contradictory, position, noted earlier, in which the moral demand of the ought is experienced but the capacity to respond to it is lacking. We seem to be caught in a disjunction in which we are unable to affirm either side.

Clearly, we must seek a more dialectical approach, one that will do justice to the valid insights that belong to each side of the disjunction. In fact, we do find in the theological tradition further ideas that can be helpful in leading toward a more adequate dialectic.

Some Christian theologians (myself included) have held that any doctrine of original sin needs to be counterbalanced by a doctrine of original righteousness.[11] In the biblical stories of the creation and the fall, man was created good before he fell into evil. So long as he remains man, some trace of this goodness remains also, if only in the form of an image of who he ought to be —an image that we have already linked with the notion of an *imago Dei*.[12] As Paul Ricoeur has expressed it, "However radical evil may be, it cannot be as primordial as goodness." [13] Evil is essentially secondary and parasitic, and it is doubtful whether there could be a "total depravity." Something of an original righteousness remains, even if it is heavily impaired by sin.

To acknowledge the reality of an original righteousness that persists along with original sin and is even more fundamental is also to acknowledge that there is a kind of grace in creation itself. We may call it, if we wish to use an expression sometimes employed in the history of theology, a "common grace." To be sure, "grace" and "nature" are relative terms, and some people might argue that a common grace belonging to creation itself is simply nature. But the use of the word "grace" expresses the giftlike character of that original righteousness or desire for the good, which is never extinguished in man. Existence itself is a gift, for we did not make ourselves, and in this sense there is a grace of existence, a grace that is prior to particular experiences of grace within a community or a religious faith.

In its treatment of sin and grace, much of our traditional theology has been guilty of a twofold distortion: it has laid more stress on original sin than on common grace; and it has tended to regard both sin and grace in objectified, mythological ways—sin as a kind of taint or stain, and grace as a kind of mysterious essence that is "infused" into the human soul or that somehow takes possession of a person's will.

As against this distortion, we must advance a contrary two-fold claim: that sin and grace are always present, and that they must be understood in nothing less than personal or existential terms. That is to say, while indeed they may support or deflect the agent, as the case may be, they do not infringe on his personal responsibility. In the theology of the Christian life, sin and grace constitute a dialectic within which responsible human action takes place. Something of this dialectic is expressed by St. Paul when he writes: "Work out your own salvation with fear and trembling, for it is God who works in you. . . ." [14] Yet, in talking of an original sin and of a common grace, I am also maintaining that the dialectic of sin and grace (even if it may not be called this) is not peculiar to the Christian life but characterizes all moral striving. Everywhere, enabling and disabling forces work upon the human will, though without destroying our ultimate personal responsibility. These enabling and disabling forces, wherever they are found, are akin to what the Christian calls "grace" and "sin." Since the Christian believes that grace is more primordial than sin, then, without denying or minimizing sin, he also maintains the essential hopefulness of the moral struggle.

NOTES

1. Romans 2:14-15.
2. Sigmund Freud, *An Outline of Psychoanalysis,* tr. James Strachey (London: Hogarth Press, 1949), pp. 3-4.
3. Heidegger, *op. cit.,* p. 314.
4. Friedrich Nietzsche, *The Will to Power: An Attempted Transvaluation of All Values,* tr. Anthony M. Ludovici (Edinburgh: T. N. Foulis, 1909), Vol. I, p. 226.
5. *Butler's Works,* ed. W. E. Gladstone (Oxford: Clarendon Press, 1896), Vol. II, pp. 121-35.
6. See pp. 60ff.
7. Romans 7:15-19.
8. W. G. Maclagan, *The Theological Frontier of Ethics* (London: Allen & Unwin, 1961).
9. *Ibid.,* p. 29.

10. *Ibid.*, p. 111.
11. Cf. my *Principles of Christian Theology* (New York: Scribner's; London: S.C.M. Press, 1966), p. 245.
12. See p. 87.
13. Ricoeur, *The Symbolism of Evil,* p. 156.
14. Philippians 2:12-13.

13 Conscience and Superego: A Key Distinction

JOHN W. GLASER

Theology and psychology are subjects: that is, fields
of thought that have a history and literature. It is
easy to study these subjects and forget that both are
dealing with human beings and that somehow both
have to be reconciled within personal experience.
Such reconciliation is difficult because there are few
scholars who are able to accept the truths of each
field and then relate them in a meaningful way.
Glaser has done this difficult task by describing the
superego, assuming its natural place in human development, and then showing how it can be falsely
equated with religion or how it presents problems for
the religious person.* He has also described conscience, showing how it functions differently from
the superego and toward different goals. Specific pastoral problems are described with these differences,
thus illuminating several normal human situations.

The superego first came to my attention when
I did not know what to call it. The occasion
was a relatively harmless instance: an Army officer and his wife,
who were by virtue of their military status dispensed from Friday
abstinence, told me how it had taken them almost a year to be able
to eat meat on Friday without feeling somewhat guilty about this
—in spite of their dispensation.

But another experience (which I shall take up later in this
article) bared the vicious set of incisors this source of pseudo-moral

* From *Theological Studies*, Vol. 32, 1971, pp. 30-47. Reprinted by
permission.

guilt could have. I saw how this source of unconscious guilt could actually cripple a person; it could keep the individual from seeing the genuine values at stake—values which alone could creatively call the person beyond his present fixation and the destructive circle of defeat, depression, "repentance," and further failures.

In this article I want to (1) briefly describe moral conscience; (2) then in some detail describe an entirely different but deceptively similar-looking reality: the superego; (3) finally reflect on a number of areas where recognition of the radical difference between genuine conscience and superego is extremely important and illuminating, where a failure to recognize this can do considerable harm.

Before beginning the discussion itself, it might be pointed out why the difference between conscience and superego has managed to escape much notice outside the circle of psychologists.[1] In a merely superficial consideration these two realities have functions which appear strikingly similar: both have been described as primarily nonverbal, preconceptual; commanding, prohibiting; accusing, approving; seeking reconciliation if norms are violated. This describes some superficial similarities between conscience and superego; the radical differences should become clear from what follows.

I
MORAL CONSCIENCE

These drastically brief remarks concern conscience as it functions in the situation of grave moral decision—core freedom. Any other use of the term conscience should be considered as analogous to this primary meaning.[2]

If we can assume (1) that *the* moral action of man is love (the unity of the love of God and love of neighbor) and that this very action is, seen from the agent's point of view, the act of his own cocreation, his answering himself into abiding existence; and if we can assume (2) that this invitation to love occurs in ever deeper invitations, at not entirely predictable *kairoi* of God's loving initiative in each person's salvation history; and if we can assume (3) that this tridimensional "object" of man's freedom (God's self-offering; the created, personal other which mediates this divine initiative; the individual himself as offered possible abiding love) is primarily, though not necessarily exclusively, present to the agent's consciousness in a preconceptual manner of knowing (each dimension of this "object" in its own mode of preconceptual knowledge), then we can describe moral conscience as the preconceptual recognition of an absolute call to love and thereby to cocreate myself genuine future, or as the nonverbal insight into a radical invitation to love God in loving my neighbor and thereby become myself abiding love. This is a description of the positive, invitation aspect of *conscientia antecedens,* often described, less than ideally, as the command of conscience. The negative aspect, the prohibition of *conscientia antecedens,* can then be logically described as the preconceptually perceived ultimate futurelessness and absurdity of being invited to radically abiding growth in love and rejecting this invitation.

Conscientia consequens (a "good conscience"), in such a context, can be described as the preconceptually experienced harmony existing between the ultimate ground of reality, the created values, and that existence which I am, cocreated by my free act. A "bad conscience" can be described as the preconceptually experienced disharmony between the abiding futureless and futile existence that my freedom has caused in the very situation which invited me to cocreate myself abiding love.

In short, conscience is an insight into love; the call issued by the ultimate value and promise of love; the warning of the destructive power of indifference or hostility to this invitation; the peace (not self-satisfaction) that results from the creative yes to love; the disharmony and disintegration of existing as an abiding contradiction to this call of love which my whole being is made to answer affirmatively.

II
THE SUPEREGO

The superego deals not in the currency of extroverted love but in the introversion of *being lovable.* The dynamic of the superego springs from a frantic compulsion to experience oneself as lovable, not from the call to commit oneself in abiding love.

To understand the superego, we have to begin there where

every human being begins—as a child. The child is faced with a problem: he is a bundle of needs, desires, and impulses. They cannot all find satisfaction; very often the fulfilment of one excludes the satisfaction of another (e.g., if a child's desire to grab everything within reach is satisfied, he finds himself confronted with the displeasure and disapproval of his parents, i.e., with the frustration of another of his desires). These desires, needs, and impulses manifest a decided hierarchy of importance and power. Eicke indicates that opinions vary on *the* primary drive, but says that most psychologists seem to see the need to be loved, to enjoy approval and affection, as the strongest, most fundamental of these drives.[3] He goes on to say that the child experiences disapproval, temporary withdrawal of love, as a kind of annihilation. Therefore this fear of punishment is not so much an aversion to physical pain as it is panic at the withdrawal of love. Freud has remarked that being loved is equivalent to life itself for the ego.[4] In these terms the child experiences the disapproval of his parents as a mitigated withdrawal of life itself. In such a situation the child needs a means of so organizing and ordering his various desires that his main need, to be loved, does not get run over by the others. Since there is not yet enough mature psychic equipment at the child's disposal to handle this conflict, the problem is handled by a more primitive (i.e., less personal) mechanism. An instance of censorship forms on this prepersonal level; its function is to so regulate the conduct of the child that he does not lose the primary object of his desires: love, affection, and approval.[5]

One point should be made clear beyond all misunderstanding: the commands and prohibitions of the superego do not arise from any kind of perception of the intrinsic goodness or objectionableness of the action contemplated. *The* source of such commands and prohibitions can be described positively as the desire to be approved and loved or negatively as the fear of loss of such love and approval.[6]

Even this prepersonal instance of censorship manifests stages of development. It has been observed that during the first few years of a child's life the commands and prohibitions of parents are so identified with the parents themselves that the commands, as it were, leave the room with the parents. These norms are only really effective when the mother or father is actually present.[7]

But even during this time a process of internalization is taking place by which the orders of authority are assimilated in the child and eventually arise from within the child himself. This process involves the psychological mechanisms of introjection and identification.[8] Eicke sums this up thus:

Through identification a value emerges, a value which I am for myself; but this is also a value according to which I must conduct myself. If I fail to act according to this norm, I experience fears and feelings of guilt; more exactly, fear of not being loved, of being abandoned or persecuted; feelings of not having done the right thing, of not having made myself lovable. As Freud says: "Consciousness of guilt was originally fear of punishment by parents; more exactly, fear of losing their love." [9]

Several things characterize this process of introjection. It is a spontaneous mechanism whose commands speak with a remarkable power (which we will discuss shortly). It is also striking how graphically (almost "photographically" at times) the authority figure takes up a place within the child himself, so that not only the content but also the very voice and formulation of this external person arises from within the child. Zulliger recounts the comment of the nineteenth-century Swiss author Rodolphe Toepffer: "For a long time I was unable to distinguish the inner voice of my conscience from *that of my teacher*. When my conscience spoke to me, I thought I saw it before me in a black cape, with a teacher's frown and glasses sitting on its nose." [10]

Allport brings a delightful and illuminating example which illustrates this process of introjection and the controlling influence it exercises:

I am indebted for this example to my colleague, Henry A. Murray. A three-year-old-boy awoke at six in the morning and started his noisy play. The father, sleepy-eyed, went to the boy's room and sternly commanded him, "Get back into bed and don't you dare get up until seven o'clock." The boy obeyed. For a few minutes all was quiet, but soon there were strange sounds that led the father again to look into the room. The boy was in bed as ordered; but putting an arm over the edge, he jerked it back in saying, "Get back in there." Next a leg protruded, only to be roughly retracted with the warning, "You heard what I told you." Finally the boy rolled to the very edge of the bed and then roughly rolled back, sternly warning himself, "Not until seven o'clock!" We could not wish for a clearer instance of interiorizing the father's role as a means to self-control and socialized becoming.[11]

The only exceptional thing about such an instance is that it happened to be observed by an adult, and by one who saw the psychological significance of the event. Zulliger offers numerous examples of the same phenomenon.[12]

The superego as discussed up to now could be characterized as having functions similar to those of what is traditionally known as *conscientia antecedens:* it commands and prohibits certain concrete possibilities in a given situation. The superego, however, also functions in a way similar to *conscientia consequens:* it accuses the offender, it condemns him when he fails to obey. The fury of the violated superego is described by Bergler: "The extent of the power yielded by the Frankenstein which is the superego is still largely unrealized. . . . Man's inhumanity to man is equaled only by man's inhumanity to himself." [13]

The reason for this violent reaction has already been touched upon. The superego must, on the psychological, subconscious level, provide for a person's being loved; it is the guardian of the individual's sense of value. We have already referred to Freud's statement that, for the ego, being loved is equivalent to life itself. Hence the violence of the offended superego arises from the panic of having lost one's right to be loved; on a primitive, psychological level he has "lost his life." [14] The fact that this plays itself out on a nonconceptual level of consciousness in terms of panic, fear, and guilt feelings makes it all the more difficult to cope with, if one is armed only with the weapons of reason and conceptual reflection.

Zulliger spells out the guilt feelings produced by the superego in terms of isolation. "When a child does something wrong, disobeys a command, etc., he experiences a feeling of isolation." [15] He feels that he is "bad" and isolated from those who are "good." Describing such guilt in terms of an experienced isolation helps us find a plausible and consistent explanation of several other phenomena closely connected with such guilt. There is no need here to recount the many examples offered by Zulliger, but by means of these examples several things are made clear: there is a powerful subconscious drive to re-create one's sense of belonging and being accepted by his community, of re-establishing the harmony and solidarity he has forfeited by his fault.

This drive to rejoint the "good" and thus regain one's sense of value, this drive to break out of the panic of isolation, can express itself in a variety of ways. Besides the direct approach of confessing to some authority figure and accepting punishment, there are various indirect ways of attempting to escape the tyranny of an offended superego. Zulliger enumerates three main indirect solutions. First, there is the unconscious betrayal of guilt. This drive to be found out (which is ultimately a drive to be reconciled), though conflicting with the conscious effort to escape detection, finds ways of exposing one's fault and in this way of indirectly confessing and ultimately being reconciled. Another substitute compensation takes the form of seeking punishment.[16] The original misdeed against the norms of the superego is not itself confessed and punished. Rather, the individual provokes punishment through further misdeeds and through this punishment for further and distinct failures attempts to quiet his need for punishment for the original unpunished misdeed. Through a further and distinct misdeed (whose real goal is the reconciliation to follow) he attempts to break out of the isolation created by the original misdeed. His subconscious goal is to have the second misdeed result in punishment-reconciliation and also take care of the original alienation. Finally, there is the indirect escape from isolation which takes the form of creating a new community where the individual will be accepted. This implies provoking others to deeds similar to his own. Instead of re-establishing harmony with the "good," he tends to create a group which will accept him with his misdeeds and even esteem him precisely on their account.[17]

Zulliger's description of the power of the superego in terms of flight from a feeling of acute alienation—an alienation from that group represented by the authority figures in his life, who "belong"—helps us see how much the formal structure of the superego differs from conscience. Conscience is precisely the call of genuine value which can well call one to an extremely isolated position. Motivating an individual's activity on the basis of "acceptance" serves well the socialization and normalization of individuals to prevailing norms; but as a basis of Christian morality (in the mature sense of this word), which should be characterized by a creative thrust into the future, i.e., into the not-yet-ready-to-be-thought, its dynamics are strikingly inadequate. The superego performs well in the process of socialization—training one to function well within a given set of limits; it works well and adequately in toilet-training an infant or housebreaking a pup (both useful results, without which life would be far less pleasant), but its legitimate function deals with the more primitive levels of psychic life. Görres points out that the relationship between superego and id is not so much that of spirit to instinct or rider to horse; rather, it concerns the relationship between instinct and training. "The superego, in Freud's sense, is primarily a function of organization of the primitive levels of psychic life. This is supported by the fact that higher animals are said to have a superego when they have been trained." [18]

The superego is basically a principle of prepersonal censorship and control. This does not mean that it has no meaningful function for man. On the contrary, the role of the superego in the life of an infant is quite meaningful and necessary. It is a primitive stage on the way to the development of genuine conscience and value perception.[19] Even in the life of a mature adult the superego is not superfluous. In certain sectors of life it provides for a conservation of psychic energy and ease of operation. Görres remarks: "When the superego is integrated into a mature conscience . . . it relieves an individual from having constantly to decide in all those situations which are already legitimately decided by custom, taste, and convention 'what one should do' and 'what one should not do.' " [20]

Psychologists are in agreement, however, that this organic development from the primitive and prepersonal censor of the infant to a mature and personal value perception does not automatically and infallibly take place. This means that the activity of superego in the average adult is not limited to the healthy and integrated function described above by Görres. In fact, Görres himself maintains that it is the task, not only of psychiatry but of education and pastoral practice as well, to reduce the influence of this childish censor more and more and thereby allow genuine value perception to grow.[21]

While it is true that the workings of the superego are generally discussed in the context of the child or the neurotic, Görres reminds us that the differences here between the neurotic and the "healthy" person are those of degree and not of kind.[22] According to Odier and Tournier, there are two moral worlds existing in the normal person: a genuine moral world and a world of false or pseudo morality and religiosity.[23] Both of these authors have written extensively on this subject precisely to call attention to the existence and influence of this all too often overlooked world of childish morality in the life of the average adult.[24] Felicitas Betz points out that the struggle to grow up in this regard does not cease at the end of childhood or adolescence but confronts us with a lifelong battle. "The maturing of one's conscience is a task that takes a lifetime; it is with us far beyond the end of adolescence. For one who has been the object more of conscience training than conscience education, this task of arriving at mature conscience will be particularly difficult, if not impossible." [25]

We might draw up some contrasting characteristics which exist between the superego and genuine conscience:

SUPEREGO	CONSCIENCE
commands that an act be performed for approval, in order to make oneself lovable, accepted; fear of love-withdrawal is the basis	invites to action, to love, and in this very act of other-directed commitment to cocreate self-value
introverted: the thematic center is a sense of one's own value	extroverted: the thematic center is the value which invites; self-value is concomitant and secondary to this
static: does not grow, does not learn; cannot function creatively in a new situation; merely repeats a basic command	dynamic: an awareness and sensitivity to value which develops and grows; a mind-set which can precisely function in a new situation
authority-figure-oriented: not a question of perceiving and responding to a value but of "obeying" authority's command "blindly"	value-oriented: the value or disvalue is perceived and responded to, regardless of whether authority has commanded or not
"atomized" units of activity are its object	individual acts are seen in their importance as a part of a larger process or pattern
past-oriented: primarily concerned with cleaning up the record with regard to past acts	future-oriented: creative; sees the past as having a future and helping to structure this future as a better future

urge to be punished and thereby earn reconciliation	sees the need to repair by structuring the future orientation toward the value in question (which includes making good past harms)
rapid transition from severe isolation, guilt feelings, etc., to a sense of self-value accomplished by confessing to an authority figure	a sense of the gradual process of growth which characterizes all dimensions of genuine personal development
possible great disproportion between guilt experienced and the value in question; extent of guilt depends more on weight of authority figure and "volume" with which he speaks rather than density of the value in question	experience of guilt proportionate to the importance of the value in question, even though authority may never have addressed this specific value

In light of this less than exhaustive list of contrasts, it should be clear that failing to distinguish these two realities will cause considerable confusion. This confusion is multiplied if one has taken superego data and allowed it to be the weightier element in understanding man as *free,* precisely because it arises from the pre-personal, prefree dimension of an individual. The pastoral and ascetic practice which flows from such a superego-weighted interpretation of guilt, etc., will be to a great extent in radical conflict with man's genuine freedom.

In the following section I want to reflect on some areas where it seems to me we have been mistaken in drawing theological conclusions or in projecting conduct (pastoral, ascetic, sacramental) from data of the superego. These remarks vary in their importance and are less systematically developed than might be desirable; they must stand as the fragmentary reflections that are prompted by my present situation. Hopefully they will stimulate further reflection and application, which will be, among other things, corrective of the following remarks.

III

Problem Areas Where Superego is Part of Problem

All the following reflections could be subsumed under one rubric: too much theory and practice in the Church arises from data whose source is the superego. Many problem areas which have emerged in the recent past can be traced to a failure to recognize the nature, presence, and power of the superego. This is not an accusation.[26] But given today's vantage point, this is a situation which can be overcome and should not be further tolerated.

Notion of God

Precisely because the voice of the superego is somehow cosmic, vast, and mysterious, arising as it does from the subconscious, it can easily be mistakenly called God's voice. This is true especially if our religious education trains us from childhood on to call this voice of the subconscious God's voice. This I see as the major danger of failing to distinguish conscience from superego. To associate the mystery of invitation, the absolute yes to man's future, the radical call to eternally abiding love—God—with the hot and cold, arbitrary tyrant of the superego is a matter of grave distortion. It reaches into the totality of a person's explicitly religious life and poisons every fresh spring of the Good News. Such a God deserves to die.

Gregory Baum's comments are much to the point on this question:

A second reason why the image of the God the punisher has flourished in the Christian and even post-Christian imagination is drawn from personal pathology. The idea of God as judge on a throne, meting out punishment, corresponds to a self-destructive trend of the human psyche. On a previous page we have mentioned man's primitive conscience or, as Freud called it, his superego. The person who is dominated by his superego—and no one is able to escape it altogether—has the accuser, judge, and tormentor all wrapt in one, built into his own psychic make-up. When such a person hears the Christian message with the accent on God the judge, he can project his superego on the divinity and then use religion as an instrument to subject himself to this court and, unknown to himself, to promote his own unconscious self-hatred. As we mentioned more than once in these pages, Jesus has come to save men from their superego. God is not punisher; God saves.[27]

Age of Reason and Transition between Grace and Sin

The theological literature on the fundamental option has drastically revised the common Catholic ideas concerning the "age of reason" and the frequency with which the transition between grace-sin-grace-sin can occur.[28] The speculation of theologians like Rahner, Schüller, Metz, and Mondin has so radically changed the atmosphere in which speculation on core freedom takes place that one is puzzled how thoughts on the "age of reason" (emergence of core freedom) and the frequency of core decisions—which were common fare in moral theology until the recent past—were ever possible. How could we have really thought that ten-year-olds could sin seriously? Or what ever possessed us to think that we could move through serious sin and grace with the frequency that we change shirts?

One major reason why such thoughts were thinkable is surely because theology failed to recognize various kinds of guilt experience and release from this guilt. Theology simply accepted all guilt experience and its release as theological data, as data arising from man's freedom. The nature of superego guilt and its radical difference from genuine moral guilt went unrecognized.

A striking example of this appears in Maritain's *Range of Reason*.[29] Maritain uses an excellent analysis of preconceptual knowledge of God to make a far from excellent explanation of why a child can engage his core freedom. At one point in his discussion of this question Maritain seems to reveal, at least in part, the source of his conviction that children can make core-freedom decisions. In what he seems to consider a phenomenological justification for his position he says:

Yet in some rare cases, the first act of freedom will never be forgotten, especially if the choice—however insignificant its object—through which the soul was introduced into moral life occurred rather late. In other cases there is a remembrance of some childish remorse, whose occasion was unimportant but whose intensity, out of proportion with its object, upset the soul and awakened its moral sense.[30]

To one aware of the dimensions of an act of core freedom on the one hand, and familiar with the nature of the superego on the other, the data described by Maritain is clearly relegated to the area of the superego, not genuine freedom. This acceptance of all guilt data as genuine theological data—which Maritain reveals in the quoted passage—remained for moral theology a silent but functioning presupposition in its consideration of the "age of reason." This error, coupled with an exaggerated conceptualistic model of conscience, helps explain in large part the now incredible conviction with which most of us grew up: children can commit serious sin.

The idea that an individual could sin seriously, repent only to sin seriously again, repent again—and this within a matter of days—also finds at least partial explanation in the fact that super-ego guilt and its remission by an authority figure was mistaken for genuine moral guilt and its remission. A very common phenomenon, familiar to anyone who has done pastoral work with Catholic adolescents, certainly *seems* to support the theory that the transition between grace and serious sin can occur relatively frequently. We might describe this datum as the "storm and sunshine phenomenon." It occurs especially in questions of sexual morality. The individual experiences severe guilt feelings after a failing against the sixth commandment: the storm phase. Upon confessing, he experiences a wonderful release from his guilt: the sunshine phase. Such a moving between storm and sunshine might well occur on a weekly basis. The guilt feelings involved represent very often the most severe experience of guilt the individual has ever known; the freeing from this guilt through confession is often the most intense experience of liberation.

Such an undeniable phenomenon seems to offer more than enough concrete evidence that an individual can fluctuate frequently between grace and serious sin. It can do this, however, only if we are ignorant of the nature of the superego; only if we overlook the fact that the area of sexuality is notoriously susceptible to the tyranny of the superego; and only if we fail to realize the vast dimensions of the transition between sin and grace. Because these very facts were not operative in reflection on core freedom (mortal sin), it is easy to understand why traditional moral theology and confessional practice took their theoretical and pastoral-practical categories from the superego-dominated data and found in such data unquestioned support for the conviction that the transition between grace and sin could occur with almost assembly-line frequency.

Diminishing Confessions

From the foregoing it is clear that at least some essential dimensions of confessional practice are based on the nature and laws of the superego and not of genuine freedom. It seems to me that these are not merely two exceptional, isolated instances, but two areas which are better seen as examples where confession's debt to the superego is more blatantly obvious. They are pocket-sized editions of what is true of confessional practice as a whole: it is, as traditionally realized, predominantly, though not exclusively, a service of the superego needs of individuals.

In traditional confession practice, therefore, we have an institution based on heavily-weighted nonfree (superego) data which purports to be an institutionalization but actually is a contradiction of genuine freedom. Now this genuine freedom and its categories of being, growing, etc., are not simply nonconscious, beyond all awareness; they are somehow present to man's awareness because of the essential relationship between freedom and knowledge. Hence we have an awareness, a consciousness "divided" against itself, contradicting itself on various levels. On the preconceptual level we have an awareness of the true nature and structure of freedom—its laws of growth, the "units" of core freedom, their duration and possible frequency, etc. On the conceptual level we have categories which attempt to represent this freedom but are actually derived to a great extent from the superego.

Since the categories drawn from the superego are far shallower, a much "thinner brew" (see the characteristics mentioned earlier), the person in question experiences present confessional practice as a trivialization of his genuine freedom. He experiences himself as dealing with the reality of his freedom—experienced preconceptually in its real depth, richness, laws of growth and engagement, etc.—in institutionalized categories derived from a far cheaper reality; hence the institutionalized categories are too cheap and too trivial for the reality to which they supposedly correspond and from which they supposedly derive.

The experience of this "misfit" is recognized, not necessarily in a reflexively formulated way, but in the depth of consciousness. It is, then, no wonder that a person reacts in a corresponding way; a person simply finds himself, in an unplanned and unarticulated way, distancing himself from the practice of confession.

This means that the phenomenon of diminishing confessions, is, at least in part, a healthy recognition of the misfit existing between genuine freedom and a system of categories—institutionalized in the traditional practice of confession—derived to a great extent from the superego. Therefore this phenomenon, far from being regrettable, is a sign of health and insight. It cannot be reversed by mere rhetoric; the very nature of genuine freedom does not prompt us to attempt to reverse it. The more nuanced understanding of man's freedom does, however, prompt us to find more adequate forms for the sacrament of penance. Finding these new forms—be they communal and/or "private"—does demand that we recognize the reality of the superego for what it is and thereby avoid merely creating forms of serving the infantile needs of the superego in a new way.

Superego Can Blind to Genuine Value

In discussing some of the pastoral implication of the foregoing pages, I have often heard the comment: "Maybe an individual needs the dynamics of the superego to help himself avoid doing what he really wants to avoid, but cannot—e.g., masturbation. If we take this away, we may be robbing him of a real help."

Several observations on such a comment: First, there is the question of what such "support" is doing to his whole conception of God and his life of partnership with God. Second, the superego is far more infallible as a tormentor of failure than as a source of effective motivation. Hence the question: What is such support doing to his own self-concept? More often than not the superego will be ineffective in overcoming the urge to masturbate; but it will, with inexorable certainty, provide a self-devouring gloom following such an act. The disproportionate guilt will set up the very situation which immerses the individual in even deeper depressions, sense of failure and frustration, fixation on this matter, etc.; in short, the very situation which is most conducive to further masturbation.

Finally, the superego orientation can quite effectively block off the ultimate values at stake. The superego handles individual acts; it demands that these past actions be "confessed" to an authority figure and thereby erased. Such a frame of reference keeps the individual from seeing the larger and more important *process,* which is always the nature of genuine human growth.

Instead of experiencing the individual acts precisely as part of a future-oriented growth process, concerned with values that of their inherent power call to growth, the center of attention is focused on righting past wrongs, seen as atomized units.

A counselor told me of a case in which a happily married man with several children had been plagued by masturbation for fifteen years. During these fifteen years he had dutifully gone the route of weekly confession, Communion, etc. The counselor told him to stop thinking of this in terms of serious sin, to go to Communion every Sunday and to confession every six weeks. He tried to help him see his introversion in terms of his own sexual maturity, in terms of his relationship to his wife and children. Within several months this fifteen-year-old "plague" simply vanished from his life. By refusing to follow a pattern of pastoral practice based on the dynamics of the superego, this counselor was able to unlock a logjam of fifteen years; by refusing to deal with the superego as if it were conscience, he freed the genuine values at stake; he allowed them to speak and call the person beyond his present lesser stage of sexual integration. We can pay rent to the superego but the house never becomes our own possession.

The same is true especially in questions of premarital sex. Fostering the mortal sin-grace horizon and plugging it into the confession-Communion-sin network can keep the person from doing the most important thing of all: honestly looking at the delicate, nuanced, process-structured values which are involved; and it is only by becoming increasingly sensitive to these values that one can be helped, through good and bad experience, to continue to grow. Allowing the superego to dominate this pattern of conduct, to atomize the acts, to deal with their guilt and its release in terms of past serious offenses against God which are set right by some authority figure can be the very manner of dealing with the problem which keeps the operative values from ever emerging and calling creatively to further growth.

Departures from Active Ministry and Religious Life

Understanding the superego also sheds some light on the phenomenon of increasing departures from the active ministry and religious life—a phenomenon badly in need of illumination from whatever source we can find. Understanding the superego helps us see a very positive side of this phenomenon—which does not mean that it is solely a positive reality or that such a consideration provides the only or primary horizon for understanding this extremely complex reality.[31] But I am convinced that the superego and its dynamics are involved to a considerable extent in this complex process.

First, I want to consider a striking example which Zulliger provides and which at first blush might seem to have little to do with departures from ministry and religious life. He recounts an incident that happened when he was a counselor at a boys' camp.[32] He was in charge of a small group of boys camping out together. One of the boys reported to Zulliger that money had been taken from his tent. Since a campfire and games had been planned for that same evening, Zulliger decided to include the Indian "swallow ordeal," never suspecting how well it would work. He explained to the boys gathered in the circle of light around the campfire that money had been taken and that the American Indians had a way of uncovering a thief in such a situation. They passed a cup of water around; each one had to take a big swallow of the water; the man who could not swallow the water was the thief. Then Zulliger proceeded with the "game," expecting no results. The cup moved smoothly, the whole group watching as each boy took the cup, filled his mouth, and swallowed. At one point a boy filled his mouth and struggled to swallow, only to choke on the water and spit it out. Zulliger made nothing of this at the time. After the games, when the boys were getting ready to bed down for the night, the boy who had almost strangled came to Zulliger, produced the stolen money, admitted he had stolen it, and asked to be forgiven and punished.

What does this example "prove"? First, it has its full weight only in the context of the many other examples Zulliger offers. Seen by itself, it could strike the reader as a fantastic coincidence; seen in the fuller context, it is a striking example of several characteristics of the superego: (1) its surprising power over an individual, touching even his ability to swallow; (2) the ratio that exists between this power to control an individual and the isolation of the social "accepting" group from a larger context.

In this example the power of the superego touches the delicate process of swallowing normally. As we have seen, the force of the superego can also affect the delicate process of seeing, perceiving, knowing.[33] Hence it can demand conduct, punish for disobedience by inducing guilt feelings, and at the same time suppress the very insight which could and should contradict and correct such tyranny.

Further, the power to influence the individual is in direct proportion to how much the immediate context of acceptance represents "all of reality." The more a person is cut off and isolated from a larger context, the more powerful will be the influence of the small and limited world which acts as the point of reference for guilt and isolation to produce such guilt experiences.

Apply this to the question of departures from ministry and religious life. When we reflect on the "world" in which those presently departing grew up (seminaries, novitiates, houses of study), we realize that these houses constituted "all of reality," an island of the "really-real" for those living there. Isolated from a larger context in principle and practice, they were institutionalized models of the campfire far from home on a dark night. So they had the power of hydraulically multiplied force to introject values; they could produce intense guilt over trivialities; they could control conduct with the subtleties of a raised eyebrow or a slightly chilled greeting.

As long as this "campfire isolation" can be maintained, the degree to which the superego operates can go unchallenged by the larger context of reality and can go unnoticed by those under its influence. But once this narrowly circumscribed context opens to a larger horizon, the misfit between superego demands punishments and the genuine values at stake emerges in one's consciousness. As we saw in the case of confession, this misfit need not be conceptually articulated; it can remain a nonverbal but deeply intellectual experience of disproportion, discomfort, etc.

Using this frame of reference to understand departures from ministry and religious life, I would say that many, not all, are simply freeing themselves from a superego-dominated way of life. They are growing in genuine value perception and find that they never really embraced the values in question and cannot bring it off now. They find themselves in the situation of others who left the religious way of life at earlier stages, or of those who never entered such a way of life because they recognized that this particular incarnation of Christian values was not what God wanted of them. So they depart. In so far as this is the heart of many departures, we as Christians can only rejoice in the event. It must be affirmed, encouraged, and fostered, just as any other discovery of God's will is the object of our benevolence and beneficence.

Some other priests and religious grow beyond this superego-dominated conduct and in this very process encounter the real values in question and embrace them freely. This particular variation of liberation from the superego is likewise the flowering of genuine Christian freedom; it must also be affirmed, encouraged, and fostered. It should not be mistakenly assumed, however, that the difference between the prior group (those who leave) and the latter group (those who grow to freely accept this particular concrete form of Christian life) is a question of good will. The difference is simply that the prior group are freed from the superego to find their true Christian vocation "in the world"; the latter group are freed from the superego to find their specific Christian vocation, now freely embraced, in their *de facto* state.

The two poles considered here were presented as chemically pure alternatives. It should be clear that they never exist in such undiluted form; the concrete cases will always be a mixture of these various elements. But if this is kept in mind, the foregoing should provide help in understanding some aspects of the question considered. And it should reveal one frame of reference as clearly inadequate: that which would analyze the problem solely in terms of good or bad will, fidelity or infidelity. Understanding the superego shows such a limited set of categories to be a vast oversimplification which can serve neither truth nor Christian freedom. It also helps us realize how much we have to avoid any educational structures which produce conduct by superego rather than decisions of freedom.

Several points discussed in the third and final section of this article have been one-sided; they left many complexities of each question untouched. My goal was to call attention to a dimension of man whose roots can appear to be man's freedom but whose actual source is a compulsion to be accepted and lovable. To make this point with emphasis, many qualifications were deliberately omitted.

This article is meant to be a service to freedom, a service which does not relieve a man of all burdens, but hopes to locate the pain where it should be and where it can function creatively: in the context of love—the goal, reward, and best name of all freedom.

NOTES

1. There is certainly a growing number of theologians who recognize the distinction between the superego and genuine conscience, and the pastoral-practical implications of this distinction. My attention was first called to this distinction in a series of lectures on morality by Bruno Schüller in 1961. It should be noted in this context that not only theologians can be blind to certain dimensions of reality because of their specific and limited concerns. Some psychologists and psychiatrists fail to recognize that besides the superego there is also a genuine preconceptual recognition of moral values—conscience.

2. Some further amplification of these remarks on conscience can be found in the following articles: K. Rahner, "Reflections on the Unity of the Love of Neighbor and the Love of God," *Theological Investigations* 6 (Baltimore, 1969) 231-49; J. Glaser, "Transition between Grace and Sin," THEOLOGICAL STUDIES 29 (1968) 260-74; "Authority Connatural Knowledge, and the Spontaneous Judgment of the Faithful," *ibid.* 29 (1968) 742-51; "Man's Existence: Supernatural Partnership," *ibid.* 30 (1969) 473-88; "The Problem of Theoretical and Practical Moral Knowledge," *American Ecclesiastical Review* 161 (1969) 410-17.

3. Dieter Eicke, "Das Gewissen und das Über-Ich," in *Das Gewissen als Problem* (Darmstadt, 1966) p. 72; cf. also Albert Görres, *Methode und Erfahrung der Psychoanalyse* (Munich, 1965) pp. 166-72.

4. S. Freud, *Gesammelte Werke* 13 (London, 1940ff.) 288.

5. Eicke, *op. cit.,* pp. 97ff; cf. also Görres, *op. cit.*

6. Hans Zulliger, *Umgang mit dem kindlichen Gewissen* (Stuttgart, 1955) p. 30: "The primitive conscience is built on the basis of fear of punishment and a desire to earn love." Eicke, *op. cit.,* p. 79: "The superego has its source in the naked fear of retribution or withdrawal of love; its organizing function serves to protect the ego from the outside world." Melanie Klein, *Das Seelenleben des Kleinkindes und andere Beiträge zur Psychoanalyse* (Stuttgart, 1962) p. 140: "Experience of guilt is inextricably bound up with fear (more exactly, with a specific form of fear, namely, depressive fear); it drives one to reconciliation and reparation; it emerges in the first few months of an infant's life together with the early stages of the superego:" Cf. also Görres, *op. cit.,* p. 170.

7. Felicitas Betz, "Entwicklungsstufen des kindlichen Gewissens," in *Beichte im Zwielicht* (Munich, 1966) p. 33.

8. Cf. Görres, *op. cit.*, p. 166; Eicke, *op. cit.*, pp. 77-80; Zulliger, *op. cit.*, pp. 63ff; Bertha Sommer, "Über neurotische Angst und Schuldgefühle," in Wilhelm Bitter, ed., *Angst und Schuld* (Stuttgart, 1959) p. 44.

9. Eicke, *op. cit.*, p. 80.

10. Zulliger, *op. cit.*, p. 38.

11. Gordon W. Allport, *Becoming* (New Haven, 1966) p. 70.

12. Zulliger, *op. cit.*, pp. 11-45; Betz, *op. cit.*, pp. 29-39.

13. Edmund Bergler, *The Superego* (New York, 1952) p. x. A few pages earlier he says: "To get an approximate idea of the 'benevolence' of inner conscience, one has only to imagine the terms of the relationship between a dictator—any dictator—and an inmate of one of his concentration and extermination camps" (p. viii). Bergler is not given to understatement; but perhaps exaggeration in this question can serve as a needed corrective to emphasize something we have too long overlooked.

14. Klein, *op. cit.*, p. 135.

15. Zulliger, *op. cit.*, pp. 103f., 108f.

16. Besides numerous examples offered by Zulliger, cf. also T. Reik, *Geständniszwang und Strafbedürfnis* (Vienna, 1925); P. Tournier, *Echtes und falsches Schuldgefühl* (Freiburg, 1967).

17. Zulliger, *op. cit.*, pp. 108-24.

18. Görres, *op. cit.*, p. 170.

19. Cf. Tournier, *op. cit.*, p. 57.

20. Görres, *op. cit.*, p. 169. Odier also points out, besides the functions mentioned by Görres, that the superego acts as a censor in dreams, thereby preventing every dream from becoming a nightmare. This is no small service. Cf. Charles Odier, *Les deux sources consciente et inconsciente de la vie morale* (Neuchatel, 1943) p. 28.

21. A. Görres, "Über-Ich," *Lexikon für Theologie und Kirche* 10 (2nd ed.; Freiburg, 1966) 437.

22. Görres, *Methode und Erfahrung*, p. 171.

23. The very titles of their books indicate and emphasize this conviction; cf. notes 16 and 20 above.

24. Melanie Klein, speaking of guilt as naked fear of rejection, says: "With a small child this is always the case; but even with many adults the only factor that changes is that the larger human society takes the place of the father or both parents" (*op. cit.*, p. 135, n. 22). Cf. also Eicke, *op. cit.*, p. 89.

25. Betz, "Entwicklungsstufen," p. 39. Cf. also Marc Oraison, *Was ist Sünde?* (Frankfurt/M., 1968) pp. 28, 63f.; Odier, *op. cit.*, p. 60; Tournier, *op. cit.*, p. 56.

26. I am *not* interested in assigning blame or assessing negligence; I *am* interested in the lesson we should learn from this: theology should be the first discipline to have its mind blown by new discoveries in other fields; it dare not be a slow-learning and suspicious discipline, threatened by whatever findings other sciences discover because this new data reshuffles the traditional deck.

27. Gregory Baum, *Man Becoming* (New York, 1970) pp. 223f.

28. Cf. the two articles mentioned in n. 2: "Transition" and "Man's Existence."

29. J. Maritain, *Range of Reason* (New York, 1952) pp. 66ff. For two other recent authors who share this basic viewpoint and for similar reasons, see Joseph Sikora, "Faith and the First Moral Choice," *Sciences ecclesiastiques,* May-September, 1965, pp. 327-37; Herman Reiners, *Grundintention und sittliches Tun* (Freiburg, 1966) esp. p. 26.

30. Maritain, *op. cit.,* p. 68.

31. I have attempted to explore another thin slice of this question from another point of view in the article "Anonymous Priesthood," *Commonweal* 93, no. 11 (Dec. 11, 1970) 271-74.

32. Zulliger, *op. cit.,* pp. 76ff.

33. *Ibid.,* pp. 138f.

II
PSYCHOLOGICAL PERSPECTIVES

14 Elements of Personality

NEVITT SANFORD

It is important to have a theory of the elements that make up personality and how they function to form character. Although we know a lot about these matters, our information is often gained in pieces without an understanding of how the pieces fit together. Moreover, researchers are specialists who normally use their data within a theory that is restricted to their way of working. Thus, sociologists tend to emphasize the social forces that shape personality. Clinical psychologists play up the strength of the self because they help individuals overcome obstacles to growth and insight. Freud, the great theorist, was preoccupied with psychoanalysis and did not systematize his discoveries. It is the contention of Sanford in this essay * that Freud's theories can be developed into a system that relates the individual to society and accounts for the moral factor in personality.

Personality is always conceived of as a whole embracing parts or elements. Theorists differ in their conceptions of the elements and of how they are organized or patterned. In their search for elements of personality, psychologists have most often started with a general theory of behavior and then transposed to personality whatever units of analysis had been adopted—for example, "habits" for stimulus-response theories, "needs" for functionalist theories, and "regions" for Gestalt theories.

* From *Self and Society* (New York: Atherton Press, 1967), pp. 73-86. Reprinted by permission.

191

Another way to arrive at elements is to start with a conception of the whole personality and then divide it according to its structural articulation. This was the procedure of Freud when he divided the psyche into the three major systems of id, ego, and superego and then propounded a theory according to which the nature of the whole was expressed in the interactions among these systems. As we shall see, none of these systems can be defined without reference to the others and to the whole personality.

Of all proposals for the analysis of personality into basic elements none has been more durable than this scheme of Freud's. This seems to have been due partly to the fact that Freud here committed himself to some notions which numerous writers both before and after him have considered to be of fundamental importance, and partly to the fact that after several revisions he left his formulations of the three systems so vague and incomplete that they could continue to evolve in the hands of his followers. But most important is the fact that psychologists and social scientists have many occasions in their practical work to conceive of whole personalities, and for this purpose better concepts than those of Freud have not as yet come along.

Still, to use these terms in contemporary discussion is to risk failure in communication. They are at once too familiar and too esoteric. Every educated man knows the terms and perhaps must believe he knows what they mean; yet conversations with such men will often reveal that in their minds Freud's concepts are mere stereotypes. For most psychologists, on the other hand, id, ego, and superego carry a great deal of meaning, but these concepts are so closely tied in with one man's system that their use might easily imply more of a commitment to that system than one wishes to make or to be perceived as making. Psychologists by and large do not like being confronted with the meaningless question: "Are you or are you not a believer in Freud?" They accept parts and reject parts of Freud's system and would have to write books to explain just where they stand. It seems safe to say that the great majority of personality psychologists of the older generation make a great deal of use of the concepts of id, ego, and superego. Some do so explicitly, giving them place in their everyday speaking and writing; others use the terms more or less facetiously in talk with colleagues ("My superego would not allow me to work in that area"), having established that their research is concerned with "non-Freudian" matters; still others, probably the majority, keep these concepts alive in the backs of their minds, allowing them to guide thought and action in important matters such as the rearing of children or the maintenance of peace (while using more limited, precise, and specialized concepts in their research), and translating them into everyday language when writing or speaking for general scientific or lay audiences.

The present writer belongs to this last group. It has been quite a few years since I have had occasion to use these terms without definition, as if I were speaking only to the "initiated" or believed everyone was initiated. Yet the concepts have been, and still are, basic in my thought and research in the field of personality. As set down here, they represent my own conceptions of the id, the ego, and the superego—not a summary of what Freud wrote on these subjects.

[Freud's "structural theory," concerning the id, the ego, the superego, and their interactions, was developed comparatively late in his career. His first systematic formulation of the theory appeared in 1923, in his little book *The Ego and the Id*. This book is still the basic source for the "structural theory," although Freud expanded and modified his ideas on this subject in later writings (1926, 1932, 1940). Other expositions of the theory may be found in A. Freud (1936), Hartmann, Kris, and Loewenstein (1946), and Arlow and Brenner (1964).

In the present account I attach considerable importance to the growth of the id, while Freud seems to have regarded the id as "constant," both in its contents and in its modes of operation.

My account of the ego is, in general, in line with what has come to be known as psychoanalytic "ego psychology." A number of psychoanalysts, most notably Hartmann (1958, first published in 1939; 1964) and Hartmann, Kris, and Loewenstein (1946), taking as their point of departure Freud's 1923 essay, have stressed the importance of an "autonomous ego" in the development of personality. Freud, in most of his writings from 1923 on, took the position that at the beginning of life the id comprises the "whole of the mind" and that the ego develops out of the id. According to ego psychology, "apparatuses of the ego," the beginnings of abilities such as perception, memory, and inhibition, are independent of the id at birth—"primary autonomy" (Hartmann, 1964, p. xi) —and may develop, under the impact of external stimuli, independently of determinants in the id and of conflicts between id and ego. More than this, there are ego activities which, though they have their beginnings in the id or in id-ego conflicts, become functionally independent of their origins—"secondary autonomy" (Hartmann, 1964, p. xi).

Freud in one of his last publications (1940) considered that there might be an inborn core of ego processes, but he never gave much attention to activities in Hartmann's (1958) "conflict-free ego sphere." I accept and utilize the concepts of primary and secondary autonomy, and I stress far more than Freud did his idea that the ego has the aim of incorporating the id and the superego within itself. More than Freud, I stress the *contents* of the ego, which are conceived as needs that operate according to the ego's ways. This makes possible some integration of Freudian theory with other psychodynamic theories, such as that of Murray (1938, 1959). The operational definition of ego strength is, of course, a post-Freudian development in psychodynamic theory. It has also been since Freud wrote that the concept of the self has achieved prominence in psychodynamic theory; hence Freud did not attempt to relate self and ego as I do here.

These points of emphasis in the present account are, I believe, consistent with modern "ego psychology," but the major concern here is not with this new look in psychoanalytic theory. I am more concerned with retaining for the id an appropriate place in the structural theory, and in personality theory generally, and with the development of the ego in interaction with the id and the superego. I agree with Hartmann (1958, p. 8) that our need is for a general developmental psychology, and that this will require a *rapprochement* between psychoanalysis and nonanalytic psychology. But whereas ego psychology tends to move psychoanalysis closer to psychology, I am for moving psychology closer to psychoanalysis. (One's perspective here seems to depend on how one was brought up. If one was, so to speak, reared on the early Freud, or met with psychoanalysis by way of medicine and discovered nonanalytic views later, then the autonomous ego processes seem new and interesting. If, on the other hand, one was brought up in academic psychology and then came to psychoanalysis, as was the case with me, it is the most characteristic or distinctive—that is to say, the older—psychoanalytic ideas that seem most seminal.) Ego processes in the conflict-free sphere may have been neglected by psychoanalysts in the past, but they have not been neglected by psychologists nor are they being neglected now. The problem now, as always since Freud appeared on the scene, is how to keep id tendencies and the more primitive processes of the superego fully in the picture. These aspects of personality always tend to be put aside in favor of what is simpler, more observable, more reasonable, and more flattering to man's conception of himself. I should like to cultivate among psychologists, as I would among developing personalities, friendly feelings toward the id. This should favor its incorporation by the ego. Freud remarked, "Where id was, there shall ego be," but he would have been scornful of any shortcuts to this state of affairs. The id is large, complex, and potent; it is the major source of the ego's richness, and its incorporation by the ego is the individual's most important developmental task.

In the case of the superego, my account differs in important respects both from Freud and from contemporary American trends in psychoanalytic theory-making. I have been influenced by the work of Melanie Klein (1948) and hence place special accent on the role of the child's imagination. The concept of *dimensions* of the superego which can be specified at the operational level was never made explicit by Freud.]

In spite of these deviations from Freud, I believe that what follows is essentially Freudian.

The Id

The id is the aggregate of all the individual's most primitive emotional strivings. These strivings appear to be mainly an expression of man's biological inheritance, but one may not simply equate the id and the biological, because other, non-id, processes also appear to be native and it is desirable for theoretical purposes to consider that some of the id's tendencies have been modified under environmental influences.

Impulses of the id are usually unconscious, but this is not a defining characteristic of them; processes of the ego and of the superego may also be unconscious, and impulses of the id may under special circumstances break through into consciousness.

An id impulse may be defined, independently of its origins and independently of the conscious-unconscious dimension, in terms of its modes of operation. Here the essential thing is striving for immediate reduction of tension, in disregard of consequences for itself or for other impulses. Tension is subjectively painful, the reduction of tension pleasurable; the id operates in accordance with the *pleasure principle,* the organism's general tendency to avoid pain and to seek pleasure.

The organism comes into the world equipped with some mechanisms by which tension may be discharged immediately through motor activity. But not all tension can be so readily managed. Often the reduction of tension depends upon there being made available some real object—for example, food, breast, mother. With repetitions, objects which have been instrumental in reducing tension become associated in the child's mind with tension reduction, so that later when tension is built up there will be produced an image of the object which is capable of reducing it. Thus an id impulse is not pure energy, with no information; very early in the infant's life, after only a minimum of learning has occurred, such an impulse is guided by a memory image of a satisfying object or circumstance. Thus it is appropriate to speak of an id impulse as a *wish,* and to speak of the process by which the individual seeks to reduce tension merely by producing an image as a *wish fulfillment.* This is the stuff of dreams, fantasies, hallucinations, and delusions. An important characteristic of the id is that it does not distinguish between memory images and perceptions of actual objects but acts toward the former just as if they were present in reality.

Unhappily for the id, wishing does not alter facts. The degree to which tensions may be reduced by the production of wish-fulfilling images, or by reflex activity in the musculature, is severely limited. For survival and reproduction, and for the maintenance and growth of the individual, other, more effective means for reducing tension have to be developed—hence the ego, that structure of the personality which deals with realities.

Although the id does not change with time in its basic modes of operation, it nevertheless develops as the infant grows into the adult. With physical and physiological growth, more physical energy is made available to the id, and it is lent increasing power through the maturation of the motor apparatus. With time, more and more different kinds of objects are utilized in the reduction of tension, and hence through association and memory there is expansion of the domain of wish-fulfilling imagery. At the same time, there is an increase in the strength and variety of stimuli that generate tensions; fresh internal stimuli come with physical and physiological growth, most strikingly perhaps with the bodily changes of puberty, while external stimuli are brought to bear by the training and discipline which are necessary to the child's socialization. More tension, more frustration, more wishes—thus it is that the id of any individual after infancy has content of considerable breadth and complexity. And this content may vary from one individual to another, depending on the course of their upbringing. "Infantile sexuality"—that is, the child's inclination to find pleasure in the stimulation of various zones of the body and from interaction with a diversity of objects (including persons)—and various forms of aggression, rejection, dependence, passivity, rebelliousness, lust for power, and the like may be ascribed to the id, *provided* that these impulses operate in ways that are characteristic of the id. Id impulses are demanding, irrational, asocial, uncontrolled. When frustrated they seek gratification in imagination. In disregard of logic or reason or reality the id creates and usually inhabits a dream world of its own.

Despite their considerable potency id impulses can be controlled by the ego. In childhood, the ego gains and maintains its control mainly by repression—making the impulses unconscious and keeping them so. When repressed, id impulses are cut off from the maturing effects of experience. As we saw in Chapter 2, the development of the ego makes possible a relaxation of repression and the gradual absorption of the id by the ego; nevertheless, in adolescents and most adults some repressed impulses remain and may be recognized by their infantile or childish quality. Repressed impulses sometimes make brief appearances at the fringe of consciousness, and sometimes through "slips" they find some expression in overt action; in these cases they are experienced as foreign or alien to the self.

The id is a system, a whole whose parts are related. Owing

to its internal connectedness its energy may be readily displaced from one object to another. And, as we shall see, the whole system may be affected by changes in the ego or superego.

The Ego

The most essential function of the ego is to bring about reduction of tension when the primitive devices of the id fail to do so. The process in the id that produces a memory image of an object capable of reducing a particular tension was called by Freud the *primary process*. The primary process serves to give direction to the individual's striving, but it can reduce tension but little, if at all. What is required is a plan of action by which an actual object, with which the individual may interact, is discovered or produced. The process by which such plans are devised and carried out is the *secondary process*. This process operates in accordance with the *reality principle;* it takes into account circumstances that exist in the real world and seeks to govern activity in such a way as to attain in the long run a maximum satisfaction of needs.

In order for the secondary process to operate there must be some delay of energy discharge until a suitable object has been found, and this means that the ego must have some capacity to tolerate tension. This, indeed, is the most essential, as it is the distinguishing, characteristic of the ego. Given this capacity, the ego is able to bring into the service of its tension-reducing activities the basic abilities of the organism—perception, memory, thinking, and action. The beginnings of these abilities—potentialities for them—are given through biological inheritance, and to some extent they develop through maturation, but their development is mainly a product of their interactions with the environment. With experience and with training the individual's powers of discrimination become finer, and his store of usable memory images is vastly enlarged—most notably through the acquisition of a language. These developments make possible a great increase in the ability to think, for the individual is now in a position to select from a vast array of external stimuli and internal images those that are relevant to a given problem, and with language at hand he is able to deal with problems vicariously without being forced to try a variety of overt actions. There is improved judgment of the realities of a situation, and an increased ability to make decisions respecting alternative courses of action. At the same time, the individual acquires increased skill in the use of his muscles, and the ability to carry out complex patterns of movement. In short, with experience and training the ego's efforts to deal with the external environment in such a way as to obtain gratification of needs become increasingly intelligent and efficient.

But to reduce tension through accommodation to or mastery of the environment is not the only task of the ego. It must also deal with internal problems. As pointed out earlier, numerous needs or strivings operate in the personality at the same time. In order that each of these may receive its due the ego undertakes to establish schedules and hierarchies of importance. But despite its best efforts, conflicts arise, and the ego has the further task of finding ways to resolve them. The most common type of conflict, and the type that has the most far-reaching implications for the development of personality, is conflict between impulses of the id and the demands of the superego, the primitive conscience that strives for moral perfection. When id impulses are permitted direct gratification, even when there is conscious pleasure in fantasies of gratification, the superego punishes the ego by arousing guilt feelings. The pangs of conscience, as is well known, may be extremely painful. The ego seeks to avoid them, both by managing impulses in ways that are tolerable to the superego and by softening the superego itself—making it more reasonable and tolerant. Here the ego exercises its important integrative or synthesizing functions. Its ultimate aim, actually, is to incorporate the id and the superego within itself, becoming the sole channel for the expression of impulse and taking over the task of maintaining behavior on a suitably high moral level. This state of affairs is approached in the ideally developed individual. But often things do not go very smoothly. Impulses from the id may increase in intensity and threaten to explode into action; this arouses in the ego extreme anxiety lest the superego punish it, with severity to match the primitiveness of the outbreak of the id. In critical situations of this kind—and we have seen that they are common in childhood—the ego resorts to maneuvers that deny, falsify, or distort reality and hence impair development in the long run. These maneuvers, of which repression is an example, are the defensive mechanisms of the ego. Typically, they operate unconsciously.

In a sense, the sense that has been mainly discussed so far, the ego is a collection of mechanisms. It remains to be pointed out that the ego is a system, a structure having a boundary, contents, and organization. The contents of the ego are mainly needs, strivings whose goals have been set in accordance with reality and ᵥ hich proceed in accordance with the ego's way of doing things. The same kind of needs—that is, needs having the same general goal—may appear either in the id or in the ego, or in both. Consider, for example, the need for dominance. In the id there will be striving for immediate and absolute power, and fantasies of omnipotence. The ego's version of this same general need will be a temperate desire to influence people and an integrated set of techniques for attaining to and maintaining positions of leadership. In time the ego comes to embrace a great variety of particular needs, together with the cognitive schemata and action patterns that have been built up as means for satisfying them. These contents of the ego constitute a coherent unity; they are organized according to the principle that in so far as possible each need should have its due.

The ego's success in obtaining satisfaction of needs is what makes possible its control over id impulses. In the beginning, according to Freud's theory, the ego has no energy of its own. But "it commends itself to the id," as an agency for the reduction of tension, and thus energy becomes available to its mechanisms. As the ego develops and becomes more and more effective, the gains to the organism from the activities of the ego become increasingly greater than the gains that can be achieved by the id, and some of the energy inherent in the id is transferred to the ego. After this development has proceeded for a time a stage is reached at which the ego, which may function as a unit, commands more energy than is embodied in a typical id impulse; and hence the id may be confronted by a stronger force. A man who has a job, a home, friends, a place in the community, satisfying interests, is not likely to sacrifice or endanger this pattern of life, or the personality structure which underlies it, through the indulgence of some momentary passion.

The ego structure *is* endangered by each uncontrolled expression of a primitive impulse. Even if the impulse is gratified and there are not painful consequences, the ego's way of proceeding is called into question. More likely, the expression of the impulse will evoke an outraged reaction from parents or other authorities, or from their internal representative, the superego, and these agencies then act as if they would be happy to relieve the ego of all its controlling functions.

By and large, however, and particularly in childhood, external authorities and the superego are helpful to the ego in its task of controlling impulses. These agencies have force aplenty at their disposal and to some extent they represent that reality which is the most essential ally of the ego.

The ego is also lent strength by the fact that it becomes the object of self-esteem. Among the id tendencies which gradually become absorbed by the ego is primary narcissism or elemental self-love. If the ego is to find satisfaction for this need, a reasonable relationship must be developed between self-satisfaction and actual worth, as reality requires. Here the ego is helped immeasurably by the love and approval of parents and others. Almost inevitably, it seems, the ego makes a connection between these rewards and "good"—that is to say, effectively controlling and organizing—behavior; thus its regard for itself is supported, as it is shaped, by the regard of others. The fact that it may take pride in its accomplishments, and experience self-respect when it is functioning well and shame when it is not, is a circumstance highly favorable to the ego's higher activities. It is a condition necessary to the individual's ability to love other people.

"Ego strength" is a variable that has loomed large in empirical studies of personality. Fundamentally, the strength of the ego is a matter of how much energy is available to it—how much energy, if it came to that, could be set in opposition to an id impulse or to demands of the superego; and this depends upon the structure of the ego—that is, the degree of differentiation and elaboration of its mechanisms for reducing tension. The stronger the ego, the more effectively it will perform its functions; hence indices of ego strength are measures of the adequacy of performance in various spheres of activity. Accuracy of perception, objectivity, judgment, common sense, tolerance of ambiguity, self-insight, initiative, persistence, competence in solving problems, tolerance of frustration, flexibility of adaptation, ability to learn from experience, capacity for logical thinking, planning ability and foresight, ability to stick to promises and to carry out resolutions—these and many other measures of performance are indices of the degree of the ego's strength.

We have spoken of self-esteem and self-respect. Is the "self" that is esteemed and respected the same as the ego system, or do we have to deal here with a different concept? I take the position here that the self, as this concept is most commonly used in contemporary psychology, is not the same as the ego. The self as most commonly conceived is a content of awareness, an aspect of human experience. Using the subjective reports of individuals, it has been possible for psychologists to distinguish numerous variables of content and organization in this self of awareness: different features that are ascribed to it, how they are patterned, how this pattern is valued, how consistent it is over time, and so on. Since the ego, as we have seen, contains processes that are unconscious, ego and self are clearly not coextensive. More than this, what enters into the conscious self may have sources other than the ego; the individual may experience, as part of his self, processes belonging to the id or to the superego. The term "inferred self" has sometimes been used to stand for all the processes that underlie the self of experience.

Although self and ego are separate, there is clearly much overlapping of the two. Of the three systems discussed here the ego is closest to consciousness and in closest touch with the external world. When the ego is carrying out some of its major functions, such as resolving or making a decision, the individual has the impression that his self is determining what he will do. Also, tendencies from the id and from the superego which are excluded from the ego are likely to be excluded by the individual from his conception of his self. Nevertheless, by maintaining the distinction that has been made, we may avail ourselves of the explanatory power of the larger conception of ego and at the same time use self as a special explanatory concept. The individual seeks to build up and to maintain a consistent conception of his self; to do this he must behave in a way that is consistent with this conception, and therefore behavior depends to some extent upon the self-conception. The individual may make a distinction in consciousness between his self as it is and his self as he would like it to be. This ideal self may embody many of the positive goals of the ego, and thus have a large influence in determining the directions of behavior.

The Superego

The superego is a hypothetical construct invented to explain such phenomena as self-blame, self-abasement, feelings of guilt, depression, suicidal thoughts, anxiety in the absence of actual threats, oversubmissiveness to external authority, night terrors, compulsive strivings to achieve high moral standards. Most essential in this conception is the notion of an agency inside the personality that punishes antisocial actions or thoughts, and that rewards what by the prevailing social code would be called virtuous. The superego is usually more or less directly opposed to the id. Although it does not necessarily seek to inhibit all impulses, it reserves the right to decide which are acceptable or consistent with its aim of maintaining a high level of morality. Needs of the ego are also often opposed by the superego, for what may be suited to reality may nevertheless fail to conform with the superego's standards.

Although the superego is most essentially a punishing or goading force, we may ascribe content and structure to it. Individuals differ with respect to the kinds of needs or drives that the superego seeks most forcibly to suppress, and with respect to the kinds of ideals that it favors. There are also individual variations in the kinds of punishments and pressures that the superego has at its disposal. The content of this agency may be observed to resemble the ideals and values of the social group in which the individual is brought up; to some extent at least the superego's content changes as the social group changes—for example, when a nation goes to war.

There is ample evidence that the child's parents have the major role in transmitting to him the standards of the community.

They have the power to reward desirable behavior and to punish the undesirable, and, given the child's natural desire for approval and fear of punishment, the assimilation of what the parents stand for seems to follow readily enough—through simple conditioning and through the child's own basic needs; the superego, like the ego, derives its energy from the id.

It is important to note that the superego develops in childhood and that it always has the features of a childish construction. It is less like the ego than like the id, with which it shares the state of being alien to the ego. The superego operates automatically, inflexibly, unreasonably. It does not make fine distinctions, or argue points with the id or the ego; it simply says, with a tone of finality, "No," or "Do this." The parents that are internalized are not the "real" parents but the idealized or omnipotent parents that the childish mind conceives. And, similarly, the child does not adopt as a model the actual behavior of the parents; rather he is guided by his conception of what they would have him do. Although the superego commonly appears in consciousness, as conscience or as an ideal of perfection, it may also operate unconsciously, giving rise to vague anxiety or to behavior that is self-defeating or self-punishing.

As a construction of the child's mind the superego cannot be merely a copy of prevailing ideas and values as represented by the parents. It may often be noted that an individual makes stronger demands upon himself than his parents do, and that he is more severe with himself than external authorities are wont to be. The explanation appears to be that the severity of demandingness of the superego in action depends not alone upon how much energy has been channeled into it, but upon the strength of the impulses which it undertakes to counter (and upon how large a role the ego is able to play in this struggle).

This close relationship between the superego and the id has led some writers to suppose that the rudiments of a superego exist within the personality before there has been any opportunity for the incorporation of parental prohibitions and sanctions. The infant, who has only begun to distinguish between what is inside and what is outside his own body, may have occasion to fear his own impulses. When frustrated and in a mood to tear things up he may suppose that the things he would like to do might very well happen to him. According to this theory, the child who has night-mares in which animals are threatening to eat him up has not necessarily had any experience with devouring animals or even been told about them; all that is required for the generation of this internal punishing agency is that the child's own wish to bite should have become sufficiently intense. This theory seems well designed to explain anxiety and irrational fears in children who have been gently handled; it may also explain why a misbehaving child, whose impulses have got beyond his own control, welcomes the restraining—even the punishing—hand of the adult. Such a child prefers the actual punishment of the more or less reasonable parent to the punishment that he may give himself in his imagina-tion. The presence of this internal punishing force is an addi-tional reason why the child may happily internalize the prohibi-tions and sanctions that society offers, and thus build up a social superego on the basis of, or in the place of, the archaic one.

The superego may differ from one individual to another not only in the quality of its contents, as already indicated, but also along several dimensions. The dimension of *strength* refers to the amount of energy that is available, to how much force might be set in opposition to strivings of the id or ego. Strength may be inferred from the amount of anxiety that is experienced, from what the ego is forced to do in order to avoid anxiety, or from the severity of the punishments that are administered—for example, as feelings of guilt. The *breadth* or *strictness* of the superego refers to the number of different kinds of impulsive strivings that will arouse inhibiting or punitive actions and to the variety of positive goals in whose interest pressure is exerted. *Rigidity* is the tendency to act in an *all-or-nothing* manner. The superego is always rigid as compared with the ego, but some superegos are far more rigid than others. A movie actress may for years conduct her life as if she had no conscience at all and then suddenly claim that she has "found God" and begin behaving in an altogether conven-tionally moral way. The contrast would be with a superego that acts to keep the individual steadily on a more or less moral course, with occasional fallings from grace.

The superego may be more or less *internalized,* in the sense that it can operate without reinforcement by an external authority. In early childhood it often seems that only the parent can prevent the full gratification of certain impulses; a little later the child will inhibit himself, perhaps call himself bad, when the parent is present, but go on his own way otherwise; in time, as socialization proceeds, the child can inhibit his impulses without help from the parent's physical presence. Before this final stage is reached, various stages of partial internalization are passed through. Not all adults achieve complete internalization of the superego, and they may be partially characterized by noting the stage at which development ceased. Signs of an immature superego would be "social anxiety"—that is, inordinate worry about what other people might think, relative freedom from self-reproach until one is "found out" and then a severe but short-lived attack or bad conscience, a high degree of susceptibility to pressures from an immediately present social group.

A superego that has been more or less firmly internalized may later be got rid of or rendered virtually ineffective. It may be repressed by the combined forces of the ego and the id and kept in that state by a succession of delinquent or antisocial actions. Or it may be replaced by external authorities. A superego that has been based mainly upon fear and hatred of the parents remains as a pain-inducing foreign body within the personality; the ego may succeed in rendering it inoperative by permitting an external agency to take over its functions, just as the archaic superego is replaced by a social one.

A further index to be considered in the study of the superego is the degree of its *integration with the ego*. When this integration has occurred, the moral precepts of the superego are in keeping with the individual's own best judgment, and they may be supported by the ego's energy. It is sometimes argued that only under this condition can the superego be said to be genuinely internalized. It may be argued that this is the *sine qua non* for dependably moral behavior, yet apparently the superego may be fully inside the personality, and may endure there, without this integration's having occurred. Certainly this seems to be the state of affairs in depression and in those patterns of behavior dominated by compulsion. When integration with the ego has occurred, the superego is not so much internalized and durable as it is well on its way to being absorbed by the ego. Enlightened conscience, the noblest edifice of the personality, is fully in the domain of the ego.

The same may be said of character, when this is understood as the ability and the inclination to conduct oneself in accordance with principles.

It was stated that the superego may be repressed. The reference was to the superego as a whole. This agency, like the ego, is an organized totality. In inhibiting or punishing or goading the id or the ego, it acts as a unit, and it is as a unit that it may be repressed, bribed, assuaged, or evaded.

Let us now emphasize that, although the id, the ego, and the superego may be distinguished conceptually, they are but elements in a larger system, the personality, and that no one of them is ever functionally independent of the others. Both the ego and the superego derive their energy from the id. The supply of energy is not unlimited; and this means that the strength of one of these agencies varies with the strength of the others. It is particularly important to note that the strength of the ego is not absolute, but relative to the tasks that it has to perform. When it is largely taken up with defensive operations, we cannot expect of it a high level of performance in its dealings with problems set by the external environment.

Interrelations of Id, Ego, and Superego

The relations among the three systems are intimate and complicated. Each may be in conflict with, and each may be allied with, each of the others. Conflict, and id-ego and ego-superego integrations, have been noted. The alliance of the id and the superego deserves a special word. This alliance may be inferred from cases in which extreme aggression is directed against the ego, as in suicide, or, more commonly, from cases in which primitive aggressive needs appear to gain satisfaction through attacks on people who are considered to be immoral.

Patterns of relationship among the id, the ego, and the superego offer a basis for the formulation of the central core of the personality. But they by no means suffice to describe all of the individual's characteristic ways of interacting with his environment, or all of the ways in which one personality might differ from another.

In their attempts to describe personality, psychologists have most often started with the observation of behavior. Noting consistency of behavior in varying situations, and sticking as close to the facts as possible, they have conceived of traits or dispositions of personality that would account for observed consistency. Many diverse personality characteristics have thus been conceptualized, and there is no reason to believe that the possibilities of this approach have been exhausted. Personality is a vast and intricate structure built up from simple beginnings. An appropriate conception of its developed state might be that of a relatively stable inner core of relatively few basic elements, surrounded by a multiplicity of tendencies that are in closer contact with the environment. It is possible to be reasonably systematic in dealing conceptually with these outward aspects of personality. One approach is to consider that even in his most superficial interactions with the environment the individual's behavior is guided by needs, in whose service a great variety of abilities and objects are utilized. Observing behavior over a period of time, one may readily infer the existence, as personality characteristics, of: (a) needs (motives, strivings); (b) attachments to objects (things, people, ideas) or to activities that consistently satisfy needs, and rejections of objects that frustrate: hence sentiments, interests, positive and negative attitudes, tastes, preferences, fears; (c) modes and styles of overt behavior, and (d) cognitive schema, beliefs, plans that further satisfaction of needs.

This approach may be brought into line with the Freudian scheme in the following way. Most of the needs—with their integrated modes and objects—which operate in immediate contact with the environment are in the ego; they can be understood as more particular ways in which this agency carries out its functions. Things are not always so simple, however. We have seen that both the id and the superego may also be expressed more or less directly in behavior, and, not uncommonly, what we encounter at the surface are resultants from the interactions of the three central systems. The competence of the individual, as displayed for example in academic or scholarly achievement, in leadership, or in effective social relations, should not be regarded as nothing more nor less than an expression of a strong ego; the id and the superego are usually also involved in competence, though now they will have become integrated with the ego. Here as elsewhere, however, we have to recognize that the same, or at least very similar, patterns of behavior may have different sources within the personality. For example, self-assertion may be a straightforward expression of the ego's needs, or it may be an overcompensation for an inner sense of weakness. As the id, the ego, and the superego develop and carry out their functions in interaction one with another, there comes to intervene between the core and the surface of personality a vast aggregate of subsystems and secondary processes. To determine the dynamic sources of surface manifestations requires not only the accurate observation of these but the investigation of large areas of the person by special techniques.

15 Superego and Conscience

GREGORY ZILBOORG, M.D.

As we look back on the early days of psychoanalysis, we see that Freud's discoveries were an enormous burst of light on the workings of the human mind, especially its unconscious elements. Freud applied his basic ideas to many fields, including morals and religion. He considered religion to be a wish-fulfillment and morality, obedience to the superego developed in the child by his parents, particularly the father. Thus there developed the notion that if a religious belief or symbol could be explained psychologically, it did not have religious significance. Zilboorg challenges this assumption.* Using the sacrament of communion as an illustration, he points out that the intention of the believer must be considered. He also affirms that conscience is more than superego; it is an element that may be related to the ego and free to brood about one's self in relation to conduct.

It was assigned to me to talk to you on the origin and structure of the superego. Ever since Freud presented his hypothesis on the topography of the human personality or, to be more precise, the topography of the psychic apparatus, volumes have been written on the ego; but the superego, as a rule, appears to be taken for granted, almost casually. I, for one, do not know of anything in the psychoanalytic

* From *Ministry and Medicine in Human Relations,* edited by Iago Galdstone, M.D. (New York: International Universities Press, Inc., 1955), pp. 100-118. Reprinted with permission.

literature written with any detail on the superego; I find in this literature very little indeed which would serve me as a guide for a comprehensive presentation of the origin, the derivation and the structure of that which we call the superego.

I was given considerable time to prepare myself for this presentation, yet, I feel that what I have to say is little if anything more than an improvisation which is based, of course, on my clinical experience and some knowledge of the theory of psychoanalysis.

I must warn you that these improvisations are in the nature of the hypothesis which was formulated by Freud; they should not be taken as postulates of some esoteric, psychoanalytical eternal truth.

There is a tendency to assume that that which is explained in terms of psychological dynamics is explained psychologically, and that by virtue of this explanation its existence in the broad spiritual sense is thereby denied and duly refuted.

In other words, if you say that this and this stems from the superego, and the superego stems from the early relationship which you had to your father, then the whole question of morality in the religious sense becomes superfluous, and the spiritual validity of your faith is duly questioned or even refuted. And should you happen to be a man of the cloth and wear a clerical collar and understand and believe in the origin of the superego in the Freudian sense, then you must be a double hypocrite.

This attitude, though widespread, is not really tenable for many reasons. Take as an example, and I trust you will realize that it is not a sacrilegious suggestion at all, take as an example the Sacrament of Communion. Long before Freud, long before psychiatry came into existence, a sacramental ceremonial was established in which the communicant came to kneel and to receive the bread and the wine. By virtue of this, the communicant felt, and was vouchsafed to feel by the Church, that he became one with Christ—identical with the Son of God whose body and blood he received; yet at the same time he remained himself, his own mortal being.

Let us now translate this experience into terms of the psychoanalytic Freudian hypothesis. This hypothesis and its terminology is concerned with what might be called the psychological pathway, by means of which the experience (in our case the experience of the Sacrament of Communion) is psychologically performed; that is to say, it is concerned with psychological mechanisms. Therefore, the psychoanalytical hypothesis would say that the act of Communion is an act of oral incorporation of the Son of God, who is represented by the consecrated bread and wine—His body and His blood. And the person who incorporates the bread and the wine becomes that which the bread and the wine is to him in a transcendental way.

On the other hand, if you read the classical Freudian descriptions of severe depressions, of suicidal drives, if you study the dreams of those neurotics and psychotics formerly known as melancholics, if you listen to those people talk and you know how to understand the inner content of their thoughts, you will be struck at once by the fact that all those people unconsciously, unwittingly, feel as if they had swallowed, incorporated a person whom they loved as well as hated. They feel (unconsciously) that that person lives in them, and all the love which the bearer of this incorporated person ever felt is there in its fullness. But it is at the same time overcast by a terrific hatred, and that hatred they turn against the incorporated individual within themselves and therefore against themselves. Thus the murder of the incorporated person appears clinically as suicide.

Now if it is, and it does seem to be, true that the individual who commits suicide is a victim of unconscious oral incorporation, that this oral incorporation, psychologically performed, resulted directly in a suicide, are we then to consider this particular psychopathological phenomenon parallel, if not identical, with the phenomenon (psychological) of incorporation of the body and the blood of Christ? And if this is so, are we to consider the Sacrament of Communion a pagan, psychotic, "manic-depressive" mechanism? And nothing else?

I, for one, struggled with this problem for a long time, and I finally came to the rather simple conclusion that this concordistic attitude of taking psychoanalytic mechanisms and pointing out how they "concord" with religious experiences, psychoses, phenomena of social action, and crises, is methodologically untenable, clinically unjustifiable, and scientifically unpardonable.

One and the same hand can use one and the same set of muscles to give a friendly handshake and to choke a person. Now, no one would engage in the folly of considering certain muscles friendly and others murderous. The muscles in themselves and the brachial plexus which superintend the motor activity of those muscles know of no friendliness and of no murderousness. It is the intent that produces the murderous or the friendly gesture. I don't see why we do not assume the same methodological and evaluative attitude toward psychological mechanisms. All mechanisms, be they physiological or psychological (I prefer to call them biopsychological) are neutral as far as true values are concerned. The activity of these mechanisms reflects the psychological life processes of the given individual. These psychological life processes may not be confused with the individual's spiritual, moral and religious life. These psychological mechanisms are as neutral from the standpoint of higher values as any of the physiological mechanisms in the human body. It is only the goal, the direction, the application and the deeper meaning of these things, of the relation of man to man, of man to himself and to God, that have a moral meaning. The psychological mechanisms involved in the formation and expression of this deeper meaning may be exactly the same as those involved in the formation of other feelings which have nothing to do with these problems. Psychological mechanisms are no less neutral in this respect than the physics and chemistry which we find operating in the case of a fracture or diabetes.

With this rather lengthy but, to my way of thinking, very necessary introduction, I can now come to grips with the issues under the heading of superego.

It was in 1922, and again in 1924, that Freud formulated and amplified the hypothesis of the superego. This idea was not entirely novel. As a matter of fact, about one hundred years before Freud (it was in 1818, I believe), the neurologist-psychiatrist Heinroth, describing the various inner struggles of certain patients, postulated the existence of something within us which is "over-us," "super-us." Heinroth called it the *Uberuns*.

Freud himself, as soon as he began to study dreams, just at the close of the past century, found that certain feelings, thoughts and trends within us are subject to a spontaneous check which he called "censorship"—something that does not permit certain things to come out into the open, into consciousness; in dreams the censorship works hard obscuring and symbolizing those things which it wants to delete. Incidentally, I must emphasize that Freud used the term "censorship." The early translators of Freud mistakenly used the word "censor," which Freud never used. Freud's term was *die Zensur* which in English means censorship—a much more meaningful designation of an inner agency which prevents one from knowing or doing things than the anthropomorphic term, "the censor."

It was about 1898-1899 that Freud first observed that inner and unconscious struggle between the "I want" and "I ought," or "I wish" and "I oughtn't to," but it was not until almost a quarter of a century later that he found he was best able to visualize the human personality (biologist that he was) as an architectural structure. Freud himself used the word "structure." Without assigning to this structure any anatomical seat (in the brain or elsewhere), and without assigning to this topographical unit any physiological function, Freud looked upon it as a series of psychological agencies which work simultaneously with and against each other within the one human body, within the one individual personality.

I want to use a diagram which Freud's great and romantic disciple Ferenczi used to great advantage.

In a nutshell the hypothesis is this:

At birth the human individual is but a bundle of biological drives, "instinctual drives," Freud called them. They are both organismic needs and quasi-psychological trends; they are not subject to direct voluntary management; they may and may not appear purposive; if they do, they may be considered purposive from the teleological point of view but not from the point of view of an act performed by a self-aware individual. These trends or drives are a mass of strivings so arranged that we medical men find it difficult to understand them. Their chief characteristic is this:

This mass is a bundle of reactions, of needs, of strivings, of wants—all primitive, direct, elemental. There is no conception of what is logical in this bundle, opposites are confused and fused; "No" and "Yes" mean the same thing; "because" and "despite" don't find themselves in contradiction to each other. And what is most striking: this bundle of drives does not know what time means. This is something terribly difficult to conceive of, is it not—

this timelessness which reigns in the original bundle of strivings and drives. We who are biologically minded, whose thinking is determined by concepts of physics and history, we always deal with reactions which we measure in terms of time.

Well, I must repeat, in this original, primitive bundle that is man just born or about to be born, time does not exist. This bundle we continue to carry with us and within us throughout our lives, but what happened the day before yesterday and twenty years and fifty years ago are happenings which live side by side as if they were contemporaneous, or rather, simultaneous happenings. In other words, if at the age of sixty, a fifty-year-old element of that area breaks into our conscious life, it will come up with an emotional freshness and intensity as if it happened yesterday.

This was a totally new and revolutionary discovery in the field of psychobiology, this "undifferentiated state" in which neither time, nor logic, nor any conscious purposiveness exists, in which opposites coexist without conflict. This singular mixture of opposites is reflected in certain peculiarities of the human language. In a special and rather neat article, Freud pointed out how in the Egyptian or in the Latin languages opposites are denoted at times by one and the same word. In Latin, for instance, *altus* means both high and deep. In our own language the colloquial "being blessed" may connote both a benediction and curse.

This is characteristic of the original, elemental reservoir of human strivings, undifferentiated during the earliest stages of the human being's biopsychological existence. This reservoir, this bundle, Freud named the "id," a name he borrowed from Groddeck, the German internist who wrote a semipoetical work called *The Book of the Id (Das Buch vom Es)*.

On the diagram is represented: A bundle of biopsychological forces, in which are intermingled all human instincts, comes into contact with the outside world; from the moment the blanket is put around the newborn baby, the outer world establishes unfriendly contact with the id. The child at once begins to develop a protective attitude, so as to protect itself from the outer impacts and then deal with them, correlate them, do something with them, master them.

This outer world has become known in psychoanalytic litera-

ture under the philosophic term "reality," a term which has frequently caused some semantic confusion. Let us call it the outside
world.

At the area of contact with the outside world, a protective
area develops around the body of the id; this area is like an outer
core around the id, like a psychological skin which, in order to
do its job, must draw upon the energies of the id. It does two
things: it receives stimuli from the outside world and registers
them, and it protects itself against the id's breaking through and
"making a mess of things." In other words, this area around the

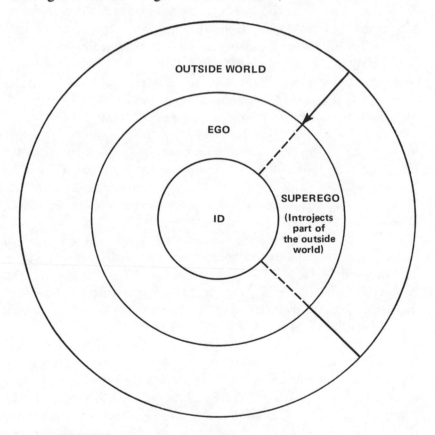

id becomes a sort of functioning organ. It deals with reality, and
masters it; it bridles to a certain extent the id itself, modulates it,
takes the energies from the id and makes them orderly. It learns
what "yesterday" is; what "tomorrow" is. It knows what "Don't-

be-a-fool and don't-do-this" means. It learns to be reasonable and rational. It knows what hot and cold is and when to blow on either or both. It learns what "I-want-to—but-I've-got-to-wait-till-later" means. It is just the opposite of the child who does not know what "tomorrow" is and wants what it wants when it wants it.

This particular part of ourselves Freud has called the "ego." When I say: *I* feel, I feel with the ego (on diagram) and not with the "id" (on diagram). As you can see, the id is never in contact with reality, and it never knows what reality is. The id is a reservoir of constantly sustained fire within us, which is kept in quiet abeyance, but with the embers always hot. But the id never breaks out into reality except in severe pathological conditions. Only the ego deals with reality.

The ego is the only part of the human personality, of the psychic apparatus, which deals with perceptions coming from without and with the apperceptions coming from within, in accordance with all the laws of the biopsychological needs of human existence.

Now an interesting thing occurs. There are people around the child; they are a part of reality—the father, the mother. Thus operative as a part of reality, is the family, the father and the mother, perhaps the nurse, the teacher, who all stand watch over the youngster. Gently or roughly, insidiously and persistently, they try to impose their authority, which means their standards, on the child. I shall limit myself merely to mentioning in passing the more or less known anthropological hypotheses which Freud propounded in *Totem and Taboo,* nor am I going to do more than mention the details of the development and of the passing of the oedipus complex, which Freud considered of paramount importance in the formation of superego.

Let us then look at this. The parents, any authority which is close to the child, are a part of that harsh reality which the child does not at first like at all. Let us say that child plays with a toy; the nurse stands watch. The nurse does not want the child to touch a certain sharp object; she says, "No" and puts the toy to one side. For a moment the child desists; then he goes back to it and the nurse again says, "No"—ever so gently. A moment finally comes when the child quickly removes its own hand from the toy the moment he hears the nurse's "No."

Someone calls the nurse out of the room. When she comes back she may find the child has returned to the forbidden toy. However, from now on as long as the nurse is present the child shows no interest in the toy, and as soon as she leaves the room, the child returns to the toy. This is a very interesting stage in the development of the human personality: at this stage, the physical presence of the inhibiting agent seems to be absolutely necessary for the child to do what is required of him. The ego of the child accepts the authority only as long as that authority is actually, physically present.

Finally a time comes when the child "learns" sufficiently, and he refrains from touching the forbidden object even when the authority is out of the room. To put it in another way: the child accepts the presence of the nurse and of her demand, even when the nurse is absent. It is as if the child has made the nurse's demands a part of his own.

Soon we might notice that should the little brother come over and try to touch the sharp toy, the little child after a while says "No" just as the nurse did. The child has thus become the nurse, as far as this demand is concerned. The child does not say: "The nurse does not want you to do it." The child says: "Don't do it," or "I don't want you to do it," or "It is bad to do it." The underlying psychological process may be presented as a gradual incorporation by and into the child of the outside demands. The ego of the child accepts the demands and makes them his very own.

Thus gradually, unconsciously, many social, cultural demands become a part of the ego, and this particular part of the ego demands of our whole ego that we do the right thing. It stands there with its "don'ts" and "do's" and "be careful" and "you ought to be ashamed of yourself" and "go to sleep" and "don't talk so much or so loud." This demanding part of the ego stands *over* the whole ego. It is the superego. In the Freudian sense, it is the precipitate of all the demands and commands and particularly of the taboos connected with what is known as "the oedipus complex."

This is the superego. You will note on the diagram something very striking: The superego is a part of the ego, and like the ego it is in direct contact with the id. The id you will remember is the reservoir of instinctual drives. Some of these drives, for reasons of constitution or accident, might prove to be extremely strong. This is of great clinical importance, because the stronger the drives, the harsher the superego which feeds on them. A child may have a mild father, realistically a kind person. But should the child for some reason or other possess intense sadistic drives, those drives will become involved in the formation of the superego, and he will develop the harshest superego in the world.

The complexity with which the superego feeds on the id has not yet been sufficiently studied. This is how matters stand. Dr. Leo Alexander, for instance, spoke of the superego and of the id. He used the Freudian term superego, in the widespread but erroneous sense whereby "superego" is equated to "conscience" as if the two were one and the same thing. Freud himself used these terms interchangeably; in *The Ego and the Id,* Freud refers to the superego as conscience; he also calls it "the ideal of the ego" and "the ideal ego" (*das Idealich*). In other words, the person has the feeling of what he is, ideally (the ideal ego), of what ideal he would like to pursue, what he would like to become, ideally (the ego ideal), and he is also aware of what the demands are that are made upon him and force him to restrict his ego and his id (the superego).

All this may be a little confusing to you. I will tell you this, and I speak with authority when I tell you, that it is a little confusing to me too. The reason for this confusion is not far to seek. First of all, take a look at the diagram, and you will at once see that neither the ego nor the superego possesses any energy charges of their own in the real sense of the word. The source of their energy, and the quality too, come from the unbridled, anarchic mass called the id, which is bottled up by the ego and the superego. Should the id break through into the ego and take possession of the latter, one becomes a pervert, a criminal, a psychotic; should those very same forces break through into the superego, we would see a truly cruel superego, violent, sadistic. It sounds confusing, does it not, when we describe conscience in terms of unconscionable sadism? Whatever terms we may find appropriate for our description, the ego and the superego are endowed with psychobiological energy, with strength, with dynamic power, which is related to reality and/or to its internalized demands, and which follows the regular psychophysiological circuit: stimulation, perception and response.

But when we speak of the ego ideal, or the ideal ego, we are speaking of contemplative, not always conscious, in fact, mostly unconscious aspirations. They may have a certain amount of emotional coloring, but they do not seem to be activated in the direction of immediate and spontaneous activity. They behave always indirectly, and always in the name of and through the superego.

The man who almost twenty-five years ago first noticed that there was a possible discrepancy here was Franz Alexander, and it is a pity that since that time his interests have run to other things. In his *Psychoanalysis and the Total Personality* he makes a rather casual but potent remark to the effect that he is rather inclined to believe that the ego ideal belongs to the ego, and not to the superego. This said, he dropped the matter, which is not a very good thing to do with ego ideals, but that is what he did.

A rather serious methodological error was committed by many in the consideration of the whole problem. The ego is partly unconscious and partly conscious, but the superego is primarily unconscious. The paradoxical thing is that the superego is not always good and virtuous. It is this fact which made Alexander speak once of the possibility of a criminal superego in certain criminals. By "criminal superego" he meant a superego formed by incorporated images of criminal parents, or criminal environment. And in saying this Alexander, by implication, although quite obviously, dropped the concept of conscience out of the superego.

It is perhaps of more than passing interest that both Charles Odier in Switzerland and myself, who occupied themselves with this problem for some years, were pupils of Alexander in his Berlin days, not his Chicago days.

In 1945 Charles Odier wrote a book, the title of which was a paraphrase of one of Bergson's: *The Two Sources, Conscious and Unconscious, of Morality and Religion*. In this book Odier points out the fundamental methodological error which was perpetuated by many psychoanalytical theoreticians since Freud formulated his hypothesis of the topography of the personality: this error being on the one hand the insistence on equating superego with conscience, and on the other hand equating both with the ego ideal and the ideal ego.

Conscience ought to be considered in terms and with understanding of the older, traditional meaning of the word *conscientia*. (See Paul Tillich's excellent reference to this; it is related to "being conscious.") Whatever vices or values human beings possess and whatever inhibitions they follow in obedience to the superego, values, problems of morality and conscience are in the final analysis problems of being "conscious of." That of which we are unconscious is not subject either to voluntary control or to spontaneous, direct, rational evaluation.

We must think of the superego as a psychobiological unit as much as the ego of which it is a part, and as much as the id. And it is the superego and not conscience—much as it manifests itself under the guise of conscience, as if it were a conscience— that appears in quasi-pathological and pathological conditions, in depressions and anxiety states. The superego, if it is properly integrated with the ego, and if together with the ego it is integrated in a regulatory way with the id, remains an unconscious part of the psychic apparatus which is biological in nature; and, of course, the superego does bear the earmarks of cultural influences too, for it came originally from the environment which was incorporated, and this environment with all its imagos—of father, mother, nurse, teacher, school—presents all the mores and traditions and culture as a whole.

It is here that the sociologist could be of great help, if only he would remember that the superego is unconscious of those values which we consider as a part of morality. Two groups of values might be recognized: (1) the group which has to do with mores, with tradition, with the socialization of our behavior are partly ego reactions, utilitarian, pragmatic in nature, and partly superego reactions; (2) those values which properly belong to morality are "seated" elsewhere. Here I seem to cease being a psychologist, and I am on the threshold of the ethico-religious field.

This, as a matter of fact, is the gist of what Leo Alexander said, except that he created a sort of dichotomy when he said that the religious leader works on the spiritual level while the psychiatrist works on the psychological level. He thus seems to take the spiritual away, as it were, organically from the individual human being. I doubt whether this dichotomy could be considered valid without reservations. The spiritual level cannot be taken away from the human being, any more than you can take the human mind away from him and leave him still a human being.

Values are indivisible from the rest of the psychic apparatus

—yet they may not be molten together with this apparatus, even though they must use the latter to express themselves. The secret of a possible true cooperation between the religious leader and the psychiatrist will be uncovered not when they come to a verbal compromise as to who will do what and when and in what manner, but when they each come to understand in each given act of man the differential characteristics between superego and conscience; between the psychobiological aspects of man and that source of morality of which Paul Tillich speaks so movingly and yet so simply. That source is fundamentally transcendental and therefore not identifiable by any psychobiological means.

As you see, I have failed to fulfill my assignment, for I was unable to describe to you the structure of the superego. The superego, I am inclined to believe, is fundamentally amorphous. The superego is fundamentally everything to everybody. It serves every master it meets: the superego obeys (it is) the teacher, and the imagined father and mother, and the bad servant and the good stranger. The superego is a product of incorporation without choice and at times, almost always, without pure love. There is a lot of hatred in the superego; there is a lot of intolerance; there is little if any charity.

As a matter of fact, almost twelve or thirteen centuries before Freud there was a man who recognized the sadistic role the superego can play and thus make a perverted masochist of man. It was, I believe, Pope Alexander III who specifically proclaimed that anyone who tried to torture himself and derives pleasure from this torture in anticipation of sainthood should be anathemized.

The various forms of flagellations, the cruelty of the Inquisition, the murderous Holy Wars demonstrate beyond any doubt how far a superego may be removed from conscience, and how far removed its practices may be from charity and sainthood even if these practices appear in the guise of religious faith, piety and fealty to God. To put it a little more sharply: Yes, there may be a strong superego in a Christian which has nothing in common with Christian conscience.

This is the point at which the psychiatrist and the religious leader not only can come together but must get together, because here we touch at the very source of the conflict between us as scientists and as adherents of a religious faith. It is by deliberations such as these that one might come to some true light as far as our basic error is concerned. The psychiatrist's error is that he thinks that because he can explain man's behavior psychologically there is no morality outside psychoanalytic, scientific dialectics. But, please note, the parish priest, the theologian also makes similar mistakes when he seems to assume that if one knows how a thing works biologically and psychologically, then the workings belong no longer in the field of spiritual values. The error is committed by the psychoanalyst to be sure, but the burden of sin by concurrence lies on the shoulders of a number of religious leaders. No, scientific analysis is not an impure hand of depravity, and in no way does its sagacious touch impair either the purity or the depth of spiritual values.

I know of only one or two books written on the subject thus far. And recently the French journal *L'Esprit* has done a magnificent job of presenting the issues involved in a special volume. Unfortunately, this volume has neither been translated nor reviewed in English. It represents what *L'Esprit* calls a global synthesis of spiritual and moral issues in relation to modern medicine and psychiatry. Clinicians, physiologists, pathologists of all shades and schools took part in this synthesis, or rather in offering the material which the skillful and very thoughtful editors put together extremely well.

In this volume of *L'Esprit* it comes out clearly how little we understand one another. We really have no quarrel. We work in different fields, and we produce a number of semantic and conceptual difficulties. These difficulties come from the clinician who tends to speak of spiritual things in physiological terms, and from the religious leader who hates to hear of the physiological aspects of spiritual values, and who seems to wish to express so many psychobiological phenomena only in theological, moralistic terms.

16 Guilt and Guilt Feelings

Martin Buber

That psychotherapy can relieve a person's guilt feelings so that he may function within tolerable limits in ordinary daily affairs has been demonstrated in many cases. But can psychotherapy help a person understand and accept existential guilt? Buber answers that question by showing that one must first go beyond the conceptions of Freud and Jung to a recognition that there is real guilt that is different from—and yet intertwined with—neurotic guilt.* The therapist is not expected to go with the patient into this realm unless the doctor understands that he is changing his role and relationship. Needless to say, the conscience associated with real guilt is different from the one that produces guilt feelings.

The boundaries set by the psychotherapist's method do not, in any case, suffice to explain the negative or indifferent attitude that psychotherapy has so long taken toward the ontic character of guilt. The history of modern psychology shows us that here deeper motives are at work that have also contributed to the genesis and development of the methods. The two clearest examples of it are provided us by the two most noteworthy representatives of this intellectual tendency: Freud and Jung.

Freud, a great, late-born apostle of the enlightenment, presented the naturalism [1] of the enlightenment with a scientific sys-

* From *The Knowledge of Man,* translated by Maurice Friedman (London: George Allen and Unwin, Ltd., 1965), pp. 123-136. Reprinted with permission.

tem and thereby with a second flowering. As Freud himself recognized with complete clarity,[2] the struggle against all metaphysical and religious teachings of the existence of an absolute and of the possibility of a relation of the human person to it had a great share in the development of psychoanalytic theory. As a result of this basic attitude, guilt was simply not allowed to acquire an ontic character; it had to be derived from the transgression against ancient and modern taboos, against parental and social tribunals. The feeling of guilt was now to be understood as essentially only the consequence of dread of punishment and censure by this tribunal, as the consequence of the child's fear of 'loss of love' or, at times when it was a question of imaginary guilt, as a 'need for punishment' of a libidinal nature, as 'moral masochism'[3] which is complemented by the sadism of the superego. 'The first renunciation of instinctual gratification', Freud stated in 1924, 'is enforced by external powers, and it is this that creates morality which expresses itself in conscience and exacts a further renunciation of instinct.'[4]

Of an entirely different, indeed diametrically opposed, nature is the teaching of Carl Jung, whom one can describe as a mystic of a modern, psychological type of solipsism. The mystical and religio-mystical conceptions that Freud despised are for Jung the most important subject of his study; but they are such merely as 'projections' of the psyche, not as indications of something extrapsychic that the psyche meets. For Freud the structure of the psyche culminates in the superego, which represents, with its censory function, only the authoritative tribunals of family and society; for Jung it culminates or rather is grounded in the self, which is 'individuality in its highest meaning'[5] and forms 'the most immediate experience of the divine which can be grasped at all psychologically'.[6] Jung does not recognize at all any relationship between the individual soul and another existing being which oversteps the limits of the psychic. But to this must be added the fact that the integration of evil as the unification of the opposites in the psyche is put forward as a central motif in the process of 'individuation', of the "realization of self".[7] Seen from this vantage point, there is in Jung's panpsychism, as in Freud's materialism, no place for guilt in the ontological sense, unless it be in the relationship of man to himself— that is, as failure in the process of individuation. In fact, in the whole great work of Jung we learn nothing of guilt as a reality in the relation between the human person and the world entrusted to him in his life.

With the other psychoanalytic doctrines it stands, in general, much the same. Almost everyone who seriously concerns himself with the problem of guilt proceeds to derive the guilt feelings that are met with in analysis from hidden elements, to trace them back to such elements, to unmask them as such. One seeks the powerful repressions in the unconscious as those that hide behind the phenomena of illness, but not also the live connection the image of which has remained in the living memory, time and again admonishing, attacking, tormenting, and, after each submersion in the river of no-longer-thinking-about-that, returning and taking up its work anew.

A man stands before us who, through acting or failing to act, has burdened himself with a guilt or has taken part in a community guilt, and now, after years or decades is again and again visited by the memory of his guilt. Nothing of the genesis of his illness is concealed from him if he is only willing no longer to conceal from himself the guilt character of that active or passive occurrence. What takes possession of him ever again has nothing to do with any parental or social reprimand, and if he does not have to fear an earthly retribution and does not believe in a heavenly one, no court, no punishing power exists that can make him anxious. Here rules the one penetrating insight—the one insight capable of penetrating into the impossibility of recovering the original point of departure and the irreparability of what has been done, and that means the real insight into the irreversibility of lived time, a fact that shows itself unmistakably in the starkest of all human perspectives, that concerning one's own death. From no standpoint is time perceived so like a torrent as from the vision of the self in guilt. Swept along in this torrent, the bearer of guilt is visited by the shudder of identity with himself. I, he comes to know, I, who have become another, am the same.

I have seen three important and, to me, dear men fall into long illnesses from their failing to stand the test in the days of an acute community guilt. The share of the psychogenic element in the illness could hardly be estimated, but its action was unmistakable. One of them refused to acknowledge his self-contradiction before the court of his spirit. The second resisted recognizing as serious a slight error he remembered that was attached to a very serious chain of circumstances. The third, however, would not let himself be forgiven by God for the blunder of a moment because he did not forgive himself. It now seems to me that all three needed and lacked competent helpers.

The psychotherapist into whose field of vision such manifestations of guilt enter in all their forcefulness can no longer imagine that he is able to do justice to his task as doctor of guilt-ridden men merely through the removal of guilt feelings. Here a limit is set to the tendency to derive guilt from the taboos of primeval society. The psychologist who sees what is here to be seen must be struck by the idea that guilt does not exist because a taboo exists to which one fails to give obedience, but rather that taboo and the placing of taboo have been made possible only through the fact that the leaders of early communities knew and made use of a primal fact of man as man—the fact that man can become guilty and know it.

Existential guilt—that is, guilt that a person has taken on himself as a person and in a personal situation—cannot be comprehended through such categories of analytical science as 're-pression' and 'becoming conscious'. The bearer of guilt of whom I speak remembers it again and again by himself and in sufficient measure. Not seldom, certainly, he attempts to evade it—not the remembered fact, however, but its depths as existential guilt—until the truth of this depth overwhelms him and time is now perceived by him as a torrent.

Can the doctor of souls function here as helper, beyond professional custom and correct methods? May he do so? Is he shown at times another and higher therapeutic goal than the familiar one? Can and may he try his strength, not with conscious or unconscious, founded or unfounded guilt feelings, but with the self-manifesting existential guilt itself? Can he allow himself to recognize, from this standpoint, that healing in this case means something other than the customary, and what it means in this case?

The doctor who confronts the effects on the guilty man of an existential guilt must proceed in all seriousness from the situation in which the act of guilt has taken place. Existential guilt occurs when someone injures an order of the human world whose foundations he knows and recognizes as those of his own existence and of all common human existence. The doctor who confronts such a guilt in the living memory of his patient must enter into that situation; he must lay his hand in the wound of the order and learn: this concerns you. But then it may strike him that the orientation of the psychologist and the treatment of the therapist have changed unawares and that if he wishes to persist as a healer he must take upon himself a burden he had not expected to bear.

One could protest that an existential guilt is only the exception and that it is not proper to frighten the already overburdened therapist with the image of such borderline cases. But what I call existential guilt is only an intensification of what is found in some measure wherever an authentic guilt feeling burns, and the authentic guilt feeling is very often inextricably mingled with the problematic, the 'neurotic', the 'groundless'. The therapist's methods, naturally, do not willingly concern themselves with the authentic guilt feeling which, in general, is of a strictly personal character and does not easily allow itself to be imprisoned in general propositions. It lies essentially nearer to the doctrine and practice to occupy itself with the effects of repressed childhood wishes or youthful lusts gone astray, than with the inner consequences of a man's betrayal of his friend or his cause. And for the patient it is a great relief to be diverted from this authentic guilt feeling to an unambiguous neurotic one that, favoured within this category by the school of his doctor, allows itself to be discovered in the microcosmos of his dreams or in the stream of his free associations. To all this the genuine doctor of souls stands opposed with the postulative awareness that he should act here as at once bound and unbound. He does not, of course, desist from any of his methods, which have in fact become adaptable. But where, as here, he becomes aware of a reality between man and man, between man and the world, a reality inaccessible to any of the psychological categories, he recognizes the limits that are set here for his methods and recognizes that the goal of healing has been transformed in this case because the context of the sickness, the place of the sickness in being, has been transformed. If the therapist recognizes this, then all that he is obliged to do becomes more difficult, much more difficult—and all becomes more real, radically real.

I shall clarify this statement through the example of a life history that I have already made use of before, although all too briefly.[8] I select it from among those at my disposal because I was a witness, sometimes more distant, sometimes nearer, to the happenings, and I have followed their sequence. The life course I have in mind is that of a woman—let us call her Melanie—of more intellectual than truly spiritual gifts, with a scientific education, but without the capacity for independent mastery of her knowledge. Melanie possessed a remarkable talent for good comradeship which expressed itself, at least from her side, in more or less erotically tinged friendships that left unsatisfied her impetuous rather than passionate need for love. She made the acquaintance of a man who was on the point of marriage with another, strikingly ugly, but remarkable woman. Melanie succeeded without difficulty in breaking up the engagement and marrying the man. Her rival tried to kill herself. Melanie soon afterwards accused her, certainly unjustly, of feigning her attempt at suicide. After a few years Melanie herself was supplanted by another woman. Soon Melanie fell ill with a neurosis linked with disturbances of the vision. To friends who took her in at the time, she confessed her guilt without glossing over the fact that it had arisen not out of a passion, but out of a fixed will.

Later she gave herself into the care of a well-known psychoanalyst. This man was able to liberate her in a short while from her feelings of disappointment and guilt and to bring her to the conviction that she was a 'genius of friendship' and would find in this sphere the compensation that was due her. The conversion succeeded, and Melanie devoted herself to a rich sociality which she experienced as a world of friendship. In contrast to this, she associated in general with the men with whom she had to deal in her professional 'welfare work' not as persons needing her understanding and even her consolation, but as objects to be seen through and directed by her. The guilt feelings were no longer in evidence; the apparatus that had been installed in place of the paining and admonishing heart functioned in model fashion.

Now that is certainly no extraordinary fate. We recognize again the all too usual distress of human action and suffering, and there can be no talk here of existential guilt in the great sense of the term. And yet, the guilt feeling that grew up at that time in the illness and that so fused with the illness that no one could say which of the two was the cause and which the effect, had throughout an authentic character. With the silencing of the guilt feeling there disappeared for Melanie the possibility of reconciliation through a newly won genuine relationship to her environment in which her best qualities could at the same time unfold. The price paid for the annihilation of the sting was the final annihilation of the chance to become the being that this created person was destined to become through her highest disposition.

Again one may raise the objection that it cannot be the affair of the psychotherapist to concern himself about this kind of thing. His task is to investigate malady and to heal it, or rather to help it toward healing, and it is just this that the doctor who had been called in had done. But here lies an important problem. Stated generally, one can formulate it somewhat as follows: Shall a man who is called upon to help another in a specific manner merely give the help for which he is summoned or shall he also give the other help that, according to the doctor's knowledge of him, this man objectively needs?

However, what is the meaning here of the help that one objectively needs? Clearly this, that his being follows other laws than his consciousness. But also quite other ones than his 'unconscious'. The unconscious is still far less concerned than the conscious about whether the essence of this man thrives. Essence—by this I mean that for which a person is peculiarly intended, what he is called to become. The conscious, with its planning and its weighing, concerns itself with it only occasionally; the unconscious, with its wishes and contradictions, hardly ever. Those are great moments of existence when a man discovers his essence or rediscovers it on a higher plane; when he decides and decides anew to become what he is and, as one who is becoming this, to establish a genuine relation to the world; when he heroically maintains his discovery and decision against his everyday consciousness and against his unconscious. Should the helper, can the helper, may the helper now enter into an alliance with the essence of him who summoned him, across this person's conscious and unconscious will, provided that he has really reliably recognized the need of this essence? Is something of this sort at all his office? Can it be his office? Particularly where the helping profession is so exactly circumscribed by principles and methods as in modern psychotherapy? Does not the danger threaten here of a pseudo-intuitive dilettantism that dissolves all fixed norms?

An important psychologist and doctor of our time, the late Viktor von Weizsaecker, laid down, in very precise language, a sober admonition on this point. There the 'treatment of the essential in man' is simply excluded from the realm of psychotherapy. 'Just the final destiny of man', he writes, 'must not be the subject of therapy.' [9] And my lay insight must concur with this declaration. But there is an exceptional case—the case where the glance of the doctor, the perceiving glance that makes him a doctor and to whom all his methods stand in a serving relation, extends into the sphere of the essence, where he perceives essential lapse and essential need. There, to be sure, it is still denied him to treat 'the essential' in his patients, but he may and should guide it to where an essential help of the self, a help till now neither willed nor anticipated, can begin. It is neither given the therapist nor allowed to him to indicate a way that leads onward from here. But from the watchtower to which the patient has been conducted, he can manage to see a way that is right for him and that he can walk, a way that it is not granted the doctor to see. For at this high station all becomes personal in the strictest sense.

The psychotherapist is no pastor of souls and no substitute for one. It is never his task to mediate a salvation; his task is always only to further a healing. But it is not merely incumbent upon him to interest himself in that need of the patient which has become symptomatically manifest in his sickness—to interest himself in it as far as the analysis conducted according to the therapist's method discloses to him the genesis of this illness. That need is also confided to him which first allows itself to be recognized in the immediacy of the partnership between the patient who is having recourse to the doctor and the doctor who is concerned about the recovery of the patient—although occasionally this need remains veiled, even then.

I have already pointed to the fact that the doctor, in order to be able to do this adequately, must for the time being lift himself off the firm ground of principles and methods on which he has learned to walk. One must not, of course, understand this to mean that he now soars in the free ether of an unrestrained 'intuition'. Now too, and only now really, he is obliged to think consistently and to work exactly. And if he may now surrender himself to a more direct vision, it can still only be one that realizes its individual norms in each of its insights—norms that cannot be translated into general propositions. In this sphere of action, too, even though it seems left to his independent direction, the man of the intellectual profession learns that a true work is an affair of a listening obedience.

But in order that the therapist be able to do this, he must recognize just one thing steadfastly and recognize it ever again: there exists real guilt, fundamentally different from all the anxiety-induced bugbears that are generated in the cavern of the unconscious. Personal guilt, whose reality some schools of psychoanalysis contest and others ignore, does not permit itself to be reduced to the trespass against a powerful taboo.

We cannot now content ourselves, however, with allowing this knowledge, which was long under a ban, to be conveyed to us by this or that tradition which is holy to us. It must arise anew from the historical and biographical self-experience of the generation living today. We who are living today know in what measure we have become historically and biographically guilty. That is no feeling and no sum of feelings. It is, no matter how manifoldly concealed and denied, a real knowledge about a reality. Under the schooling of this knowledge, which is becoming ever more irresistible, we learn anew that guilt exists.

In order to understand this properly we must call to mind one fact, no accessory fact but the basic one. Each man stands in an objective relationship to others; the totality of this relationship constitutes his life as one that factuality participates in the being of the world. It is this relationship, in fact, that first makes it at all possible for him to expand his environment (*Umwelt*) into a world (*Welt*). It is his share in the human order of being, the share for which he bears responsibility. An objective relationship in which two men stand to one another can rise, by means of the existential participation of the two, to a personal relation; it can be merely tolerated; it can be neglected; it can be injured. Injuring a relationship means that at this place the human order of being is injured. No one other than he who inflicted the wound can heal it. He who knows the fact of his guilt and is a helper can help him try to heal the wound.

One last clarification is still necessary. When the therapist recognizes an existential guilt of his patient, he cannot—that we have seen—show him the way to the world, which the latter must rather seek and find as his own personal law. The doctor can only conduct him to the point from which he can glimpse his personal way or at least its beginning. But in order that the doctor shall be able to do this, he must also know about the general nature of the way, common to all great acts of conscience, and about the connection that exists between the nature of existential guilt and the nature of this way.

In order not to fall into any error here, however, we must bear in mind that there are three different spheres in which the reconciliation of guilt can fulfil itself and between which noteworthy relations often establish themselves. Only one of these spheres, that which we shall designate as the middle one, directly concerns the therapist whom I have in mind.

The first sphere is that of the law of the society. The action begins here with the demand, actually made or latent, which society places on the guilty man according to its laws. The event of fulfilment is called confession of guilt. It is followed by penalty and indemnification. With this sphere the therapist, naturally, has nothing to do. As doctor, an opinion is not even accorded him as to whether the demand of the society is right or not. His patient, the guilty man, may be guilty toward the society or he may not be; its judgment over him may be just or it may not be. This does not concern the doctor as doctor; he is incompetent here. In his relation to the patient this problematic theme can find no admission, with the exception of the unavoidable occupation with the anxiety of the patient in the face of the punishments, the censure, the boycotts of society.

But the third and highest sphere, that of faith, also cannot be his affair. Here the action commences within the relation between the guilty man and his God and remains therein. It is likewise consummated in three events which correspond to the three of the first sphere, but are connected with each other in an entirely different manner. These are the confessions of sin, repentance, and penance in its various forms. The doctor as such may not touch on this sphere even when he and the patient stand in the same community of faith. Here no man can speak unless it be one whom the guilty man acknowledges as a hearer and speaker who represents the transcendence believed in by the guilty man. Also when the therapist encounters the problem of faith in the anxiety concerning divine punishment that is disclosed in the patient's analysis, he cannot interfere here—even if he possesses great spiritual gifts—without falling into a dangerous dilettantism.

The middle sphere, as we have said, is one to the sight of which the therapist may lead—up to it, but no farther. This sphere, about which he must *know* for this purpose, we may call that of conscience, with a qualification which I shall shortly discuss. The action demanded by the conscience also fulfils itself in three events, which I call self-illumination, perseverance, and reconciliation, and which I shall define more exactly still.

Conscience means to us the capacity and tendency of man radically to distinguish between those of his past and future actions which should be approved and those which should be disapproved. The disapproval, in general, receives far stronger emotional stress, whereas the approval of past actions at times passes over with shocking ease into a most questionable self-satisfaction. Conscience can, naturally, distinguish and if necessary condemn in such a manner not merely deeds but also omissions, not merely decisions but also failures to decide, indeed even images and wishes that have just arisen or are remembered.

In order to understand this capacity and tendency more exactly, one must bear in mind that among all living beings known to us man alone is able to set at a distance not only his environment but also himself. As a result, he becomes for himself a detached object about which he can not only 'reflect', but which he can, from time to time, confirm as well as condemn. The content of conscience is in many ways determined, of course, by the commands and prohibitions of the society to which its bearer belongs or those of the tradition of faith to which he is bound. But conscience itself cannot be understood as an introjection of either the one authority or the other, neither ontogenetically nor phylogenetically. The table of shalts and shalt-nots under which this man has grown up and lives determines only the conceptions which prevail in the realm of the conscience, but not its existence itself, which is grounded in just that distancing and distinguishing—primal qualities of the human race. The more or less hidden criteria that the conscience employs in its acceptances and rejections only rarely fully coincide with a standard received from the society or community. Connected with that is the fact that the guilt feeling can hardly ever be wholly traced to a transgression against a taboo of a family or of society. The totality of the order that a man knows to be injured or injurable by him transcends to some degree the totality of the parental and social taboos that bind him. The depth of the guilt feeling is not seldom connected with just that part of the guilt that cannot be ascribed to the taboo-offence, hence with the existential guilt.

The qualification of which I spoke, accordingly, is that our subject is the relation of the conscience to existential guilt. Its relation to the trespassing of taboos concerns us here only in so far as a guilty man understands this trespassing more strongly or weakly as real existential guilt which arises out of his being and for which he cannot take responsibility without being responsible to his relationship to his own being.

The vulgar conscience that knows admirably well how to torment and harass, but cannot arrive at the ground and abyss of guilt, is incapable, to be sure, of summoning to such responsibility. For this summoning a greater conscience is needed, one that has become wholly personal, one that does not shy away from the glance into the depths and that already in admonishing envisages the way that leads across it. But this in no way means that this personal conscience is reserved for some type of 'higher' man. This conscience is possessed by every simple man who gathers himself into himself in order to venture the breakthrough out of the entanglement in guilt. And it is a great, not yet sufficiently recognized, task of education to elevate the conscience from its lower common form to conscience-vision and conscience-courage. For it is innate to the conscience of man that it can elevate itself.

From what has been said it already follows with sufficient clarity that the primeval concept of conscience, if only it is understood as a dynamic one rather than as a static, judging one, is more realistic than the modern structural concept of the superego. The concept of the superego attains only an orienting significance and one, moreover, which easily orients the novice falsely.

If we now wish to speak of actions in the sphere of conscience in this high and strict sense, we do not mean thereby the well-known synthesis out of the internalization of censure, torment, and punishment that one customarily regards as the proper factual content of conscience—that pressuring and oppressing influence of an inner high court on an 'ego' that is more or less subject to it. Rather this tormenting complex has, for our consideration, only the character of an angelic—demonic intermezzo on which the high dramatic or tragicomic act of neurosis may follow, and the whole affair may end with a therapy that passes for successful. What concerns us here is another possibility, whether it be the true process of healing after the neurosis, or whether it be without a neurosis preceding it. It is that possible moment when the whole person who has become awake and unafraid ascends from the anguishing lowland of the conscience to its heights and independently masters the material delivered to him by it.

From this position a man can undertake the threefold action to which I have referred: first, to illuminate the darkness that still weaves itself about the guilt despite all previous action of the conscience—not to illuminate it with spotlights but with a broad and enduring wave of light; second, to persevere, no matter how high he may have ascended in his present life above that station of guilt—to persevere in that newly won humble knowledge of the identity of the present person with the person of that time; and third, in his place and according to his capacity, in the given historical and biographical situations, to restore the order-of-being injured by him through the relation of an active devotion to the world—for the wounds of the order-of-being can be healed in infinitely many other places than those at which they were inflicted.

In order that this may succeed in that measure that is at all attainable by this man, he must gather the forces and elements of his being and ever again protect the unity that is thus won from the cleavage and contradiction that threaten it. For, to quote myself, one cannot do evil with his whole soul, one can do good only with the whole soul.[10] What one must wrest from himself, first, is not yet the good; only when he has first attained his own self does the good thrive through him.

NOTES

1. Freud himself described psychoanalysts as 'incorrigible mechanists and materialists' (Sigmund Freud, 'Psycho-analysis and Telepathy', in *The Standard Edition of the Complete Psychological Works of Sigmund Freud,* XVIII (London: Hogarth Press, 1955), pp. 177-193.

2. See, for example, 'A Philosophy of Life', ch. 7 in Freud, *New Introductory Lectures on Psycho-Analysis* (London: Hogarth Press; New York: W. W. Norton, 1933).

3. Freud, 'The Economic Problem in Masochism', in *Collected Papers* (London: Hogarth Press, 1948), pp. 255-268.

4. *Ibid.,* p. 267.

5. Carl Jung, *Von den Wurzeln des Bewusstseins,* Psychologische Abhandlungen, IX (Zurich: Rascher, 1954), pp. 296f.

6. *Ibid.,* p. 300.

7. Carl Jung, *Von der Wurzeln des Bewusstseins,* Psychologische Abhandlungen, IX (Zurich: Rascher, 1954). For a fuller analysis of Jung, see Martin Buber, *Eclipse of God,* Section 2, 'Religion and Modern Thinking', and 'Supplement: Reply to C. G. Jung', trans. by Maurice Friedman.

8. See my Preface to Hans Trüb's posthumous work, *Heilung ans der Begegnung: Eine Auseinandersetzung mit der Psychologic C. G. Jungs,* ed. by Ernst Michel and Arie Sborowitz (Stuttgart: Ernst Klett Verlag, 1952). This Preface appears in English as 'Healing through Meeting' in Martin Buber, *Pointing the Way,* pp. 93-97.

9. *Herztliche-Fragen* (1934), p. 9.

10. Martin Buber, *Good and Evil: Two Interpretations* (New York: Charles Scribner's Sons, paperback, 1961), p. 130. British edition, *Images of Good and Evil* (London: Routledge, 1952).

17 The Development of Moral Values in Children

E. MANSELL PATTISON, M.D.

In spite of the differences among psychologists about conscience, there is a general recognition that the self is defined to some extent by society and that the conscious self (ego) has a sphere of activity of its own rather than being merely a referee between the id and the superego. Sometimes called ego drives, this part of the mind is concerned to make sense out of experience. Properly directed, a person's self-awareness will continue to interact with the ready-made values and belief system of his social milieu to form and reform personal moral convictions. Pattison traces these new trends in child development and applies them to conscience.* His careful definition of four kinds of guilt, for example, is helpful because each has a different source and process of resolution.

O ne of the traditional roles of the church has been that of definer, sustainer, and enforcer of moral values. In primitive societies religious institutions represent the major social embodiment of the morality of the culture. The same was true for much of the history of Christianity in relation to Western society. That cannot be said of Christianity today, for there have been serious and far-reaching challenges to the claim of Christian religion as a moral agency.

Sigmund Freud, father of psychoanalysis and our "psychodynamic" age, may rightly be given credit (some would say

* From *Pastoral Psychology*, February, 1969, pp. 14-30. Reprinted by permission.

238

blame!) for the reevaluation of the moral claims of Christianity which have taken place in our century. Freud has sometimes been accused of being unconcerned with morality, although Philip Rieff devoted an entire book, *Freud: The Mind of the Moralist* to the demonstration of the centrality of moral issues in Freud's thought. Freud was dissatisfied with traditional and conventional morality. He was looking for a more viable, more consistent, more humane morality; a morality that was not mere ethnocentric assertion.

Freud noted that religious morality was not necessarily constructive, but was often oppressive and destructive. This view is in part correct and needs little documentation. For example, in *The True Believer* Eric Hoffer trenchantly describes the inhumanities perpetrated by the believer who uses his religious morality to justify his own means to a personal end. The negative judgment which Freud placed on Christian religion as a moral agency was supported by his observation of religious persons' behavior; namely, that persons who affirm the strongest moral convictions may act in ways which totally contradict what they affirm. Recent research evidence has substantiated and extended Freud's clinical observations.

A few illustrations must suffice. In *Christian Beliefs and Anti-Semitism* sociologists Glock and Stark reported a strong relationship between Christian belief and ethnic prejudice. In other studies I have found that Christian belief is highly correlated with anti-humanitarianism, authoritarian personality, high degrees of interpersonal hostility, punitive social attitudes, etc.[13,16,17] Studies of children have similarly demonstrated that there is little correlation between the moral precepts they have been taught in their church and how they behave in both test situations and real life situations.[1,7] It is beyond the scope of this paper to deal with the complexities of these studies here. But I do wish to indicate that there is a large quantity of research that calls into question the value of religious education in producing children who will consequently act according to the moral principles presented in their religious education.

In this paper I plan to: (1) discuss the definition of moral values, (2) present an analysis of various psychological dynamics of morality, (3) present an analysis of the dynamics of guilt and forgiveness, and (4) suggest some applications of these concepts to the role of the church as a moral agency.

I
TOWARD A DEFINITION OF MORALITY

Morality has been taken to be an individual matter by both psychology and theology. For Freud, morality was the superego—the inculcation of parental prohibitions. In theology, morality was the response to conscience, the still small voice of feeling guilty. In both instances, morality was a question of guilt. However, this individual emphasis on morality overlooks the fact that morality is as much a social issue as a personal one. The late anthropologist Clyde Kluckhohn states the issue clearly:[8]

There is the need for a moral order. Human life is necessarily a moral life precisely because it is a social life, and in the case of the human animal the minimum requirements for predictability of social behavior that will insure some stability and continuity are not taken care of automatically by biologically inherited instincts, as in the case with the bees and the ants. Hence there must be generally accepted standards of conduct, and these values are more compelling if they are invested with divine authority and continually symbolized in rites that appeal to the senses.

No society, then, can function without a specific morality. The relationship of morality to culture is further extended by sociologist Philip Rieff: [18]

To speak of a moral culture would be redundant. Every culture has two main functions: (1) to organize the moral demands men make upon themselves into a system of symbols that make men intelligible and trustworthy; (2) to organize the expressive remissions by which men release themselves in some degree from the strain of conforming to the controlling symbolic, internalized variant readings of culture changes at its profoundest levels may be traced in the shifting balance of controls and releases which constitute a system of moral demands.

Moral values provide a core of integrative concepts for the development of personality and for the maintenance of society. Morality, in these terms, is not a question of prohibitions or musts, but rather the values and definitions of appropriate behavior by which man governs his behavior, and protests against destructive social mores.[15]

It can readily be seen that "values" range along a continuum from the most relative to the most absolute. We can list them in the following hierarchy:

1. Idiosyncratic values—held only by one person in the group under consideration, i.e. personal preferences.
2. Group values—which are distinctive of some plurality of individuals, whether this be family, clique, association, tribe, nation, or civilization.
3. Personal values—a private form of group values.
4. Operational absolutes—values held by members of a group to be absolute in their application for them.
5. Tentative absolutes—those operational absolutes found to exist in all societies.
6. Permanent absolutes—assumptions that may be asserted but unknowable in any scientific sense.

Anthropologists no longer hold to the radical cultural relativism of a quarter-century ago. Rather, there is growing consensus that tentative absolutes do exist—interestingly, a rough parallel to the Mosaic Decalogue. This is not at all at odds with the emphasis of the situational ethicists, for the Decalogue may be seen as the negative definition of love as the defining ethic. That is, the Decalogue spells out the conditions of non-love. But the problem with both traditional Christian morality and with situational ethics morality is that both assume that ideal moral norms are self evident in their social application. Rather, I would suggest that moral absolutes must be defined and translated into appropriate behavior by each group. In other words, absolute values must be translated into operational and group values that are to be taken as the moral norms of behavior. Briefly, absolutes must be reduced to a relative definition, and these relative definitions must assume absolute functions. For example, a tentative absolute value is the right of personal property, or, negatively stated, stealing is immoral. However, the behavior to be labeled as stealing varies with societies and with a given society over time; yet a given consensual social definition must be a fairly inviolable norm for that society.

With this in mind, any specific behavior in terms of a moral evaluation is culture-bound. Or more psychologically—relative group and operational values are incorporated by the child and become part of a psychologically absolute moralistic system. This results in the familiar concept of morality with which we have lived for many centuries. I feel guilty about that which I have been trained to feel guilty. I seek means to assuage my guilt and call that forgiveness. (I shall comment on this later.)[14] My "moral system" in actual operation may bear little relation to any mature or ideal moral values.

The Christian church long has been part of this system of psychological ethnocentric moralism—for I do not consider this mature morality. Thus it is not surprising that Christian religious education has failed to produce a consistent morality in its constituency.

What then is morality? Lawrence Kohlberg, a research psychologist, has been able to construct a scale of moral development that consists of 6 stages: [9]

Stage 1: Obedience and punishment orientation. Egocentric deference to superior power or prestige, or a trouble-avoiding set.
Stage 2: Naively egoistic orientation. Right action is that instrumentally satisfying the self's needs and occasionally others'.
Stage 3: Good-boy orientation. Orientation to approval and to pleasing and helping others.
Stage 4: Authority and social-order maintaining orientation. Orientation to "doing duty" and to showing respect for authority and maintaining the given social order for its own sake.
Stage 5: Contractual legalistic orientation. Duty defined in terms of contract, general avoidance of violation of the will or rights of others, and majority will and welfare.
Stage 6: Conscience or principle orientation. Orientation not only to actually ordained social rules but to principles of choice involving appeal to logical universality and consistency.

Not all, or perhaps even a majority of persons reach stage 6, much less operate consistently at this most mature and ideal level. Perhaps that is not so much a concern as the fact that much of the thrust of Christian education as actually implemented produces a morality that only fits into the earlier stages of Kohlberg's categories. Some of the reasons for the confusion between high purpose and low accomplishment will become evident as we turn to an analysis of the psychological dynamics involved.

II
EGO MORALITY

For working purposes I shall give a brief summary of four major intrapsychic parts of the self to be discussed: superego, ego-ideal, narcissistic self, and ego.

Superego may be understood as the internalization of pro-hibitions exerted on the child. Thus the parent slaps the child's hand and says "naughty" when the two-year-old reaches in the cookie jar. At age three the child will reach in the cookie jar, slap its own hand and say "naughty" to itself. By age four the child will reach in the cookie jar and now feel "guilt." This is the progression of internalization of the external prohibition into the internalized experience of "feeling guilty."

Ego-ideal may be seen as the positive counterpart of the above. Thus when we perform in approved manners we feel a sense of self-approbation; if we fail to achieve a norm we experi-ence "shame." Shame and guilt then are different dimensions of the psychological dimensions of "moral feeling." It is obvious that these "moral feelings" are capricious and no necessary guide to moral action. Yet when we speak of conscience we most typically refer to these feeling states. In the concept of morality I wish to develop, I prefer to refer to conscience in a much more personal-ized, and self-conscious sense. That is, conscience not as feeling, but rather *conscience as the moral commitment which a person makes as a mature judgment.*

Narcissistic self may be seen as the universal given psycho-biological substrata of personality. Thus hunger, cold, sexuality, etc. represent aspects of need and drive that influence the be-havior of all men. The narcissistic self is one of the component parts of personality that make up the survival needs of the human or-ganism.

Ego may be defined as that part of self related to self-consciousness, decision-making, and experiencing of both internal and external states. It is the executive agency of the self.

The contributions of the superego, ego ideal, and the narcis-sistic self are more or less unconscious, predetermined by our childhood experiences, and in the need of realignment in accord with the requirements of reality and the adult values to which one chooses to commit oneself.

Existentialists have long emphasized the role of personal freedom, responsibility, and decision in contrast to the unconscious, determined, irrational aspects of behavior emphasized by classic psychoanalytic formulations. In recent years these two approaches have been at least partially synthesized in our theories of ego function. I have summarized this previously: [16]

Although couched in various terms, there is a growing consensus that personality development reflects not only physiological needs, but also value needs. Such needs to 'make sense out of the world' have been termed the 'quasi-needs' of the ego (von Bertalanffy) the will to meaning (Frankl) ego efficacy (White), cognitive coherence (Festinger). Now, according to Hartmann's formulation of ego development, there is an initial undifferentiated id-ego matrix from which emerges aspects of ego function separated apart from instinctual drive processes; and these autonomous ego activities are involved in the process of developing a coherent effective adaptation to the external world.

These autonomous ego functions assume the function of 'ego drives' in contradistinction to 'instinctual drives.' These ego drives are dependent upon the beliefs and values of the culture and these drives become important if indeed not the overriding determinants of behavior. Thus it can be seen that belief systems or value systems are the data that the ego uses to organize individual behavior. The lack of such cultural value data results in the failure to develop an effective coherent ego structure; or the cultural value system may result in significant distortions in the formation of ego structure. Belief systems, whether they be religious or otherwise, then are both necessary and influential in the development of personality.

The autonomous adult ego, then, chooses the values, morals, norms and standards by which the person shall live. These consciously chosen values, however, must be related to the unconscious values of one's superego, ego ideal, and narcissistic self. The capacity to pursue moral behavior in adulthood optimally occurs when there is a synchronous alignment between all four derivative forces: superego, ego ideal, narcissistic self, and autonomous ego values.

Morality has been usually thought of in terms of static rules, and has been defined as a negative behavior to avoidance of punitive superego sanctions or meeting ego-ideal demands.

In contrast, the concept of morality developed here is a

dynamic concept emphasizing the selection of goals and values and the process by which the person makes value choices . . . although including avoidance behavior, it emphasizes the positive goal-person directed behavior of the ego. This concept of ego morality posits that there is an evaluating and coordinating structure and function of the ego which is part of its autonomous function, concerned with defining and directing one's life in accord with the values one has chosen.

This latter function of the ego is related to what Engel [3] calls *signal-scanning affect*. His description of the nature and function of this ego mechanism bears directly on our theoretical model of ego morality.

The *signal-scanning* affects have as their distinguishing characteristics a warning or signal function and a 'how am I doing?' or scanning function, yielding information to self and to the environment of good or bad, success or failure, pleasure or unpleasure. They serve as signals and means of reality testing for orientation to both external reality and internal reality 'in a continuum extending in all shadings from massive affect experience to mere signals and even signals of signals' (Rapaport). They have both *regulatory and motivational properties* . . . the signal-scanning affects operate to provide information which is then used by the self-inspection part of the ego as a guide for subsequent ego activities in the service of the reality principle.

This phenomenological view of the observing, evaluating, and motivational self does not tie in neatly with psychoanalytic theory. Nonetheless, at this stage of formulation it seems reasonable to think in terms of a self-aware aspect of ego which is involved in the issues of moral values, and which experiences what Freud had termed "moral anxiety."

The role of the ego in morality is also differentiated by Piaget in his studies on the development of moral concepts in childhood.[11] Early first morality is "moral realism" which is absolute and a morality of constraint. This morality is superego moralism. The child's morality is based on authority and fear of punishment. Morality is a static set of absolute rules. In contrast, in adolescence the child begins to develop a "morality of cooperation" which is a relativistic concept. Morality here is related to ego functions of perception, evaluation, and determination of both consequences and desires. It is a relativistic morality in that the adolescent learns to guide his value choices and behavior in terms of his commitments to others and to the ideals and goals he posits for himself.

Chassell [2] notes that "children who were fixed in a state of moral realism by their peculiarly strong ties to their parents were unable to pass on to moral relativism, and remained bound by the moral realism of the superego."

Recent studies on the development of moral character and moral ideology have found that ego-strength and "good moral character" are closely associated. *It is ego-strength rather than superego that results in moral behavior.* Thus the ego variables associated with moral capacity include:

1. The ability to withstand temptation and to behave honestly.
2. To act in conformance with social norms that require impulse control.
3. Capacity to defer immediate gratification in favor of more distant rewards.
4. Maintain focused attention on one task.
5. Ability to control unsocialized phantasies.

Reviews of child rearing practices reveal that parental attempts at specific training in "good" habits fail to produce consistent moral behavior; whereas effective nurturance of a child as a significant, lovable individual with the use of firm, kind, consistent discipline does produce "moral capacity."

Parenthetically it is of note that scholars in the Roman Catholic church have urged their leaders to redefine the preadolescent concept of sin in the light of this evidence, for they argue that moral capacity does not develop until after the ego of the adolescent has coalesced into the capacity to make moral commitments and discriminations in the mature sense we have described.[12]

To conclude in a less theoretical vein, Erikson [4] writes:

The true ethical sense of the young adult at its best encompasses moral restraint and ideal vision, while insisting on concrete commitments to those intimate relationships and work associations by which man can hope to share a lifetime of productivity and competence. Truly ethical acts enhance a mutuality between the doer and the other—a mutuality which strengthens the doer even as it strengthens the other. Thus, the 'doer unto' and 'the other' are one deed. Developmentally, this means that the doer is activated in whatever strength is appropriate to his age, stage, and condition, even as he activates in the other the strength appropriate to his age, stage, and condition.

For mature ego morality to develop, the person must modify the absolutes laid down in the superego, ego ideal and narcissistic self to fit one's mature moral commitments.

In ego morality, the ego continually balances and weighs one's actions in terms of how general absolute values can be put into action in terms of one's group values in accord with one's personal values.

The so-called "new morality" or situation ethics is an attempt by theologians to reconstruct a system of morality since psycho-analysis demonstrated the vagaries and immorality of traditional moralism. However, theologians like Fletcher have failed to come to grips with the need for man to rely on more than personal integrity in social context as he sees it. Although they stress love as the penultimate ethic, they fail to recognize that man, left to his own devices, no matter how noble his intent, deludes and defeats himself. Sociologists and philosophers alike have criticized the situational ethicists on this count. Not that the situational ethicists are wrong in criticizing the traditional approach to moral-ity, but rather that the situational ethic fails to take account of the fact that morality is not merely an individual matter. Indeed, individual morality stands in interdependence with group morality.

The concept of ego morality implies that each individual is not alone in determining his value commitments and determining moral choices. The individual is molded by both his culture and his upbringing. His mature commitments are influenced by his social matrix, and his mature moral decisions are not his alone to make, but interdependent on the judgments and evaluations of his peers. This is what theologians are now calling "contextual" or "consensus" ethics.

Again, Erikson [5] implies this interdependence in his discus-sion of the roots of virtue. He notes that man is not guided by a comprehensive and conclusive set of instincts but must learn to develop what he calls the eight cardinal virtues of Hope, Will, Purpose, Skill, Fidelity, Love, Care, and Wisdom. He goes on:

The cog wheeling stages of childhood and adulthood are truly a system of generation and regeneration—for into this system flow and from this system emerge those attitudes which find permanent structure in the great *social institutions*. I have tentatively listed these social attitudes as reverent, judicious, moral, technical, ideological, interpersonal, productive and philosophical. Thus the basic virtues—these miracles of everyday life—seem to provide a test for universal values, and to contain the promise of a possible morality which is self-corrective as it remains adaptive.

What Erikson intimates, and what ego morality posits, is that the individual optimally acts to integrate one's behavior into the commitments to oneself and to one's society according to a whole range of social values. In some instances only a matter of personal preference is involved, while in others it is a question of decision for one's whole culture.

III
THE DYNAMICS OF GUILT AND FORGIVENESS

From the central axiom of ego morality stem certain corollaries in regard to guilt, responsibility and forgiveness. I define four types of guilt: 1.) civil objective guilt; 2.) psychological subjective guilt-feelings; 3.) existential ego guilt; 4.) ontological guilt.

Civil guilt is arbitrary and impersonal. It is the violation of objective rules. Such guilt may or may not be related to morality. For example, the Jewish martyrs to Nazi justice were objectively guilty of violating Nazi law; or a small child may be objectively guilty of property damage. Many instances of civil guilt involve other types of guilt. However, objective civil guilt does not in itself indicate either the morality of the act or the moral consequences for the person.

Psychological guilt is an affect or guilt-feeling. It is the subjective experience of internal condemnation of oneself by one's superego. Guilt-feelings bear no necessary relationship to either existential ego guilt or civil objective guilt. To avoid confusion, I do not believe that the common word "conscience" should be used for either guilt-feelings or for superego function, since these latter concepts refer to specific intrapsychic dynamics.

Existential ego guilt is a violation of relationship between man and man. This guilt, too, is objective, for it is a condition of estrangement between two persons. Existential ego guilt is ultimately a reflection of man's denial of his values and commitments, a denial of his true situation, and a withdrawal into narcissistic isolation from others. Existential ego guilt is not a feeling but is a situation.

Ontological guilt may be understood in theological terms as original sin, that is, man's basic responsibility for his life and behavior. In *The Brothers Karamazov,* Dostoevsky puts it that man is responsible for everything and therefore guilty of everything. Sartre pessimistically notes that man can only face himself in making decisions; he has nowhere to turn to affirm that his decisions are right or moral. Ontological guilt is a reflection of the original state of man in the human condition of inadequacy—the fatal flaw of human character that leads man to damn himself—the classic theme of "hubris" of the Greek tragedians—the leitmotif of our contemporary novelists like William Golding in his *Lord of the Flies*—the basic contention of both ancient theology and the modern formulations of theologians like Reinhold Niebuhr.

Ontological guilt, in summary, is a situation, a reflection of man's awareness of what he is. One contemporary psychoanalyst, Allen Wheelis, in his metaphorical analysis of the limitations of self-enlightenment, *The Illusionless Man,* concludes that the ontological quest for meaning in life is crucial, yet unanswerable and certainly untreatable by the psychotherapist.

With these definitions of guilt we may now look at the solutions of guilt—the problem of forgiveness.

A typical ploy has been to assume that behavior must be based on choice to be moral, and that one should not feel guilty about one's behavior which has been unconsciously determined. The assumption here is that guilt and morality are integral to each other. However, this view does not account for the variety of circumstances that we call "guilt." Indeed psychotherapists have for the most part concerned themselves with reducing guilt feelings, but ignored the "existential guilt situation."

In contrast I propose that morality is only tangentially related to guilt feelings and is primarily involved with existential guilt . . . that is, the issue of relating to others in terms of my ego commitments to them.

Out of existential human incapacity rises the conflict between one's own conscious aspirations and one's own unconsciously determined behavior. Indeed, St. Paul's classic self-confession states:

"I do not do the good things that I want to do, but I do practice the evil things that I do not want to do" (*Romans* 7:19, Williams translation).

Long ago Freud pointed out that our behavior was more determined by our unconscious than we were willing to admit and that we were more responsible and able to change our behavior than we were willing to accept. Despite the philosophical arguments about determinism and free will, recent studies of psychotherapy indicate that Freud's maxim holds true.

Gatch and Temerlin [6] compared psychoanalytic protocols from both existential and classic psychoanalysts. Interestingly, there was no actual difference between the two groups—both treated events in the patient's past as if they had been determined and not the patient's responsibility, while both treated the decisions for the future as totally a matter of free choice of the patient who had the responsibility for making those decisions.

It seems fatuous to assume that by rational process we can analyze our behavior into determined and chosen components. As I have indicated previously, one's moral choices are a *combination* of conscious and unconscious motives and norms, and a combination of determined and free choices. I suggest that we never know, in any conscious rational sense, fully what our motives are or why we choose the way we do. The concept of a rational man is at best a partial truth—the only people that seriously attempt to live by reason alone are paranoids! I assert that we need to rely upon and utilize in an integrated fashion our unconscious and irrational aspects of self as well as our conscious and rational self.

Furthermore, I submit that we are often faced with situations where we cannot determine either beforehand or afterwards whether the alternative we chose was more moral than the other. In Sartre's [19] analysis, we often cannot look to arbitrary external norms, or to others, or to a scientific analysis. Rather, we must accept the fact that existential choice is made by us. That alone may on occasion define our choice as moral. *I have chosen with integrity and that makes it moral.* A person must be able to take the consequences of and be willing and able to answer for what he thinks, feels, or does; to acknowledge and feel that this is a part of himself. Ego morality implies that one makes one's choices with as much integrity as one has, and accepts the consequences of those choices with the same integrity.

We are responsible for everything that we are and do. But responsibility does not imply that we should be punished even if guilty, in the sense of blamable. Superego moralism condemns the self as worthless and bad; whereas ego morality appraises oneself with integrity without rejecting or punishing oneself. Superego moralism says *"I feel guilty"*; whereas ego morality says *"I am guilty."*

The task then is not to assuage guilt feelings, although that is often a necessary preamble to real forgiveness. Rather, the task is to help the person to see himself and his relationships with others in the light of how he violates the relationships to which he is committed. The resolution of guilt feelings does not change the basic violation of relationship which is existential guilt. People would quite willingly settle for pacification of their superego, but are reluctant to undergo the pain of changing their pattern of relationship so that they no longer need to feel guilty!

The Development of Forgiveness

The need for forgiveness stems from the ambivalence of the early child-parent relationship. All parental restrictions frustrate the self-centered, pleasure-oriented child. He fears punishment from the parent if he breaks the rules but is angry at the frustrations. Yet to express that anger may also bring punishment, so the child deflects his frustrated anger from the parent onto himself. If the child violates restrictions in the pursuit of pleasure, he experiences anxious fear of retaliation by the parent, reinforced by his own deflected anger at the frustrating rules. These two sources of anger, parental and child, become internalized as the superego.

Forgiveness is sought to relieve the anxious fear attendant to seeking gratification in defiance of the rules. But this mechanistic pattern of forgiveness is a misnomer, for the resolution of guilt is by punishment, not forgiveness. The parent is a thing, not a person. The relationship, in Buber's terms, is an I-It relationship rather than an I-Thou one. The only concern is a narcissistic one. Therefore I have called this the *punitive model* of forgiveness, which is not forgiveness at all, but only the payment of a price for narcissistic gratification.

Only gradually does the child develop what Piaget calls "moral realism." The child develops relationships with the parents as persons. He finds that morality does not primarily involve acts, but the underlying attitudes. The anxiety is not over punishment but over estrangement; the driving force for the resolution of guilt is the deprivation of love. Identification with the parental expectations becomes internalized as the ego ideal, so that violations do not produce guilt but elicit shame—the fear of contempt by the parent and ultimate abandonment. Here the process of forgiveness is that of reconciliation in the I-Thou of love. But the previously established superego condemnation leads the child to anticipate punishment as the requisite for forgiveness. Yet no payment of sacrifice will bring forgiveness; one can only seek to reestablish the I-Thou. Likewise, the forgiver can only accept back the forgiven into the love relationship. If the forgiver demands payment, he is violating his end of the I-Thou. I call this the *reconciliation model* of forgiveness which involves the *ought*—the conscious willfulness of forgiver and forgiven to seek reunion.

The punitive model can never lead to true forgiveness, for it misconstrues the I-Thou guilt in terms of I-It relationships. The person with a punitive infantile superego may attempt to placate the superego demands for punishment as a misguided attempt to obtain forgiveness. Note the neurotic mechanisms by which superego guilt is evaded: reparation, confession, repression, projection, and rationalization. These mechanisms may effectively dissipate conscious guilt at the expense of neurotic symptoms, but unconsciously the superego guilt remains.

The guilt of the punitive model is poorly tolerated in the person and is defended against by layers of fear or hate. If by fear, the guilty person may develop physiologic reactions—anxiety attacks or psychosomatic states. If by hate, the original hostility is turned upon the self; it may lead to suicide, the ultimate failure to forgive oneself. The superego never forgives, it can only be satiated. Neurotic and psychotic symptoms are often a reflection of superego guilt. O. H. Mowrer is partially correct when he insists that psychologic disease stems from real guilt, that is, real events in patients' lives. But the punitive superego does not discriminate among those events which call for forgiveness and those which do not. Forgiveness is not a superego phenomenon.

The Nature of Confession

Confession may be defined as the recognition of personal responsibility. It is the perception of the estrangement in the I-Thou, the acknowledgment of one's initiative in violating the I-Thou, and is a prelude to remedial steps to reestablish the I-Thou.

But confession may be used to deny responsibility rather than to affirm it. In Alcoholics Anonymous the alcoholic confesses that he is helpless within the clutches of a disease. He need feel no responsibility. However, this denial of responsibility leads to a continued dependence on A.A. rather than bringing the alcoholic to a condition of self-acceptance and mature responsibility.

Confession can be used to diminish responsibility or punishment; it acts as a defense against acknowledging the true guilt. Confession is made of pseudo-guilt and is ineffectual. For example, in civil court one may confess to a lesser crime to avert a conviction with a severer penalty. In Alcoholics Anonymous the alcoholic gives a stock confession of his drinking so that he does not have to confess to his omnipotent fantasies, his shame of inadequacy, and his frustrated anger. Or one may confess to the group so that they will share in one's guilt. For example, a husband in marital group therapy confessed his shortcomings to the group and felt guilty no longer because the group registered no disapproval. He mistook group acceptance for approval. The confession was also a disarming mechanism, for his wife could not upbraid him in the face of his having "come clean" in front of everybody.

The most obvious distortion of confession is the "scrupulosity syndrome." The scrupulous person is bothered by incessant feelings of guilt and depression over his religious behavior. He fearfully confesses repetitively but obtains no feeling of relief because he confesses to pseudo-guilt for specific acts which obscures the defiant hostility. Confession of the acts is a defense against recognition of the attitude.

The patient was a thirty-year-old Holiness minister who found it increasingly difficult to preach because he felt hypocritical. He demanded perfection of himself because holiness meant making absolutely no mistakes. He dreaded that one mistake would send him plunging to hell. He prayed incessantly but found no forgiveness. He wept at the altar rail to no avail. He hated himself for failing and experienced dread anxiety before each sermon. Alternately he felt that he could achieve a flawless existence superior to any of his colleagues. During therapy he revealed his hatred toward his alcoholic father. Father was projected as God, demanding perfection. The patient desired perfection as an omnipotent identification and simultaneously hated the father-God for demanding what he could not be.

Confession may be masochistic—a relentless exposure of one's faults to gain the attention, sympathy, and love of others.

A husband in marital group therapy came every week to proclaim loudly that the marital problems were all his fault; he relished detailing his failures as a husband. His confession brought only attention.

In this light we may consider the recent enthusiasm for the return of the Protestant confessional, and recall Flugel's observation that Protestantism has exchanged the tyranny of the external superego of the Catholic Church for the greater tyranny of the individual's internal superego. In many Holiness churches the altar rail has been a masochistic wailing wall, and in many confessionals only the superego has been appeased. One patient of mine returned from confessional cursing the cleric for not imposing severe penance. He felt he had been robbed of the chance to absolve his guilt! The confession can placate but it cannot reconcile. Confession is a first step, but we may use institutionalized forms of confession as a neurotic defense.

The Nature of Remorse

Although in confession one may acknowledge and accept one's responsibility, it need not follow that one feels sorrow, remorse, or contrition for one's behavior. I have seen many a sociopath defiantly confess and readily accept the responsibility for his behavior. He is sorry that he got caught but not sorry for what he did.

Remorse is not regret. It is the recognition of the hostility expressed toward the Thou and the desire to be reconciled in love. True remorse is not self-condemnation as an attempt to extract sympathy, or is it a wallowing self-pity. Contrition is the opposite of obsessive remorse; it is the objective appraisal of one's state, not the punitive condemnation of one's behavior. Remorse is the motivating spur to reconstitutive action rather than the occasion for punitive self-flagellation. If one is operating by the punitive model of forgiveness, remorse is but the turning on oneself of anger originally directed at the frustrating person. Hence depression and suicide reflect the failure to move from remorse to reconciliation.

The Nature of Restitution

It is here that the distinction between the punitive and reconciliation models of forgiveness is most clearly seen. In the punitive model, restitution is a payment to avoid retaliation. In the reconciliation model, restitution reestablishes the conditions of the I-Thou. If I have stolen your purse and then seek forgiveness, I must return the purse. Not because I will not otherwise be forgiven, or because it is demanded by the forgiver. Rather, I return the purse because my love compels me to restore what belongs to Thou. To keep the purse is self-preference and repudiates the love of Thou. Restitution consists of returning to Thou anything I have taken in disregard of Thou.

From this it is evident that restitution is not always a condition of forgiveness. Mechanical replacement is meaningless. Restitution of things is meaningful only as it reflects the relationship. If one insists on non-existent, impossible, or undesired restitution this is again a response to the punitive impulses within oneself—a failure to accept the fact that love accepts one as one is. The obsessive-compulsive is a good example of the distortion of restitution. One patient of mine slaps her mouth when she starts to say a forbidden word, becomes apologetic, makes absurd offers to make up for allegedly hurting me, and tries to undo her actions like a child piecing together a broken plate. These attempts at restitution are based on her narcissism, for she is attempting self-atonement without realizing that I accept her as she is, without her having to make herself acceptable.

The attempt to undo one's actions is a neurotic failure to distinguish between punitive demands and the need for reconciliation. A good example again is Alcoholics Anonymous. In the Twelfth Step, the alcoholic is to repay others as he is able to assist other alcoholics. The continual repayment in terms of time and energy in A. A. rescue activities is an attempt to undo the past, negate one's condition, and prove by present activity the falseness of the past. Further, the rescue activities play upon the rescue fantasies of the dependent alcoholic who vicariously saves himself by saving others. This exchange of an alcoholic neurosis for an A.A. neurosis may be a social gain, but I cannot agree with those who see such an affiliation as a society of forgiveness.

We are reluctant to forsake a notion of punishment and see forgiveness as purely a function of love. Witness attempts to find theologic justification for an angry God who punishes for sin so that man can be reconciled. This misperceives the nature of sin, for *sin is a relational concept*. The Biblical idea of wrath and judgment refers not to Divine hostility, but to the settled opposition of holiness to evil. We anthropomorphize God's personality and project the punitiveness of our superego onto God. The demand for death is man's hatred of the loving God, and the only really radical judgment of sin is pure love. Meyerson and Stoller, analyzing the crucifixion in psychoanalytic terms, aptly note that the cross stands as a warning to man that he is a narcissistic creature with an inability and fear to love [10]. Man would rather take punishment than admit to Christ's demand for total love and accept that love as the measure of forgiveness.

The Nature of Mutual Acceptance

The guilty one follows the previous steps by himself, but now the process must include the forgiver as well. Here we see the pathology of the failure to forgive in contrast to the failure to be forgiven. As we shall see, the failure to forgive others is ultimately the failure to forgive oneself.

In *acceptance,* the guilty one accepts the implication of dependence on the love of the other. Unqualified love is threatening for it highlights the nature of one's inadequacies. Those with children will recognize that sometimes the child repudiates the advance of love. He fears the implication of surrendering his rebellious autonomy, fearful that he will become the slave of the loving parent, rather than seeing the nurturing growth available within that love. In *accepting,* the forgiver must share the guilt, anguish, and estrangement of the sinner. To forgive is to extend one's love to the person who has violated it. To accept another, one must accept within oneself and experience the meaning of mutual separation. Note the reaction of the mother as she begins to feel the estrangement of, and from, the naughty child, and goes to envelop the child in her arms.

To demand the "pound of flesh" as the condition of forgiveness is a hostile retaliation. Or one may forgive as a duty, which is a condescending gesture. In these instances one is gratifying the narcissistic desire to retaliate against the one who hurt us. The forgiveness is a facade. It is a receipt for payment, but it is not reconciliation.

Another pattern is the need to forgive others. This is a masochistic maneuver aimed at gratifying one's omnipotence. Every church has at least one such morally masochistic wife who demonstrates her saintly ability to forgive her alcoholic husband for thirty years, although she unwittingly provokes him to offend her. This wife keeps her husband an alcoholic so that she can maintain her masochistic forgiving role. One can also be *too forgiving,* denying the other person's guilt, minimizing it, or forgetting it. That occurs when we fear rejection by the guilty one. For example, the child may readily excuse the parent for an obvious error. Ready forgiveness may be a defense against one's actual anger and wish for retaliation.

Still another pattern is the omnipotent person who aspires to perfection . . . the "unforgiving legalist." He cannot accept himself or forgive himself for being imperfect and hates others for reminding himself of his status. He is particularly intolerant of others who accept themselves more casually, for they represent a desire for self-gratification he cannot indulge. The member of Alcoholics Anonymous cannot accept the premise that treated alcoholics may drink normally because it represents a desire he must repudiate in himself. Here we see anxiety lest one's deluded perfectionism be exposed for what it is. Or one may fail to forgive because of one's own guilt. The offender is a convenient target for minimizing one's own guilt by making the other person appear guiltier. This is the scapegoat mechanism. Projecting one's own guilt onto another allows one to punish them instead of oneself. Such is the course of prejudice.

Mutual acceptance, then, does not overlook the gravity of the estrangement, nor seek payment of punishment, nor use the occasion for self-justification. It is the mutual realization of the I-Thou estrangement and the mutual yearning for reunion.

The Nature of Reconciliation

Reconciliation is the completed act of restoration to an I-Thou. The punitive model of forgiveness, based upon *superego morality,* can never lead to reconciliation, for in the I-It model only the self exists. Whereas the reconciliation model of forgiveness is based on an *ego morality* in which both personal and spiritual forgiveness are contingent upon recognition and reconciliation between two people. The establishment of autonomous ego values allows one to react to others in terms of one's actual moral commitment, freed from the obligation to act upon infantile desire. Realistic anxiety aroused by estrangement is constructive anxiety as it spurs forgiver and forgiven to moral action. Therefore true forgiveness is a willful process involving both the forgiver and the forgiven. As such, one makes the conscious decision not to choose retaliation but to seek restoration of the I-Thou. The love of forgiveness endures the hostility of sin and remaining unqualified in its capacity to receive the guilty back into relationship.

Superego guilt says "I feel guilty," whereas *ego guilt* says "I am guilty." The punitive model of forgiveness applies to the first, the reconciliation model to the second. Theology and psychology overlap in that they share the reconciliation model of forgiveness for guilt which is the hostile, defiant, rejecting *attitude* toward authority, one's own integrity, and one's true being. The therapist accepts the patient as he is and forgives the patient for being what he is . . . that is, the therapist accepts the patient into a relationship regardless of the patient's condition. Later the patient forgives the therapist . . . that is, for not being the idealistic figure whom the patient desired, and accepts the therapist for what he is. Eventually the therapist and patient can come to a conscious mutuality of recognition and acceptance. In reconciliation forgiveness, the acceptance is already present in parent, therapist, God waiting to be accepted by the child, patient, sinner. The state of forgiveness is waiting. The forgiven need only enter into that state.

IV
THE ROLE OF THE CHURCH IN THE DEVELOPMENT OF MORAL VALUES

In this section I shall briefly outline some applications of the previous theories to the educational efforts of the church.

First, it seems clear that a major mechanism of moral teaching has been to inculcate superego sanctions. This has produced the sort of moral inflexibility that leads to moral irrelevancy when time and circumstance change. Further, it produces a guilt assuaged by punishment instead of reconciliation. Indeed superego dynamics can be seen in some popular theological theories of the atonement. The child does need kindly, but firm limits. I am not at all suggesting that moral education should consist of some paltry relativism. But rather the child must be continually pushed toward the replacement of immature concepts of morality by more mature concepts as he goes through stages of moral development. Perhaps an example will illustrate the point. A four-year-old must learn most definitely that he must not cross streets against a red light. However, the ten-year-old must be taught that there is no absoluteness about red lights. Yet the ten-year-old must still respond to red lights as a meaningful and relevant directive for behavior. In other words, at different ages the same moral problem must be reevaluated in terms of its meaningfulness and how the individual should deal with moral prescriptions.

Second, the ego-ideal teachings of the church need to stress realistic and tenable models of moral behavior. A common perversion, particularly in the pietist traditions, has been the model of Christ as the ego-ideal. The consequences are two-fold. If the child takes the model seriously he tries to become a paragon of virtue that he cannot attain. He may then demean himself and fail to accept himself for his realistic worth. Since no one can live without some self-acceptance the child will attempt to affirm his worthiness by scapegoating others—here lie the roots of religious prejudice. Or if the child takes the Christ paragon as really attainable he may develop a supercilious superiority and be unwilling and unable to see the real defects of any human personality—hence leading to the inevitable pride that culminates in a fall. The model of Christian virtue implied is that of self-accepting honesty, of willingness to accept and love oneself for what one is, and yet see that the virtuous life is an existential process—one is always "becoming."

Third, in terms of the narcissistic self the church must look towards the development of a Christian concept of pride. It is my observation that the problem of hostility so often observed in religious people reflects the fact that they do not love themselves, hence cannot love others. It is noteworthy that the Great Commandment of Christ is: Love thy neighbor *as thyself*. A respectful love and nourishment of self must occur before Christian charity can be implemented toward others.

Fourth, in regard to the ego it should be recalled that mature morality is related to the degree of personality maturity and personality integrity which the person develops. Many of the criminals whom I have treated in prison gave me a history of a "religious" upbringing. The stern enforcement of moral injunctions does not produce morality. The teaching of "moral principles" to young children is probably irrelevant. More important is that children experience a relationship with adults, and with the institution of the church, which fosters the sense of relatedness, belonging, and mutuality or responsiveness to others.

The Christian religion that promises "freedom in Christ" has instead produced participants hounded by fear, guilt, and anxiety. It seems to me that the message of Christ may be seen as affirming the reconciliation of man to his Creator, thus affirming man's opportunity to freely choose his life without fear of condemnation. Or in Sartre's terms, man in Christ no longer has to justify his existence. Yet we shrink from that freedom to be and to choose.

Let me give one final example of the dilemma that faces children in learning the freedom of existence and moral opportunity. I returned from a trip with a bag of lollipops for my children. They clamored for the goodies, but instead of grabbing the clutch of candies I held out to them they hesitated. "Daddy, which should I choose?" "Daddy, will I like the red or green one best?" "Daddy, you know best, tell me which one to take." When I said that the choice was theirs to make they became petulant and angry! They refused the proffered freedom. They did not want to bear the consequence of taking a lollipop they might not like, or one which wasn't as good as another they might have chosen!

Here then is the moral dilemma. Too often the church has taken the position of telling its children how and what to choose, as if it had the answers to which "lollipop" was best. And the churches' children bought this security. I am reminded of Erich Fromm's comment in *Escape From Freedom*: that men would rather have the security of false truth than the freedom of ambiguous reality.

As I see it, the task of moral education for the church is to teach its children how to deal with the ambiguities of life with integrity, with fortitude, and the willingness to grapple with the consequences of choice. Moral education then is not the task of transmitting precepts, but teaching principles in terms of the ever-changing exigencies of the contemporary society each child will face.

The church in this sense, and Christian education in this sense, aims not at transmission of the moral values per se, but at providing a vehicle for responsible moral dialogue, and presenting children with a model for grappling with morality as an ongoing existential process.

REFERENCES

1. Allinsmith, W., "Conscience and Conflict: The Moral Force in Personality," *Child Devel.* 28:469-476, 1957.
2. Chassell, J. O., "Old Wine in New Bottles: Supcrego as a Structuring of Roles," *Crosscurrents in Psychiatry and Psychoanalysis.* R. W. Gibson (ed.) Philadelphia, Lippincott, 1967.
3. Engel, G. L., "Towards a Classification of Affects," *Expression of the Emotion in Man.* Knapp, P. H. (ed.) New York, Inter. Univ. Press, 1963.
4. Erikson, E. H., "The Golden Rule and the Cycle of Life," *Harvard Med. Alumni Bull.* Winter, 1963.
5. Erikson, E. H., "The Roots of Virtue," *The Humanist Frame.* Huxley, J. (ed.) New York, Harper, 1960.

6. Gatch, V. M. & Temerlin, M. K., "The Belief in Psychic Determinism and the Behavior of the Psychotherapist," *Rev. Exist. Psychol. Psychiat.* 15:16-33, 1965.

7. Hartshorne, H. and May, M. A., "Studies in the Nature of Character," 3 vols. New York, Macmillan, 1928-30.

8. Kluckhohn, C. "Introduction," *Reader in Comparative Religion: An Anthropological Approach.* 2nd. Ed. W. A. Lessa & E. Z. Vogt (eds.). New York, Harper & Row, 1966.

9. Kohlberg, L., "Development of Moral Character and Moral Ideology," *Review of Child Development Research.* Vol. 1, M. D. Hoffman & L. W. Hoffman (eds.) New York, Russell Sage Fdn., 1964.

10. Meyerson, O. G. and Stoller, L., "A Psychoanalytic Interpretation of the Crucifixion," *Psychoanal. Rev.* 49:117-122, 1962.

11. Nass, M. L., "The Superego and Moral Development in the Theories of Freud and Piaget," *Psychoanal. Stud. Child.* 15:51-63, 1966.

12. O'Neill, R. P. and Donovan, M. A., "The Question of Pre-Adolescent Sin," *Insight: Quart. Rev. Rel. M.H.* 4:1-10, 1966.

13. Pattison, E. M., "Social and Psychological Aspects of Religion in Psychotherapy," *J. Nerv. Ment. Dis.* 141:586-597, 1965.

14. Pattison, E. M., "On the Failure To Forgive or To Be Forgiven," *Amer J. Psychother.* 19:106-115, 1965.

15. Pattison, E. M., "Ego Morality: An Emerging Psychotherapeutic Concept," *Psychoanalytic Rev.* 52:187-222, 1968.

16. Pattison, E. M., "The Effects of a Religious Culture's Values on Personality Psychodynamics." Read to Section H—Anthropology: Amer. Assn. Adv. Sci. Berkeley, 1965.

17. Pattison, E. M., "The Closed Mind Syndrome," *Christ. Med. Soc. J.* 18:7-11, 1966.

18. Rieff, J. *The Triumph of the Therapeutic: Uses of Faith After Freud.* New York, Harper & Row, 1966.

19. Sartre, J. P. *Existentialism and Human Emotions.* New York, Philosophical Lib., 1957.

18 The Development of the Normal Conscience

Dorothea McCarthy

Because conscience is fundamental to any consideration of human behavior, psychologists of every school have speculated or conducted research about its development. The data thus produced are baffling, confusing, and sometimes contradictory. This situation reflects the current status of psychology: for each school of thought has favorite methods of gathering data which also contain assumptions about human beings. Therefore, the task of analyzing psychological data and sorting out their meaning is formidable. McCarthy has surveyed this vast field of knowledge, seeking as a major concern what is known about the development of conscience in normal people.* Toward the end of her article she applies these data to church educational policies.

It may be appropriate for me to mention that my approach is that of a developmental psychologist. I shall try to describe what psychologists have contributed to our knowledge of the developing conscience of the child and how they approach the subject. Then I shall point out some of the limitations of methodology and the need for further research in this vitally important area.

In terms of normative outlining of how the child's conscience develops, this area, and the whole broader sphere of moral development, has lagged behind other aspects of child development

---

* From *Conscience: Its Freedom and Limitations*, edited by William C. Bier, S.J. (New York: Fordham University Press, 1971), pp. 39-61. Reprinted with permission.

such as motor behavior and language development. It has frequently been subsumed, even among authors who recognize the area, under the general rubric of socialization of the child, and hence has been given very limited treatment within that context. Until about ten or fifteen years ago the textbooks in child psychology rarely, if ever, mentioned moral development or conscience. This was probably a result of the fact that, as psychology was trying to establish itself as a science, especially by using objective methods, the earlier work was done on the more readily objectifiable aspects of child behavior rather than on this elusive, sensitive area of conscience. In the period when behaviorists were dominating the field of psychology, consciousness and other subjective phenomena were not considered readily subject to scientific investigation. In more recent years, however, learning theorists, psychoanalysts, and developmental psychologists have developed techniques for the study of conscience and various aspects of moral development in children. And in 1968 the topic was considered of sufficient import to be the focus of a conference at the National Institute of Child Health and Human Development. It brought together developmental psychologists as well as psychiatrists, theologians, and clergymen of many denominations (National Institute of Child Health and Human Development, 1969).

PSYCHOLOGISTS' DEFINITIONS OF CONSCIENCE

Much depends on the theoretical orientation of the investigator as to how he defines conscience, what dimensions of it he will choose to investigate, and how he will interpret his data.

In some of the attempts of psychologists to define conscience, one notes a certain self-consciousness and uncertainty in their efforts, for most of them have no religious affiliation and the term has been heard too frequently in religious contexts in which most behavioral scientists are not usually at ease. Sears in his essay on the growth of conscience states:

The meaning of *conscience* is not very precise in western culture, but the word has an approximate aura which nearly everyone understands. It refers to the standards of right and wrong, and the motivation to abide by these standards, that every normal person carries within himself. It is the incontrovertible dogma of obligation and responsibility, the not-to-be-argued-with moral sense, the deep-lying self-control of plea-sure-seeking principles [Sears 1960, p. 92].

Jersild admits that ". . . from a psychological point of view, the conscience is a rather nebulous thing. . . . The conscience usually does not represent a unitary, internally consistent set of principles or sanctions. It has many facets" (Jersild, 1968, p. 512). Sears (1960) identified three such facets as resistance to temptation, feelings of guilt, and the positive side of the moral ledger which he also calls conscience in a narrow sense. Jersild points out that the conscience may be rigorous in some things and too lenient in other matters; it may be strong and prevail over temptation, or weak and succumb to temptation. He even indicates that it may be only the voice of expediency or a sort of gadfly which merely prevents a person from enjoying what he knows he should not do, but often does not keep him from doing it.

Kohlberg offers the following comment on the meaning of conscience:

Current investigators consider morality or conscience to be the set of cultural rules of social action which have been internalized by the in-dividual. . . . In spite of loose agreement on the notion of internalized rule, there have been important differences of emphasis in researchers' conception of morality [Kohlberg, 1964a, p. 277].

One difficulty of definition frequently encountered in the literature stems from the etymological definition of morality which derives from *mores* or social customs of the group. In tests of moral knowl-edge, authors often lump together matters of serious violations of moral standards which most societies would agree are wrong— such as stealing or assault—with trivial matters of politeness with only minimal ethical implications—such as spitting on the side-walk. Much confusion in the literature can result from such super-ficial labeling and grouping under the same term of behaviors of such diverse implications.

PROBLEMS OF METHODOLOGY

Before reviewing recent research in the various schools of thought, I should draw attention to certain limitations of method-ology. In order for a psychologist to gather data on any aspect of behavior he must develop a method with which to measure or observe and quantify the trait or characteristic. He must also cope with the problem of the validity and reliability of his method. Two of the most careful pieces of research I know of in the area of moral development are doctoral dissertations which have been done at Fordham University: one by Father Pius Riffel (1967) on scrupulosity, and another by Father William Novicky (1959) on fraternal charity. In both of these investigations great care was taken to define the dimensions being studied and to validate the scales used for measuring them.

Many laboratory studies have been conducted in efforts to isolate various dimensions of moral development. Some have concentrated on the self-critical ability of the child, others on evidences of guilt shown by the child who has transgressed; from such evidence the presence of a conscience is inferred. Other studies have concentrated on resistance to temptation especially in cheating and lying, and still others on ability to delay gratification. Some of these studies use methods which seem so devious and contrived that many thoughtful readers consider them superficial and doubt the validity of the results as well as the meaning attributed to them. The "ray gun" or shooting-gallery technique developed by Grinder (1961), and subsequently used in a number of other investigations, in which the child has an opportunity to falsify his score and earn a badge of dubious motivational value, is typical of such studies.

Another methodological difficulty concerns the samples used in the various investigations. Since there are no norms nationally or culturally for really large groups, only very limited generalizations can be made from the particular samples involved. Strangely enough, the vast majority of studies on moral behavior have used only males as subjects. Some which have used female subjects, however, have emerged with different results for the two sexes. Yet these researchers, considering the role of the parents in moral training of children, usually find that for preschool- and elementary-school-age children the mother is the chief disciplinarian in our American culture.

Typical of studies concerned with children's moral values is the study by Gump and Kounin (1961) in which over 200 children were asked: "What is the worst thing a child can do at home?"; "Why is that so bad?" and "What is the worst thing a child can do at school?"; "Why is that so bad?" The responses fell into the categories of violation of rules, assaults on other children, breaking and damaging property, non-conformity with the adult leader, and miscellaneous items. Breaking and destructiveness showed the greatest difference between home and school, with the more destructive behavior at home. Boys always reported more assaults on children in school. Talking in school was reported by 1 girl in 4 in first grade, but by third grade this was reduced to only 1 in 8. Play with fire was more frequently reported by boys than by girls, and at third grade 1 in 4 boys reported it at home, and 1 in 16 at school. These authors report that children were increasingly concerned about harm to others and with morally serious incidents with increase in age and less frequently referred to adult punishment as they became older. Especially was there less frequent mention of corporal punishment among the older children than among the younger.

Many of the investigations on the child-rearing attitudes and techniques of parents also leave much to be desired from the standpoint of methodology, for they often depend on retrospective reports of parents, sometimes going back several years, about the methods of control they formerly employed. Another large group of studies depends on a variety of projective techniques such as story completions, and the like, which may not reflect what the child really would do if he were confronted with the actual situation described in the story stem. Ingenious as many of these techniques are in attempting to find the key to this important area, they often do not yield solid scientific data.

Most of the better studies recognize the multifaceted nature of the concept of conscience and attempt to investigate only one content area, such as Eberhart's (1942) study on attitude toward property, Durkin's (1959) study of children's concepts of justice, or Ausubel's (1955) attempt to distinguish between guilt and shame.

RESEARCH AND THEORIES
BEARING ON MORAL DEVELOPMENT

As Mussen, Conger, and Kagan (1969) point out in their recent text, although developmental psychology has amassed a vast amount of information about persons of all ages throughout the life span, the field is relatively deficient in explanatory theory. The major influences are those of the cognitive theorists, emphasizing the trait-organization approach; the learning theorists, who stress the active internalization of rules in the process of moral development. Each of these systems offers partial theories of various aspects of psychological development, and moral development is treated to a limited extent by each of them. As yet no one theory affords sufficiently unifying explanations or hypotheses either of psychological development in general or of moral development in particular.

The Cognitive Theorists

In 1928 there appeared the first volume in the monumental and now classic works of Hartshorne and May (1928-1930) involving studies in deceit and in service and self-control. A variety of situations were set up so that deception, cheating, and lying of various sorts could be detected. Older children were found somewhat more deceptive than younger; there was no difference between boys and girls. In general, brighter children were more honest in the experimental situations than duller ones. Children who were emotionally more unstable on other personality indices were more likely to be deceptive, and children of upper socio-economic levels were less deceptive than those of lower socio-economic levels. These studies, although considered daring and ingenious, were severely criticized. The rather consistent indications were that honesty was not a unitary trait, but was very specific to the situation, since none of the children was always honest and none was always deceitful. Those moral and religious educators who were oriented toward the cultivation of the virtue of "honesty" were rather dismayed by such results indicating the importance of specific environmental factors.

In 1963 Burton applied factor-analytic techniques to the old data of Hartshorne and May and found evidence for some degree of generality in regard to the concept of honesty. His work suggested a model for the further investigations of Nelson, Grinder, and Mutterer (1969), who gathered new data by presenting six tasks to sixth-grade children. The correlational data essentially confirmed the results of Hartshorne and May, although the data were gathered forty years later, with different subjects performing different tasks. However, in applying Burton's factor-analytic procedures to the new data these investigators also found evidence for conceptualization of a disposition toward honesty *vs.* transgression across a variety of temptation situations. They also applied the more recently developed techniques of analysis of variance and were able to tease apart statistically the influence of persons and of situations. Persons accounted for about 15-26 per cent of the total variance, and tasks for about 14 per cent. The remainder of the variance was accounted for by error and inter-action scores (60-71 per cent). These findings have important methodological implications, for the relatively low indices of internal consistency suggest that any *single* behavior measure holds little or no validity as a measure of a general trait of honesty.

The Learning Theorists

Recognizing that conscience is a learned phenomenon, psychologists have been ingenious in developing techniques to try to discover how the child learns to behave in a moral way. As Kohlberg (1964a) puts the question, "How does the amoral infant become capable of morality?" Traditionally there is the explanation of the learning theorists who see the answer in terms of learning good habits by positive reinforcement (or reward) of good or approved behavior and by negative reinforcement (or punishment) of bad or disapproved behavior. Such writers as Eysenck (1960), Sears, Maccoby, & Levin (1957), Mowrer (1950), and Bandura and Walters (1963) regard learning in the moral sphere as similar to learning in other areas, with Eysenck's view being the most simplistic and closest to that of the associationists. Learning in the moral sphere is, however, much more complex than the learning of a motor skill or the learning of the meaning of a word, and more dynamic and motivational forces must be recognized as operative in moral learning. These writers generally agree that morality is conformity to cultural norms; but the learning theorists stress that the child learns to behave in a moral way by the process of reinforcement resulting in modeling behavior, and that the child gradually actively internalizes the standards of society through the societal imposition of restrictions on his behavior. The emphasis is on the environment.

Psychoanalytic Theorists

Writers with a psychoanalytic orientation, such as Freud himself and Erikson (1950), agree with the learning theorists that morality represents conformity to cultural standards, but they tend to stress the affective and motivational aspects involved in developing such conformity. The acquisition mechanism is different in learning theory and in psychoanalytic theory, in the latter the dynamics of family influences being brought in, for the parents are regarded as the transmitters of the culture. By the process of identification the child forms an ego-ideal in terms of consistency with the parent of the same sex. Incidentally, those theories have been much more fully developed for boys than for girls. In today's society more and more children are growing up without the opportunity for parental influence in the traditional sense, and hence become victims of amorality and experience identity crises. The psychoanalytic point of view stresses the child's active efforts to cope with the process of incorporating the rules of society. It is less through an environmental impact of specific rewards and punishments as is the case with the learning theorists, and the internalization of the rules of society is tied in with the formation of the super-ego and the resolution of the Oedipal conflict. The child is seen as the active internalizer of rules rather than as a passive recipient of environmental experience. Freudian theory has led to a number of interesting experimental studies of the child-rearing antecedents of various groups of children. These researches have been very ably summarized by Hoffman (1963).

Another theorist who stressed the affective aspects of moral development, but whose work has not led to much experimental verification, is Erikson (1950) [1] who has presented the only developmental theory of the formation of the ego. The well-cared-for infant learns very early that when his mother is there, making certain sounds in getting his bottle ready, he will be fed, and that everything will be all right. The child thus learns to wait and trust his mother, and in so doing he also learns to defer immediate gratification of his desires. This has been described by Goldfarb (1955) as the basis of all character formation. Certainly the child who learns to wait and to defer gratification is the one who learns to control impulsivity. Bender (1947) has pointed out that the psychopath has no conscience, and she relates this character deficiency to his never having learned to defer immediate gratification—or to trust others, in Erikson's terms. Some children are also very deficient in their concepts of time and show very slow development of time-words (Brock & Del Giudice, 1963). One cannot help but wonder, therefore, how meaningful legal penalties in terms of "doing time" really are for such persons when they become teenagers and young adults.

DEVELOPMENTAL COGNITIVE THEORIES

In addition to the trait-oriented cognitive theorists already mentioned, there are developmental cognitive theories which deserve consideration. As the name would suggest, these theories stress the developmental nature of morality and try to define the stages characteristic of such progress. The best-known of these theories are those proposed by Piaget and Kohlberg.

The Theory of Jean Piaget

Modern workers in the field regard Piaget's volume *Moral Judgment of the Child* (1932) as a milestone in research on moral development. Concentrating on the cognitive aspects of moral development and using his typical clinical-interview technique, Piaget studied approximately 100 children from six to twelve years of age and identified two distinct stages in the child's moral judgment. The first he called "heteronomous" and the second "autonomous," with the transition between the two occurring at about *seven* years of age in normal children. (It is indeed interesting that developmental psychologists, using their sophisticated techniques, find and describe in their own jargon important qualitative changes in the child's cognitive development around seven years of age which traditionally has been used by wise old Mother Church as "the age of reason.")

Children in these two stages, Piaget reports, have different concepts of right and wrong, and different concepts of justice. In the "heteronomous" stage they judge the seriousness of offenses against property, for example, in terms of the amount of damage done (how many cups broken, regardless of the accidental nature of the event), whereas the "autonomous" children judge the seriousness of the offense in terms of the *intent* of the offender. Similarly, the less mature children were found to believe in immanent justice and the need for expiation. The more mature children tend to believe in naturalistic causation and in the need for restitution rather than for expiation. These trends were found to show increase with age and to hold for many Western cultures.

Piaget not only identified the above-mentioned two major stages in moral development, but on the basis of rather scanty evidence outlined in some detail five types of moral realism and six attributes of the sense of justice. His work in broad outline has been verified by other investigators, but the details of the sequences he postulates have not been substantiated.

Kohlberg (1964a) agrees that eight of Piaget's eleven stages are consistent enough to be considered "genuine developmental dimensions," increasing regularly with age regardless of the culture or situation. He also maintains that the other three dimensions described by Piaget, which are less cognitive, do not appear to be genuine developmental dimensions. Studies of the relations of moral judgment and social pressure and of the child's attitude toward authority yield no support for Piaget's theory. Although the latter's theory leads to the expectation of a positive relationship between peer-group participation and an orientation toward reciprocity, Kohlberg found a trend in the opposite direction, for children who were social isolates made more use of the concept of reciprocity in their moral thinking than those who identified with a peer group. Kohlberg concludes:

Piaget's theory is . . . validated only in its description of the young child's morality as oriented to obedience and to punishment and as ignoring subjective ends and values, and in its assumption that these features of child morality decline with age and development in various cultural settings [Kohlberg, 1964a, p. 320].

The Theory of Lawrence Kohlberg

After a critical review of Piaget and the psychoanalytically oriented identification theory, Kohlberg (1964a) turns to the developmental approach, which he espouses, in which moral learning is viewed in terms of age-related sequences of changes by which moral attitudes emerge from qualitatively different pre-moral attitudes and concepts. He sees these differences in *description* of moral learning as being associated with differences in conception of the *process* of moral learning, regardless of content. The developmentalist, Kohlberg explains, does not accept the "super-ego strength" view of the social environment as "stamping into" the child given cultural rules which persist as internal moral structures throughout life; environment is seen rather as a social world including rules which the child comes to understand through conceptualized role-taking. He concludes:

The mere process of role-taking the attitudes of others in organized social interaction is believed to transform concepts of rules from external things to internal principles [Kohlberg, 1964a, p. 314].

In Kohlberg's own developmentally oriented research based on lengthy free interviews with 100 boys aged seven to seventeen years concerning ten hypothetical moral-conflict situations, he identified six stages which, he claims, define a genuine sequence in individual development. He concludes that moral internalization relates closely to cognitive development of moral concepts, and that this contrasts markedly with the prevailing ideas of learning theorists interested in overt behavior, psychoanalysts interested in fantasy, and of Piaget who was interested in moral judgment. He points out that these theorists have all assumed that the basic features of adult conscience have developed by early childhood between five and eight years of age and claims that moral judgment data indicate that anything clearly like "conscience" develops relatively late.

Kohlberg (1964b) studied children's ability to judge action in terms of moral standards by asking them to evaluate certain deviant acts which they were told were followed by rewards, and certain conforming acts which they were told were followed by punishment. Each act was judged as good or bad by four-year-olds in terms of the reward or punishment rather than in terms of a rule. Between five and seven years of age, the children generally evaluated the act in terms of its moral label rather than in terms of its reinforcement in the story. It was not until pre-adolescence that the majority of children were able to make "disinterested" moral judgments and to formulate a concept of a good self. Kohlberg's studies support a developmental point of view, and he maintains that moral judgment cannot be explained by a "nondevelopmental" view of moral learning as simply internalization of cultural rules through verbal learning, reinforcement, or identification. Relating his work back to the earlier findings of Hartshorne and May, he points to a "view of overt adolescent moral conduct as a product of the development of broad social-cognitive capacities and values rather than of a 'superego' or of 'introjection of parental standards'" (Kohlberg, 1964a, pp. 324-325). He concludes as follows:

The development of a morality of identification with authority is dependent upon "natural" social role-taking and the development of concepts of reciprocity, justice, and group welfare in the years from four to twelve [Kohlberg, 1964a, p. 323].

As a final point, Kohlberg, after identifying five types of ego-strength variables from the experimental literature, drew the following conclusion which is very relevant to our concern about the development of conscience:

The above findings in the aggregate provide some support for the interpretation of moral character as ego, rather than superego strength. This interpretation implies that the major consistencies in moral conduct represent decision-making capacities rather than fixed behavior traits. It is thus consistent with the findings on situational variation which suggested that moral conduct was the product of a situational decision [Kohlberg, 1964b, pp. 391-392].

OTHER DEVELOPMENTAL STUDIES

In an effort to answer the developmental question of whether the early formation of conscience is predictive of good behavior over long periods of the life span, the studies of MacFarlane, Allen, and Honzik (1954), and of Kagan and Moss (1962) may be cited. These studies showed no substantial stability between ages six and thirteen on such traits as parents' ratings of selfishness and psychologists' ratings of aggressiveness over time.

In the Nobles County (Minnesota) longitudinal study reported by Anderson (1960) a "sense of responsibility" as measured by the Harris (1957) scale revealed early improvement in responsibility from nine to eleven years, followed by a plateau until thirteen years of age, and a second growth spurt from thirteen to sixteen years of age. Peck and Havighurst (1960) found considerable stability in moral character as shown by the ratings of community informants over the ages of ten to seventeen. As Kohlberg (1964) points out, however, this may be the result of an increasingly favorable reputation and halo effect in ratings obtained in the small city where the data were gathered, rather than to any real stability in the deeper aspects of moral character. According to Parke (1969), such data "argue against a learning theory interpretation of moral judgments as products of direct cultural instruction." He adds that "a learning theory approach may be more appropriate for explaining moral conduct data, which in contrast to moral judgments, vary greatly with situational and background differences" (Parke, 1969, p. 513). This illustrates the complexity of the field and how difficult it is to isolate different aspects for separate investigation.

In discussing the very sensitive and ingenious study of Aronfreed (1963) on self-criticism (which is essential to the formation of conscience) and reparation, Parke states:

Self-critical responses are more likely to be made when the socialization agent provides the child with explicit standards of evaluation than when cognitive structure is minimized. Reparation, however, tends to occur when the child, rather than the agent, has active control over the corrective or punitive consequences of transgression [Parke, 1969, p. 512].

Ausubel (1955), in a very insightful presentation on guilt and shame in the socializing process, points out that guilt is one of the most important psychological mechanisms through which an individual becomes socialized and without which child-rearing would be extremely difficult. He conceptualizes guilt as a special kind of negative self-evaluation, when an individual acknowledges that his behavior deviates from a given moral value to which he feels obligated to conform. By conscience Ausubel means an abstraction referring to a feeling of obligation to abide by all internalized values.

Before guilt feelings can be experienced, Ausubel (1955) hypothesizes that certain developmental conditions must have occurred: a) the individual must have accepted certain standards as his own, b) he must also have accepted the obligation to regulate his behavior to conform to those standards and must feel accountable for any lapses from them, and c) he must possess sufficient self-critical ability to recognize when a lapse has occurred. Ausubel (1955) also makes an interesting distinction between moral behavior and conformity to ethical standards. He claims that conformity may be only an indication of submission to authority rather than acceptance of it, and that behavior can first be regarded as manifesting moral properties when a sense of obligation is acquired.

Aronfreed (1964) studied the timing of punishment and found that an undesirable response was more likely to be inhibited if the punishment came at the onset of the action rather than afterwards. The punishment after the deviant behavior had occurred was more effective in producing the acquisition of self-critical responses. Parke concludes that the general implication of Aronfreed's research is that different reactions to transgression "should be treated as distinct moral phenomena and not equivalent reflections of an underlying unitary phenomenon such as conscience" (Parke, 1969, p. 512).

Three other studies of particular relevance deserve special mention, not only because of their scope and careful methodology, but also because of their practical implications for child-rearing. The first of these is *Anger in Young Children* by Goodenough (1930), in which over 1800 anger outbursts were observed and recorded in detail by the mothers of 42 children. Anger outbursts were found to be related to time of day, state of the child's health, what activity the child was engaged in, and so forth.

Perhaps the most pertinent results of Goodenough's study in the context of moral behavior and conscience concern the parents' methods of handling outbursts. Many of the methods which brought the outbursts to an immediate end were not effective for long-term training in moral development, as they rewarded the child for his misbehavior (bribing, giving in to the child's desire, and the like would come under this category). Many verbal methods such as reasoning, scolding, coaxing, and the like did not terminate the outbursts, but nearly always had to be followed by other methods. This is interpreted as indicating that children often have temper tantrums as a means of getting parental attention, and these verbal methods do just that—give the child plenty of attention! The most effective methods were those usually described by investigators in the field of parent-child relations as withdrawal of love—namely, ignoring or isolation for the severe occurrences. When these techniques are used with a well-adjusted child, the child should always know that he will be back in the family circle as soon as he is ready to behave himself, and what he has to do to reingratiate himself. Small incidents with very young children are often better handled by distraction and a change of activity.

A longitudinal analysis of the individual records kept over a period of several weeks revealed interesting data regarding the consistency of parental discipline. When the cases were divided into those who had more than the average number of outbursts and those who had less, it was found that, with one exception, every case in the former group had parents who used inconsistent discipline so that the children had no opportunity to learn what would happen as a result of their misbehavior. Most after-effects, such as pouting and resentment, were found in the children whose parents were *inconsistent* in their handling. Thus children resent, and consider unfair, punishments based on whims which vary from day to day. After meticulous analysis of her data by statistical techniques, Goodenough concluded with the wise adage which might have been heard from the pulpit generations ago: "Self-control in the parents is after all the best guarantee of self-control in the child" (Goodenough, 1930, p. 247). Although Goodenough's analysis seems to have been suggested by learning theorists, her conclusion is certainly relevant to the modeling and identification aspects of the psychoanalytic tradition.

A rather parallel study on discipline in the home was reported by Clifford (1959) which involved 120 mothers of 60 boys and

60 girls from both upper and lower socio-economic levels. The children were three, six, and nine years of age. The three-year-olds were involved in disciplinary incidents on the average of once a day, the six-year-olds approximately once every other day, and the nine-year-olds only once every fourth day. For all the dimensions examined, age was the most important variable. Disciplinary incidents arose in situations concerning daily routines, establishing sibling and adult relationships, and in displaying behavior adults deem inappropriate. Mothers were primarily responsible for handling the incidents requiring discipline, and the fathers participated only minimally. Evidence was found that parents shift their disciplinary methods with the age of the child. This is attributed to the child's increasing communication skills, for as he becomes older he can communicate his needs and desires more effectively and can better understand the limitations imposed by, and expectations of, the parents. Clifford concludes that the child proceeds from rudimentary concepts to those which are more differentiated, and that the degree to which the child comes to establish his own set of behavioral standards is really the best measure of the success of the discipline. Since the older child was found better able to get along with others, better able to follow routines, and better able to participate in activities without requiring disciplinary measures, Clifford believes that his study showed that the older subjects had learned self-discipline.

A third study by Eberhart (1942) was based on 850 boys in grades 1 to 12 from the West Side of Chicago. Using the method of paired comparisons, he developed a scale of children's attitudes regarding the seriousness of offenses against property. Some of the offenses which were regarded as more serious by older than by younger children were "to swipe flowers from a park," "to swipe your mother's wrist watch and pawn it," "to sneak a rubber ball from a dime store counter." Offenses which older children regarded as less serious than younger children regarded them were: "to keep $1.00 you find on the street without trying to find the owner," "to help yourself to chocolates from a box in your sister's room," "to ride on the street car for half fare when you should pay full fare." About ten per cent of the boys were interviewed in order to determine some of the criteria for the moral judgments they expressed on the written test. Here the findings agreed with Piaget's report of increasing concern with intention and motivation. Offenses were judged more serious in proportion: as they were more likely to bring punishment; as they involved more valuable property; when the property was owned by someone toward whom an obligation was felt; when they injured an actual person; when they must be called stealing rather than "borrowing"; or insofar as they damaged the moral character of the offender. The absence of these features rendered offenses less serious in the judgment of the children. In general, younger boys reported fear of punishment more frequently, and in the upper grades the reason given most frequently was unwillingness to injure others.

PARENT–CHILD RELATIONSHIPS

Hoffman succinctly summarized the studies on the influence of family relationships and child-rearing practices on the child's development of a conscience as follows:

Affection contributes to identification: psychological discipline which capitalizes on the affectionate relationship (and its resulting identification) fosters the development of internalized moral structures in general; and variations in type of psychological discipline may then account for the particular kind of internalized moral structure that develops [Hoffman, 1963, p. 312].

The same author goes on to conclude that, although in early childhood there may be little behavioral generality and little dynamic consistency, both tend to increase with age. The morality of the young child may be more a matter of rote learning of relatively specific acts and avoidances, but as the child grows older his standards become more integrated around broad principles and are more likely to be generalized from one situation to another.

In summarizing a related group of investigations dealing with children's reactions to transgressions, the same author concludes:

Despite the diversity of theoretical approaches, measuring instruments, and moral content areas . . . , results have a common core of agreement that is encouraging. . . . We may tentatively conclude that an internalized moral orientation is fostered by an affectionate relationship between the parent and child, in combination with the use of discipline techniques which utilize this relationship by appealing to the child's personal and social motives [Hoffman, 1963, p. 305].

On the other hand, after reviewing a number of investigations on parental punitiveness, Kohlberg (1964a) concludes that there is a consistent positive relationship between conscience and parental punitiveness. Indeed, punitive aggression by the parent leads to aggression by the child, but it does not lead to moral learning. In spite of the experimental and naturalistic evidence of imitation of parental behavior based on power and prestige, it appears, according to Kohlberg, that there is almost no evidence that variations in parental power influence strength of conscience or strength of identification with parents. He also found that there is little evidence for a relationship between the sex of the dominant parent and various measures of conscience.

Probably the most devastating type of parental behavior for children's moral development is that which deliberately and openly flouts the moral principles which parents verbalize and try to instill in their children. The "white lies" parents tell, or ask children to tell for them, and the frequent forgotten or broken promises can do more to undermine a child's trust than preaching and religious education can counteract. Children are very wise and sense inconsistency and insincerity in the behavior of adults at an early age. This is the kind of thing which is present in large amounts in too many homes and which often counteracts the better moments and the good outside influences of school and religious educators. Parents who punish bad language by children, yet constantly present such a language model to their children, or who insist that children attend church, but do not go themselves, are guilty of this type of inconsistency.

One of the most baffling problems for parents, teachers, and religious educators concerned with helping children to develop a right conscience in a variety of areas, is the discrepancy between moral knowledge and conduct. Parents frequently admonish children for wrongdoing with the comment "You should know better!" —and indeed the culprit often does know better. But as so often happens at all ages, we "know better and do worse." This has been one of the greatest pitfalls to the clergy who usually are verbalists par excellence, steeped in abstractions of philosophy and theory during their long years of training, but who find themselves utterly frustrated and incapable of spelling out the abstractions and principles which they have absorbed in sufficiently concrete and specific terms to make them meaningful to small children.

Mothers, too, often become hopelessly entangled in semantic problems as they have become overly attached to the words of prayers or the catechism and find themselves unable to communicate spiritual and moral values to young children in language which they can understand. Children at first think very concretely in terms of their own limited experience. When they first begin to define words, around six years of age, their definitions are most often in terms of use, such as "a hat is to wear," "a stove is to cook on," or "an orange is to eat." Still later, the definitions are in descriptive terms of shape, color, size, or material, and only much later—about ten to twelve years of age—do they think categorically and say that "an orange is a fruit" or "a hat is an article of clothing."

Too often, parents, the clergy, and religious educators give the principles and expect children to be able to apply them in their everyday life situations. For the eight-year-old it is a far cry from learning to love one's neighbor to not hitting Charlie back, on the playground; or from learning to verbalize about respect for the property of others to not taking fruit from a fruitstand or the necessity of paying for candy in the supermarket. Much of the attempted moral training of children has resulted in disappointment because it is too much oriented to the intellectual approach, and when he *knows* better, the child's parents and teachers are baffled by the psychological problem of the motivation for disapproved behavior.

On the other hand, many childish transgressions are committed in utter ignorance that the specific act is dishonest, cruel, or impure according to his as yet imperfectly internalized standards. How often has a young child been called "a little liar" for something he said when he himself has no idea of what "a liar" is. It has been found that about 50 per cent of the lies children tell are told out of fear, usually as quite natural defensive reactions to the threat or expectation of severe punishment. Another high percentage of the lies of four- and five-year-olds are merely fanciful imaginative tales of children who are looking for attention or approval, and who have no intention of deceiving a listener. A great deal of psychological harm is often done to children by well-meaning adults who attempt to read moral meanings into innocent events or extract confessions even in the face of objective facts, or who label as lies the fanciful imaginative stories of creative children who need help in distinguishing between the real and the unreal. Extracting confessions is of little or no value. It often amounts to mental cruelty and never replaces the broken object.

SOCIO–ECONOMIC STATUS AND DELINQUENCY

Burton (1963) cites the work of Kohn (1959) who noted that different value systems have been found to characterize families from different social levels. Working-class families tend to stress the immediate implications of a child's act and want the child to stay out of trouble by not doing the "wrong" thing. In essence their approach seems to be entirely negative and to emphasize the "don'ts." On the other hand, middle-class parents try to help their children to understand the implications of their own behavior, to show them *why* they should not do certain things and to enable them to *choose* to do the "right thing." This fits in with MacRae's (1954) postulation that there are two distinct processes of moral development, the cognitive and the emotional. It would seem that the middle-class families, with their greater language skills enabling better communication and interpretation and generalization about ways to behave, tend to develop the cognitive aspect of moral behavior earlier and to a more effective level; whereas the lower socio-economic families are more concerned with the immediate control of their impulse-ridden children who have not learned to wait, and to trust, and to defer immediate gratification, as required in Erikson's (1950) and Goldfarb's (1955) conceptualizations.

The voluminous literature on delinquency may be mentioned briefly in this connection as it exemplifies the failure of the development of a normal conscience. The evidence is quite impressive that delinquents tend to come from homes where an excessive amount of corporal punishment has occurred. Rejecting parents have relied almost exclusively on physical punishment, often administered in anger with the children not knowing what they were being punished for. "Oh, she was always beatin' on me" is typical of delinquents' descriptions of home discipline. Eventually the children get too big for this kind of blind, unreasoned handling; the necessary affective bond for the normal identification is never formed, and respect for authority is not established in such children. The result is open rebellion in the form of delinquency and serious conduct-problems. In these cases there is no formation of a healthy conscience, and recidivism is common. Hewitt and Jenkins (1946) describe this type of child as the "unsocialized aggressive" youngster who is not helped by the usual psychotherapeutic techniques because

> . . . he does not have too much superego: he has too little. One does not need to analyze a superego, rather it is necessary to synthesize one. One does not seek to relieve guilt-anxiety. One seeks to create it. This is done in essentially the same way that taboos are planted at any time of life, whether in the early training period of childhood when the process is normally most intense or in later life adjustments as upon induction into the Army. It requires the use of authority, firmness, planned limitation, and at times punishment. What is necessary for success is, first of all, a warm accepting attitude on the part of the parent or parent substitute [Hewitt & Jenkins, 1946, p. 86].

Since the parents of the above-described children often do not or cannot love them, the job usually falls to a counselor, teacher, or other parent-surrogate. It is necessary first to convince such a child that one has an interest in his welfare. It usually takes a very exceptional personality to be able to tolerate and maintain a warm relationship with these difficult children. The slow process of retraining such children usually has to be done in an institutional setting where *all* transgressions can be corrected. If these children are treated by methods suited to overinhibited, withdrawn children in permissive-play therapy, which leads to further open expression of aggression, behavior only becomes worse.

Not all children who engage in delinquent behavior are of this unsocialized aggressive type. Hewitt and Jenkins (1946) also identified a group of children who were called socialized delinquents who subscribe to the code of the peer group. These children are often the products of parental *neglect* rather than parental *rejection* who have developed gang loyalty which must be redirected. Either the individual children must be isolated from the group, or the whole group treated effectively by strong masculine personalities with capacities for warmth, fairness, and generosity of feeling. More recent work by Kohlberg found a

> . . . morality of reciprocity and equality . . . to be associated with lack of respect for adult authority, but with peer group participation. Judgements in terms of reciprocity, relativism and equality were found to

differentiate delinquents from working class controls [Kohlberg, 1964a, p. 320].

RELIGIOUS TRAINING

The developmental psychologist who is trained to deal with the whole child in all the complexities of the total organism has difficulty in accepting the intellectual compartmentalizing of the person engaged in by philosophers and theologians. Piaget, for example, stresses only the cognitive aspects of moral judgment, yet developmental psychologists, clergy, educators, and parents are concerned with the moral conduct and behavior of children. In trying to help children develop a right conscience about their behavior, adults must be concerned also with the emotional and affective aspects of their lives as well, which include the feelings of guilt or shame as elements of conscience, and which to the developmentally oriented psychologist cannot be reduced to isolated intellectualized distinctions used by theologians.

In the home of religious parents, the child's religious motives can also be appealed to, for parents who have a deep, abiding faith in God and who recognize that their authority over their children is God-given inculcate in their children a belief in the Creator. Such parents can appeal to their children's love for their heavenly Father, which is a powerful means of accomplishing conformity to the standards of behavior they are trying to maintain in their home. Emphasis on the positive motivation of conformity because of the love of God and desire to please Him is much sounder psychology than the all-too-frequent and strong emphasis on negative motivation to be good because of fear of God's punishments. It is an aid in achieving perfect contrition rather than imperfect contrition and is much less likely to lead to problems of scrupulosity and overwhelming guilt feelings.

There are a few psychological studies which present some evidence on the influence of religious training. Of special interest in this connection is the study by Boehm (1962) who gave four Piaget-type stories to children from six to nine years of age and found a marked tendency for the children from Catholic parochial schools to make more mature moral judgments in responding to the stories, answering much more often in terms of intentionality than children in public schools. In similar articles on the same populations she had found differences related to intelligence and to socio-economic level. The differences in relation to intelligence and social class were not found in the Catholic school children, as the more mature moral interpretations seemed to have been communicated to the children of the working class in such settings as well as, or sometimes better than, to the children from the middle class.

A somewhat different dimension of what may be conscience as broadly conceived was studied by Novicky (1959) in his research on fraternal charity in Catholic students in parochial and in public schools. The students were matched on background factors so as to minimize the likelihood of finding positive results in favor of the parochial school children. The instrument was carefully validated and was highly reliable. At all grade levels studied —five, seven, nine and twelve—the parochial school children showed strikingly higher scores of fraternal charity. The trait measured by this instrument showed growth over these grades in both school systems, with some slackening at ninth grade and with the girls earning scores superior to those of the boys,

In an interesting study by Kuhlen and Arnold (1944), 547 children and adolescents, aged twelve, fifteen, and eighteen years, responded to a questionnaire consisting of 52 statements representing various religious beliefs and 18 statements dealing with religious issues. Many important age trends appeared in contrasting the beliefs of the twelve- and eighteen-year-olds, indicating an increasing tolerance and a discarding of many specific beliefs as they grew older. Catholics, all of whom were in public schools, wondered about fewer beliefs and checked fewer problems than did non-Catholics. One wonders if the same trend would be found since Vatican II. The study did indicate that many children had religious problems with which they wanted help, but they were dissatisfied with conventional church services and with the help available to them through their churches. In another study, Farber (1959) found that the presence of a mentally retarded child in the home had a less disintegrating effect on Catholic families than on families of Protestant or Jewish background.

An interesting volume by a psychologist (O'Neil) and a priest (Donovan) entitled *Sexuality and Moral Responsibility* shows the strong impact of Piaget's writings on some of the newer thinking in theology. The basic contention of the book is that "a viable morality must be solidly grounded in the established principles of the behavioral sciences" (O'Neil & Donovan, 1968, p. ix). These authors attempt to build a bridge between psychological findings on cognitive growth and moral development in children and recent theological thinking on the nature of mortal and venial sin. It is on the basis of material of this sort that such controversial changes as deferral of the Sacrament of Penance have gone into effect in some dioceses.[2] The problem of masturbation has also been reinterpreted especially in reference to the age of the penitent and to a morality of intention rather than of specific acts,

In the past, religious educators have often been disappointed that the catechetical method produced mere mouthings about theological concepts which young children did not really comprehend. The great needs seem to be to translate the abstract material or content into sufficiently concrete language to make it really meaningful to the immature minds of children, and then to find techniques for carrying children through the difficult growing-up and doubting period of adolescence when religious material formerly accepted on the authority of adults becomes accepted as mature beliefs, well integrated with scientific and other areas of knowledge.

It seems that from the psychological point of view religious educators in their current haste to innovate may be discarding something very precious in the early training of the young at their most impressionable age. Because previous methods of teaching have often produced difficult cases of scrupulosity even among the very young, and because of the increasing shortage of priests and the increasing numbers of children to cope with, Piaget's placing of the cognitive stage of "logical operations" as late as eleven to thirteen years has seemed to provide a welcome psychological justification for postponing the reception of the Sacrament of Penance until the adolescent or preadolescent years, when intellectually in Piaget's schema the necessary stage of cognitive growth has been reached for making the moral judgments necessary for an adequate examination of conscience, using the theological definitions of sin both mortal and venial.

Yet, as has been shown, much younger children can do wrong and they give evidence of feelings of guilt about their wrongdoing. It seems as though the early training for confession, when properly given, serves two very useful psychological purposes: *a*) it gives the child a way of disposing of his guilt at frequent intervals instead of cumulating it to be unloaded on the therapist's couch in adulthood; and *b*) it gives him a feeling of reverence in preparing himself for the reception of the Eucharist. This feeling is also in danger of being lost in the newer methods. Whether these practices have theological validity is another matter, but psychologically it will be very difficult suddenly to expect certain religious practices at eleven to thirteen years of age, when the conscience has not been developed and trained gradually in small matters from the very beginning.

Because religious education has not always used the most effective methods is no reason for deferring the whole process during the child's most important formative years. There will always be a few obsessive-compulsive personalities who will develop problems of scrupulosity regardless of specific content taught. The number and seriousness of these deviations can be lessened by placing the stress on the positive aspects of love of God rather than on the negative aspects of fear of punishment.

Many adults never really achieve Kohlberg's highest level in moral development and frequently rely on techniques and crutches they learned as children, for they never learned to communicate on the level of conscience in an adolescent or adult manner. Individual differences are great, and faulty methods of religious education can be responsible for fixations at immature levels. The techniques and curricula must grow with the child, always a step ahead to challenge him, yet timed not to be so advanced as to be beyond his grasp, but never so repetitious as to bore him. Furthermore, it is only when parents and teachers exemplify in their own lives the principles they are trying to inculcate that they can avoid the current well-deserved accusation of hypocrisy, leveled by the younger generation.

Just as Piaget claims that the psychologist should not tell the educators how or what to teach, but should merely present them with the facts that research has discovered regarding the child's intellectual development, so Kohlberg draws similar conclusions regarding the moral development of children. He wisely points out that "Social scientists can contribute to *clarification* of moral education decisions both of ends and techniques, without imposing their values on others" (Kohlberg, 1964b, p. 424). Such clarification demands the communication of accurate and comprehensive information regarding moral development and functioning to parents and educators in terms they can understand and apply in everyday-life situations in their relationships with children.

NOTES

1. The integration of Erikson's theory with Catholic philosophy is well developed by McLaughlin (1964).
2. The focal point of the controversy is the reception of First Communion without antecedent reception of the Sacrament of Penance. In this connection, it is emphasized that Penance and Eucharist are two distinct and separate sacraments. It is appropriate, therefore, that pastoral concern should be separately directed to the best initial reception of each. Guide lines adopted, for instance, in the Diocese of Brooklyn state: "The theological understanding of sin, the experience of priests and catechists and the studies of developmental psychology lead to the conclusion that young children are not capable of mortal sin. Hence they should not be obliged to confess before First Communion." In keeping with this viewpoint, initial reception of the Sacrament of Penance might be postponed until the age of ten or even early adolescence, because it is judged, largely on the basis of evidence from developmental psychology, that the individual does not have the self-possession or freedom to sin gravely until this time. An indication of how sharply controverted this viewpoint is may be seen from the interchange of articles and letters on this subject appearing in *The Tablet* (Brooklyn) during October, November, and December, 1969, and January, 1970.—Ed.

REFERENCES

Anderson, J. E., "Prediction of Adjustment over Time," I. Iscoe & H. Stevenson (Eds.), *Personality Development in Children.* Austin, Texas: University of Texas Press, 1960. Pp. 28-72.

Aronfreed, J., "The Nature, Variety, and Social Patterning of Moral Responses to Transgression," *Journal of Abnormal and Social Psychology,* 1961, *63*, 223-240.

Aronfreed, J., "The Effects of Experiential Socialization Paradigms upon Two Moral Responses to Transgression," *Journal of Abnormal and Social Psychology*, 1963, *66*, 437-448.

Aronfreed, J., "The Origin of Self-Criticism," *Psychological Review*, 1964, *71*, 193-218.

Ausubel, D. P., "Relationship between Shame and Guilt in the Socializing Process," *Psychological Review*, 1955, *62*, 378-390.

Bandura, A., & Walters, R. H., "Aggression," *The 62nd Yearbook of the National Society for the Study of Education*. Pt. I. *Child Psychology*. Chicago: University of Chicago Press, 1963. Pp. 364-415.

Bender, L., "Psychopathic Behavior Disorders in Children," R. M. Lindner & R. V. Seliger (Eds.), *Handbook of Correctional Psychology*. New York: Philosophical Library, 1947.

Boehm, L., "The Development of Conscience: A Comparison of Students in Catholic Parochial Schools and in Public Schools," *Child Development*, 1962, *33*, 591-605.

Brock, T. C., & Del Giudice, C., "Stealing and Temporal Orientation," *Journal of Abnormal and Social Psychology*, 1963, *66*, 91-94.

Burton, R. V., "Generality of Honesty Reconsidered," *Psychological Review*, 1963, *70*, 481-499.

Clifford, E., "Discipline in the Home," *Journal of Genetic Psychology*, 1959, *95*, 45-82.

Durkin, D., "Children's Acceptance of Reciprocity as a Justice Principle," *Child Development*, 1959, *30*, 289-296.

Eberhart, H. C., "Attitude toward Property," *Journal of Genetic Psychology*, 1942, *60*, 3-35.

Erikson, E., *Childhood and Society*. New York: Norton, 1950.

Eysenck, H. J., "The Development of Moral Values in Children: The Contribution of Learning Theory," *British Journal of Educational Psychology*, 1960, *30*, 11-22.

Farber, B., "Effects of Severely Mentally Retarded Child on Family Integration," *Monographs of the Society for Research in Child Development*, 1959, *24* (Whole No. 71).

Goldfarb, W., "Emotional and Intellectual Consequences of Psychologic Deprivation in Infancy: A Revaluation," P. Hoch & J. Zubin (Eds.) *Psychopathology of Childhood*. New York: Grune & Stratton, 1955. Pp. 105-119.

Goodenough, F. L., *Anger in Young Children*. Minneapolis: University of Minnesota Press, 1930.

Grinder, R. "New Techniques for Research in Children's Temptation Behavior," *Child Development*, 1961, *32*, 679-688.

Gump, P. V., & Kounin, J. S., "Milieu Influences in Children's Concepts of Misconduct," *Child Development*, 1961, *32*, 711-720.

Harris, D. B., "A Scale for Measuring Attitudes of Responsibility in Children," *Journal of Abnormal and Social Psychology*, 1957, *55*, 322-326.

Hartshorne, H., & May, M. A., *Studies in the Nature of Character*. Vol. I. *Studies in Deceit*. Vol. II. *Studies in Self-Control*. Vol. III. *Studies in the Organization of Character*. New York: Macmillan, 1928-1930.

Hewitt, L. E., & Jenkins, R. L., *Fundamental Patterns of Maladjustment: The Dynamics of Their Origin*. Springfield, Ill.: State of Illinois, 1946.

Hoffman, M. L., "Child Rearing Practices and Moral Development: Generalizations from Empirical Research," *Child Development*, 1963, *34*, 295-318.

Jersild, A. T., *Child Psychology*. (6th ed.) Englewood Cliffs, N.J.: Prentice-Hall, 1968.

Kagen, J., & Moss, H. A., *Birth to Maturity: A Study in Psychological Development*, New York: Wiley, 1962.

Kohlberg, L., "Moral Development and Identification," *The 63rd Yearbook of the National Society for the Study of Education. Pt. I. Theories of Learning and Instruction*. Chicago: University of Chicago Press, 1964. Pp. 277-327. (a)

Kohlberg, L., "Development of Moral Character and Ideology," M. L. Hoffman & L. W. Hoffman (Eds.), *Review of Child Development Research*. New York: Russell Sage Foundation, 1964. Pp. 383-432. (b)

Kohn, M. L., "Social Class and Parental Values," *American Journal of Sociology*, 1959, *64*, 337-351.

Kuhlen, R. G., & Arnold, M., "Age Differences in Religious Beliefs," *Journal of Genetic Psychology*, 1944, *65*, 291-300.

MacFarlane, J., Allen, L., & Honzik, M. P., *A Developmental Study of the Behavior Problems of Normal Children between 21 Months and 14 Years*. Berkeley: University of California Press, 1954.

MacRae, D., Jr., "A Test of Piaget's Theories of Moral Development," *Journal of Abnormal and Social Psychology*, 1954, *49*, 14-18.

McLaughlin, B. (S.J.), *Nature, Grace, and Religious Development*. Westminster, Md.: Newman Press, 1964.

Mowrer, O. H., *Learning Theory and Personality Dynamics*. New York: Ronald Press, 1950.

Mussen, P. H., Conger, J., & Kagen, J., *Child Development and Personality*, (3rd ed.) New York: Holt, Rinehart & Winston, 1969.

National Institute of Child Health and Human Development, *The Acquisition and Development of Values: Perspectives on Research*. Report of a Conference, May 15-17, 1968, Washington, D.C. Washington, D.C.: U.S. Government Printing Office, 1969.

Nelson, E. A., Grinder, R. E., & Mutterer, M. L., "Variance in Behavioral Measures of Honesty," *Developmental Psychology*, 1969, *1*, 265-279.

Novicky, W. A., "A Comparison of the Attitudes of Fraternal Charity between Catholic Children with Two Kinds of Educational Background," Unpublished doctoral dissertation, Fordham University, 1959.

O'Neil, R. P., & Donovan, M. A., *Sexual and Moral Responsibility*. Washington, D.C.: Corpus Books, 1968.

Parke, R. D., "Introduction: Moral Development," R. D. Parke (Ed.), *Readings in Social Development*. New York: Holt, Rinehart & Winston, 1969. Pp. 507-515.

Peck, R. F., & Havighurst, R. J., *The Psychology of Character Development*, New York: Wiley, 1960.

Piaget, J. *The Moral Judgement of the Child* (trans. by M. Worde). New York: Harcourt, Brace & World, 1932.

Riffel, P. (S.J.) *A Psychological Study of the Personality Characteristics of the Pastorally Scrupulous*. (Doctoral dissertation, Fordham University) Ann Arbor, Mich.: University Microfilms, 1967. No. 67-11, 496.

Sears, R. R., "The Growth of Conscience," I. Iscoe & H. Stevenson (Eds.), *Personality Development in Children*. Austin, Texas: University of Texas Press, 1960. Pp. 92-111.

Sears, R. R., Maccoby, E. E., & Levin, H., *Patterns of Child Rearing*. Evanston, Ill.: Row Peterson, 1957.

Teriel, E., "Developmental Processes in the Child's Moral Thinking," P. H. Mussen, J. Langer, & M. Covington (Eds.) *Trends and Issues in Developmental Psychology*. New York: Holt, Rinehart & Winston, 1969. Ch. 5, pp. 92-131.

19 How Conscience Is Formed

ROBERT SEARS, ELEANOR MACOBY
AND HARRY LEVIN

Conscience is complicated: no single fact or factor
is adequate to explain its formation. The giving of
rewards for good behavior and punishments for unacceptable conduct will account partly for the internal control a child develops. The values of the
peer group in which the child lives will also have a
direct effect on his moral code. These and other
processes are integrated in a theory of "identification" whereby the child creates a mentality similar
to that of his parents or other adults with whom he
has close association. The following selection *
shows how identification involves imagination, motivation, and practice in role-playing. It also indicates
through recorded interviews how normal parents
create the conditions in which conscience is formed.

At the beginning of a child's life, nearly all
the control of his changeworthy actions
comes from the parents. They watch what he does and decide
whether they like it. In a sense, they are required to play constantly the role of policeman.

This direct control is essential at first, of course, for the child
has had no opportunity to discover what is wanted of him. He is
ignorant of adult standards; he has not yet learned how to do
the "right" things. But this would be an intolerable state of affairs
if it continued very long. Mothers cannot spend all their time

* From *Patterns of Child Rearing* (Chicago: Row, Peterson and Company, 1957), pp. 362–380. Reprinted by permission.

watching and guarding. The child must learn to control himself. He must develop his own standards of conduct. He must apply sanctions to his own behavior. He must, in other words, develop a conscience.

One can distinguish three kinds of control. First, there is the external type that requires constant surveillance and direct intervention. The child does as he wishes until someone stops him. The year-and-a-half-old baby crawls toward the fireplace and his mother picks him up and puts him elsewhere. The children quarrel and the mother says, "Stop that fighting with your brother!"

Second, there is the child's self-control that is based on fear of punishment or hope of reward. This is simply an extension of external control. It is dependent on the immediate (or near future) presence of someone who can punish or reward. When a youngster is punished often enough for a misdeed, he may learn not to do it any more. At least, he may if punishment is fairly certain and the mischief is self-announcing, like marking the wallpaper with crayons. Control by fear has certain disadvantages, obviously, for there are many kinds of misconduct that involve little risk of being caught. Children learn, inevitably, to appraise the realistic probabilities that they can get away with such matters as filching cookies, pinching the baby, masturbating in bed, or jumping on the sofa when mother is in the back yard. Furthermore, to be at all effective, punishment must be fairly frequent or very severe; and we saw, in the chapters on dependency and aggression, some of the unattractive consequences of such methods of training.

Third, there is the child's inner control that appears to come from a genuine acceptance of the parents' standards of conduct as his own. Deviation from these carries its own punishment from within the child himself; going counter to his self-instruction makes him feel guilty, ashamed, or self-derogating. The term *conscience* is applied to this kind of internal control.

Control by fear and control by conscience are both learned, of course, and every normal child develops some of each. For certain kinds of behavior he may have no internalized standards but only a fear of getting caught. For other kinds, the standards of his parents may be fully accepted as his own, and he acts in accord with them, whether or not there is risk of punishment.

It is difficult to judge what would be an ideal balance between these two for children in our society. Too heavy a reliance on fear tends to make a child opportunistic and unpredictable, while a too severe conscience tends to inhibit him beyond the requirements of social living. A lack of either kind leaves him with changeworthy behavior that is unacceptable to his peers in childhood, and is viewed as infantile and irresponsible in adulthood. It is clear that without *some* conscience, the individual could not live with others.

As with any other learned behavior, the development of internal control is a gradual process. The year-old baby seems to have little of it. What he wants to do, he does. As he gets more skill at locomotion, he must be watched fairly continuously, for he shows little sign of realizing that ash trays and magazines and figurines are not for touching. In spite of continuous instruction, he goes about his exploration and manipulation with an expression of intent concern and an utter disregard of all threats or pleadings. "Nothing in the house is safe if he can reach it!"

Like the two-o'clock feeding, however, this stage will pass. In the middle of their second year, most children begin to show a few signs of restraint. Ash trays and trinkets are not yet inviolate, but on rare occasions a child may be seen to reach for something—hesitate—and withdraw. At first glance, this self-control may seem a simple matter, no more than a kind of primitive self-protection from expected criticism or restraint. No doubt some of his compliance with adult wishes is exactly this and no more (and always will be), but on occasion a parent may be lucky enough to overhear and note the muted birth-cry of conscience itself. Here is an example:

Martha's parents brought her along one Sunday afternoon when they came for a visit. She was seventeen months old, full of curiosity and mischief. While we had coffee and cookies, she thirstily drank down a glass of milk, ate half a cookie, and began an eager exploration of her surroundings. Toddling most of the time, crawling occasionally, she left trails of crumbs and tipped-over cups wherever she went. One of the floor lamps fascinated her especially. It was tall and straight, made of a single glossy round of wood just the right size for Martha to get a good grip on. When she stood up against it, clutching happily, the lamp teetered and swayed in what was obviously an entrancing fashion for Martha.

Twice her father had to put down his cup and leap across the room to prevent a crash. Twice he said clearly and distinctly, "Now, Martha, *don't touch!*" Each time he took her by the hand and led her over to some toys. These distracted her only briefly.

After the second interruption, Martha began a general exploration of the room again. Now she went a little slower, and several times glanced at her father. As she came closer to the lamp, however, she stopped looking his way and her movements were all oriented toward the lamp. Deliberately she stepped toward it, came within a couple of feet of it, and lifted her arm partly, a little jerkily, and then said sharply, commandingly, *"Don't touch!"*

There was an instant of struggling silence. Then she turned and stumbled across the room, flopped down on the floor, and started laughing excitedly. Her father, laughing with her, and obviously adoring, reached out and hugged and snuggled her for several minutes.

Why was this a beginning of conscience? Why not assume, more simply, that Martha was afraid her father would punish her if she touched the lamp again? The difference between fear and conscience lies in the *self-instruction* and the incorporation, in the child herself, of the values expressed by the parents. Martha was playing the parental role when she said sternly to herself, "Don't touch!" Had she continued to look furtively at her father as she got close to the lamp—had she oscillated back and forth in her approach—had she been whimpery or silent and withdrawn after the moment of decision—we would have said she was responding to the dangers of the situation by simple avoidance. But at the crucial moment, she did not have to look at her father; she looked to herself for guidance, and the behest she followed was her own.

This episode gave no real opportunity to observe the two most significant characteristics by which conscience control can be recognized. One is the maintenance of control, in the face of temptation, when there is no one present to insist, and when there is little danger of being caught. The other is the occurrence of guilt-feelings on those occasions when temptation is not overcome, when the child does deviate from his own standards of what is right or wrong. Guilt is difficult to observe, in any case, and occurs only when conscience control fails, or the temptation is strong enough to make the child recognize his wish to perform the forbidden act.

These criteria of conscience control become more and more frequently evident as children grow through their preschool and early school years. The three-year-old becomes trustworthy with respect to handling delicate objects—most of the time. The four-year-old can be left alone with the baby safely, even when the baby is a provocative nuisance—most of the time. Mothers gradually find themselves giving fewer admonitions, making fewer threats of direct control. They hear more frequently a sobbing and spontaneous confession of mischief, and they discover the doubtful satisfaction of being able to tell when a misdeed has occurred by the child's typical hangdog expressions of shame and guilt. Mothers learn, too, that such episodes produce pain and insecurity for a child. He may revert briefly to an earlier stage of dependency, sidling up to her, thumb in mouth, seeking reassurance and expressions of love. Or his self-inflicted pain may be so great that he actively seeks punishment; the spanking may be a better alternative than guilt and remorse. As one mother put it:

M. I spanked her, and I think it did her good. This idea . . . if you feel guilty, you feel better if you're punished for it. If you're not punished, you feel that you've missed something. . . . Until you have paid retribution, you are upset.

Conscience, then, does not develop all in one piece. The word itself refers not to a "thing" but to a process—the internal control of impulses that would lead to parentally disapproved action. From the second year, more and more impulses come under such control; more and more of the parents' qualities of behavior and standards of conduct are incorporated in the child's own repertory of actions. Even into adulthood, there is a continuing crystallization of beliefs and values, and the discovery of new areas of action that can be subjected to ethical interpretation.

This growing *scope,* or inclusiveness, of conscience control only partially corresponds to the *process* of conscience development, however. So far as we can tell, there is a learning of internal control that goes on mainly in the years before puberty, perhaps even chiefly in the first six to ten years of life, which establishes the extent to which conscience will operate throughout all the rest of life. As the child matures, and as he develops an understanding of more and more complex forms of social behavior (e.g., religious, political, economic, familial) under the categories of childhood behavior that he has already brought under internal control. Thus the adolescent may work out—often not consciously—an ethical belief that aggressive competition is evil; he may control firmly all his own impulses toward such behavior, even to the extent of refusing to join in competitive sports. It seems likely, however, that these later judgments of right and wrong are the direct successors to his early-childhood incorporation of parental strictures against aggression in the family. The *content* of the new values (i.e., avoiding competitive sport) is determined by the new experiences of maturity, but the *process* of internal controlling of impulses was learned long since. Even the *general category* (aggression control) probably was established as a category subject to such control in the first four or five years of life.

By their sixth year, children are well into the process of developing internalized control, although there are great differences among them in the rate at which this development takes place. Some children, especially some girls, appear to incorporate maternal values very early and to behave like "model" children long before they reach school age. Others have more of a struggle with such learning, and still show considerable evidence of depending on direct external control well after the age of six. What produces these differences? What child-rearing practices are associated with the rapid development of conscience?

We can approach this question best through the theory of *identification,* a process that has been hypothesized by psychoanalytic observers to account for the development not only of conscience but of several other aspects of behavior as well. The theory will help suggest which practices to examine as possible sources of conscience development. In succeeding sections we will then describe the measure of conscience we have been able to cull from the interviews and what child-rearing practices seem to have been associated with the more rapid and intense development of such behavior.

Identification

Long ago, psychoanalytic therapists discovered that many qualities in their adult patients' personalities seemed to be direct imitations of the same qualities in the patients' parents. Persistent probing of the feelings connected with these similarities brought out recollections of powerful emotions—love, anxiety, hatred—that seemed to stem from the earliest years of life and to be connected with both the love and disciplinary relationships the child had had with his parents. Many of the similarities, particularly those having to do with moral standards and values, apparently had developed in a context that made them seem almost like the products of direct parental demands. There was ample evidence that the process of absorbing parental values and adopting some forms of parental behavior was not a passive one. On the contrary, it was associated with very vigorous motives and emotions, and the qualities thus learned were so strongly established that the normal experiences of adult life could influence them but little.

Direct observation of young children, however, has suggested that much of this "learning" occurs without any specific "teaching" from the parents. A child, from his second year, begins to display interests and attitudes similar to theirs; he develops their values, and places their demands on both himself and others. Fantasy, too, shows this. The child acts out the adult role in his play with dolls, making mothers spank babies or require children to eat their cereal or hang up their clothes. He tries out adult-role behavior in his play with other children, trying on parents' clothes, pretending to have their occupations and responsibilities.

Perhaps the most pervasive of these patterns is that of sex-typing, i.e., the development of social behavior appropriate to the child's own sex. The great bulk of boyish behavior displayed by a boy, we suspect, is absorbed in the absence of any direct tuition whatever. Somehow he learns what occupations are male ones; he selects those occupations in his play and in his dream-plans for the future. When a mixed-sex group of three-year-olds is playing house, there may occasionally be a crossing of sex roles—a boy may be "nurse" or even "grandmother"—but this very rarely happens at kindergarten age. Boys are males by then, and girls are females. And they both know how to act appropriately. How did they learn if the parents did not teach them?

We can distinguish three main kinds of learning which occur in connection with social and emotional behavior of the complex level we are considering here. One of these is *trial and error.* Another is learning by *direct tuition,* what we called guidance in the last chapter. The third is *role practice,* the discovery and learning of new actions by observing what others do, and then practicing it by pretending to *be* the other person. The word "pretending" gives us an important clue to the character of role practice as it occurs in childhood: most of this practice occurs as fantasy, and much of it is covert. That is, it occurs in daydreams as well as in active play. We call the third method role practice rather than simple imitation partly because it may not manifest itself in overt, but only imagined, imitative behavior at the time it occurs. But beyond this, it involves the child's adopting the other person's role and then trying to act *altogether* like the other person acts in that role. He does not imitate just single aspects of his model's behavior; he takes on the role itself, at least momentarily, with all the feelings, attitudes, values, and actions that he attributes to the person who actually occupies the role.

All three kinds of learning require the same basic conditions. First there must be motivation. The child must want something. Second, he must perform some action. And third, that action must be reinforced; it must bring about a rewarding state of affairs. The difference between learning by direct guidance and by role practice is that in the latter the child's selection of what actions to perform stems from his own observation of what the role requires rather than from the instructions of his parents (or others). Role practice is more complex than simple trial and error because it requires the child to perceive and imagine himself in the place of a model. We are inclined to doubt that much learning of social behavior or values ever occurs by simple trial and error. We are concerned here, rather, with the distinction between learning by direct tuition and learning by role practice, i.e., learning without direct tuition.

Identification is the name we choose to give to whatever process occurs when the child adopts the method of role practice, i.e., acts as though he were occupying another person's role. Our chief problems in analyzing the process will be the discovery of what motives lead the child to role playing, and what satisfactions he gets from it. Within the framework of our present study, discovering the motives means discovering the kinds of learning experiences—maternal child-rearing practices—that are associated with a tendency to engage in such role practice.

We surmise that an important motive leading to role practice is the child's desire *to reproduce pleasant experiences*. Just as we rehearse in our own minds the compliments people have paid us, to savor once again the pleasure they gave us, so the child will enjoy playing the parental role in fantasy if parental actions have been nurturant, supportive, accepting. A related motive may be the child's *worry about whether he has his parents' affection and approval*. He can reassure himself by play-acting supportive behavior on his parents' part. These considerations lead us to examine especially the dependency relation between child and mother, to see if it has any bearing upon what we have called identification.

The normal physical dependency of the infant provides the conditions for development of a dependency motive. The constant association of the mother with the rewarding experiences of infancy also establishes a strong love for her. By the time a child is a year old, he has become related to his mother in such a way that not only do many of his satisfying actions require her presence and co-operation, but her very orientation toward him—indeed, her simple existence near him—is a source of pleasure. He *loves* his mother; he is emotionally dependent on her.

The nature of a mother's responsibilities is such, however, that she must gradually withdraw her attention. Perhaps she has another baby, or she must go to work, care for the house, devote herself more to her husband. She must return to her customary role as an individual in her own right. This gradual withdrawal of attention and support interferes with the child's satisfactions. He becomes *deprived*, in the technical sense of the word, even though his own growth of independence and desire for mastery of his world offer something of a substitution. Quite naturally, as with any frustration, he seeks methods of recovering what he has lost, and of overcoming the barriers that have been in his way.

One obvious method of doing this is to perform acts that delight and please the mother, especially those that she herself specifies. Any device that helps the child select and learn such acts will ultimately be rewarded. During the latter part of their first year and the beginning of their second, children start to imitate the behavior of their parents. The rewards for imitation are not hard to discover; the infant being subjected to socialization pressures can use parental behavior as a model and thus can learn more readily the rewarded ways of behaving.

This kind of modeling is still, in a sense, learning by direct tuition. That is, the mother rewards the child, perhaps not for specific actions but for generally patterning himself upon his parents. But there are other satisfactions in practicing parental roles, beyond the satisfaction of winning direct approval for it. Indeed, much role practice goes on when the parents are not present and cannot reward it—when the child is alone playing with dolls, when he is talking to himself in his crib, and when he is playing outdoors with playmates.

Our hypothesis is that a child will be most likely to practice his parents' roles extensively (even in those situations where his behavior is not directly rewarded) if his dependency motivation is strong. He wants to make sure that his mother loves him, and in an effort to do so, he may even perform some of the acts, himself, that his mother ordinarily performs. He can babble and talk, snuggle against his own arms, or offer himself a thumb to suck. He wants his mother near him, and when she is not there, he brings her closer by imagining her soothing words and actions.

If the strength of the child's identification is related to his level of dependency, we must consider again what child-rearing practices produce a strong motive of this kind. In Chapter Five we reported that the mother's warmth and her affectionate demonstrativeness were very slightly related to the amount of dependency the child showed ($r's = .08$ and $.13$). We expect, then, that these same aspects of maternal behavior will be related to the child's tendency to practice parental roles.

Second, we might examine the influence of the mother's method of discipline. If she used *love-oriented* techniques, we would expect that the child's efforts to rehearse love-expressions from her would be more vigorous than if she used techniques such as physical punishment or the deprivation of privileges, which could be adapted to by flight or hiding or by independent activity designed to recover the withheld objects or privileges.

In these comments, we have talked of the mother as the identificand. But whom does the child use as a model? With whom does he identify? The conditions described above suggest that the main *caretaker* will be the identificand. In American culture, this is almost always a woman, and usually it is the mother. Both boys and girls, according to this theory, form their first identification with a female. This is quite acceptable for a girl, for she will do well to possess feminine personality characteristics throughout her life. For the boy, however, it poses a problem. He must shift to a masculine identification, sometime in his early years, if he is to develop a normally masculine personality.

There are several possible reasons why he makes such a shift. The first is that he receives direct rewards from both his parents and his peers for behaving in the way his parents expect, that is, acting like a young male.

A second factor that seems to help boys to shift from a feminine to a masculine identificand is the defensive process described by Anna Freud (1937) as *identification with the aggressor*. During the latter part of the preschool period, boys rather commonly develop some degree of hostility toward their fathers, who may be viewed as rivals for their mothers' affection. This hostility creates an expectation of counter-hostility and a fear of retaliation. As a defense against this fear, the boy may adopt the "father role." There may be several things that conduce to this choice. For one, playing the father role may place the boy in what he perceives to be a more favored competitive position for the mother's attention. For another, he gains some fantasy control over the dangerous father, control in the sense that he now can "make the father do what he wants." He *is* the father. Still another factor is the power advantage that characterizes the father role. Quite aside from the competitive advantage for the mother's affection, the boy gains greater disciplinary and manipulative power within the family when he plays the father's role. This may not be a factor that would *initiate* the boy's more than the girl's identification with the father, but it is a reward that may often serve to maintain such identification when once the other factors have started it.

Still another factor in a boy's sex-typing, we suspect, is the greater number of opportunities he has to behave in a masculine way than in a feminine one. Also, he is more often rewarded for it. People around him *expect* a boy to be masculine; they gear their own activities to this expectation, and hence he is led into appropriate masculinity quite involuntarily. Then—because he does what is expected of him—the other people are satisfied and tend to provide him with the satisfaction he wants. This means, simply, that a boy probably gets more rewarded practice for his masculine identification than for his feminine one. Moreover, not all the contents of others' roles that we practice in fantasy see the light of day in our real-life actions. Many of us know how to take the oath of office for President of the United States, having watched inaugurations, but few of us will be called upon to put our stored-up knowledge into effect. Similarly, we believe that there is a great deal of potential behavior which a boy learns through identification with his mother which he never has an opportunity to employ. A boy can and does employ the learning that involves his mother's values, of course, but not such strictly feminine bits of behavior as putting on lipstick. The items a boy has rehearsed when practicing his *father's* role, however, are much more likely to be appropriate to the expectations others have of his behavior, and therefore are more likely to find their way into overt expression.

These views about identification can be recapitulated quite simply. We suggest that role practice develops in response to a number of motives, a major one being dependency—the child's need to assure himself of the continuance of the affection and nurturance to which he has become accustomed in early infancy. He chooses as his initial identificand the person—usually the mother—who has been his chief source of reward in these respects. He practices especially those aspects of the maternal role that bring important evidences of approval. The moral values and strictures, the attitudes and behaviors that are offered him as replacements for his changeworthy behavior, are the attributes of the adult role which prove particularly useful to him in this process. These include what we characterized earlier as *internal control* and *conscience.*

Along with the adoption of these specific learnings, the process of identification leads to the practice of many other aspects of the role of the identificand. Included are the appropriate sex-typed behaviors and attitudes. These begin to appear by age three in most children, because there is not only immediate reward for adopting the correct role, but there are also ample opportunities for practicing it in interaction with other people who have expectancies for the child to behave appropriately. Certain other behaviors that are part of the identificand's role—such as behaving maternally toward smaller children—may develop more slowly and may not be fully displayed until the child reaches adulthood himself. The reason for this lies in the lack of appropriate qualities in the environment; nobody expects him to behave in parental fashion or provides him the opportunity to be a fully responsible caretaker. Nevertheless these behaviors are practiced in some degree, even in very early childhood (primarily in fantasy), and are ready for evocation when the appropriate changes occur in the environment.

Obviously, we are assuming that the child-rearing practices of mothers are significant determinants of these various developments in the child. Equally obviously, we mean to suggest that differences among mothers' behaviors toward children will produce differences in the rapidity and intensity with which role practice will develop. Our next problem is the measurement of the differences in the extent to which identification has occurred. We will be concerned, in what follows, with one of the major consequences of this process, what we have called conscience. Extensive practice of parental roles enhances conscience, we believe, because in the course of such role play the child practices the value statements of his parents and thus makes them his own.

Conscience, as was mentioned in connection with the example of Martha, is demonstrated in behavior by two characteristics: the success with which temptation is resisted when no "policeman" is present; and the expression of confession and guilt after temptation has not been resisted. Our interviews provided no adequate information concerning the children's resistance to temptation, and reluctantly but necessarily we leave this behavior quality to later research. We have been able to secure a measure of the extent to which the children showed signs of guilt and confession, however. This aspect of behavior is but a limited representation of the effects of the identification process, and indeed is even a limited representation of conscience itself. As will be seen in the next section, our measure of this quality was based on the mothers' reports of how their children acted—whether with guilt signs and confession or with flight and denial—after having broken a rule or having committed some other misdeed. We might well suppose that those mothers whose children had the strongest capacity for resisting temptation would have the least evidence to contribute for our confession measure!

This fact, coupled with the usual problem of non-independence of our measures of the child's behavior and the mother's child-rearing practices, requires us to be particularly cautious in interpreting the findings we will present here. In addition, we must recognize that there are other possible factors besides those we have discussed in connection with the identification process that may determine the extent to which a child will confess his misdeeds—and perhaps seek absolution. These will be discussed in connection with the description of our measure of conscience.

Signs of Conscience

By and large, the mothers had little to suggest as to the best conditions for conscience development; they did not appear to think of this aspect of behavior in terms of their own responsibility for training. They were nonetheless acutely aware of conscientious behavior. Nearly all were able to describe clearly what they had observed with respect to their children's confessions and guilt reactions to deviation.

What are the symptoms by which we can recognize the growth of internal controls in a child? One, of course, is that he more and more often resists temptation, even when he is not being closely watched by a potential punisher. As we indicated above, we were not able to measure this quality from the interviews. A second indication of his having accepted his parents' standards as his own is his effort to teach these standards to his friends and siblings, i.e., *to act the parental role*. For example:

M. And I've taught him never to touch a medicine cabinet. I showed my little boy the bottles—medicine bottles—and I've told him. He was sick, oh, about a year ago, in the hospital, and he's never forgotten it, and I don't think he ever will. He's told his brothers about it plenty of times. And I told him, "If you took your medicine bottle, you're going to get sick like you did then." He won't go near that medicine cabinet. And if he sees one of his brothers going to touch it, he'll tell him, "You'll go to the hospital, and you'll stay in the hospital for a long, long time; and you won't see Mommy or Daddy. And you won't have no toys to play with—just lay in bed all the time and get needles." And now none of them will go up there. I think he's really the one that broke them of going to the medicine cabinet.

This child was taking a parental role in real-life interaction with his brothers. Such role playing is even more common in play situations. Every mother has heard little girls, when playing with their dolls, adopt their mothers' tones of voice and phrases, sometimes with embarrassing precision. This play acting, this pretending that one *is* one's father or mother, appears to be one of the major ways in which children come to understand what their parents' values are and to learn to accept them as their own. Since we did not inquire directly about the mothers' observations of this kind of behavior, we had only scattered examples reported and so were unable to use them for measurement.

A third indicator of conscience is the way a child acts *after* he has done something wrong. Some children, those who are primarily concerned with the avoidance of external punishment, will try to get out of their parents' sight, hide the evidence of the misdeed, and deny the act when asked directly about it. The child with a well-developed conscience cannot escape so easily, for he is troubled by self-blame as well as by the fear of punishment. He applies his parents' disapproving evaluation of his behavior to himself. He can feel better only after he has made up for his misdeed in some way, and been forgiven. He acts guilty and sheepish. He may hang around his mother, acting in such a way that she will know something is wrong. Sometimes he will arrange things so she is sure to find out what he has done, even though he does not actually confess. Or he may simply come to her and tell her about it openly. Following is an example of a child who showed *confession* as a sign of conscience:

I. We'd like to get some idea of how Sid acts when he's naughty. When he deliberately does something he knows you don't want him to do when your back is turned, how does he act?
M. Very seldom does that. But a few times that he has done something

that he shouldn't do, that I don't know anything about, if I'm in the other room, he just can't hold it in very long. And finally he comes in to me and he says, "Mother,"—and I'll say, "What?"—"I did something I shouldn't have done." Instead of leaving it and getting away with it, he usually comes over and tells me what he's done. He usually comes, I mean, and it's not very long after he's done it. He can hardly hold it in to himself, you see.

I. Are there any situations in which he doesn't do this? In other words . . .

M. Never come across one that he didn't. Even when he does something outside that he shouldn't do, and I don't even know about it, he could very easily not say a word to me. Instead he comes and he says, "You know what I did?" And if something goes wrong in school he'll say, "Something happened today. My teacher had to speak to me." And he doesn't have to tell me, but he does; he comes right over and tells me. I don't know why. I should think if I were a child I'd keep it to myself but he doesn't; he comes and tells me and I would never know about it. I mean it—you know the old saying, "What you don't know won't hurt you." He evidently doesn't know it yet.

I. When you ask him about something he's done that he knows he's not supposed to do, does he usually admit it, or deny it?

M. He always admits it. I can always tell, of course, with Sid. I can always tell when he's trying to fabricate something. I mean if I say, "Did you do this?" And he says, "No." Well, I mean, it's just natural for a child to say "no." Remember that when a child is accused, even a grownup accused of something, if you said, "Did you do this?" Immediately the first answer that comes is "no." You say, well, that person's a liar. It's not that at all, it's just an immediate reaction to say "no." That's the first reaction any person has, and it's not only for a child; a grownup will do the same thing. But I can always tell when he says "no" and doesn't mean it because—but he can't tell—I don't know whether he'll accomplish it later—but he cannot tell a story. He can't fabricate at all. Or prevaricate. He just gets this silly grin on his face and I know that he's telling it and I'll say—and he'll just sheepishly put his eyes down and grin; he can't help it, he just can't tell a lie. Some people can and some people can't. He just can't.

I. What have you done about it, if he denies something that you're pretty sure he's done?

M. No, not too many things have happened, but when they have, it's been almost a puppy-dog fashion in that he's been very quiet and has led me to it.

Another child with a highly developed conscience confessed and took a spanking rather than risk his mother's continued disapproval:

M. He knows he has incurred our displeasure, and he says that he's sorry, he apologizes. Right away when he incurs this displeasure, he gets discouraged, because right away he puts his arms around you and says,

"I love you so much, I love you, and I won't do it again." And I say, "You've said that now, and if you do it again, *that* time you're going to have to be punished." And that's what happened. I've forgotten what it was, but it was something that I figured was not safe, so he did do it again, and he came and told me, and I said, "Now, what's going to happen?" and he said, "I guess I have to be spanked." I said, "That's right. Because it's too much to expect you to remember; and it would be dangerous for me to go along on that assumption, because I would be the one that would be sorry if you were hurt. I would never forgive myself, because I slipped up in not teaching you the danger. It's a sorrowful thing to me to have to teach you through pain."

At the other extreme, however, there were children of the same age who went to great lengths to avoid having their misdeeds found out.

A

I. We'd like to get some idea of how Billy acts when he's naughty. When he has deliberately done something he knows you don't want him to do, when your back is turned, how does he act?
M. Well right now he is lying. If he is caught, he will lie his way out, which is very disturbing to me. If there is anything I can't stand it's lying. I just want him to face the fact he's been naughty, and I will be much kinder with him; but sometimes if he's very bad, I just put him up in his room, which has a terrible effect on him. Sometimes I just give him a good scolding, and sometimes I fall back on the old dodge of telling him when his father gets home he will deal with him, which I know is wrong, but I just don't know how to handle him. I'll admit he is a problem.
I. What about if he does something when your back is turned, how does he act then?
M. And I find out afterwards? Well, that is usually the story, and it will come to my attention that he has broken something, and I will call him and try to get him to tell me why he did it; and I will admit I don't get very far. I don't know how to handle Billy.
I. Does he ever come and tell you about it without your having to ask him?
M. No, he would never admit that he has done something. It is only when Dick tells me or I just discover it.
I. When you ask him about something he has done that he knows he's not supposed to do, does he usually admit it or deny it?
M. He denies it. He will do anything to get out of admitting it.

B

M. Jack is inclined to be a little sneaky. Now that's another problem I don't like about him. For example, the things that annoy you, he will do more the minute your back is turned, and of course I don't like that at all. In other words, he thinks he is outsmarting you—kind of cute and not aboveboard.

I. If he does something, will he usually come and tell you about it?
M. Oh, he wouldn't tell you unless he was caught. He really wouldn't.
I. When you ask him about it, will he admit it or deny it?
M. Oh—well—for example, just two days ago, there was a lot of scribbling all over the window sill in his room, which hadn't taken place for about two years, and there was an awful lot of it, and I saw it and I immediately asked who did it—so Lee spoke right up and said, "Well, *I* didn't." And Jackie said, "Well, I didn't!" I found out later he did do it. He'll admit it if you tell him you're going to take away his television if he doesn't, but as far as getting right up and saying, "I did it," he's no George Washington.

Confession, of course, is not always a sign of conscience. It may indicate a greater fear of the consequences for *not confessing* than of the actual punishment for the misdeed. For example:

I. What do you do about it if she denies something you are pretty sure she has done?
M. She may deny it at first, but she'll usually tell me. She's deathly afraid of being punished—not by me—but we've always told her that any little girl who tells a lie, God always does something terrible to them, and she's deathly afraid of that. Like, for instance, up the street a little boy was hit by an automobile, and Cathy was quite sure it was because he did something wrong at some time and God punished him. Maybe it's not the right thing, but we let her believe it.

In general, however, a child's ability to admit that he was in the wrong, and to apologize or to make restitution, is an important step along the road to the development of internal controls. It means that he is willing to risk external punishment in order to recover his self-esteem and the esteem of his parents.

20 Personality Formation in the Kibbutz

BRUNO BETTELHEIM

Almost all discussion of human development assumes that the child is raised in a family-type arrangement and that morality is incorporated through a process of identification with adults. In psychoanalytic literature the Oedipus situation—a child's (especially male) dynamic struggle around the age of five or six with his parents—is central in the formation of conscience, and a nuclear family is presupposed. The only place where we have a living demonstration of a deliberate effort to form character by an environment other than the family is in the Israeli kibbutz. The nature of conscience formed under these circumstances is not completely known, but enough experience has been accumulated to suggest the main characteristics.*

Freud, for his own reasons, was not too concerned with the problem of how the particular culture within which an individual grows up, shapes his personality. But Karen Horney, in the very title she gave her first book, *The Neurotic Personality of Our Time,*[1] stressed the time-bound, and by obvious implication, the culture-bound nature of our personality. I am sure Freud was aware that each culture determines its norms, and hence also what constitutes deviation from it. But, having been the first to illuminate how and why deviation occurs and how personality develops, he was more interested in what is universal to man rather than what is specific to one culture. There-

* From *The American Journal of Psychoanalysis*, Vol. 29 (Netherlands: Henkes Press, 1970), pp. 3-9. Reprinted by permission of the Sonia Shankman Orthogenic School, Chicago.

fore, Horney's stressing the time-bound nature of the forms of neurosis was a signal contribution to our understanding of man in his society. This is why, when I was so singularly honored by being asked to present this, the Sixteenth Annual Karen Horney Lecture, I decided to ask you to consider with me how personality is formed differently from ours in a culture that is both extremely closely related to our own, and at the same time very different from it.

This selection of a topic was further suggested to me when, after having received your kind invitation, I thought best to look at what some of my predecessors in this series had to say. Here I found that Dr. Lidz,[2] in the Fifteenth Karen Horney Lecture, remarked that psychoanalysis "has not considered the influence of the totality of the interpersonal environment impinging upon the individual, causing reaction and counter-reaction which altered the behavior of the entire group and each member of it." I could not more heartily agree. But, after having thus stressed the culture-bound nature of behavior, and with it, I must assume, the particularity of a culture's ideas, then he relinquishes such sound views about the relativity of any culture's attitudes and proceeds to say: "The family is everywhere society's agent for protecting, nurturing and indoctrinating the new generation," which statement in its absolute form contradicts his much more culture-bound premise. This presents another reason to invite you to consider a subculture where the family does not exercise these functions. I am referring to child-rearing as practiced in the communistic Israeli Kibbutzim.

Scriptures tell that for forty years the Jews had to wander through the desert. Our civilization begins with the image that only a new generation, raised very differently from their parents, can create a new society—which is exactly what the Israeli kibbutz strives for: to breed a new personality type by raising children in ways that are radically different. These children, from birth on, do not live with and are not reared by their parents, but live in children's houses, in groups, taken care of by educators called *metapelets*. (Caretaker is a close approximation of the Hebrew word, *metapelet*. It is used here as meaning those who execute the mothering and functional rearing of the child.) Most of what we consider to be the parental functions of caring for and protecting the children are performed by the kibbutz, with far-reaching effects on the nature of the children's attachment to their parents. While many of the children are breast-fed, their mothers visit them only for these feedings, and all babies are expected to be weaned from breast or bottle before six months. Thereafter children will be with their parents for only about two hours a day when they visit with them. Contrary to such regulated nursing and early weaning, toilet training is relatively late and very lenient. Thus, in regard to orality and anality, standards and timing are very different from what is typical with us.

Reflecting on the intimate relation between the character of a society and its way of raising children, David Rapaport[3] remarked that, "The upbringing of children in the agricultural collectives in Israel is for the social scientist what an 'experiment of nature' is for the natural scientist."

None of the reports on how kibbutz children grow up, he felt, had yet shown what it "can teach us about the relationships between instinctual drives, ego, and environment, that is, about the relationship between the life of a society and the upbringing and development of children in it."[3] To which I would add: Nor have we explored yet, what revision of psychoanalytic theories on early childhood development follow from the success of kibbutz education.

Psychologists and psychoanalysts have predicted that a system which removes the infant from his family, particularly from his mother, and raises him in institutions must result in total failure. Bowlby,[4] Spitz,[5] and others, for example, believe it "essential for mental health that the infant and young child should experience a warm, intimate, and continuous relationship with his mother." Bowlby feels it is particularly damaging to the child's mental health if 1) during the first three years of life, there is no chance to form a close relationship to a mother figure; if 2) maternal deprivation or separation trauma occurs; and 3) if there are changes from one mother figure to another.

If he were right on all three counts, kibbutz children should be in poor mental health. Since there are frequent changes in the *metapelets* who care for a group, intermittent mothering prevails in the kibbutz. And the children, too, move first from the infants' house to the toddlers' house, then to the kindergarten, the house of the grade school children, and again later to the house of the youth society. There is lack of closeness to the mother because her visits are quite restricted even while she still nurses, and much more so later on. Thus the child's separation from the mother is a daily occurrence. Yet the effects of these three conditions are by no means pathogenic. Kibbutz children who are raised in groups from infancy on, fare very well in life. There is no delinquency, homosexuality, alcoholism or drug addiction among kibbutz youth and work morale is extremely high.

In objective tests (Rabin [6]) children so raised compared very favorably with corresponding American youth. As adults they are hard-working, responsible citizens, stable in marriage and devoted to their community and nation. In at least one respect kibbutz education has certainly succeeded: It has disproved the critics. It has been even more successful in creating a radically new personality in a single generation.

Compared to the personality of some of their parents, the kibbutz-raised generation seems less complex; but when compared with their parents in regard to mental health, they are much more stable, much less neurotic. While less attached to their parents, they are deeply attached to their peers; their holding on to each other, their inability to contemplate a life apart, suggests that there is also some bondage in this relationship. This goes so far that some, like twins, feel themselves only half a person when alone. But when together, their excellent performance in all tasks of life shows they are most effective as a group. Yet if intensity of attachment to the group may lessen individuation, it prevents that anomie which plagues modern man in competitive society.

These are competent, successful people, secure within their limitations. They remind me of what Grinker [7] found in his study of mentally healthy college youth—that they seemed uninteresting. Though intelligent, they were rather a dull group.

How come, then, that they manage so well, though in infancy and childhood they spend most of the day and all night away from their parents? The two most important theoretical questions this raises are: What exactly constitutes the love and tender care a child needs for developing well? Can something just as effective take the place of our type of mothering?

The kibbutz suggests that our view of what are the necessary ingredients of love and tender care may be in need of revision. According to Erikson [8] the infant needs love and tender care because these create in him a sense of basic trust. But the kibbutz instills basic trust though there is much less sameness and continuity in the person who provides for the infant than our theories call for. Trust in oneself also develops even when there is no threat of the outside provider's leaving to enforce inner control over one's asocial urges. Self-control can grow out of a wish to keep the goodwill and companionships of the peer group.

Perhaps we can better understand what is needed for basic trust if we ask what the inner experience of the infant must be rather than ask what the environment must provide.

The kibbutz example suggests that the inner experience the infant needs for successful growth—and which is designated as "mother love" or "love and tender care"—can be divided into at least two separate entities: security and companionship.

Security at this age derives firstly from the fact that adults provide for the infant's essential needs like food, shelter, rest, etc., with only the mildest demands for returns. Secondly, it derives from a devotion to his needs that makes him feel sure he will not be deserted but will always be well taken care of. These are the necessary conditions, but they are not enough by themselves to assure successful growth.

To them must be added *companionship* which implies age-correct stimulation and challenge, and a responsiveness from others. These provide for spontaneous and guided growth in line with the infant's natural endowment and his potentials for socialization. A companionship that in one setting consists mainly of the sameness and continuity of the person who is also the provider (the mother), may in another setting (the kibbutz), be built up of other ingredients. If all these are available to the infant, he feels basically secure and develops an attitude of trust.

Basic security, then, is the assurance of survival. Only he who has the power to assure it can truly offer security. We must come to terms with him who holds such power, or identify, if we are utterly dependent. To be dependent also means to be in the power of the one on whom we depend. And since the infant's dependence in the nuclear family is not only physical but also emotional and social, he is in another person's power on all counts. Dynamically, the obverse of the security derived from the sameness of the provider is separation anxiety, the fear of desertion. But the more dependent the child is on the security derived from this single provider, the more devastating the anxiety and the basic mistrust that arises when this person deprives emotionally or leaves physically. What counts here is the ratio between security derived from a single provider, and the unrelieved separation anxiety when deserted by the one on whom all security depends.

In the kibbutz, parents have transferred all parental powers to the community. All children are in a very serious manner viewed and cared for as "children of the kibbutz." To the children, in an emotional sense, the kibbutz as a whole stands for the providing, controlling and educating parent. The kibbutz gives them all they need, shapes and plans their present and future life.

In all the countless ways in which our middle-class parent educates his children—from toilet training to bedtime, to how they should eat, sit at the table, talk, arrange their day, play with others—the kibbutz, through its *metapelets* and the peer group, educates the child. Though children refer to no one but their real parents as parents, they are intensely aware, both consciously and unconsciously, that all these extremely important functions—which we view as typically parental—are exercised, not by their parents, but by the community, with the important difference that to them these are not parental, but community functions.

To kibbutz children, then, basic security is provided not by their parents but by the kibbutz, and hence derives from it. For them, basic trust does not require that its source be a particular person, the mother, or whoever stands in her place. The kibbutz offers a much more favorable balance between security and insecurity than does many a middle-class family.

The story is different for individuation (the being uniquely oneself), and its correlate, true intimacy (the being uniquely oneself with another). Individuation depends on internalizing and identifying not with a group, but with particular persons. Of course, the less individuation there is, the less need there is for this kind of intimacy. Therefore, perhaps the kibbutz-reared person, by reaching a lower level of individuation than is theoretically possible in our society, and also having less ability to be intimate, is not any worse off. Having less of the one he has less unsatisfied longing for the other, a longing which many of even the best in our society suffer from acutely.

I have concentrated on the earliest experiences because critics allege that it is the infant whom the kibbutz deprives most severely. Unfortunately time keeps me from touching on how other stages of development unfold in the kibbutz—on latency which, in my opinion, is the happy age in the kibbutz, or on adolescence which is as difficult there as it is with us, though differently so. Instead, I shall try to summarize what I found essentially different about personality formation between our system of child-rearing and theirs.

As I have just described, in the very beginning of life basic trust derives not so much from *the* maternal person as from a number of maternal persons and from the kibbutz itself. In the kibbutz, the infant's essential experience is that he gets, but he is not expected to give in return to the mother. True, if the infant reaches out to his caretakers, he will receive more from them. But since there are several caretakers, there will be less of a uniform reaction from them, and it will make much less difference whether or how he gives in return.

The differences are more marked in the development of autonomy, and of shame and doubt. In our culture they derive mainly from the impact of the parents, in the kibbutz, from the peer group. Thus the peer group, which with us does not make itself felt as a major force until puberty, is, in the kibbutz, of very great importance during the earliest stage of development. "Law and order" do not derive from being toilet trained by parents, as with us, but from the "laws" of the group and how the kibbutz orders the child's life.

One example may illustrate the difference. Some of the problems that beset parent and child in the toddler period are the child's passion to explore. In consequence, the parents have to put poison out of reach, make the infant leave things alone, make him stay in bed. Battles are fought around these issues that leave infant and parent emotionally scarred for life. In the kibbutz there is nothing in the infant house he must not touch, no property to be protected. Since nothing goes on around him after bedtime, staying in bed is no problem for the child. With far fewer do's and don'ts and much more lenient toilet training, there is much greater autonomy and very little shame and doubt. The internalized feeling for law and order that develops is less stringent. It is not the strong and uniquely consistent parental voice that is internalized as conscience, but the much more diffuse voice of the group and of the kibbutz that utters the do's and don'ts. This voice is much less threatening, but often equally or even more compelling. And the consequent fear is of being shamed by others, rather than of guilt.

The child in our culture forms himself in the image of his parents. They appear to him very powerful and often also quite unreasonably threatening. But to the kibbutz child his parents certainly do not appear to him as very powerful, and even less as being dangerous. The most powerful persons to the kibbutz child of this age are the *metapelets*. And typically, if the children play the roles of adults, the girls play at being *metapelets*, while both boys and girls play at being the kind of person who carries high prestige in the kibbutz, such as a truckdriver.

Thus at a much earlier age the identification is with the society's "culture carriers" rather than with the individual parent. And in the kibbutz these culture carriers represent the culture much more closely than does the parent in our society, or the cowboy, Indian, or sports hero of television. Identification with what the group admires and what the kibbutz stands for takes precedence over the identification with one's own parents or with any individual. The child's wish is not to become a unique person —a wish that is likewise suppressed in his parents and *metapelets* —but to become a good comrade. This tallies with his parents' ego ideal and with the moral valuation of the whole society.

The guilt feelings the kibbutz child develops are very different than with us because they derive from transgressing the rules of the children's community, not from violating the values of a nuclear family. There the essential experience creating guilt is to go against the values of the group. In the kibbutz initiative in the manipulation and mastery of the external world is much more encouraged—as opposed to internalization of experiences—because the children must fend for themselves to such a great extent, and because the entire life of their community is an open book to them. (The single exception here is the private life of adults, including their sexual life.) There is continual challenge to do things and no challenge to sit and think and feel.

As to private possessions, children raised in the nuclear

family want to possess their friends, and infants want to possess their parents. The root of the oedipal conflict is that the wish for such possession is thwarted, But in the kibbutz all private possession is shunned, whether of property, persons, or experiences. It may very well be that the wish to possess the parent is reinforced by other experiences with having and owning what stays with us always (the child's bottle, his blanket, his bed), and most of all by the parent's feeling that to possess things is desirable. To the kibbutz infant, it is obvious that any private possession is undesirable, that everything is owned by the community, to be used and shared by it. He cannot possess his *metapelets* or his parents since his being with them is so strictly regulated. And he cannot possess a friend because the group will not stand for it, and the *metapelet* would try to break up such a twosome (as will the youth group later). Thus the feeling is deeply ingrained that to wish to possess is wrong, and the guilt about even having such a wish interferes with the desire for exclusive belonging.

The lives of our latency-period children are deficient in experiences of having a useful and meaningful place in the world, while for the kibbutz child it is just the opposite. Even as a toddler he contributes to kibbutz economy by growing things, or raising animals. From the beginning of school age he works industriously on the children's farm.

With so much more chance for industry in matters that count in his society, the youngster feels no sense of inferiority. Since he can fully satisfy his desire for industry, and enjoys a sense of competence the average kibbutz child is much happier than a typical child of his age in our society. But, not having to resolve crises of great depth he does not develop the greater inner resources needed to weather them, nor the greater depth of personality this would bring. But with all that, the nature of his early experience adapts him mainly to his own society. In any other he will feel out of place and awkward, but still inwardly superior because he is convinced of the moral superiority of his way of life.

Much greater mastery in doing things and relating to others is expected of the kibbutz child rather early in life, although the circle of relations will not grow much later on. With us, the young child relates only to few, but the circle of relationships that must be mastered increases continuously as he grows older. This is just one indication of how any educational system, compared to another, pushes certain developments and slows others down, with far-reaching consequences for the type of personality it will finally produce.

The adolescent struggle to become a unique individual does not exist in the kibbutz. A struggle for personal identity would have to take the adolescent caught up in it away from the kibbutz. Nor is there any danger of identity diffusion. Those who fit into kibbutz life have no need to struggle for identity of a personal nature, since the community so largely defines their identity. In this way the kibbutz adolescent escapes the identity diffusion that afflicts so many of our middle-class adolescents.

In conclusion, I might add that it was the high degree of individuation among the founding generation that enabled them to feel so deeply the anomie in their living. For their children they wanted both, utter egalitarianism, and highest individuation. Finding that these are contradictory values is difficult for them. The more they became an integrated group, truly a kibbutz, the less became the individuation. (Those who set personal self-realization higher than the value of consensus, excluded themselves from the kibbutz and left.)

Things were simpler for the kibbutz-born second generation. Knowing nothing of alienation, they had never striven for an individuation that would compensate, through a rich inner life for what was missing in their social life. And things seem to be much simpler for the third generation which has never even known through their parents the inner conflicts of the first generation.

Final answers will have to wait until this third generation has grown up. For only they will have been raised without the pressures of ambivalence from their parents, without desires strongly felt and strongly repressed. Since this third generation has not yet reached maturity, the final results of kibbutz education are uncertain as yet. But already there is reason to believe that in view of the kibbutz experience we need to re-examine our views of what childhood experiences make for a healthy personality.

REFERENCES

1. Horney, K., *The Neurotic Personality of Our Time.* New York: W. W. Norton & Co., 1937.

2. Lidz, T., "Psychoanalytic Theories of Development and Maldevelopment: Some Reconceptualizations," *Am. J. of Psychoan.*, Vol. 27, 1967, pp. 115-126.
3. Rapaport, D., "The Study of Kibbutz Education and Its Bearing on the Theory of Development," *Am. J. of Orthopsych.*, Vol. 28, 1958, pp. 587-597.
4. Bowlby, J., *Maternal Care and Mental Health.* Geneva: World Health Organization Monograph, 1951; "The Nature of the Child's Tie to His Mother," *Int. J. of Psycho-Analysis,* Vol. 39, 1958, pp. 350-373; "Separation Anxiety," *Int. J. of Psycho-Analysis,* Vol. 41, 1960, pp. 89-111.
5. Spitz, R., "Hospitalism: An Inquiry into the Genesis of Psychiatric Conditions in Early Childhood," *The Psychoanalytic Study of the Child.* New York: International Universities Press, 1945, Vol. 1, pp. 53-74.
6. Rabin, A. I., *Growing Up in the Kibbutz.* New York: Springer Publishing Co., Inc. 1965.
7. Grinker, R., "Mentally Healthy Young Males (Homoclites)," *Arch. of Gen. Psychiat.,* Vol. 6, 1962, pp. 405-453.
8. Erikson, E. H., "Identity and the Life Cycle—Selected Papers," *Psychological Issues,* Vol. 1, No. 1, 1959.

21 Changes in Conscience During Adolescence

IRENE M. JOSSELYN, M.D.

By middle adolescence physical growth is almost complete, sexual maturation is established, and mental development in the sense of ability to do logical reasoning and to understand historical perspective is adult-like. But in the realm of self-understanding, an adolescent is uncertain and insecure. This condition is caused in part by our society which extends dependence into the third decade of life through schooling and which expects no social responsibility or work from youth. It is also caused by the inherent difficulty of a person's working through his childhood morality in order to find his own standards. Because this process is basically a struggle to change the content of one's conscience, it is slow, uneven in growth, and characterized by ambivalent and irrational behavior.*

During adolescence a struggle with the conscience occurs. The conscience develops in early childhood and reaches a discernible form at the time of the resolution of the conflicts centering in the family triangle. The conscience is the result of the incorporation into the child's unconscious psychological structure of the standards imposed by the parents. The child is thereby enabled to avoid the danger of rejection or punishment by the parents. He assumes a role previously carried by his parents, becoming his own monitor and disciplinarian.

* From *The Adolescent and His World* (New York: Family Service Association of America, 1952), pp. 67-75. Reprinted by permission.

321

In Freud's formulation of the concept of the superego—or conscience—he states that the superego may be subsequently modified.[1] The child is influenced by other adults as well as by siblings and other children. Clinical observation of children during the latency period indicates that a modification does occur. At this period, certain prohibitions imposed by the parent and incorporated into the formulation of the conscience are abandoned. As the child seeks gratification from social contacts outside the family, he finds himself exposed to the rejection or punishment of his group if he does not accept certain standards that may be in addition or contradictory to those of his family.

Cleanliness is a simple example of this change. Parents' standards imposed during the early period of the child's life, if unmodified, would result in every boy's being an immaculate and faultlessly dressed Little Lord Fauntleroy. The group helps him to escape this fate by denying the value of cleanliness. Most parents accept this change without protest, seeing it as evidence of growing up. It is, however, a significant change. The child's unconscious attitude toward cleanliness is modified in order to achieve acceptance by the peer group. The modification of the superego during latency, and the role of the peer group in initiating the change, have real significance during adolescence.

Rebellion against Infantile Conscience

A major psychological struggle in the process of maturation, which occurs in adolescence, is rebellion against the infantile conscience. The infantile conscience was adequate for the adjustment of a small child; its structure was determined by the needs and requirements of childhood. The same standards of adjustment are not satisfactory for adult living, and because the conscience is a part of childhood, it becomes a barrier against maturation. An adolescent feels he must free himself from infantile modes of behavior; he rebels against his own conscience.

This rebellion against his conscience plays a part in the determination of two characteristics of adolescence which are often alarming. The adolescent flaunts his new freedom from his conscience; he verbalizes his contempt for its demands and acts out token proof that he is free of it. In seeking a symbol of his conscience against which to strike, he most frequently chooses the persons who were the determinants of the original pattern for his conscience—his parents. A significant part of the adolescent's rebellion against parental control is actually a symbolic rebellion against the no longer serviceable part of his own unconscious demands upon himself.

If the structure of the infantile conscience is considered in detail, it becomes obvious why the adolescent must rebel against it. Heterosexuality is forbidden by the infantile conscience. It was the need to find an efficient means of repressing parent-forbidden impulses, especially the early sexual impulses directed toward the parent of the opposite sex, which resulted in the crystallization of the infantile conscience. The early sexual feelings were in embryonic form, the beginning of ultimate adult heterosexuality. Sexual feelings must be freed of the chains by which they were bound in childhood before mature heterosexuality can be attained. Also, in other areas of development the conscience has imposed unwarranted restrictions. As the child moves into adulthood, activities, drives, and impulses that were forbidden to him as a small child now become permissible. To the infantile conscience, that which was once bad is always bad. It protests against any act that was forbidden in childhood and is deaf to the approval expressed by a more flexible reality world. This is true because of the nature of the repression that took place. It is characteristic of repressed drives and feelings that they remain unconscious but unchanged in structure and in power. The repressing force therefore tends also to remain unchanged in structure and in power. This concept, familiar in our understanding of the neuroses, is equally true in the psychological format of the so-called normal individual.

The rebellion against the conscience is frightening to the child. Previously the conscience gave the individual a sense of ease with himself. He felt assured that his impulses would not be expressed in a form that would jeopardize his security since the pattern was molded by internal standards that mirrored the demands of the external world. Impulses now strengthened by new energy are difficult to hold in check by former methods; whereas to abandon the protection of the former methods is to invite chaos. As the anxiety mounts, the adolescent has need to strengthen old defenses. The conscience then becomes overly severe toward himself—a swing in the opposite direction from his earlier abandonment to impulsive behavior. The adolescent suddenly becomes a prig.

In one phase, the adolescent may be frighteningly free of inhibitions, and, in the alternate phase, may be deprived of all normal spontaneity by unrealistic, self-imposed prohibitions. A girl was referred to a psychiatrist because of her unconventional behavior which had resulted in her being branded as the "bad girl" of the community. Her dress, her mannerisms, and her verbalization seemed to flaunt her defiance of all conventional standards. When the psychiatrist, in a comment, implied that he thought she permitted boys to kiss her, she left treatment. As an adult she recalled this episode. She could remember her horror at the thought that the psychiatrist had so little respect for her decency that he would believe it possible that she behaved in this manner—a manner completely unacceptable to her.

The adolescent often handles this conflict between the wish to be free of the conscience and slavish devotion to it by verbalization of defiance but with complete compliance to standards in actual behavior. Sometimes, however, the defiance is not only verbal but is acted out, with serious consequences. Usually, then, the acting out that occurs during the phase of defiance results in an overwhelming guilt reaction when the conscience is again in control. The conscience did not succeed in prohibiting the behavior, but once the act is committed, it must use all its force to punish. Such behavior is difficult to evaluate, diagnostically, in adolescence. It resembles the clinical picture of adults who act out impulses in order to be punished, and of those who, by their chronic defiance provoke retaliation. With adolescents, the need for punishment plays a part in their acting-out behavior, but it is questionable whether it is usually a dominant factor. A significant difference should be taken into account. The character formation of the adolescent is not structuralized but is still fluid. As a result, he acts out his defiance of his conscience in order to have a sense of freedom from it. His goal is not chiefly to gain punishment. Frightened by his freedom, however, he abandons his defiance and submits to his conscience. The conscience then behaves as parents behave when they punish a child for an act committed in their absence. Once the conscience is back in control, external punishment is sought or self-punishment is administered.

Parents as Symbols of the Conscience

As was pointed out earlier, the rebellion against the infantile conscience does not remain internal. The pattern of the conscience was determined by the parent-figures of infancy. This close relationship between internal and external forces makes possible a point of focus for the revolt. Parents may serve as a symbol of the conscience. As a result of the symbolization, part of the struggle can be externalized. The adolescent rebels against the parents and parent-surrogates not only because parents are restrictive but also because they are symbols of the infantile conscience from which the child must be partially free in order to reach maturity.

The adolescent's behavior toward his parents is as confused as it is toward his own conscience. At times he resents his parents' authority and flaunts his contempt for their beliefs and their pattern of living. At other times he seeks their controls, demands restrictions, and slavishly follows the family mores. He often violates those requirements that will bring punishment upon himself. The logical restrictions, which in themselves may not be too important in his daily living, are used for another purpose. He uses them as an excuse for rebellion, in trying to free himself of chains that are invisible but can be symbolized by the parent. At the same time, he values the restrictions since they assure him that external restraint against unfettered freedom exists and that punishment will follow if he oversteps the rules.

The value in violation of justifiable familial restrictions and in the resultant punishment was clearly shown in the following incident. George was 15 years old. His general pattern of behavior was characterized by constructive conformity both to the demands of his family and to those of his environment. The parents had only one major complaint. The trouble focused on the use of the family car. George was allowed to use the car at any time it was not needed by his mother. Frequently she would allow him to have it when she was aware that she would need it later in the day. Although ordinarily he was very reliable, on occasion he failed to return it on time. The parents finally punished him by refusing him the use of the car on the subsequent day, but he did not "learn his lesson," and failed again to return the car promptly. When his mother decided to handle the situation by completing her errands first and allowing him to have the car afterwards for an unrestricted period, a new source of irritation developed. Before he would use the car he insisted that his mother set a time for his return. He was able to verbalize a feeling of uneasiness and dissatisfaction if he drove off without a limit put on the time he could be gone.

Alice, who was 14, created a somewhat similar situation. She was also very reliable. Her mother had overheard her, on several occasions, complain to her girl friends that her mother was too strict—that she made Alice come home from parties at a certain hour rather than allowing her to remain until the parties broke up. The mother decided that she herself undoubtedly had been unreasonable. One night, as Alice was leaving for a party, she asked what time she was to return. The mother suggested that they not set a definite time but that Alice use her own judgment. Alice immediately rejected her mother's liberality. She asked her mother to state a definite time, explaining that even though she fussed at this restriction, actually she would feel uneasy if it were not imposed. She could not decide with any conviction what was the right time to leave. She preferred that her mother carry the burden. Alice also admitted that the restriction set by her mother served a further purpose. The time that her mother set usually coincided with her own wishes. If she should tell her friends that she wanted to go home they might criticize her. If she said that she had to go home because her mother was restrictive, she could save face with her friends by blaming her mother and at the same time could carry out her own wishes. She also confessed that sometimes when no restrictions had been imposed she pretended they had been—if her group wanted to do something that she did not wish to do. She would say that her mother would not let her, even though this placed her mother in an unpleasant light. By this subterfuge, Alice consciously avoided the responsibility for failure to follow the group, transforming her distaste for an activity into a prohibition by her mother.

Although, in this instance, the subterfuge was used consciously, the same mechanism can be used unconsciously. When the adolescent wishes both to obey and to defy the conscience, he often externalizes the conscience by using the parent as its symbol. Such symbolic use of the parent may lead to a naive interpretation of an adolescent's report of parental controls. He may say that a certain act would be prohibited by the parents when actually they have no objection. Superficially, such statements may be a result of simple misunderstanding of the parents' attitude, and sometimes may not be more complicated. In other instances, however, the adolescent is actually revealing the role of his own censor. He does not feel comfortable in carrying out the impulse behind the act and projects the disapproval onto the parent. Reassurance that the parent does not disapprove may lead to the conviction on the part of the adolescent that the act is proper and therefore should be accepted. On the other hand, unless he understands his own role in the prohibition, reassurance may only add to his anxiety and confusion.

The complex interaction of the role of the conscience, the role of the parent per se, and the role of the parent as a projection of the conscience, as well as the satisfaction that lies in the revolt against both the parent and the conscience, were illustrated by Jean's reaction to a rather simple situation. Jean's parents were well aware that high school girls and boys smoked. In discussion with her, the parents expressed their opinion that there was no convincing proof that smoking was either injurious or desirable for young people, but that, probably, it was wise to delay smoking as long as possible. They added that she very shortly would find herself with friends who smoked and they suggested that she might like to try it at home. They told her there was no need to hide the fact that she was smoking but that she might join them in an after-dinner cigarette. She did not accept the invitation, but eventually her parents became aware that she was smoking in her room. One evening after dinner her father passed her a cigarette, suggesting that since she was already smoking she might as well smoke with them. Jean blushed and very self-consciously took a cigarette and smoked it briefly. It took several days before she could smoke relaxedly in front of her parents. Her self-consciousness was not due to lack of skill; she no longer appeared an amateur once she was comfortable with her parents. She herself later described her feelings. She explained that she felt that she was doing something wrong in smoking in front of her parents even though her parents had not forbidden it. When she smoked prior to their knowledge she had a gratifying feeling of doing something wrong. When she no longer had to keep smoking a secret from her parents she noticed the enjoyment in smoking was much less. The simple episode evidently involved an unconscious prohibition against smoking, a prohibition which she identified with her parents and against which she secretly revolted.

Influence of the Peer Group

During the period of early adolescence, when the rebellion against the infantile superego seems to threaten all previously accepted standards of behavior, the modification of the superego by the mores of the peer group becomes apparent. The peer group, during latency, has not completely destroyed the earlier superego. It has only introduced certain modifications. Many parental standards are valued by the group as they are by the family structure. Stealing, for example, is prohibited by the family. Although a group frequently experiments with pilfering, in most instances it learns that stealing not only brings punishment from others as well as the parents, but jeopardizes the possessions of the group itself. Pressure against stealing comes from the group and ultimately results in a strengthening of the unconscious restraining force within the individual. The average social group, wishing to be accepted in the social structure, does not abandon the more important prohibitions that parents imposed earlier upon each individual. The acceptance by the child of this group-formulated pattern of behavior gives the child a sense of security in his world of classmates and friends.

Security with peers becomes extremely significant at adolescence. The panic resulting from unresolved conflicts at this age is handled in part by the individual's seeking a haven in the security his peer group offers. Frightened by his own impulses, and by the hazards of seemingly necessary complete repression, or alternatively, by the free expression of these impulses, he turns to the peer group for support and for answers to his questions. In the peer group he can discuss his mixed feelings and find solace in the identical suffering of others. He can formulate tentative answers to his perplexities, exposing them to the check of the equally tentative formulations of his peers. Most important, he can participate in the formulation of restrictions upon his behavior, which will assure him of protection from a chaotic expression of desires without the apparent dangers inherent in depending on the restrictions outlined by the parents.

Adolescent groups frequently have seemingly ridiculous rules of conduct as a part of the mores of their own world. There was, for example, a period in which an adolescent girl would have preferred walking down the street in a bathrobe to appearing with a cardigan sweater worn with the buttons in front. The group had decreed that to be "proper" a cardigan should be buttoned in back. The normal adolescent is a slave to the rules and fashions of the group.

The absurdities of the group-imposed restrictions frequently provoke expressions of ridicule or censorship from the adult world. The value of the group control is not always properly estimated. The group not only determines how a cardigan should be worn, but, more important, it tempers the effect of the rebellion against the infantile conscience. As a result of the mutual soul-searching that the individuals in the group experience, standards of the group concerning more basic concepts of social living take shape. Attitudes toward questions of morality, ethics, and social customs take form. The standards are rigidly held to by the individuals in the group and gradually become a part of the "conscience" of each member. The character of the group attitudes is influenced to a large degree by the past experiences of its members. If the past experiences have been generally satisfactory, the resulting group attitudes will not be strikingly different from parental standards. Some variations, of course, will occur. These variations often become known as "social progress" twenty years later. The group structure, however, has served in the meantime as a relative island of security in a tumultuous world. It has protected the individual from becoming lost in the tortuous paths and possibly the blind alleys of the psychological maze of adolescence.

NOTES

1. Sigmund Freud, *An Outline of Psychoanalysis,* W. W. Norton & Co., New York, 1949, Chapt. 1.

22 The Struggle of Conscience in Youth

KENNETH KENISTON

In the introduction to this reader it was stated that it may be closer to the truth to say a person *is* a conscience, rather than that he *has* a conscience. That is, a person creates from his self-hood and his interaction with society his ethical standards and his desire to live by them. In this essay * Keniston shows how changes in society have formed the adolescent stage of development and how contemporary changes in society are forming a new stage of "youth." The basic struggle in the youth stage is moral in that it represents an effort to define one's life; and it is about morals, for youth is a stage when decisions are reached about what is worthwhile. This process of "individualization" requires both concentration and diligent work in order for a person to grow into his developing self-image and also courage to break with his parents and others who tend to hinder the development of autonomy.

Before the twentieth century, adolescence was rarely included as a stage in the life cycle. Early life began with infancy and was followed by a period of childhood that lasted until around puberty, which occurred several years later than it does today. After puberty, most young men and women simply entered some form of apprenticeship for the adult world. Not until 1904, when G. Stanley Hall published his monumental work, *Adolescence: Its Psychology and Its Relations to*

* From "Youth: A 'New' Stage of Life," in the *American Scholar,* Fall, 1970, pp. 631-648. Reprinted by permission.

Physiology, Anthropology, Sociology, Sex, Crime, Religion, and Education, was this further pre-adult stage widely recognized. Hall's work went through many editions and was much popularized; "adolescence" became a household word. Hall's classic description of the *sturm und drang,* turbulence, ambivalence, dangers and possibilities of adolescence has since been echoed in almost every discussion of this stage of life.

But it would be incorrect to say that Hall "discovered" adolescence. On the contrary, from the start of the nineteenth century, there was increasing discussion of the "problem" of those past puberty but not yet adult. They were the street gang members and delinquents who made up what one nineteenth-century writer termed the new "dangerous classes"; they were also the recruits to the new public secondary schools being opened by the thousands in the late nineteenth century. And once Hall had clearly defined adolescence, it was possible to look back in history to discover men and women who had shown the hallmarks of this stage long before it was identified and named.

Nonetheless, Hall was clearly reflecting a gradual change in the nature of human development, brought about by the massive transformations of American society in the decades after the Civil War. During these decades, the "working family," where children labored alongside parents in fields and factories, began to disappear; rising industrial productivity created new economic surpluses that allowed millions of teenagers to remain outside the labor force. America changed from a rural agrarian society to an urban industrial society, and this new industrial society demanded on a mass scale not only the rudimentary literacy taught in elementary schools, but higher skills that could only be guaranteed through secondary education. What Hall's concept of adolescence reflected, then, was a real change in the human experience, a change intimately tied to the new kind of industrial society that was emerging in America and Europe.

Today, Hall's concept of adolescence is unshakably enshrined in our view of human life. To be sure, the precise nature of adolescence still remains controversial. Some observers believe that Hall, like most psychoanalytic observers, vastly overestimated the inevitability of turbulence, rebellion and upheaval in this stage of life. But whatever the exact definition of adolescence, no one today doubts its existence. A stage of life that barely existed a century ago is now universally accepted as an inherent part of the human condition.

In the seven decades since Hall made adolescence a household word, American society has once again transformed itself. From the industrial era of the turn of the century, we have moved into a new era without an agreed-upon name—it has been called post-industrial, technological, postmodern, the age of mass consumption, the technetronic age. And a new generation, the first born in this new era of postwar affluence, television and the Bomb, raised in the cities and suburbs of America, socially and economically secure, is now coming to maturity. Since 1900, the average amount of education received by children has increased by more than six years. In 1900, only 6.4 percent of young Americans completed high school, while today almost eighty percent do, and more than half of them begin college. In 1900, there were only 238,000 college students: in 1970, there are more than seven million, with ten million projected for 1980.

These social transformations are reflected in new public anxieties. The "problem of youth," "the now generation," "troubled youth," "student dissent" and "the youth revolt" are topics of extraordinary concern to most Americans. No longer is our anxiety focused primarily upon the teenager, upon the adolescent of Hall's day. Today we are nervous about new "dangerous classes" —those young men and women of college and graduate school age who can't seem to "settle down" the way their parents did, who refuse to consider themselves adult, and who often vehemently challenge the existing social order. "Campus unrest," according to a June, 1970, Gallup Poll, was considered the nation's *main* problem.

The factors that have brought this new group into existence parallel in many ways the factors that produced adolescence: rising prosperity, the further prolongation of education, the enormously high educational demands of a postindustrial society. And behind these measurable changes lie other trends less quantitative but even more important: a rate of social change so rapid that it threatens to make obsolete all institutions, values, methodologies and technologies within the lifetime of each generation; a technology that has created not only prosperity and longevity, but power to destroy the planet, whether through warfare or violation of nature's balance; a world of extraordinarily complex social organization, instantaneous communication and constant revolution. The "new" young men and young women emerging today both reflect and react against these trends.

But if we search among the concepts of psychology for a word to describe these young men and women, we find none that is adequate. Characteristically, they are referred to as "late-adolescents-and-young-adults"—a phrase whose very mouth-filling awkwardness attests to its inadequacy. Those who see in youthful behavior the remnants of childhood immaturity naturally incline toward the concept of "adolescence" in describing the unsettled twenty-four-year-old, for this word makes it easier to interpret his objections to war, racism, pollution or imperialism as "nothing but" delayed adolescent rebellion. To those who are more hopeful about today's youth, "young adulthood" seems a more flattering phrase, for it suggests that maturity, responsibility and rationality lie behind the unease and unrest of many contemporary youths.

But in the end, neither label seems fully adequate. The twenty-four-year-old seeker, political activist or graduate student often turns out to have been *through* a period of adolescent rebellion ten years before, to be all too formed in his views, to have a stable sense of himself, and to be much farther along in his psychological development than his fourteen-year-old high school brother. Yet he differs just as sharply from "young adults" of age twenty-four whose place in society is settled, who are married and perhaps parents, and who are fully committed to an occupation. What characterizes a growing minority of postadolescents today is that they have not settled the questions whose answers once defined adulthood: questions of relationship to the existing society, questions of vocation, questions of social role and life-style.

Faced with this dilemma, some writers have fallen back on the concept of "protracted" or "stretched" adolescence—a concept with psychoanalytic origins that suggests that those who find it hard to "settle down" have "failed" the adolescent developmental task of abandoning narcissistic fantasies and juvenile dreams of glory. Thus, one remedy for "protracted adolescence" might be some form of therapy that would enable the young to reconcile themselves to abilities and a world that are rather less than they had hoped. Another interpretation of youthful unease blames society, not the individual, for the "prolongation of adolescence." It argues that youthful unrest springs from the unwillingness of contemporary society to allow young men and women, especially students, to exercise the adult powers of which they are biologically and intellectually capable. According to this view, the solution would be to allow young people to "enter adulthood" and do "real work in the real world" at an earlier age.

Yet neither of these interpretations seems quite to the point. For while some young men and women are indeed victims of the psychological malady of "stretched adolescence," many others are less impelled by juvenile grandiosity than by a rather accurate analysis of the perils and injustices of the world in which they live. And plunging youth into the "adult world" at an earlier age would run directly counter to the wishes of most youths, who view adulthood with all of the enthusiasm of a condemned man for the guillotine. Far from seeking the adult prerogatives of their parents, they vehemently demand a virtually indefinite prolongation of their nonadult state.

If neither "adolescence" nor "early adulthood" quite describes the young men and women who so disturb American society today, what can we call them? My answer is to propose that *we are witnessing today the emergence on a mass scale of a previously unrecognized stage of life,* a stage that intervenes between adolescence and adulthood. I propose to call this stage of life the stage of *youth,* assigning to this venerable but vague term a new and specific meaning. Like Hall's "adolescence," "youth" is in no absolute sense new: indeed, once having defined this stage of life, we can study its historical emergence, locating individuals and groups who have had a "youth" in the past. But what is "new" is that this stage of life is today being entered not by tiny minorities of unusually creative or unusually disturbed young men and women, but by millions of young people in the advanced nations of the world.

To explain how it is possible for "new" stages of life to emerge under changed historical conditions would require a lengthy excursion into the theory of psychological development. It should suffice here to emphasize that the direction and extent of human development—indeed the entire nature of the human life cycle—is by no means predetermined by man's biological constitution. Instead, psychological development results from a complex interplay of constitutional givens (including the rates and phases of biological maturation) and the changing familial, social, educational, economic and political conditions that constitute the matrix in which children develop. Human development can be obstructed by the absence of the necessary matrix, just as it can be stimulated by other kinds of environments. Some social and historical conditions demonstrably slow, retard or block development, while others stimulate, speed and encourage it. A prolongation and extension of development, then, including the emergence of "new" stages of life, can result from altered social, economic and historical conditions.

Like all stages, youth is a stage of transition rather than of completion or accomplishment. To begin to define youth involves three related tasks. First, we need to describe the major *themes* or issues that dominate consciousness, development and behavior during this stage. But human development rarely if ever proceeds on all fronts simultaneously: instead, we must think of development as consisting of a series of sectors or "developmental lines," each of which may be in or out of phase with the others. Thus we must also describe the more specific *transformations* or changes in thought and behavior that can be observed in each of several "lines" of development (moral, sexual, intellectual, interpersonal, and so on) during youth. Finally, we can try to make clear what youth is *not*. What follows is a preliminary sketch of some of the themes and transformations that seem crucial to defining youth as a stage of life.

Major Themes in Youth

Perhaps the central conscious issue during youth is the *tension between self and society*. In adolescence, young men and women tend to accept their society's definitions of them as rebels, truants, conformists, athletes or achievers. But in youth, the relationship between socially assigned labels and the "real self" becomes more problematic, and constitutes a focus of central concern. The awareness of actual or potential conflict, disparity, lack of congruence between what one is (one's identity, values, integrity) and the resources and demands of the existing society increases. The adolescent is struggling to define who he is; the youth begins to sense who he is and thus to recognize the possibility of conflict and disparity between his emerging selfhood and his social order.

In youth, *pervasive ambivalence* toward both self and society is the rule: the question of how the two can be made more congruent is often experienced as a central problem of youth. This ambivalence is not the same as definitive rejection of society, nor does it necessarily lead to political activism. For ambivalence may also entail intense self-rejection, including major efforts at self-transformation employing the methodologies of personal transformation that are culturally available in any historical era: monasticism, meditation, psychoanalysis, prayer, hallucinogenic drugs, hard work, religious conversion, introspection, and so forth. In youth, then, the potential and ambivalent conflicts between autonomous selfhood and social involvement—between the maintenance of personal integrity and the achievement of effectiveness in society—are fully experienced for the first time.

The effort to reconcile and accommodate these two poles involves a characteristic stance vis-à-vis both self and world, perhaps best described by the concept of the *wary probe*. For the youthful relationship to the social order consists not merely in the experimentation more characteristic of adolescence, but with now more serious forays into the adult world, through which its vulnerability, strength, integrity and possibilities are assayed. Adolescent experimentation is more concerned with self-definition than are the probes of youth, which may lead to more lasting commitments. This testing, exacting, challenging attitude may be applied to all representatives and aspects of the existing social order, sometimes in anger and expectation of disappointment, sometimes in the urgent hope of finding honor, fidelity and decency in society, and often in both anger and hope. With regard to the self, too, there is constant self-probing in search of strength, weakness, vulnerability and resiliency, constant self-scrutiny designed to test the individual's capacity to withstand or use what his society would make of him, ask of him, and allow him.

Phenomenologically, youth is a time of alternating *estrangement and omnipotentiality*. The estrangement of youth entails feelings of isolation, unreality, absurdity, and disconnectedness from the interpersonal, social and phenomenological world. Such feelings are probably more intense during youth than in any other period of life. In part they spring from the actual disengagement of youth from society; in part they grow out of the psychological sense of incongruence between self and world. Much of the psychopathology of youth involves such feelings, experienced as the depersonalization of the self or the derealization of the world.

Omnipotentiality is the opposite but secretly related pole of estrangement. It is the feeling of absolute freedom, of living in a world of pure possibilities, of being able to change or achieve anything. There may be times when complete self-transformation seems possible, when the self is experienced as putty in one's own hands. At other times, or for other youths, it is the nonself that becomes totally malleable; then one feels capable of totally transforming another's life, or creating a new society with no roots whatsoever in the mire of the past. Omnipotentiality and estrangement are obviously related: the same sense of freedom and possibility that may come from casting off old inhibitions, values and constraints may also lead directly to a feeling of absurdity, disconnectedness and estrangement.

Another characteristic of youth is the *refusal of socialization* and acculturation. In keeping with the intense and wary probing of youth, the individual characteristically begins to become aware of the deep effects upon his personality of his society and his culture. At times he may attempt to break out of his prescribed roles, out of his culture, out of history, and even out of his own skin. Youth is a time, then, when earlier socialization and acculturation is self-critically analyzed, and massive efforts may be made to uproot the now alien traces of historicity, social membership and culture. Needless to say, these efforts are invariably accomplished within a social, cultural and historical context, using historically available methods. Youth's relationship to history is therefore paradoxical. Although it may try to reject history altogether, youth does so in a way defined by its historical era, and these rejections may even come to define that era.

In youth we also observe the emergence of *youth-specific identities* and roles. These contrast both with the more ephemeral enthusiasms of the adolescent and with the more established commitments of the adult. They may last for months, years or a decade, and they inspire deep commitment in those who adopt them.

Yet they are inherently temporary and specific to youth: today's youthful hippies, radicals and seekers recognize full well that, however reluctantly, they will eventually become older; and that aging itself will change their status. Some such youth-specific identities may provide the foundation for later commitments; but others must be viewed in retrospect as experiments that failed or as probes of the existing society that achieved their purpose, which was to permit the individual to move on in other directions.

Another special issue during youth is the enormous value placed upon change, transformation and *movement,* and the consequent abhorrence of *stasis.* To change, to stay on the road, to retain a sense of inner development and/or outer momentum is essential to many youths' sense of active vitality. The psychological problems of youth are experienced as most overwhelming when they seem to block change: thus, youth grows panicky when confronted with the feeling of "getting nowhere," of "being stuck in a rut," or of "not moving."

At times the focus of change may be upon the self, and the goal is then to *be moved.* Thus, during youth we see the most strenuous, self-conscious and even frenzied efforts at self-transformation, using whatever religious, cultural, therapeutic or chemical means are available. At other times, the goal may be to create movement in the outer world, to *move others:* then we may see efforts at social and political change that in other stages of life rarely possess the same single-minded determination. And on other occasions, the goal is to *move through* the world, and we witness a frantic geographic restlessness, wild swings of upward or downward social mobility, or a compelling psychological need to identify with the highest and the lowest, the most distant and apparently alien.

The need for movement and terror of stasis often are a part of a heightened *valuation of development* itself, however development may be defined by the individual and his culture. In all stages of life, of course, all individuals often wish to change in specific ways: to become more witty, more attractive, more sociable or wealthier. But in youth, specific changes are often subsumed in the devotion to change itself—to "keep putting myself through the changes," "not to bail out," "to keep moving." This valuation of change need not be fully conscious. Indeed it often surfaces only in its inverse form, as the panic or depression that accompanies a sense of "being caught in a rut," "getting nowhere," "not being able to change." But for other youths, change becomes a conscious goal in itself, and elaborate ideologies of the techniques of transformation and the *telos* of human life may be developed.

In youth, as in all other stages of life, *the fear of death* takes a special form. For the infant, to be deprived of maternal support, responsiveness and care is not to exist; for the four-year-old, nonbeing means loss of body intactness (dismemberment, mutilation, castration); for the adolescent, to cease to be is to fall apart, to fragment, splinter, or diffuse into nothingness. For the youth, however, to lose one's essential vitality is merely *to stop*. For some, even self-inflicted death or psychosis may seem preferable to loss of movement; and suicidal attempts in youth often spring from the failure of efforts to change and the resulting sense of being forever trapped in an unmoving present.

The youthful *view of adulthood* is strongly affected by these feelings. Compared to youth, adulthood has traditionally been a stage of slower transformation, when, as Erik H. Erikson has noted, the relative developmental stability of parents enables them to nurture the rapid growth of their children. This adult deceleration of personal change is often seen from a youthful vantage point as concretely embodied in apparently unchanging parents. It leads frequently to the conscious identification of adulthood with stasis, and to its unconscious equation with death or nonbeing. Although greatly magnified today by the specific political disillusionments of many youths with the "older generation," the adulthood = stasis (= death) equation is inherent in the youthful situation itself. The desire to prolong youth indefinitely springs not only from an accurate perception of the real disadvantages of adult status in any historical era, but from the less conscious and less accurate assumption that to "grow up" is in some ultimate sense to cease to be really alive.

Finally, youths tend to band together with other youths in *youthful counter-cultures,* characterized by their deliberate cultural distance from the existing social order, but *not* always by active political or other opposition to it. It is a mistake to identify youth as a developmental stage with any one social group, role or organization. But youth *is* a time when solidarity with other youths is especially important, whether the solidarity be achieved in pairs, small groups, or formal organizations. And the groups dominated by those in this stage of life reflect not only the special configurations of each historical era, but also the shared developmental positions and problems of youth. Much of what has traditionally been referred to as "youth culture" is, in the terms here used, adolescent culture; but there are also groups, societies and associations that are truly youthful. In our own time, with the enormous increase in the number of those who are entering youth as a stage of life, the variety and importance of these youthful counter-cultures is steadily growing.

This compressed summary of themes in youth is schematic and interpretive. It omits many of the qualifications necessary to a fuller discussion, and it neglects the enormous complexity of development in any one person in favor of a highly schematic account. Specifically, for example, I do not discuss the ways the infantile, the childish, the adolescent and the truly youthful interact in all real lives. And perhaps most important, my account is highly interpretive, in that it points to themes that underlie diverse acts and feelings, to issues and tensions that unite the often scattered experiences of real individuals. The themes, issues and conflicts here discussed are rarely conscious as such; indeed, if they all were fully conscious, there would probably be something seriously awry. Different youths experience each of the issues here considered with different intensity. What is a central conflict for one may be peripheral or unimportant for another. These remarks, then, should be taken as a first effort to summarize some of the underlying issues that characterize youth as an ideal type.

Transformations of Youth

A second way of describing youth is by attempting to trace out the various psychological and interpersonal transformations that may occur during this stage. Once again, only the most preliminary sketch of youthful development can be attempted here. Somewhat arbitrarily, I will distinguish between development in several sectors or areas of life, here noting only that, in fact, changes in one sector invariably interact with those in other sectors.

In pointing to the self-society relationship as a central issue in youth, I also mean to suggest its importance as an area of potential change. The late adolescent is only beginning to challenge his society's definition of him, only starting to compare his emerging sense of himself with his culture's possibilities and with the temptations and opportunities offered by his environment. Adolescent struggles for emancipation from external familial control and internal dependency on the family take a variety of forms, including displacement of the conflict onto other "authority figures." But in adolescence itself, the "real" focus of conflict is on the family and all of its internal psychic residues. In youth, however, the "real" focus begins to shift: increasingly, the family becomes more paradigmatic of society than vice versa. As relatively greater emancipation from the family is achieved, the tension between self and society, with ambivalent probing of both, comes to constitute a major area of developmental "work" and change. Through this work, young people can sometimes arrive at a synthesis whereby both self and society are affirmed, in the sense that the autonomous reality, relatedness yet separateness of both, is firmly established.

There is no adequate term to describe this "resolution" of the tension between self and society, but C. G. Jung's concept of *"individuation"* comes close. For Jung, the individual man is a man who acknowledges and can cope with social reality, whether accepting it or opposing it with revolutionary fervor. But he can do this without feeling his central selfhood overwhelmed. Even when most fully engaged in social role and societal action, he can preserve a sense of himself as intact, whole, and distinct from society. Thus the "resolution" of the self-society tension in no way necessarily entails "adjusting" to the society, much less "selling out"—although many youths see it this way. On the contrary, individuation refers partly to a psychological process whereby self and society are differentiated internally. But the actual conflicts between men and women and their societies remain, and indeed may become even more intense,

The meaning of individuation may be clarified by considering the special dangers of youth, which can be defined as extremes of *alienation, whether from self or from society*. At one extreme is that total alienation from self that involves abject submission to society, "joining the rat race," "selling out." Here, society is affirmed but selfhood denied. The other extreme is a total alienation from society that leads not so much to the rejection of society, as to its existence being ignored, denied and blocked out. The result is a kind of self-absorption, an enforced interiority and subjectivity, in which only the self and its extensions are granted live reality, while all the rest is relegated to a limbo of insignificance. Here the integrity of the self is purchased at the price of a determined denial of social reality, and the loss of social effectiveness. In youth both forms of alienation are often assayed, sometimes for lengthy periods. And for some whose further development is blocked, they become the basis for life-long adaptations—the self-alienation of the marketing personality, the social alienation of the perpetual drop-out. In terms of the polarities of Erikson, we can define the central developmental possibilities of youth as individuation vs. alienation.

Sexual development continues in important ways during youth. In modern Western societies, as in many others, the commencement of actual sexual relationships is generally deferred by middle-class adolescents until their late teens or early twenties: the modal age of first intercourse for American college males today is around twenty, for females about twenty-one. Thus, despite the enormous importance of adolescent sexuality and sexual development, actual sexual intercourse often awaits youth. In youth, there may occur a major shift from masturbation and sexual fantasy to interpersonal sexual behavior, including the gradual integration of sexual feelings with intimacy with a real person. And as sexual behavior with real people commences, one sees a further working-through, now in behavior, of vestigial fears and prohibitions whose origin lies in earlier childhood—specifically, of Oedipal feelings of sexual inferiority and of Oedipal prohibitions against sex with one's closest intimates. During youth, when these fears and prohibitions can be gradually worked through, they yield a capacity for genitality, that is, for mutually satisfying sexual relationships with another whom one loves.

The transition to genitality is closely related to a more general pattern of *interpersonal development*. I will term this the shift from *identicality* to mutuality. This development begins with adolescence [1] and continues through youth: it involves a progressive expansion of the early-adolescent assumption that the interpersonal world is divided into only two categories: first, me-and-those-who-are-identical-to-me (potential soulmates, doubles and hypothetical people who "automatically understand everything"), and second, all others. This conceptualization gradually yields to a capacity for close relationships with those on an approximate level of *parity*, or similarity with the individual.

The phase of parity in turn gives way to a phase of *complementarity,* in which the individual can relate warmly to others who are different from him, valuing them for their dissimilarities from himself. Finally, the phase of complementarity may yield in youth to a phase of *mutuality,* in which issues of identicality, parity and complementarity are subsumed in an overriding concern with the other *as other*. Mutuality entails a simultaneous awareness of the ways in which others are identical to oneself, the ways in which they are similar and dissimilar, and the ways in which they are absolutely unique. Only in the stage of mutuality can the individual begin to conceive of others as separate and unique selves, and relate to them as such. And only with this stage can the concept of mankind assume a concrete significance as pointing to a human universe of unique and irreplaceable selves.

Relationships with elders may also undergo characteristic youthful changes. By the end of adolescence, the hero worship or demonology of the middle adolescent has generally given way to an attitude of more selective emulation and rejection of admired or disliked older persons. In youth, new kinds of relationships with elders become possible: psychological apprenticeships, then a more complex relationship of mentorship, then sponsorship, and eventually peership. Without attempting to describe each of these substages in detail, the overall transition can be described as one in which the older person becomes progressively more real and three-dimensional to the younger one, whose individuality is appreciated, validated and confirmed by the elder. The sponsor, for example, is one who supports and confirms in the youth that which is best in the youth, without exacting an excessive price in terms of submission, imitation, emulation or even gratitude.

Comparable changes continue to occur during youth with regard to *parents*. Adolescents commonly discover that their parents have feet of clay, and recognize their flaws with great acuity. Childish hero worship of parents gives way to a more complex and often negative view of them. But it is generally not until youth that the individual discovers his parents as themselves complex, three-dimensional historical personages whose destinies are partly formed by their own wishes, conscious and unconscious, and by their historical situations. Similarly, it is only during youth that the questions of family tradition, family destiny, family fate, family culture and family curse arise with full force. In youth, the question of whether to live one's parents' life, or to what extent to do so, becomes a real and active question. In youth, one often sees what Ernst Prelinger has called a "telescoped re-enactment" of the life of a parent—a compulsive need to live out for oneself the destiny of a parent, as if to test its possibilities and limits, experience it from the inside, and (perhaps) free oneself of it. In the end, the youth may learn to see himself and his parents as multidimensional persons, to view them with compassion and understanding, to feel less threatened by their fate and failings, and to be able, if he chooses, to move beyond them.

In beginning by discussing affective and interpersonal changes in youth, I begin where our accounts of development are least precise and most tentative. Turning to more cognitive matters, we stand on somewhat firmer ground. Lawrence Kohlberg's work on *moral development,* especially on the attainment of the highest levels of moral reasoning, provides a paradigmatic description of developments that occur only in youth, if they occur at all.

Summarized over-simply, Kohlberg's theory distinguishes three general stages in the development of moral reasoning. The earliest or *pre-moral* stage involves relatively egocentric concepts of right and wrong as that which one can do without getting caught, or as that which leads to the greatest personal gratification. This stage is followed, usually during later childhood, by a stage of *conventional* morality, during which good and evil are identified with the concept of a "good boy" or "good girl," or with standards of the community and the concept of law and order. In this stage, morality is perceived as objective, as existing "out there."

The third and final major stage of moral development is *post-conventional.* It involves more abstract moral reasoning that may lead the individual into conflict with conventional morality. The first of two levels within the postconventional stage basically involves the assumption that concepts of right and wrong result from a *social contract*—an implicit agreement entered into by the members of the society for their own welfare, and therefore subject to amendment, change or revocation. The highest postconventional level is that in which the individual becomes devoted to *personal principles* that may transcend not only conventional morality but even the social contract. In this stage, certain general principles are now seen as personally binding although not necessarily "objectively" true. Such principles are apt to be stated at a very high level of generality: for example, the Golden Rule, the sanctity of life, the categorical imperative, the concept of justice, the promotion of human development. The individual at this stage may find himself in conflict with existing concepts of law and order, or even with the notion of an amendable social contract. He may, for example, consider even democratically-arrived-at laws unacceptable because they lead to consequences or enjoin behaviors that violate his own personal principles.

Kohlberg's research suggests that most contemporary Americans, young or old, do not pass beyond the conventional stage of moral reasoning. But some do, and they are most likely to be found today among those who are young and educated. Such young men and women may develop moral principles that can lead them to challenge the existing moral order and the existing society. And Kohlberg finds that the achievement of his highest level, the stage of personal principles, occurs in the twenties, if it occurs at all. Moral development of this type can thus be identified with youth, as can the special moral "regressions" that Kohlberg finds a frequent concomitant of moral development. Here the arbitrariness of distinguishing between sectors of development becomes clear, for the individual can begin to experience the tension between self and society only as he begins to question the absolutism of conventional moral judgments. Unless he has begun such questioning, it is doubtful whether we can correctly term him "a youth."

In no other sector of development do we have so complete, accurate and convincing a description of a "development line" that demonstrably characterizes youth. But in this area of *intellectual development,* William Perry has provided an invaluable description of the stages through which college students may pass. Perry's work emphasizes the complex transition from epistemological dualism to an awareness of multiplicity and to the realization of relativism. Relativism in turn gives way to a more "existential" sense of truth, culminating in what Perry terms "commitment within relativism." Thus, in youth we expect to see a passage beyond simple views of Right and Wrong, Truth and Falsehood, Good and Evil to a more complex and relativistic view; and as youth proceeds, we look for the development of commitments within a universe that remains epistemologically relativistic. Once again, intellectual development is only analytically separable from a variety of other sectors—moral, self-society and interpersonal, to mention only three.

In his work on *cognitive development,* Jean Piaget has emphasized the importance of the transition from concrete to formal operations, which in middle-class Western children usually occurs at about the age of puberty. For Piaget the attainment of formal operations (whereby the concrete world of the real becomes a subset of the hypothetical world of the possible) is the highest cognitive stage possible. But in some youths, there seem to occur further stages of cognitive development that are not understandable with the concept of formal operations. Jerome Bruner has suggested that beyond the formal stage of thought there lies a further stage of "thinking about thinking." This ability to think about thinking involves a new level of consciousness—consciousness of consciousness, awareness of awareness, and a breaking-away of the phenomenological "I" from the contents of consciousness. This breaking-away of the phenomenological ego during youth permits phenomenological games, intellectual tricks, and kinds of creativity that are rarely possible in adolescence itself. It provides the cognitive underpinning for many of the characteristics and special disturbances of youth, for example, youth's hyperawareness of inner processes, the focus upon states of consciousness as objects to be controlled and altered, and the frightening disappearance of the phenomenological ego in an endless regress of awarenesses of awarenesses.

Having emphasized that these analytically separated "lines" of development are in fact linked in the individual's experience, it is equally important to add that they are never linked in perfect synchronicity. If we could precisely label one specific level within each developmental line as distinctively youthful, we would find that few people were "youthful" in all lines at the same time. In general, human development proceeds unevenly, with lags in some areas and precocities in others. One young woman may be at a truly adolescent level in her relationship with her parents, but at a much later level in moral development; a young man may be capable of extraordinary mutuality with his peers, but still be struggling intellectually with the dim awareness of relativism. Analysis of any one person in terms of specific sectors of development will generally show a simultaneous mixture of adolescent, youthful and adult features. The point, once again, is that the concept of youth here proposed is an ideal type, a model that may help understand real experience but can never fully describe or capture it.

What Youth is Not

A final way to clarify the meaning of youth as a stage of life is to make clear what it is not. For one thing, youth is not the end of development. I have described the belief that it is—the conviction that beyond youth lie only stasis, decline, foreclosure and death—as a characteristically youthful way of viewing development, consistent with the observation that it is impossible truly to understand stages of development beyond one's own. On the contrary, youth is but a preface for further transformations that may (or may not) occur in later life. Many of these center around such issues as the relationship to work and to the next generation. In youth, the question of vocation is crucial, but the issue of work—of productivity, creativity, and the more general sense of fruitfulness that Erikson calls generativity—awaits adulthood. The youthful attainment of mutuality with peers and of peerhood with elders can lead on to further adult interpersonal developments by which one comes to be able to accept the dependency of others, as in parenthood. In later life, too, the relations between the generations are reversed, with the younger now assuming responsibility for the elder. Like all stages of life, youth is transitional. And although some lines of development, such as moral development, may be "completed" during youth, many others continue throughout adulthood.

It is also a mistake to identify youth with any one social group, role, class, organization, or position in society. Youth is a *psychological* stage; and those who are in this stage do not necessarily join together in identifiable groups, nor do they share a common social position. Not all college students, for example, are in this stage of life: some students are psychological adolescents, while others are young adults—essentially apprentices to the existing society. Nor can the experience of youth as a stage of life be identified with any one class, nation or other social grouping. Affluence and education can provide a freedom from economic need and an intellectual stimulation that may underlie and promote the transformations of youth. But there are poor and uneducated young men and women, from Abraham Lincoln to Malcolm X, who have had a youth, and rich, educated ones who have moved straightaway from adolescence to adulthood. And although the experience of youth is probably more likely to occur in the economically advanced nations, some of the factors that facilitate youth also exist in the less advanced nations, where comparable youthful issues and transformations are expressed in different cultural idioms.

Nor should youth be identified with the rejection of the status quo, or specifically with student radicalism. Indeed, anyone who has more or less definitively defined himself as a misanthrope or a revolutionary has moved beyond youthful probing into an "adult" commitment to a position vis-à-vis society. To repeat: what characterizes youth is not a definitive rejection of the existing "system," but an ambivalent tension over the relationship between self and society. This tension may take the form of avid efforts at self-reform that spring from acceptance of the status quo, coupled with a sense of one's own inadequacy vis-à-vis it. In youth the relationship between self and society is indeed problematical, but rejection of the existing society is not a necessary characteristic of youth.

Youth obviously cannot be equated with any particular age-range. In practice, most young Americans who enter this stage of life tend to be between the ages of eighteen and thirty. But they constitute a minority of the whole age-grade. Youth as a developmental stage is emergent; it is an "optional" stage, not a universal one. If we take Kohlberg's studies of the development of postconventional moral reasoning as a rough index of the "incidence" of youth, less than forty percent of middle-class (college-educated) men, and a smaller proportion of working-class men have developed beyond the conventional level by the age of twenty-four. Thus, "youths" constitute but a minority of their age group. But those who are in this stage of life today largely determine the public image of their generation.

Admirers and romanticizers of youth tend to identify youth with virtue, morality and mental health. But to do so is to overlook the special youthful possibilities for viciousness, immorality and psychopathology. Every time of human life, each level of development, has its characteristic vices and weaknesses, and youth is no exception. Youth is a stage, for example, when the potentials for zealotry and fanaticism, for reckless action in the name of the highest principles, for self-absorption, and for special arrogance are all at a peak. Furthermore, the fact that youth is a time of psychological change also inevitably means that it is a stage of constant recapitulation, reenactment and reworking of the past. This reworking can rarely occur without real regression, whereby the buried past is reexperienced as present and, one hopes, incorporated into it. Most youthful transformation occurs *through* brief or prolonged regression, which, however benignly it may eventually be resolved, constitutes part of the psychopathology of youth. And the special compulsions and inner states of youth—the euphoria of omnipotentiality and the dysphoria of estrangement, the hyperconsciousness of consciousness, the need for constant motion and the terror of stasis—may generate youthful pathologies with a special virulence and obstinacy. In one sense those who have the luxury of a youth may be said to be "more developed" than those who do not have (or do not take) this opportunity. But no level of development and no stage of life should be identified either with virtue or with health.

Finally, youth is not the same as the adoption of youthful causes, fashions, rhetoric or postures. Especially in a time like our own, when youthful behavior is watched with ambivalent fascination by adults, the positions of youth become part of the cultural stock-in-trade. There thus develops the phenomenon of *pseudo-youth*—preadolescents, adolescents and frustrated adults masquerade as youths, adopt youthful manners and disguise (even to themselves) their real concerns by the use of youthful rhetoric.

Many a contemporary adolescent, whether of college or high school age, finds it convenient to displace and express his battles with his parents in a pseudo-youthful railing at the injustices, oppression and hypocrisy of the Establishment. And many an adult, unable to accept his years, may adopt pseudo-youthful postures to express the despairs of his adulthood.

To differentiate between "real" and pseudo youth is a tricky, subtle and unrewarding enterprise. For, as I have earlier emphasized, the concept of youth as here defined is an ideal type, an abstraction from the concrete experience of many different individuals. Furthermore, given the unevenness of human development and the persistence throughout life of active remnants of earlier developmental levels, conflicts and stages, no one can ever be said to be completely "in" one stage of life in all areas of behavior and at all times. No issue can ever be said to be finally "resolved"; no earlier conflict is completely "overcome." Any real person, even though on balance we may consider him a "youth," will also contain some persistent childishness, some not-outgrown adolescence, and some precocious adulthood in his makeup. All we can say is that, for some, adolescent themes and levels of development are *relatively* outgrown, while adult concerns have not yet assumed full prominence. It is such people whom one might term "youths."

The Implications of Youth

I have sketched with broad and careless strokes the rough outlines of a stage of life I believe to characterize a growing, although still small, set of young men and women. This sketch, although presented dogmatically, is clearly preliminary; it will doubtless require revision and correction after further study. Yet let us for the moment assume that, whatever the limitations of this outline, the concept of a postadolescent stage of life has some merit. What might be the implications of the emergence of youth?

To most Americans, the chief anxieties raised by youth are over social stability and historical continuity. In every past and present society, including our own, the great majority of men and women seem to be, in Kohlberg's terms, "conventional" in moral judgment, and, in Perry's terms, "dualistic" in their intellectual outlook. Such men and women accept with little question the existing moral codes of the community, just as they endorse their culture's traditional view of the world. It is arguable that both cultural continuity and social stability have traditionally rested on the moral and epistemological conventionality of most men and women, and on the secure transmission of these conventional views to the next generation.

What, then, would it mean if our particular era were producing millions of postconventional, nondualistic, postrelativistic youth? What would happen if millions of young men and women developed to the point that they "made up their own minds" about most value, ideological, social and philosophical questions, often rejecting the conventional and traditional answers? Would they not threaten the stability of their societies?

Today it seems clear that most youths are considered nuisances or worse by the established order, to which they have not finally pledged their allegiance. Indeed, many of the major stresses in contemporary American society spring from or are aggravated by those in this stage of life. One aspect of the deep polarization in our society may be characterized psychologically as a struggle between conventionals and postconventionals, between those who have not had a youth and those who have. The answer of the majority of the public seems clear: we already have too many "youths" in our society; youth as a developmental stage should be stamped out.

A more moderate answer to the questions I am raising is also possible. We might recognize the importance of having a *few* postconventional individuals (an occasional Socrates, Christ, Luther, or Gandhi to provide society with new ideas and moral inspiration), but nonetheless establish a firm top limit on the proportion of postconventional, youth-scarred adults our society could tolerate. If social stability requires human inertia—that is, unreflective acceptance of most social, cultural, and political norms—perhaps we should discourage "youth as a stage of life" in any but a select minority.

A third response, toward which I incline, seems to me more radical. To the argument from social stability and cultural continuity, one might reply by pointing to the enormous *in*stabilities and gross cultural *dis*continuities that characterize the modern world. Older forms of stability and continuity have *already* been lost in the postindustrial era. Today, it is simply impossible to return to a bygone age when massive inertia guaranteed social stability (if there really was such an age). The cake of custom crumbled long ago. The only hope is to learn to live without it.

In searching for a way to do this, we might harken back to certain strands in socialist thought that see new forms of social organization possible for men and women who are more "evolved." I do not wish to equate my views on development with revolutionary socialism or anarchism, much less with a Rousseauistic faith in the goodness of the essential man. But if there is anything to the hypothesis that different historical conditions alter the nature of the life cycle, then men with different kinds of development may require or be capable of living in different kinds of social institutions. On the one hand, this means that merely throwing off institutional shackles, as envisioned by some socialist and anarchist thinkers, would not automatically change the nature of men, although it may be desirable on other grounds. "New men" cannot be created by institutional transformations alone, although institutional changes may, over the very long run, affect the possibilities for continuing development by changing the matrix in which development occurs.

But on the other hand, men and women who have attained higher developmental levels may be capable of different kinds of association and cooperation from those at lower levels. Relativism, for example, brings not only skepticism but also tolerance of the viewpoints of others, and a probable reduction in moralistic self-righteousness. Attaining the stage of personal principles in moral development in no way prevents the individual from conforming to a just social order, or even for that matter from obeying unreasonable traffic laws. Men and women who are capable of interpersonal mutuality are not for that reason worse citizens; on the contrary, their capacity to be concerned with others as unique individuals might even make them better citizens. Examples could be multiplied, but the general point is obvious: higher levels of development, including the emergence on a mass scale of "new" stages of life, may permit new forms of human cooperation and social organization.

It may be true that all past societies have been built upon the unquestioning inertia of the vast majority of their citizens. And this inertia may have provided the psychological ballast that prevented most revolutions from doing more than reinstating the *ancien régime* in new guise. But it does not follow that this need always continue to be true. If new developmental stages are emerging that lead growing minorities to more autonomous positions vis-à-vis their societies, the result need not be anarchy or social chaos. The result might instead be the possibility of new forms of social organization based less upon unreflective acceptance of the status quo than upon thoughtful and self-conscious loyalty and cooperation. But whether or not these new forms can emerge depends not only upon the psychological factors I have discussed here, but even more upon political, social, economic and international conditions.

NOTE

1. Obviously, interpersonal development, and specifically the development of relationships with peers, begins long before adolescence, starting with the "parallel play" observed at ages two to four and continuing through many stages to the preadolescent same-sex "chumship" described by Harry Stack Sullivan. But puberty in middle-class Western societies is accompanied by major cognitive changes that permit the early adolescent for the first time to develop hypothetical ideals of the possibilities of friendship and intimacy. The "search for a soulmate" of early adolescence is the first interpersonal stage built upon these new cognitive abilities.